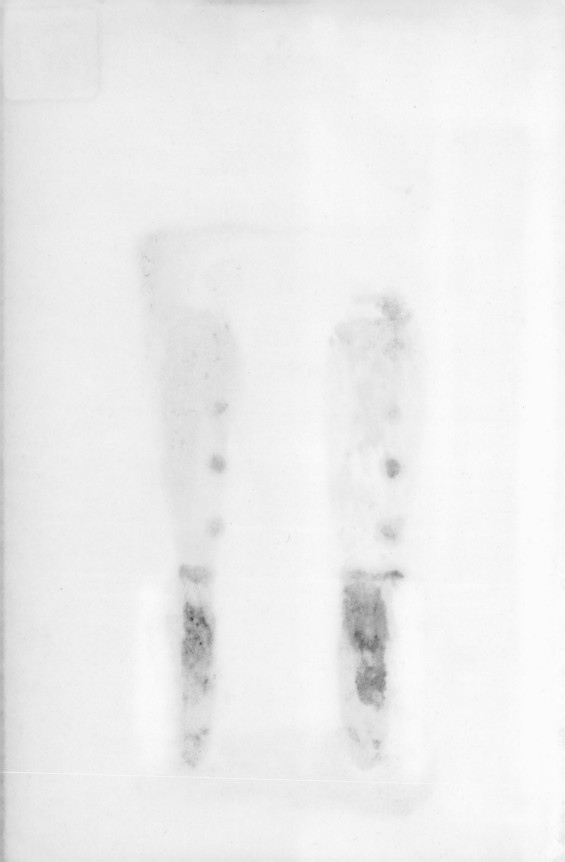

My World of Birds:

Memoirs of an Ornithologist

Lake of the Clouds on Mt. Mansfield, Vermont—nestled like a glistening jewel among the balsams and spruces that provide nest sites for the rare and elusive Bicknell's Gray-cheeked Thrush. Photo from Alice Wallace Wonders.

My World of Birds:
Memoirs of an Ornithologist

by

GEORGE J. WALLACE

DORRANCE & COMPANY • *Philadelphia and Ardmore, Pa.*

To all who helped with this book: teachers, students, colleagues, family, and friends.

Contents

Illustrations

Preface

MY WORLD OF BIRDS is the story of my lifelong experiences with birds—boyhood's ceaseless quest for new species, academic training during the university years, nearly half a century trying to instill acquired knowledge into others, and travels to faroff places to seek more background. Birds have been my main obsession, but not exclusively so. In my early years I had a mania for identifying everything out-of-doors, from mushrooms to stars, ever making new discoveries by rambling about in the woods and fields of Vermont. During the difficult university years, I wavered from time to time from my main goal, but ultimately settled down to a career in teaching and research in ornithology. I have never regretted it.

Many people, often unwittingly, have contributed to this book—a sympathetic mother, long since deceased; a close-knit family of brothers and sisters, virtually my sole companions in those early days on the farm; university professors who taught me to seek more scientific background; students—good, bad, and indifferent—who helped mold me; and professional colleagues, with whom I have had so many pleasant associations.

An important influence, as indicated in Chapter 2, has been an enduring friendship with Carlton F. Wells, now professor emeritus of English at the University of Michigan. He had faith in me as a struggling college freshman, encouraged me to pursue my never fully realized ambition of becoming a literary naturalist, and, more recently, has gone over the entire manuscript of this book for diction and usage. I owe him a lasting debt of gratitude.

Several of the chapters have had the additional benefit of critical reading. An older sister and brother, Lelia and Bob, went over Chapter 1 and supplied data that they remembered better than I. And brother Keith, still on the old family farm, corrected some errors my faulty memory committed. Dr. F. N. Blanchard, my major professor in graduate school, and his wife, Dr. Frieda Cobb Blanchard, helped me over many difficult hurdles; the latter read most of Chapter 2. Bartlett Hendricks, a longtime trustee at Pleasant Valley Sanctuary, and his wife, Mary, helped with the chapter on the Berkshires. The Flemings, father and son, ornithologists now living in Nepal (formerly in India) reviewed Chapter 11, as did Harold Peters, tour leader on our trip to India, Nepal, and Ceylon. Les and Alma Eyer, our traveling companions on the trip to Australia and New Zealand, checked the data in Chapter 13.

I am also grateful to the editors and staff at Dorrance and Company, Inc., for the many ways in which they helped to bring this book to completion.

And last, but never least, I am forever indebted to a hardworking and cooperative wife, who has served as secretary, business manager, housekeeper, and companion on excursions afield. Her labors in my behalf will never be fully rewarded.

George J. Wallace
Professor emeritus of zoology
Michigan State University
Grayling, Michigan
June 1978

CHAPTER 1

Boyhood's Formative Years

Vermont Beginnings

I DON'T KNOW when I first became conscious of birds or just what aroused my early interest in them. Probably it was a gradual development, perhaps abetted by a sympathetic and somewhat knowledgeable mother. All of us, a close-knit family of seven children and widowed mother, were interested in the birds around our farm in Waterbury in north-central Vermont. We knew the Barn Swallows that nested in our barns, the phoebes that built or repaired their nest each spring on the ell of the house where it was visible from the sink room window, the crows that supervised spring plowing and planting, the orioles that hung their pendulous nests in the maples beside the house, the hummingbirds that visited mother's neglected flower garden, and—an especially fond memory for me—the handsome Bobolinks that serenaded us with their melodious songs while we were planting potatoes on Memorial Day. And each spring after the long hard winter we anxiously awaited the arrival of the first robins and bluebirds, the latter then common and well-known farm and orchard birds.

It must have been soon after World War I, when I was in my early teens, that I began listing birds. My sister Lelia, three years my senior, thinks she began watching birds seriously in the spring of 1917. I probably caught on a couple of years later. My first complete annual list was for 1921, when I was in the seventh and eighth grades. But there were a few earlier lists: an undated spring list (April to June) had thirty-four species, including such imprecise items as sea gull, hawk, and woodpecker.

Several family concerns help determine the chronology of early events. In the fall of 1918, when I was eleven years old, father died of Spanish influenza, which took more lives than did German guns and wiped out a large segment of our small community. Then an ingenious older brother, who took over partial management of family affairs, devised all sorts of contests, including competitive bird, flower, tree, and mammal lists. Sometimes we kept our annual lists secret, then on December 31 we brought them out to determine the winners. After a few years, such contests were dropped, but I persisted in keeping annual bird lists, and, by spells at least, kept lists of trees and shrubs, flowers, ferns, and mammals. Lelia helped with the flowers, but my brothers usually scoffed at such "sissy" pursuits. An additional quirk of mine: by the aid of a kerosene lantern and the star charts in *Boys World,* a Sunday school paper, I learned the names of the first magnitude stars, and some second magnitude stars, as well as the constellations in the northern hemisphere.

By present-day standards my bird lists were nothing to brag about. That first annual list in 1921 had seventy-two species, three of which I later tabbed with question marks. By 1925, I reached a coveted goal of one hundred species; my accumulative Vermont list for the eight-year period from 1921 to 1928, when I left the farm for college at the University of Michigan, was one hundred twenty.

But we had ample excuses for low bird lists. We were "loners" and had no birding companions; indeed, we knew of no local person who had any real knowledge of birds. We had no binoculars and probably did not even know such aids existed. And we had no vehicular transportation other than horse and buggy, hence, we were largely limited to upland farm areas within walking distance. Our chief source of identification was a well-worn, nearly memorized Reed's *Land Birds East of the Rockies* (there were no Peterson, Pough, or Robbins field guides in those days). Later we secured Reed's *Water and Game Birds,* but it was of limited usefulness to us because there were no lakes or extensive marshes within walking distance. Occasionally we borrowed books from the town library. The only ones I remember— perhaps all the library had—were Chapman's *Handbook* and Blanchan's *Bird Neighbors.* We also got engrossed with the Burgess bedtime stories, supplied to us at first by a kindly New York lady who sent newspaper clippings that Lelia pasted in a scrapbook. Then over the years, for birthdays and Christmas, we acquired many of the Burgess *Bedtime Story-Books.*

But we had some distinct advantages for birding—freedom to roam over our 226-acre ecologically diversified farm in a strictly rural setting. We had seventy acres of fields, two pastures, two beech-maple-hemlock woodlots comprising more than one hundred acres, and three orchards, which, according to my early records, harbored some thirty-seven species of nesting birds. Usually there were no trespassing problems about venturing into neighboring properties, one of which contained a small pond and another a trout stream flowing into Little River. An exception occurred when we were quarantined to our own premises in the spring of 1922 by a local outbreak of scarlet fever—not a great hardship on a 226-acre farm with enjoyable days off from school. But a nosy neighbor blabbed to Mother when we strayed onto her property. As I recall, Mother reprimanded us—mildly and with a hidden smile; she didn't like the neighbor, who had had a crush on Dad.

Farm chores were exacting—five boys ranging in age from eight to fourteen, trying to operate a farm before and after school and on holidays. Unfortunately, it fell to my lot to clean the horse stables, an indoor task. An older brother, deaf in one ear, had the pleasanter assignment of driving the cows to pasture down a tree-bordered lane in the early morning and rounding them up again in the late afternoon for milking. He was perhaps the least interested in birds of any of us, attributable in part to his inability to distinguish bird song. But I managed to get in my precious moments of birding—on the long walks to and from our one-room country school, on short trips into the surrounding woods during the noon hour and the fifteen-minute recesses, and on our free Sunday afternoons. Often I was accused—rightly, I suppose—of shirking my work; sometimes I showed up late for a working assignment, but often with a new bird or two on my list.

We must have invented listing on our own. At least we didn't know then that there were other queer people who kept such lists. We kept our records in Champion Harvester pocket-sized notebooks, of which Father, a dealer in farm equipment, had left an ample supply. I had mostly bird lists, but I find undated lists of 14 mammals, 46 trees and shrubs, and 140 wild flowers, the latter probably an accumulative list over several years.

Some Nonbirding Activities

Perhaps I should digress momentarily to describe some nonbirding activities that helped cement family relationships in those early days. (Now, fifty years later and living in six different states, we still keep in touch by a monthly round robin.) Brother Bob, the ringleader in nearly everything, organized all sorts of competitive athletic contests among ourselves, perhaps because we had such limited contact with other boys our age. Events included the half-mile and mile runs; the 50-yard, 100-yard and 220-yard dashes; running and standing high jumps and broad jumps; pole vault; shot-put (with a 16 lb. iron maul used for driving fence posts); and pull-ups. We got really proficient at the latter by developing a swinging technique that made it easier to get our chins up over the bar. My final record, after a few years of practice, was 54. I was slim and underweight, distinct advantages, but overweight brother Bill achieved a remarkable total of 36 by swinging so violently that the shed and rafters to which the crossbar was attached threatened to collapse. Our swinging technique backfired on me, however. Much later, in a freshman gym contest at the University of Michigan, I got disqualified, in spite of advance warnings, for flexing a knee and wiggling my toes. As I recall, a supple Japanese won the coveted award with about 25 pull-ups.

We also organized a family basketball team—the Wallace All Stars. We played on the hay barn floor between the haymows (or next to empty bins in the spring), at first with a stuffed stocking cap (which wouldn't bounce) and barrel hoops for baskets; later with a real ball (a Christmas present from Mother) and real baskets mounted on a backboard by brother Bob. Sometimes we chose up sides with any neighbors available, at other times we had real games with organized teams. One I particularly remember was with a boys' group from town. We practiced long and hard for the event, even devising signals. The boys from downtown trudged through three miles of snow, mostly uphill. Then we played all afternoon—without time periods, I think. We slaughtered them unmercifully, 136-0. It went something like this: My big brother, playing center, would tip the ball to me, a forward, and I would race for the basket, often missing the shot in my haste. But then big brother Bob would come tearing down the floor, scattering any small fry in his way, retrieve the ball, and put it in the basket. In those days the ball always went back to center after a basket, so our opponents hardly touched the ball.

In Pursuit of Birds

But back to birds. In scanning my early lists I find little to quibble about. Although there were undoubtedly many misidentifications, only a few could be questioned on distributional grounds. Carolina Wren was on several lists; it probably did not occur there at that time. I am dubious about my 1922 "marsh wren." I think my first Wood Thrush was not a Wood Thrush; they appeared in later years. "Wild Goose" on my 1921 list got changed to Canada Goose in 1927 (no records for other years). Probably some of my hawk records (6 species) are questionable. The Sparrow Hawks (American Kestrels) that nested for years in a dying elm in a neighbor's pasture and the Marsh Hawks cruising over the meadows were readily identified, but not the Sharp-shinned and Cooper's hawks that appeared on most of my lists. I had a hard time deciding that the hen hawk nesting in a big beech in our lower woods was a Red-shouldered Hawk and not a Redtail.

Many birds, of course, went unidentified. But now I know that the froglike calls emanating from a roadside alder swamp came from a woodcock (we never observed the flight) and that the mysterious voice my brother Keith and I pursued all over the woods one moonlight night was a Saw-whet Owl. All we proved that night was that it could fly. Once I roosted uncomfortably near the top of a big maple, trying, mostly unsuccessfully, to identify the warblers passing through the trees. It now seems a little remarkable that my warbler list—without binoculars or a Peterson field guide—reached 22—nearly all correctly identified, I believe. But many identifications were gradually worked out over a period of time. Once I chased a small dark bird around, off and on, for about three days before I discovered that it was blue—an Indigo Bunting.

Most of our quests for birds were on our own property. But trips to town, three miles away, produced such specialties as House Sparrows and European Starlings in the village, and, more exciting, Yellow Warblers along a willow-fringed tributary to the Winooski River. The river flowed through town, causing disastrous floods at times, the worst of which was in 1927. The "sea gulls" floating over the river we finally identified correctly as Herring Gulls (Ring-bills apparently did not occur there then). More rarely we sighted an Osprey sailing over the river. Otherwise water birds were almost unknown to us. There was a small pond, however, a half-mile jaunt through the woods, and two streams—Alder Creek and Little River— a mile away. From the pond or streams we often flushed Great Blue Herons and Belted Kingfishers, less often an American Bittern and wild ducks, presumably Blacks. Spotted Sandpipers were quite common and, in migration, occasional Solitary Sandpipers. These were the only sandpipers we could identify.

But the small pond was used mainly as a swimming hole on summer days, until the town fathers banned swimming because the water was used for washing ice cut there in winter. In those days, "skin-dipping" was traditional for boys in Vermont. The pond was on the edge of the woods and not visible from the nearby road. However, when we were pressured into taking along a sister or one of her female companions we had to be encumbered with old clothes (no one had a swimming suit). My older brothers remember (alas, I don't) when a teenage neighbor girl, clad only in an old dress, jumped off a raft feet first. Her descent into the water lifted

5

her dress up over her head, much to my brothers' amusement.

Some of my earliest ornithological experiences stand out vividly. Following are some highlights:

The winter of 1917–1918 was one of the most severe on record in north-central Vermont. The hard winter killed the pear trees in our front orchard, once our father's pride and joy. It also nearly exterminated his thriving bee colony. It must have been in the winter or early spring of 1919 that we had the dead trees cleared away, leaving conspicuous piles of brush strewn about the orchard and front yard. In late March and early April these brush piles became shelters for an assortment of early seed-eating fringillids. We got out our Reed's *Land Birds* and faces glued to the often frost-lined kitchen window, we easily identified the slate-gray birds with flashing white tail feathers as juncos. Lelia finally convinced us that the streak-breasted birds we had formerly called "ground birds" or "brown birds" were really Song Sparrows and that those with unstreaked breasts and redder crowns were Tree Sparrows. Then the Red-winged Blackbirds came and made the orchard and maple trees ring with their chorus of song. They did not then remain with us over summer but departed for distant marshes.

One summer a pair of brilliant Red-headed Woodpeckers, unusual at our latitude, nested in a maple stub that served as a hammock post in our front yard. They disappeared after one summer, as often happens to birds on the northern periphery of their range, but brother Keith, who remained on the farm, says that years later they reappeared at least once and nested in the orchard.

A truly red-letter day in the life of any budding ornithologist is his first Scarlet Tanager. Near our country school was a cutover woods grown up to aspens and birch. During a recess period in mid-May one year, I discovered my first Scarlet Tanager, resplendent with his shimmering black wings and tail, on a low branch of a quivering aspen. It was breathtaking. And to make the day complete, a male American Redstart, my first, suddenly appeared in an adjacent tree, and an Ovenbird flushed from the ground onto a low branch and sang his loud "teacher-teacher" song. Climaxing the experience was my discovery of my first porcupine high up in another tree. I was late getting back to classes, but I didn't get reprimanded—a sympathetic teacher who encouraged us to keep a spring bird list, knew where I had been.

Another indelible memory came on the morning of April 20, 1925, when a belated snowstorm decked every tree and bush with soft fluffy snow. En route to school that morning, in a stand of snow-laden willows where we often collected our first pussy willows, I noticed a small yellow bird, incongruous against a background of new snow. It flitted from bush to bush at close range, wagging its tail, apparently searching for insects. Of course it was a Palm Warbler, then known as the Yellow Palm Warbler, distinguishable from the more drab western subspecies by its brighter colors. It was not there when I returned after school. Most of the snow had melted by then, and the warbler was gone. But another warbler, the fourteenth, was added to my growing list.

By now I was making excursions further afield, especially on Sunday afternoons, the only half-day block of free time I had for such pursuits. Sometimes I found neighboring woodlots or pastures more attractive than ours—at least I found some new birds in them. One neighbor had a largely uncut (or selectively cut, as were most farm woodlots) beech-maple woods with numerous butternut trees, the latter a source of envy to us because the Wallace farm had no butternut trees. A mellow, sustained, robinlike song proved, as I suspected without ever having seen or heard the singer before, to be a Rose-breasted Grosbeak. My first Black-throated Blue Warbler, ever after one of my favorite warblers, was also found in this woods. Often thereafter I revisited this woods to look—though mostly unsuccessfully—for new birds.

Another neighboring woodlot was clear cut by villager loggers who had no respect for standing trees. But it also produced a few new birds. In the early dawn before chores one morning, brother Keith discovered a Mourning Warbler's nest beside a brush-surrounded stump. Later he showed it to me. Here also, in a swampy uncut portion of the woods, I discovered my first Olive-sided Flycatcher.

Another memorable spot—a long trek from our house through woods and pastures, past a rocky ledge with a fox den and a spruce knoll with a patch of twinflowers—was an alder and willow swamp, more extensive than any on our land. An abrupt *gre-beek* (as I called it), proved, after considerable chasing, to be an Alder Flycatcher (the *E. alnorum* form), and the loud rattling chippy song, I guessed correctly, was made by a Swamp Sparrow. So far as I know, neither of these birds occurred on our premises at that time, but in later years an Alder Flycatcher did move into the lower wetter portion of the orchard behind our house.

The sugaring season in Vermont was fraught with both pleasant and unpleasant memories of long hard days and sometimes nights in the sugarbush. We had no sugarhouse at that time; grandfather's sugarhouse had burned down before my day. Before rebuilding years later in the upper woods, we sugared in the lower woods, too rough for a team of horses, so that all the sap had to be gathered by hand from scattered trees and boiled

The ancestral acres where five generations of Wallaces have lived.

The farm house, purchased by grandfather Sydney Wallace in 1866.

The avenue of maples planted by grandfather Sydney in 1871, now dying of old age, disease, and road widening.

Six of us in ascending age order: Alice, Avelyn, Keith, George, Bill, Bob. Lelia took the picture.

Baseball aspirants. Too few for a team we limited our baseball activities largely to pitching and catching and batting out flies.

down over a crude makeshift affair ingeniously contrived by my older brothers. Two large pans were suspended over the fire by iron pipes laid across two spruce poles, which sometimes caught fire.

Sugaring this way was hard work, often from early dawn to dusk or later. There were cords of wood to be cut and brought in by hand, fires to be stoked, and, of course, potential syrup to be tested frequently, not by modern methods but by sampling it long before it was ready, by cooling it in a dipper placed in snow. But hard work was interspersed with delightful signs of awakening spring. Fiddleheads of interrupted ferns were breaking through the thawing ground (we sometimes ate the roots but found them only so-so), the first robins and bluebirds appeared, and Purple Finches made the sugarbush ring with their melody. Sugaring was a prolonged and often interrupted affair, usually from late March to late April. Hermit Thrushes, Vermont's state bird, usually arrived before the end of sugaring. Their serene refrains in the evening echoed from nearby trees while we huddled over the dying embers of the fire and sugared off the rewards of the day. Red-breasted Nuthatches, less noticeable in winter, became more vocal, their haunting nasal wail so different from that of the more guttural white-breasted species. Sometimes Myrtle (Yellow-rumped) Warblers, the earliest of the warblers, appeared; a pair once started a nest near the terminus of a long low-sweeping branch of a red spruce but deserted it, perhaps because I stopped too frequently to inspect its progress. The brook that flowed along the border of the sugarbush, swollen by melting snows, gurgled merrily, and hepaticas and spring beauties burst into bloom beside a bank of lingering snow. Later, in May, after we had "pulled the buckets," many other wildflowers decorated these woods; some thirty or more species of May flowers were on my list.

For me the most rewarding, as well as the most accessible spot for bird watching, was our main orchard behind the house. Actually we had three orchards (with a pair of bluebirds in each); a small one of a dozen or more trees in a distant pasture on a neighboring farm that Dad had purchased; the mixed pear-plum-apple orchard that largely died out after an unusually severe winter, and the main orchard of about three acres, primarily apples of thirty or so different varieties—Dad had been a great experimenter—behind the house. Here the trees came up close to the house and barns, so that some birds could be seen from our sink room window. Swallows nesting in or on the barns and Chimney Swifts from the ell of the house foraged over and among the orchard trees. However, our frequent visits to the orchard, at first for green apples to be eaten with salt (in spite of Mother's dire warnings) and later for ripening Yellow Transparents, Tetoskies, and Duchess could hardly be called birding events. When the Transparents were ripening, we always made an early morning dash, before milking, for any apples on the ground. We had an unwritten but clearly understood law that we couldn't shake the tree, but in our race for fallen apples we sometimes checked our speed by using the tree trunk as a brake, thus knocking off more apples "accidentally."

The diversity in the orchard trees, from newly planted to old dying trees with knotholes for hole-nesting species, was attractive to quite a variety of birds. Moreover, the immediate surroundings added to its diversity. A double row of about sixty maples, (planted by grandfather in 1871) along the east side of the orchard, a wet lane at the lower (north) end, and fields on the west border added to the variety of birds using the orchard. Eastern Wood Pewees, Red-eyed Vireos, and woodpeckers were more closely associated with the maples than with the orchard trees. Alder Flycatchers, Gray Catbirds, and Common Yellowthroats were found in the lower portions. And Bobolinks, Vesper Sparrows, and Savannah Sparrows, although nesting in the fields, used the west border trees for singing posts.

According to my early records, about 37 species of summer resident birds nested in or along the borders of the orchard. This does not include visitors such as crows and hawks that often invaded the orchard but nested elsewhere. Also excluded are winter birds, such as Pine Grosbeaks and crossbills, and migrating transients, such as warblers.

Acutely conscious in later years of the probable differences in the bird life of old, unsprayed, diversified orchards like ours (and partly to answer an unrelenting pro-spraying critic of mine who claimed that he had "all kinds of birds" in his heavily sprayed orchard), I made a survey of the birds in an apple orchard at Michigan State University and tried to compare the results with my Vermont orchard records. The MSU orchard was a little larger (about five acres compared to three), but probably was less diversified as to its surroundings. The results are presented in the following tables. (For more detailed data, see *Massachusetts Audubon,* 54:pp. 2–10, 1970).

Summer Birds in a Vermont Orchard in the 1920's

Regular Summer Residents
(believed nesting)

Hummingbird
Flicker*
Downy Woodpecker*
Kingbird*
Crested Flycatcher*

Phoebe*
Least Flycatcher*
Wood Pewee
Tree Swallow*
Barn Swallow*

Blue Jay
White-breasted Nuthatch
Robin*
Bluebird*
Cedar Waxwing*

Red-eyed Vireo
Warbling Vireo*
Bobolink (border)
Baltimore (Northern) Oriole*
Goldfinch*

Vesper Sparrow (border)
Chipping Sparrow*
Song Sparrow*

*Nests found

Irregular Summer Residents

Black-billed Cuckoo (status uncertain)
Chimney Swift* (2 summers)
Red-headed Woodpecker* (2 summers)
Hairy Woodpecker (status uncertain)
Alder Flycatcher (border)

Cliff Swallow* (3 summers)
Black-capped Chickadee*
House Wren*
Catbird (border)
Yellowthroat (border)

Cowbird (status uncertain)
Indigo Bunting (border)
Purple Finch*
Savannah Sparrow (border)

12

Summer Birds in an MSU Orchard, June 3-11, 1968

Nesting

        Robin (nest with 4 eggs)

Potential Nesters

        Mourning Dove (all around, nested earlier?)
        Cedar Waxwing (mated pair?)
        Goldfinch (late nesters)

Visitors (seen in orchard)
        Brown Thrasher (twice)
        House Sparrow (frequent visitors from buildings)
        Starling (frequent flocks of 6 or more)
        Red-winged Blackbird (song post)
        Cowbird (once)

        Common Grackle (frequent)
        Chipping Sparrow (twice)
        Field Sparrow (song post)
        Song Sparrow (daily, on border)

Peripheral (not seen in orchard)
        Pheasant (in nearby weed field)
        Killdeer (on ploughed ground)
        Horned Lark (on ploughed ground)
        Crow (flying by)
        Bobolink (flew by)

        Meadowlark (adjacent field)
        Savannah Sparrow (adjacent field)
        Vesper Sparrow (adjacent field)

The tables, of course, do not tell the whole story. Several sharp contrasts, especially the three listed here, existed between the two orchard situations.

(1). All 37 of the Vermont species, 23 of them regularly, were believed to be nesting in or along the borders of the orchard and did a part or all of their foraging for food in or around (swifts and swallows) the orchard trees. By contrast, only one species, a robin, was found nesting in the Michigan orchard, although several others might have nested there at other times. I had no evidence that any of the thirteen birds seen in the MSU orchard were obtaining food there.

(2). All but two (goldfinch and Purple Finch) of the Vermont birds were partially or entirely insectivorous (e.g., four woodpeckers, six flycatchers, three swallows, two vireos). None of the Michigan orchard birds were primarily insectivorous.

13

(3). The numerically dominant birds associated with the Michigan orchard—Starlings, House Sparrows, Red-wings and Common Grackles—did not occur in the Vermont orchard in summer in the early 1920s. House Sparrows and Starlings, at that time, were village or lowland birds (they invaded the farm later), Common Grackles were uncommon, and the Red-winged Blackbird, a common spring migrant, nested only in distant swamps and marshes.

The conclusions are obvious: an unsprayed orchard, with considerable diversity in its surroundings, and enough old trees to provide homes for woodpeckers (we had boxes for bluebirds, Tree Swallows, a Crested Flycatcher, and a wren) is an ideal habitat for many birds; a heavily sprayed, carefully pruned commercial orchard of young trees with no cavities for hole-nesters and little or no insect food is a poor habitat for birds. This is not intended to discredit commercial orchards—the objective of an orchard is to produce fruit, not birds—but it does indicate that what was formerly nearly ideal habitat for many birds is now of limited usefulness to them.

My Vermont Bird Records, 1921-1928

The following annotated list is a summary of my early Vermont records. Unfortunately, there are many gaps in these data. I have often regretted that I didn't keep better records; my earliest lists had no dates, and specific localities are not recorded. Now I wish I knew exactly where and in what numbers various birds were seen. As a result of my early negligence I have always tried to impress on my students the importance of keeping accurate dates and locality records; they may prove to be of inestimable value in later years.

Great Blue Heron—Flushed frequently from local ice pond

American Bittern—Flushed occasionally from ice pond

Canada Goose—Occasional fall flights; a large flock on Nov. 25, 1927, none recorded in spring

Black Duck—Most wild ducks flushed from ice pond were probably this species: one positive record (originally listed as Mallard) of a lone bird perched on fence post in wooded swamp, May 2, 1922

Sharp-shinned Hawk—Probable summer resident but most identifications uncertain

Cooper's Hawk—probable summer resident; Father's "chicken hawk"?

Red-tailed Hawk—Listed for most years but I had difficulty with positive identification; the "hen hawk" of local farmers?

Red-shouldered Hawk—Nested several summers in large beech in lower woods

Marsh Hawk—Regular summer resident, listed every year

14

Osprey—Recorded most summers, usually over Winooski River, 3 miles away

Sparrow Hawk (Am. Kestrel)—Nested regularly (?) in old elm in a neighbor's pasture

Ruffed Grouse—Common permanent resident in our woods

American Woodcock—Sometimes flushed from woods and alder swamps

Spotted Sandpiper—Common summer resident around a local pond and along Alder Creek and Little River

Solitary Sandpiper—Flushed occasionally from weedy border of pond

Herring Gull—Common visitors along the Winooski River; Ring-bill not listed (it came in later years—Lelia)

Black-billed Cuckoo—Presumed summer resident, nests not found

Barred Owl—Listed for most years; the only owl positively identified (one found asleep on a low branch in a neighbor's woods on April 30, 1922.)

Whip-poor-will—Discovered belatedly (July 12, 1927 according to my records) in a neighboring pasture (Lelia thinks we had it earlier.)

Nighthawk—Occasionally seen flying over; more common in town

Chimney Swift—Common summer resident and visitor; nested several times in chimney on ell of house (stove there not used)

Ruby-throated Hummingbird—Regular summer resident around garden and orchards; nest never found

Belted Kingfisher—Frequently observed at local pond and along Alder Creek and Little River

(Common) Flicker—Common summer resident; nested several times in broken off maple stump by our mailbox

Red-headed Woodpecker—Several summer records; nested once in hammock tree; later in orchard.

Yellow-bellied Sapsucker—Summer resident in deep woods, more common in migration.

Hairy Woodpecker—Regular permanent resident in woods, sometimes in roadside maples and orchard.

Downy Woodpecker—Common permanent resident, woods, orchard, and along roadside

Eastern Kingbird—Nested in both orchards (2 pairs) every summer

(Great) Crested Flycatcher—Nested (several summers?) in old syrup can placed in orchard tree; also in sugar orchard; Lelia remembers that the nest once had a snakeskin in it

Eastern Phoebe—Nested on ell of house nearly every summer; sometimes in manure cellar under cow barn and (later) in a new shed

Alder Flycatcher—Discovered in distant alder swamp, May 14, 1924; later invaded lower part of orchard

15

Least Flycatcher—Regular summer resident in orchard and adjacent maples

(Eastern) Wood Pewee—Regular summer resident in lower sugar woods, sometimes in maples or orchard

Olive-sided Flycatcher—One record June 7, 1925, in Palmer's woods

Horned Lark—Northern form *(alpestris)* in winter, fall and spring; the prairie form *(pratincola)* a regular summer resident in later years

Tree Swallow—Nested in boxes in orchards

Bank Swallow—Frequent visitor; a pair or two in dugout just below our orchard (I believe now that these may have been Rough-wings.)

Barn Swallow—Nested each summer in three of our barns, originally one pair per barn, later sometimes several nests per barn

Cliff Swallow—A few nested irregularly (3 summers) under eaves of barn; our cats (good mousers) drove them out one summer. The farm below us had a colony until a disastrous fire burned them out one year during the nesting season.

Purple Martin—June 16, 1925, my only record, rare in north-central Vermont then

Blue Jay—Common permanent resident

Common Crow—Common resident, late February to November

Black-capped Chickadee—Common permanent resident

White-breasted Nuthatch—Regular summer resident, not often observed in winter

Red-breasted Nuthatch—Permanent resident in our woods, upper and lower, especially in conifers but often in maple groves

Brown Creeper—Observed mostly in winter and spring, but may have been a summer bird in woods

House Wren—First discovered by Keith along orchard stonewall; later nesting in syrup can placed in orchard tree (perhaps dummy nest of unmated male)

Winter Wren—Summer resident in our woods, not often observed. (Common on higher mountains)

(Gray) Catbird—Uncommon but regular summer resident

Brown Thrasher—Two records: April 26, 1925; June 13, 1926. Common later (Lelia)

American Robin—Common summer resident, March to November

Wood Thrush—First record (new?) on May 18, 1927; later a summer resident

Hermit Thrush—Common summer resident in both woods

Olive-backed (Swainson's) Thrush—First record July 18, 1927, apparently a little noted summer resident

(Bicknell's) Gray-cheeked Thrush—Summer resident on summit of nearby Camel's Hump which we climbed nearly every summer

Wilson's Thrush (Veery)—Found quite regularly in low swampy woods

Eastern Bluebird—Nested in three orchards and along field borders and pastures, sometimes in natural cavities, more often in boxes provided for them

Golden-crowned Kinglet—Winter visitor and common transient

Ruby-crowned Kinglet—Commonly observed in spring, its loud song a pleasant surprise when first identified

American (Water) Pipit—Listed for May 10, 1928; could be questionable

Cedar Waxwing—Common but irregular summer bird, sometimes nesting in our orchard

Northern Shrike—Frequently observed in early spring

Starling—Not present on our farm in the 1920's (came later), but we often saw it (one nest tree) en route to town and in village

Solitary Vireo—Observed frequently in spring, probably nested in woods

Red-eyed Vireo—Regular summer resident, roadside and woods

Warbling Vireo—Regular summer resident, orchard and maples

Black-and-white Warbler—Listed nearly every spring, probably nested

Tennessee Warbler—Listed for June 24, 1926 (probably a Camel's Hump record)

Nashville Warbler—Transient and probable summer resident

Parula Warbler—Listed for May 17, 1928 (could be questioned)

Yellow Warbler—Summer resident along river in town, not at our elevation

Magnolia Warbler—Regular summer resident, spruce and hemlock groves

Cape May Warbler—One record, May 16, 1926, in a blossoming apple tree in a pasture; a red-letter day

Black-throated Blue Warbler—Summer resident in ours and neighboring woods

Myrtle (Yellow-rumped) Warbler—Common transient, our earliest arriving warbler; common to abundant summer resident in mountains

Black-throated Green Warbler—Common summer resident, sugarbush and hemlock ridges

Blackburnian Warbler—Common spring transient, probably nested locally

Chestnut-sided Warbler—Common spring transient, probable summer resident

Bay-breasted Warbler—Recorded on June 12, 1927, and May 23, 1928

Blackpoll Warbler—Abundant summer resident in mountains (Camel's Hump)

17

Pine Warbler—Listed for May 2, 1926, might be doubtful

Palm Warbler—April 20, 1925, in a snowstorm, my only record

Ovenbird—Common summer resident

Mourning Warbler—Keith found a nest in Palmer's woods, found there regularly thereafter

Common Yellowthroat—Summer resident, mostly at lower elevations, but one nested in a blueberry patch near our house

Wilson's Warbler—Two records: May 30, 1925, and May 27, 1928

Canada Warbler—Uncommon transient and summer resident

American Redstart—Common summer resident

House Sparrow—Common village bird, especially around horse sheds, invaded our farm in later years

Bobolink—Common and much appreciated summer bird

Eastern Meadowlark—Uncommon (usually nonexistent) on our farm (regular later—Keith)

Red-winged Blackbird—Noisy singing flocks common in spring, not present as a summer resident in the 1920's but later invaded wet swales below our springs

Baltimore (Northern) Oriole—Nested in maples beside our house

Rusty Blackbird—Listed nearly every year

Bronzed (Common) Grackle—Have it listed every year but not a common summer bird on farm until later years

Brown-headed Cowbird—Have it listed for most years, but found mostly at lower elevations

Scarlet Tanager—Regular summer resident; spectacular spring transient

Rose-breasted Grosbeak—First record May 22, 1923, in Huntley's woods, regular thereafter

Indigo Bunting—Regular summer resident (hard to identify in poor light without glasses, but song, once learned, helps)

Purple Finch—Regular (?) summer resident

Pine Grosbeak—Common some winters; we fed them halved apples on the back porch

Common Redpoll—March 3, 1926, seems to be my only positive record

Pine Finch (Siskin)—Observed nearly every winter and/or spring

American Goldfinch—Irregular winter flocks; common summer resident

White-winged Crossbill—Quite regular winter visitor, sometimes lingering late in spring (possibly nesting); I had no record of Red Crossbills.

Chewink (Rufous-sided Towhee)—Listed for Aug. 5, 1925, apparently uncommon

Savannah Sparrow—Common summer resident in low meadows

Vesper Sparrow—Common summer resident, orchard border, roadside and pastures

Slate-colored Junco—Common spring and fall transient, rarely over winter; nesting commonly in nearby mountains

(American) Tree Sparrow—Common spring and fall transient, rarely in winter

Chipping Sparrow—Common summer resident

Field Sparrow—Found in Wheeler's dry pasture, not known to occur in our fields in early days

White-crowned Sparrow—A spectacular but uncommon transient

White-throated Sparrow—Common transient, uncommon summer resident in deep woods. (Common summer resident in mountains)

Fox Sparrow—Uncommon but fairly regular transient

Lincoln's Sparrow—Recorded for Sept. 30, 1926, could be doubtful

Swamp Sparrow—Discovered on June 13, 1923, in distant swamp, regular thereafter

Song Sparrow—Common summer resident, March to November

Snowflake (Snow Bunting)—Irregular winter visitor, flushed from snowy roads where horse-drawn sleighs traveled (no cars then in winter)

Supplementary Records

Ducks—Probably some Mallards (an uncommon duck in New England then) and Blue-winged Teal were among the unidentified ducks flushed from the local pond.

Ring-necked Pheasant—Not present in the 1920's, but widely introduced in later years; Waterbury was one of the major release sites

Killdeer—Not found in the 1920's, but Keith says they moved in more or less permanently in the late 1930's

Upland Plover (Sandpiper)—Not recorded in the 1920's, but appeared later in our upper field

Snowy Owl—I don't remember seeing one alive, but neighbors shot them on several occasions.

Pileated Woodpecker—Not recorded in the 1920's; noted frequently in the 1960's

Evening Grosbeak—Appeared in the late 1930's

Grasshopper Sparrow—Not recorded in the 1920's, but was found present in later years

References

Blanchan, N. *Bird Neighbors*. New York: Doubleday, 1902.

Burgess, T.W. *The Burgess Bird Book for Children*. Boston: Little, Brown & Co., 1920.

Chapman, F.M. *Handbook of Birds of Eastern North America*. New York: Appleton & Co., 1906, rev. ed. 1931 (reprinted in 1974 by Dover Publications).

Reed, C. A. *Land Birds East of the Rockies*. New York: Doubleday, Doran & Co., 1906, rev. eds. 1930, 1951.

Reed, C.A. *Water and Game Birds*. New York: Doubleday, Doran & Co., 1906, rev. ed. 1916.

Wallace, G.J. "A Changing World: Birds in Transition." *Massachusetts Audubon,* 54: (1970) pp. 2–10.

CHAPTER 2

Ann Arbor and the University Years

THE FALL OF 1928 ushered in a strange new way of life for a shy but aspiring farm boy who had never been far from home. I left home at twenty-one years of age to attend the University of Michigan. The year following high school, Keith and I had stayed home to operate the farm. We boys staggered our college educations in order to leave someone on the farm while others were in school. Mother was determined that all of us go to college, an opportunity denied both her and father. How grateful we were, a decade or so later, that she lived to see the last of her seven children graduated from college. (Grateful, also, we were that in 1976 she was listed in *Mothers of Achievement in American History,* 1776-1976.)

In addition to routine farm work during the winter and spring of 1928, Keith and I cut lumber in our woods, hired out to a neighbor to help saw his woodpile, and sold maple sugar—all to defray part of our college expenses. Beech, maple, birch, spruce, and hemlock logs at that time brought $18 to $25 per thousand board feet at the local mill. White ash, then in demand for scythe snaths and baseball bats, brought $40 a thousand. Cutting and hauling out the logs and transporting them to the mill was exacting work, but we enjoyed it. Keith took the initiative in directing operations, which gave me some opportunity to watch the few birds that frequented the Vermont woods in winter. My January-February bird list that year totalled fifteen species, perhaps all that were available there then.

To decide on a college, we pored over a selection of catalogues, largely to check tuition rates and curricular offerings. Most Eastern schools were way out of reach because of high tuition costs. Cornell University, my first choice because of the outstanding offerings in ornithology developed by Dr. Arthur A. Allen, was out of the question because of high tuition rates. In

21

contrast, tuition at my ultimate choice, the University of Michigan, was only $93 *per year,* plus a one-time $25 matriculation fee for out-of-state students. And because I was uncertain about a major course of study, the University of Michigan's almost unlimited course offerings would be useful to any student undecided about his field of study.

The Journey West

Resourceful brother Bob, who had already had three years at Ohio Wesleyan, accompanied me on my first journey to school. The chief mode of transportation for all of us in those days was hitchhiking. But by 1928 the Wallaces had acquired a car, an old Franklin given to us by our family doctor who had no further use for it. We soon understood why: sometimes it would run, sometimes it would not. Brother Bill, who had finished his four-year course at Ohio Wesleyan, was to take us on the first lap of our journey, to the New York State border, where we thought hitchhiking would be easier than on the back-road shortcut we took out of Vermont.

Hitchhiking was poor that fall, especially for two people traveling together. Motorists were getting more cautious about picking up hikers; some drivers had been held up by unappreciative hitchhikers. I had mixed emotions about our experiences on this trip. It was discouraging to stand by the roadside, sometimes for an hour or more, and see promising cars approaching, watch them whiz by without slackening their pace, then watch them receding in the distance. That whine of tires on the pavement, faint at first, then louder as cars passed, then faint again, continued to ring in my ears long after the trip was completed. Most of our rides were short hauls; one was a wild ride of eleven miles with a drunk driver who (fortunately for us) dropped us off at the next bar. But there were compensations too. Most of the drivers were friendly, sympathetic, and helpful, sometimes going out of their way to deposit us at a more favorable hiking spot or even treating us to a snack. Bob was always a diplomat, getting acquainted with strangers easily and carrying on a lively conversation with them.

Getting in and out of cities was often a problem; there were no throughways in the 1920s. But the big cities were also a thrill for me—a little frightening at times, yet fascinating. As I recall, we got stranded on the east side of Cleveland, boarded a street car, got a transfer in the center of town, and rode out to the western outskirts, a long sightseeing tour for weary travelers with tired feet. And all for five or ten cents.

On later trips, alone, I usually had better luck. I made the trip back and forth between Vermont and Michigan eleven times. Usually it took three or more days, but once I made it in two days and a half at a grand total of 55 cents. The home of our uncle, Dr. C. H. Richardson, a professor of mineralogy at Syracuse University, made a convenient halfway stop for me. Before our early morning departures, Uncle Henry always treated us to a breakfast of popovers, a specialty of his. And in the fall there was usually plenty of fruit in his backyard. During the fall of my quick-record trip, a bumper season for peaches, I bought a big bag of them at a roadside stand for five cents, which, with a box of graham crackers, sustained me until I reached Ann Arbor. However, I got stranded overnight in Toledo. A policeman to whom I confided my plight advised me to put up in a local flop house with other bums—for 25 cents. It was a frightful experience—a long row of cots in one big room. I clutched my pocketbook tightly all night (actually it had little in it), but the other bums, a few obviously drunk, ignored me completely.

Ann Arbor

Ann Arbor was an impressive sight—tree-shaded residential streets and a beautiful campus with attractive buildings. Bob helped me with registration procedures, with filling out applications for part-time jobs, and with finding a room to rent. Before he left for his school in Ohio, we dropped into a newly opened sandwich shop for a bite to eat. Typically, Bob struck up a conversation with the congenial proprietress, explaining our mission and my need for a job. That did it! She could use some help in the kitchen, and I went to work right away. I got along well with the management; when difficult times came and some of the help had to be dismissed, I was retained—indeed, often given overtime work for pay—until the restaurant went out of business later in the year.

I was not so fortunate in my choice of a room. The small garret enclosure seemed cozy enough at first, but when cold weather came, the room was inadequately heated. Sometimes the landlady—a large, fawning, almost repulsive woman—would drop in and see me huddled in an overcoat, trying to study. Then she would tell me what a nice boy I was, never complaining like some of the other tenants. She would promise to turn up the heat right away—but usually she didn't. It was also becoming increasingly difficult to scrape up the $3.50 weekly (payable in advance—there was no question about that) for the overpriced room by doing odd jobs on Saturdays. It irked me, too, that she charged the full price for the two weeks of Christmas vacation, when I was gone. She was holding the room for me, she said.

But many a dark cloud has a silver lining. At a Wesleyan Guild meeting that fall I met another student from Vermont. He was living with three elderly aunts—pro-Vermont "loyalists" because they had family connections there. He would be graduated at the end of the semester and would be leaving. Perhaps, he suggested, I could take over his room for a modest fee—enough to cover the cost of heat, water, lights, etc. The room was small, barely large enough to turn around in, but it was warm and comfortable and only four blocks from the campus. The dear ladies, a widow and her two spinster sisters who had moved into town from a farm they could no longer operate, took me in. I lived with them for five years for a dollar a week ($36 a year), payable when and if I had the cash. Once, with their approval—indeed, their suggestion—I let payment go for the whole academic year and paid it off by working the following summer. Sometimes I doubt if I could have survived those undergraduate years without the help of those kind, charitable ladies.

Another fortunate coincidence occurred that fall. During freshman week I had taken the required battery of tests that included writing a short essay. Some years earlier, in high school, I had won five dollars in a state nature essay contest; perhaps that helped me dream up something quickly. Anyway, I was put into an advanced sophomore-level rhetoric class. In a chance interview with the instructor, Carlton Wells, a young teacher still working for an advanced degree and trying to raise a family, I told him falteringly that I hoped to become a literary naturalist. He was immediately interested. He liked the out-of-doors, often took long walks, and was familiar with the writings of literary naturalists. But no one, he said, not even Dallas Lore Sharp or Walter Prichard Eaton, could make a living by writing nature essays. I would have to take up some other occupation and use writing as a sideline. Carlton Wells became my undergraduate adviser and a lifelong friend. Sometimes we took hikes together—I particularly remember the first one that October to a field full of asters, fringed gentians, and grass-of-parnassus. Once I had memorized Bryant's poem "To a Fringed Gentian," but in Vermont, despite considerable search, I had never found a fringed gentian.

A more novel experience was baby-sitting with the Wells' baby daughter. I recall one frightening episode that first year. Alone with the sleeping baby in an upstairs apartment one evening, I heard a rattling noise at one of the back windows. With my heart pounding, I peered cautiously through the kitchen window and could see a dark form apparently trying to break in through another window. Finally I mustered up enough courage to go outside and ask the man what he was doing. He was the apartment house janitor, removing screens for the winter.

Curricula and Instructors

That first semester, since I was considering (at least tentatively) a science major, I enrolled in Botany I. Not surprisingly, it was something of a letdown for an aspiring naturalist. The lectures and text were informative though not inspiring; but the laboratory work consisted mainly of drawing external and internal parts of plants, a task for which I had no talent. We did go on one field trip out into the University Arboretum. Eager to learn the names of a few unfamiliar wildflowers, I soon found out that the instructor did not know them either. Systematics was not his cup of tea.

Zoology I the following semester was a little better, but here, too, the labs were largely drawing exercises. One lab period on taxonomy, however, was more exciting. We identified and classified frogs—and didn't have to draw them. The recitation, or quiz, sections entirely separate from the lectures and labs, was interesting. We had a young unorthodox instructor who liked to raise provocative subjects—like the claim that man's beard continues to grow for three days after death.

In spite of a busy schedule that first year, I continued my never-ending quest for new birds. On and around the campus, Mourning Doves, Cardinals, and Tufted Titmice, unknown to me in north-central Vermont, were common, but I found little else that was new, even during spring migration. I still had little or no opportunity to visit local lakes and marshes where new birds could have been found. Apparently I gave up keeping annual lists during my Ann Arbor years, but I did have lists for some short trips. Unfortunately, all of these records were lost in a suitcase in the summer of 1932. Trying to remember when and where I first saw new birds during that period has proved nearly futile.

During my first three undergraduate years there was no formal course in ornithology at the university, but arrangements could be made for special work with birds at the university museum. Hence, at Carlton Wells' suggestion, I signed up for a special course with Dr. Josselyn Van Tyne, then a recent Harvard (A.B.) and University of Michigan (Ph.D.) graduate who had taken the post of Assistant Curator of Birds at the museum (Norman A. Wood, discoverer of the first nest of the Kirtland's Warbler, was head curator). Van Tyne was an impressive and to me an almost frightening figure. Six feet seven inches, gaunt and broad of frame, he seemed coldly scientific, even unfriendly. It was only years later that I learned he could be friendly, courteous, witty, and exceedingly helpful to anyone serious about information on birds.

Another student, much more advanced than I and already engaged in a

Ph.D. project on Great Horned Owls, also registered for the course. But he soon dropped out; farmers, he said, shot his owls as fast as he found new nests. Discouraged, he quit zoology entirely and switched to a major in Greek. That left me as Van Tyne's lone student. At the outset it was obvious that he was not impressed with my qualifications and he seemed to take no further interest in me. He gave a few informal lectures, assigned pertinent readings in various books, and arranged for laboratory work with the bird collections. My only examination was an oral final. As far as I know, I answered all his questions correctly. But I was not surprised, though a little disappointed and chagrined, to receive a C for my efforts—incidentally the only C I ever received in a biology course in my eight years at the university. He had summarily dismissed me as "unqualified" (one of his favorite terms) for a career in ornithology. (Later, I might add, I took an advanced course with another instructor and received an A + .) But it was nevertheless a good disciplinary experience. And as a fortunate dividend of it, I became slightly acquainted with the young instructor, a man only four years my senior, who was soon to become recognized as Michigan's leading ornithologist, and, a little later, an outstanding national and international authority on birds. (For a really profound insight into Van's character and accomplishments see Harold Mayfield's "In Memoriam: Josselyn Van Tyne.")

During that troubled semester I met Professor F.M. Gaige, a congenial and friendly man who was director of the museum. He seemed to sense my academic difficulty—a would-be naturalist not at home, as yet, with the more technical aspects of zoology. He urged me to take Dr. F. N. Blanchard's "Natural History of Vertebrates," a course, he said, that would take me out into the field, studying muskrat houses in winter, collecting salamanders at vernal pools, and listening to and taking notes on the spring choruses of frogs and toads. And even though I wasn't really eligible for the course, not having had the prerequisites, Dr. Blanchard agreed, reluctantly and with misgivings, to let me try it.

I soon realized my need for a better background, especially in comparative anatomy, though such a background was not quite indispensable. Blanchard's was one of the best courses I ever had. He was a rare naturalist and a careful observer, insistent on copious field notes and meticulous attention to details, then on writing up the results in a concise and accurate way. Every student had to keep an aluminum-covered, relatively waterproof notebook with removable pages. I still have the notebook; it has been with me, and used, on six continents.

On Blanchard's field trips I wasn't always a model student. Once I sneaked off with two other students to inspect a Long-eared Owl's nest that one of them had found earlier. It was my first Long-eared Owl. The only disciplinary action taken was that the class bus left without us, leaving us to walk the three miles back to the campus.

The indoor laboratory work was equally demanding. It entailed the identification and classification of fishes, amphibians, reptiles, and mammals (birds were largely excluded—Blanchard was soon to offer a separate course in ornithology). I already knew quite a few of the vertebrates but had to learn the scientific names, which came easily for me, much to the envy of two spinster school teachers who were really having a rough time mastering the names. The spot quizzes, exacting and sometimes tricky (I missed a juvenile milk snake—quite unlike the adult), were a challenge I greatly enjoyed.

My chief ornithological undertaking that spring, suggested by Carlton Wells, was an observational study of the mating flight of the American Woodcock. I had flushed a woodcock a few times in Vermont but had never observed the flight. Wells persuaded me to spend several evenings in April and May watching that spectacular phenomenon in a clearing in the arboretum not far from the Huron River. Several performing birds could be seen or heard at once. I watched them take off on their sudden spurt from the ground, tried to follow their dim forms on their aerial manoeuvers in the sky, and tried to pinpoint their exact landing spot so that I could sneak up more closely during the next flight. Since then, during my teaching years, I have often taken a few students at a time to observe the dramatic performance. Usually they have been equally thrilled.

At this time (1930), so far as we knew, little had been published on observations on the flight. Pettingill's monograph on the American Woodcock (a Ph.D. project at Cornell University) was to follow about six years later. Wells persuaded me to write up my observations for an ornithological journal. Both of us were pleased—and a little surprised, I think—when the manuscript was accepted for *Bird-Lore* by the editor, F. M. Chapman, then one of America's most distinguished ornithologists. I was pardonably proud at the time but somewhat deflated years later when William Sheldon published *The Book of the American Woodcock* (1967) in which his comprehensive and almost all-inclusive bibliography failed to list my earlier publication.

Since I had some background by now in natural history it seemed only logical that I should attend the University of Michigan Biological Station at Douglas Lake in northern Michigan that summer (1930). I wanted to take the beginning ornithology course, but Dr. Blanchard talked me out of it. He

University of Michigan's Angell Hall. Its massive pillars were an impressive sight to a neophyte freshman in 1928. Many of my undergraduate classes were held here. Michigan Historical Collections, Bentley Historical Library, University of Michigan.

Natural Science Building, my "home" during four graduate years. Michigan Historical Collections, Bentley Historical Library, University of Michigan.

Dr. Frank Nelson Blanchard—herpetologist, ornithologist, and naturalist engaged in a study of the four-toed salamander *(Hemidactylium scutatum)* in a swamp near Ann Arbor. Photo by Frieda Cobb Blanchard.

Blanchard Ornithology Laboratory at the University of Michigan's Biological Station at Douglas Lake in Cheboygan County, Michigan.

"Manville" at UMBS, where unmarried men students, including the author for two summers, were housed.

was right in contending that I needed other courses much more. However, I virtually took the course anyway; I couldn't resist stopping in the bird lab now and then to study the specimens and to try to help confused students— either the teaching instinct was cropping up, or, more likely, the desire to show off how much I knew about birds. And, of course, I continued my quest for new birds in this new setting. Although my summer records were lost later, at Carlton Wells' prompting I published a Douglas Lake list of one hundred species (some reported to me by other students) in the *Snowy Egret,* a mimeographed periodical published irregularly by the Olsen brothers, students at the university but also tireless observers of birds in the field. About a dozen of the one hundred species were not on my Vermont or Ann Arbor lists. The Bald Eagle at Grapevine Point and Ospreys and eagles around other lakes were particularly exciting.

I enrolled in Entomology and in Systematic Botany that summer. I had some trouble with both; I still lacked the inclination to buckle down to fine technical details. On a quiz question asking for the distinguishing characteristics of a bumblebee, for instance, I described the bee as I saw it— big, burly, noisy in flight—not by the venation of the wings or the apical spurs on the hind tibia. Most of the work in entomology, however, con- sisted of collecting insects in the field in the morning, then identifying and pinning them up in the afternoon, all the time being entertained by Dr. Hungerford's inimitable and often humorous stories about insects. I still have parts of that collection, representing about one hundred families— many specimens now minus head, wings, or legs, but many of them still in fair condition.

Systematic botany was a little easier. I already knew many of the plants but had difficulty with the technical keys in *Gray's Manual;* a previous course in plant anatomy certainly would have been helpful. However, I had my own shortcut for keying out plants: just look up the common name in the index, then turn to the page where the plant was listed and described. But "Ol' Doc Ehlers," as he was called, didn't approve of such techniques and got even with me. On the final written exam he gave each of us a specimen to key out. I think mine was a gentian that didn't look at all like a gentian—perhaps an aberrant species—and I muffed it. The final spot test in the field was also a little disconcerting. Doc told us no one had ever had one hundred percent correct on his final spot test. I thought perhaps I could do it. In the field we were lined up alphabetically from A to W, and one hundred plants were passed down the row. By the time they got to the W's some were in poor condition; one never reached me at all or else got switched with another plant en route. Another specimen came to me as a pathetic-looking twig—sans leaves, flowers, or fruit. I guessed correctly that it was a *Vaccinium* but had the wrong species designation. However, I missed another specimen with no good excuse, hence I failed to achieve that unprecedented perfect score.

By now I realized the need for buckling down to some difficult courses that didn't appeal to me. I had rebelled at the idea of taking some of them, but a fellow student, more scientifically endowed than I, used to argue with me about the necessity of such courses. He warned me particularly about Dr. Peter Okkelberg's infamous three—Comparative Anatomy, Embryology, and Histology. "They will be rough for you," he said. I would be in competition with premedical students hungry for high grades. But one had to have them, he insisted, for a zoology major. He was right. I took them and almost enjoyed them, especially comparative anatomy, which has always seemed to me so fundamental as a foundation for other biological disciplines. These three were followed by many other courses, nearly everything the department had to offer. I can't resist trying to characterize a few of the professors and their courses.

I had Prof. A. Franklin Shull, a nationally renowned geneticist and author of several textbooks, for five different courses: Zoology I; Organic Evolution; Heredity; Genetics; and Biometrics; the latter was a new course introduced by Dr. Shull. But I never felt close to the man. He was a dignified, unbending, austere individual. His lectures, precise and carefully worded, seemed stiff and humorless though clear. His apparent lack of humor was indicated one day when a student posted an amusing (or so I thought) cartoon in the genetics lab. The picture showed a mother cat with a very mixed-up litter of kittens—blacks, grays, whites, and tigers. The legend read: *Name the genotype of the father.* Dr. Shull entered the lab, looked carefully at the cartoon, and walked stiffly away without a trace of a smile. During my later teaching years I always posted cartoons that I thought were amusing takeoffs on bird watchers. Students sometimes added to the collection. One anonymous contribution was a provocative pinup of a scantily clad redhead labeled "homing pigeon."

But it was Shull's attitude toward people that disturbed me. A confirmed classifier of people as superior and inferior, in his course in heredity, he offended many Negroes by maintaining that they were intellectually inferior to whites; army tests, he said, proved it. He also frowned on working students; he seemed to contend that if their parents were not successful enough to be able to send them to college, they shouldn't go. According to his philosophy, I shouldn't have been in college because neither of my parents had had even a high school education.

31

By contrast, our eminent parasitology professor, Dr. George R. La Rue, was jovial and friendly with a characteristic twinkle in his eye. I was a little flattered at first because he called me George; later I learned that he didn't know my last name. However, he taught so thorough a course that it demanded considerable overtime in the lab. One Saturday morning I was putting in some extra time with a few other students when a white rat appeared in the lab. Always desperate for hosts to examine, I captured the rat, dispatched it, examined it for parasites, then disposed of the carcass. A little later two worried psychologists from the fourth floor came to our basement lab. They had lost a valuable, highly trained white rat. Had we by any chance seen it? I kept my mouth shut with fear and trembling. Fortunately another student, who had come in after the rat episode and was nearest the door, assured the psychologists that he hadn't seen a rat around the lab. Then Dr. La Rue came in and listened to the tale of woe. I think he surmised what had happened (he smelled a rat), but he merely told the psychologists that the parasitology lab was no place for a rat, trained or untrained, to be running around loose.

Another character much discussed among students was Dr. E. C. Case, the vertebrate paleontologist at the museum. Nearly every graduate student in zoology took his course—a full year of it—and never ceased talking about it. I was duly forewarned because my office "cellmate" and other students used to assemble in our office and discuss their problems. Although some of them were outstanding students, they were worried about their standing in the course. I think Dr. Case liked to intimidate students, especially if they pretended to know too much. He loved to get students to sound off on something about which they knew little. Then he would back them into a corner and slay them. I kept discreetly silent most of the time when I took the course and let a more brash student take the punishment, but I was a little worried because Dr. Case seemed to ignore me most of the time. However, I survived almost with flying colors, probably because I put so much effort into two required papers, one on fossil birds. Actually, although Dr. Case could be gruff and explosive at times, most students (including me) really liked and respected him very much. (The university erected a bust in his honor *before* he died. Dr. Case grumbled about the premature timing, but I rather suspect that he was appreciative of the recognition.)

During my crowded undergraduate years, I found little time for field excursions to look for birds. I even toyed with the idea of giving up zoology and taking an English major. I had had six courses in English composition and literature. Professor Wells continued to encourage me to go on with reading the literary naturalists—Burroughs, Thoreau, W. H. Hudson, Dallas Lore Sharp, Walter Prichard Eaton—but advised against an English major, which at that time didn't seem to hold much promise for a professional career.

By this time I had acquired a girl friend, a shy but determined and capable mathematics major who, like me, had a humble farm origin. She was a native Michigander from Rockford. Lacking the money for the more traditional types of entertainment, we used to go on walks. I remember showing her her first Black-and-white Warbler. She was duly impressed—at least with the bird, but I think the bird enhanced my chances. On another occasion we hiked out to the Forestry Farm, a six-mile round trip, on a balmy April day when spring flowers were bursting into bloom and newly arriving birds were singing. But there had been heavy rains and some of the paths in the woods were flooded. I carried Martha across one of the puddles (it really wasn't necessary), and I seem to remember that more clearly than any birds we saw that day. In the early morning when the tennis courts were always available we often played tennis. On those early mornings I used my *"fee-be"* whistle of the Black-capped Chickadee as a signal under her upstairs window. She was nearly always ready, but she overslept one morning. Her elderly uncle, in whose house she roomed, called up to her, "I think your boyfriend is whistling for you."

A turning point came in the first semester of my senior year, when I was still somewhat uncertain about a career. I enrolled in a newly organized ichthyology course that looked inviting. It was more than that: I almost became an icthyologist. We had a small class of dedicated students and a likable teacher, Dr. John Greeley, who had come from Cornell University that year to work with Dr. Carl Hubbs in fisheries, a curriculum that Dr. Hubbs was vigorously promoting. Greeley was a tall, lean, stoop-shouldered individual. Sometimes he apologized for his unscholarly lectures. But he had a good sense of humor and told us many amusing incidents concerning fisheries work about which, we soon realized, he was well informed. It wasn't difficult to persuade Dr. Greeley to offer a follow-up course in fisheries management, aimed at practical training in management for professional careers. At that time, during the worst of the Depression years, fisheries work was one of the few fields in biology that offered hope of future employment.

But for me a dilemma had developed. Dr. Blanchard had decided to offer an on-campus ornithology course that spring. I think it was the first one ever offered in the Department of Zoology, which at that time was separate from the museum. It conflicted with the icthyology course I had planned to take. I wavered but finally chose the ornithology. It may well have changed my career.

The ornithology course that spring was really my initiation to waterfowl and marsh birds in the field. We visited local lakes teeming with transient ducks. I think they were probably scaup, Redheads, Canvasbacks, Buffleheads, and mergansers, but I have no record of exactly what we saw. I do remember wading in Geddes Marsh, where we found rails, gallinules, coots, and Long-billed Marsh Wrens, and, in some cases, found their nests. By that time, laboratory identification posed few problems. Learning the scientific names of birds was not required in this course, but several of us, including Durward L. Allen, now so well known in wildlife fields, decided to do so anyway.

Graduate School

That summer (1932) I returned to the Biological Station for graduate work. It proved to be a rough summer. I elected to take a full load of courses, plus to work in the kitchen for meals and to put in considerable overtime. "Fresh Water Algae," taught by Dr. George Nichols from Yale University, suffered some for lack of time and perhaps inclination, but I gave my best for the plant ecology and advanced ornithology courses.

Dr. Frank Gates, well-known ecologist from Kansas State University, taught the ecology course. (His son David, then a small boy, is now the station's director.) We studied sand dunes (an overnight trip to the Sleeping Bear Dunes), aquatic habitats in various stages of succession, aspen associations and their gradual transition to pines, climax beech-maple communities, and orchid-filled bogs. Then we had to write up detailed reports on all of these, which often kept us up most of the night.

The ornithology field trips were much like those so aptly described by Theodora Nelson (1956) and Pettingill (1974). (Beloved Teddy Nelson was Blanchard's assistant that summer. Dr. Pettingill took over the class in 1938 after Blanchard's death.) Some of our field trips were to areas close by— around the lake, among the aspens, pines, and hardwoods, and to local bogs. But other trips, often starting in the early morning with the stars still shining and with both breakfast and lunch eaten in the field, took us farther away to Indian River, where we paddled or pushed flat-bottomed boats among the cattails and rushes, finding nests of Least Bitterns, Black Terns (I was nearly scalped by one), various ducks, and, of course, screaming Red-wings. We went to Cecil Bay and Duncan Bay to look for shorebirds and to Wilderness State Park for a little of everything. An additional assignment was to make a nesting study of a local bird. Mine, on the Hermit Thrush, was only partially successful. The first nest, safely snuggled, it seemed, in a dense lowbush blueberry patch, was broken up in the egg stage; a second nest was looted by a garter snake. I caught it removing a nearly grown bird from the nest.

Back on campus for what would stretch over another four years, I faced severe financial problems. I had hoped for a graduate assistantship, but there were none that year, nor, I think, in the following two years. There was a three-year Depression freeze on assistantships. Then in my last year things seemed to open up with quite a few vacancies. I thought an assistantship for me was inevitable, after waiting for three years. But the acting chairman of the department, who was largely responsible for filling the vacancies, said I was no longer eligible. Assistantships, he said, were apprenticeships for new incoming students (he had several). It was little consolation (but some salving of wounded feelings) that several of the apparently ill-chosen apprenticeship students flunked out that year.

There were, however, some redeeming aspects. Graduate assistants took half-time schedules (or less) and thus required longer to complete their studies. Some who hung on to assistantships for six years or more never did finish their Ph.D.'s Naturally I was eager to get out as soon as possible, so I always loaded up with a full schedule, defraying expenses by a variety of menial tasks. Martha's uncle, a kindly, benevolent, white-haired gentleman who helped many students through school by giving them jobs in his well-known and highly regarded Freeman's Dining Room, had passed away in 1931, leaving the dining room in the hands of his widow, Martha's Aunt Eva. She was a frugal, sometimes impatient, but kind-hearted woman. Somehow I got into her good graces (many people didn't) and worked for her for my four remaining years in Ann Arbor, a better deal than I had had during my last two undergraduate years working in the Michigan Union Cafeteria. We think she sometimes invented things for me to do for much-needed extra money. The odd-jobs paid only thirty cents an hour—Depression rates—but even that was welcome.

I worked, too, at the University's Botanical Gardens. Dr. Frieda Cobb Blanchard (daughter of Dr. Nathan A. Cobb, an internationally known nematodologist in the U.S. Department of Agriculture) was assistant director at the gardens and often found work for me there, including full-time work in the summer of 1934. This paid forty cents an hour, which prompted Mrs. Freeman to give me a ten cent raise when working for her.

Another break came with Roosevelt's NRA and FERA programs, which provided Federal funds for student employment. I obtained part-time work at the museum, rearranging some of the bird collections. Pierce Brodkorb, a museum assistant with some previous curatorial experience (but, like me, a struggling graduate student) supervised the work. (Now he is one of the world's leading avian paleontologists.) From the museum's standpoint I probably wasn't a very efficient worker because I spent so much time studying the labels on unfamiliar birds.

Somehow I managed to survive those difficult years. Employment in biology in those days, even with a master's degree, was virtually unobtainable—perhaps a blessing in disguise. Had a good job come my way, I might never have finished work on my Ph.D. Martha faced a similar predicament; she had a master's degree in mathematics and a teacher's certificate, but most high school math jobs went to men who could double as athletic coaches. But in September of 1934 we decided to get married anyway; my summer job at the gardens had netted enough to buy a wedding ring.

Like most of my colleagues in zoology, I made several false starts on a Ph.D. project. One on meadowlarks at the Botanical Gardens was abandoned when I learned that George Saunders at Cornell was just completing a three-year study on meadowlarks. A Cardinal study in the arboretum was also dropped; someone else had started a similar project. I toyed with robins for a while and had a few nests under study, but Van Tyne, by now a useful adviser, pointed out that the world literature on the cosmopolitan genus *Turdus,* to which the American Robin belongs, was so extensive that it would be exceedingly difficult to explore it thoroughly. At that time it was felt that if a student overlooked an obscure reference, even in a foreign language, his examining committee would give him a hard time. Today if a student lists all the available literature on a given topic, he is accused of padding his thesis with unnecessary references.

During these explorations for possible research projects, I had always kept in mind a little-known thrush, then known as Bicknell's Thrush in the Green Mountains of Vermont. Actually I had gone back in the summer of 1933 and camped on Mt. Mansfield for a couple of months but had arrived too late for the main nesting season. The one belated nest I found came to grief from an unknown cause, so I had given up the project, at least temporarily, as impractical. However, after our marriage in the fall of 1934, and having acquired a balky Model T Ford (for $20.00), we dreamed of the possibility of going back to the mountains for a more thorough study of that elusive thrush, a subspecies of the better-known and more widespread Gray-cheeked Thrush. During the academic year of 1934 to 1935 I explored all the available literature—fortunately not very extensive—

and Martha typed hundreds of reference cards, letters of inquiry to many thrush specialists, and even pertinent articles from the literature. Martha had finished work on her master's degree and was working for her Aunt Eva, doing the laundry for the dining room.

The long story of our travels East, to visit museums with pertinent collections, our acquaintance with many helpful co-workers, and that belated honeymoon in the mountains is the subject matter of the next chapter.

References

American Mothers Committee. *Mothers of Achievement in American History, 1776–1976*. Rutland, Vermont: Charles E. Tuttle Co., 1976.

Mayfield, H. "In Memoriam: Josselyn Van Tyne." *Auk,* 74: (1957) pp. 322–332.

Nelson, T. *The History of Ornithology at the University of Michigan Biological Station*. Minneapolis: Burgess Publ. Co., 1956.

Pettingill, O.S., Jr. "The American Woodcock *Philohela minor* (Gmelin.)" *Memoirs Boston Society Natural History,* 9:(1974) pp. 167–391.

_____. *Ornithology at the University of Michigan Biological Station and the Birds of the Region*. Kalamazoo: Kalamazoo Nature Center, 1974.

Sheldon, W.G. *The Book of the American Woodcock*. Amherst, Massachusetts: University of Massachusetts Press, 1967.

Wallace, G.J. "Birds of the Douglas Lake Area." *Snowy Egret,* (1930) pp. 1–2.

_____. "The Mating Flight of the Woodcock." *Bird-Lore,* 33: (1931) pp. 111–112.

CHAPTER 3

Vermont, Mt. Mansfield, and "Bicknell's" Thrush

On Our Way

DURING THE WINTER and spring of 1935 in Ann Arbor, we formulated plans for visits to the few Eastern museums that had pertinent collections of Bicknell's Thrush. Then we would continue on to Vermont for a field study of thrushes on Mt. Mansfield during the summer. Packing was a minor problem; we had very little to pack. Martha's brother, a good mechanic, overhauled the Model T for us, putting in new clutch, brake, and reverse bands, and giving the car a good tuneup.

Nevertheless, we had mishaps on the trip. We hadn't anticipated the ruggedness of the mountains that had to be crossed to get to Washington, D. C., where some of the important thrush specimens were housed. With a Model T one grinds up steep hills in low gear by pressing the clutch pedal firmly down to the floorboards; then one descends by alternately using the brake and the reverse pedal; the latter is done cautiously to minimize wear and tear on the brake bands. In time, with such treatment, all the bands—clutch, brake, and reverse—become so worn they no longer function.

We made good progress at first and were in high spirits; but eventually—inevitably—we got stalled halfway up a steep mountain in Pennsylvania. We couldn't go forward—no clutch; it would be unsafe to turn back—no brakes. So we parked for the night beside the road. Big trucks came grinding down the mountain, their headlights blinding us. It looked as if they would crash into us, yet they always missed us, sometimes it seemed by inches. Our little car shook with each passing vehicle. Martha says I slept soundly through it all (I doubt it), but that she didn't sleep a wink.

In the morning I hiked up the mountain for help. Fortunately, there was a garage at the top and a mechanic on duty. He came down the mountain with his tow truck, towed us to his garage, and put in new clutch, brake, and

38

reverse bands. I watched operations with apprehension, fearing we wouldn't have money enough to pay the bill. The total bill—for the long haul up the mountain, new bands for the gears, and the labor for installing them—came to three dollars!

Other difficulties involved encounters with the police. Once, when we were parked by the roadside to cool the motor by draining and refilling the radiator with water from a nearby stream, a patrolman stopped to check up on us. He questioned the legality of our 1934 license plates, which, according to a new Michigan law—a concession to motorists in the Depression years—were good until September 1935. Although still dubious, he let us go. Later, another cop was not so accommodating. Even if 1934 plates were legal in Michigan, he said, they were not acceptable in his state and we couldn't go on. He ordered us into court in the next town, but the local judge was more considerate. If our license was legal in Michigan, he said, it was all right in other states.

Some Eastern Museums

Our first business was at the Carnegie Museum in Pittsburgh to consult with Mr. W. E. Clyde Todd, curator of birds at the museum. Todd had three critical skins of male thrushes in breeding plumage from the Canadian Labrador (the north shore of the Gulf of St. Lawrence), which, with two skins of females collected earlier by Townsend, he thought represented a new subspecies. By his own confession, Todd was a "splitter," accused of naming "millimeter races," and this new thrush was apparently one of them. We had had some previous correspondence about the relationship of these North Shore birds to those in New England. Obligingly, he confided to me what information he had about the situation, but, he warned, it was with the distinct understanding that I was not to publish anything about it in advance of "his report." Later some of Todd's colleagues who knew him well advised me to ignore this request, since Todd might never get around to publishing his paper. (He did—twenty-eight years later—in 1963, when he was eighty-nine.)

Todd was a fussy but likable individual. His bird skins were perfect, laid out in neat rows in trays. He was reluctant to have me or anyone else handle them. I needed measurements of the specimens; I don't remember whether he finally permitted me to take the necessary measurements or whether I depended on those he had taken. He also gave me specific instructions on how to remove a book from a shelf in Pittsburgh. His books were kept in closed cases, in spite of which soot accumulated on the tops of volumes.

39

When I innocently removed one from a case, he told me to look at my index finger; it was black and there was a fingerprint on the top of the book. In Pittsburgh, he warned me, one removes a book from a shelf by lifting it out from the bottom, not the top.

Todd had many other pecularities, but I always liked and respected him, although I soon came to disagree with him about the validity of his North Shore subspecies. Devoutly religious Todd was a confirmed teetotaler; he abstained from coffee and tea as well. Once, in a receiving line in England, when he was sixty years old, he was handed a cup of tea. He looked at it, hesitated, then gulped it down—his first and only cup of tea. Because he lacked a college education, he refused honorary degrees. For those who would like further insight into Todd's virtues and eccentricities, I recommend Ken Parkes' classic in the *Auk* (1970): "In Memoriam; Walter Edmond Clyde Todd."

Our next official business was in Washington to examine the specimens in the Biological Survey and National Museum collections (then kept separately). I needed to confer with H. C. Oberholser, A. H. Howell, and Herbert Friedmann, with each of whom I had had previous correspondence about Bicknell's Thrush. I also had a cousin, George Dodge, chief clerk in the Bureau of Printing and Engraving, with whom we could stay during our several days in the city. Cousin George was a perfect host and guide. He proudly showed us all sights around the mall, carefully explained the Government's complicated functions, and took us down into the vault, where briefly, we were allowed to hold a million dollars (in stocks and bonds) in each hand. We were highly impressed with Washington; an impression that stayed with us for many years but has deteriorated since then.

Of the many people with whom I corresponded about Bicknell's Thrush, Dr. Oberholser was one of the most helpful. He had an uncanny memory for details. Often he could recall exactly where, when, and under what circumstances critical specimens had been collected, and he always showed a keen interest in the progress of my work with thrushes. At that time he and A. H. Howell, who had collected specimens of Bicknell's Thrush on Mt. Mansfield, held the view that the two sympatric color phases (as they proved to be) in New England might be separate species—a view that irritated J. L. Peters at the Museum of Comparative Zoology in Cambridge, who was not a "splitter" like Oberholser and Howell.

Oberholser seemed to take an interest in everybody and everything. While we were chatting about thrushes, two young boys, obviously twins, burst into the office in great excitement. They had discovered a Peregrine Falcon's nest along the Potomac and wanted to tell Oberholser all about it.

When they left Oberholser grinned approvingly. "Great little boys," he said. "They will go a long ways." They were the Craighead brothers, now so well known for their work with raptors, grizzly bears, and other wildlife.

After examining and measuring the specimens in the Survey collection, we tackled the collections in the National Museum. Martha recorded the data while I took the measurements. Dr. Friedmann, the curator, and his trustworthy assistant, J. H. Riley, were very helpful. We also met Dr. Ira Gabrielson, newly appointed chief of the Biological Survey and later director of the Fish and Wildlife Service. He had just returned from a trip to Vermont and said that Mt. Mansfield, our destination, was covered with snow.

On our journey north from Washington we bypassed the Academy of Natural Sciences in Philadelphia. I had borrowed their two breeding specimens from Carter's Dome, N.H. We also bypassed the Princeton Museum. Mr. C. H. Rogers, the curator, had sent me measurements and other data on the specimens in his care.

At the American Museum of Natural History in New York we encountered some difficulty gaining access to the bird collections, which were not open to the public. I believe it was Dr. Mayr (then at the American Museum) who finally got us admitted; J. L. Zimmer, as I recall, was working on his South American flycatchers and was not interested in my thrushes. However, it was Mr. O'Brien who did the legwork for us. He located and brought out the trays that contained the specimens I needed to examine—not a simple task when dealing with the world's largest collection of birds. In spite of the large collections, however, for me the specimens in the American Museum were not as critical as those in Washington and Cambridge.

While in New York we visited the Brooklyn Museum to try to settle an enigma that had bothered me for some time. The 1931 A.O.U. Check-list stated that Bicknell's Thrush wintered in Haiti and Venezuela, but I hadn't been able to run down a Venezuelan specimen. I had written to nearly every member of the checklist committee and to various museum curators, but none knew the source of the Venezuelan bird. At one stage a letter from L. B. Bishop of Pasadena, California, mentioned that he had a Bicknell's Thrush from Venezuela in his collection that was stored in his former home in New Haven, Connecticut; but when I borrowed Bishop's superb collection of thrushes, the specimen in question proved to be one of the larger Graycheeks, not the smaller subspecies. But a list I had received from the Brooklyn Museum included two specimens of Bicknell's Thrush from Venezuela, hence my desire to verify them.

With some difficulty we found our way to the Brooklyn Museum. It had been converted into a children's museum and appeared to have little use for scientific skins. However, an obliging attendant took us to a little-used storage room containing some old "Cambridge cans" (museum cases) of bird skins. He lifted a dust-covered can labeled "Thrushes" from an upper shelf and opened it. It contained the two thrushes in question, but they were wrongly identified. It was no great surprise to me to find that they were Olive-backed (Swainson's) Thrushes, which winter in northern South America. Thus ended my long quest for Bicknell's Thrush in Venezula. (Ironically, the 1957 A.O.U. Check-list reinstated Venezuela as a part of the winter range for Bicknell's Thrush, I think on the basis of specimens in the Phelps collection. I have not examined them.)

We looked forward to our visit to the Museum of Comparative Zoology in Cambridge, where the most critical specimens were housed. And we welcomed the opportunity to meet J. L. Peters, a leading authority on the taxonomy of birds and author of the first six volumes of *Check-list of Birds of the World.* I had had some correspondence with Peters about the specimens at MCZ, and he had written that it would be impractical to send them to me. I would have to come there to examine them. I soon understood why. He brought out tray after tray of specimens—those from the MCZ collection and those from the Batchelder, Bent, Thayer, and several other private collections, all housed in different areas of the range room. These all had to be assembled so that I could sort out the specimens I needed.

Needless to say, Peters' help here was indispensable. But for other reasons also both Martha and I have a warm spot in our hearts for him. He not only received us cordially but, better still—particularly at that point in time—he took us to lunch at the Harvard Club, the first complete meal we had had since leaving my cousin's home in Washington.

In addition to getting important data on the many thrushes in the collections at Harvard (and later those in the Boston Society of Natural History), two astonishing revelations came to light. The type specimen for Bicknell's Thrush, which had already had a long and complicated nomenclatural history, was still misidentified; and the Batchelder collection, which I had not seen before, solved another mystery.

The original type specimen for Bicknell's Thrush *(Turdus minimus),* unfortunately, was a trade skin from Bogotá, Colombia (thus not necessarily collected at Bogotá). Described by Lafresnaye in 1848 (in Latin and French), it was generally ignored, and Prince Bonaparte soon united it with *Turdus minor* (then the name for the Olive-backed Thrush), where it remained buried in synonymy for nearly seventy years. In the meantime, in

1858, Baird had described *Turdus aliciae,* the Gray-cheeked Thrush. And still later, (1881) Ridgway, on the basis of specimens obtained by Eugene Bicknell in the Catskills, named the Bicknell's Thrush *Hylocichla* (a generic change from the original *Turdus*) *aliciae bicknelli.* Things remained thus for another forty years, until Outram Bangs, in going over a series of old skins in the MCZ, chanced upon Lafresnaye's long-neglected *Turdus minimus* and erroneously reinstated it as the type specimen of Bicknell's Thrush.

By this time, however, I had established a new standard of measurements, based on more specimens than had ever been used before. My data clearly indicated that the old Bogota skin was not a Bicknell's Thrush but one of the larger Gray-cheeks. Oddly, none of the earlier examiners of the Lafresnaye bird had published any wing measurements, the only reliable morphological criterion. The left wing was broken off at the tip, but the right wing measured 99 mm, well above the maximum even for males of Bicknell's Thrush (the Bogotá skin was not sexed). Color was of little use in subspecific determination, because the Bogotá skin, according to Oberholser, had once been mounted and thus exposed to light, then later made into a study skin.

Happily (for me at least), the A.O.U. accepted my recommendations for changes, and the two forms became known as *Hylocichla minima minima* for the Northern Gray-cheeked Thrush and *Hylocichla minima bicknelli,* the Bicknell's Gray-cheeked Thrush. (More recently most of the genus *Hylocichla* has been merged with the neotropical genus *Catharus*).

The other surprising revelation came in examining Batchelder's fine collection of 43 Gray-cheeks from Newfoundland. In examining specimens of migrant Gray-cheeks in various museums I had been puzzled by occasional brown-phased birds of the larger northern form. It had long been known that *bicknelli* in New England consisted of overlapping and sympatric gray-phase and brown-phase forms, but this biphase color condition apparently had not been noted in the larger subspecies. The mystery was almost immediately solved when I saw Batchelder's specimens from Newfoundland: all or nearly all were brown-phase birds. This suggested a distinct Newfoundland race, which I later described—appropriately, I think— as *Hylocichla minima batchelderi,* but Peters persuaded me *not* to publish it. He argued—and I finally agreed—that the Newfoundland birds were merely a localized color phase not meriting recognition as a new subspecies. Later, John Aldrich, curator of birds at the National Museum, remarked to me that I had presented all the data for a new subspecies and then failed to name it. Still later (1958), Todd did describe the Newfoundland birds as a separate race, but so far as I know it has not yet been accepted by the A.O.U.

Mt. Mansfield and Its Thrushes

Now, at last, we were ready to undertake a study of the living birds in their mountain haunts, which, until I ran into the nomenclatural problems described above, had been my sole intention. En route to Mt. Mansfield we stopped at the home farm in Waterbury where Mother and brother Keith still lived, almost under the shadow of Mt. Mansfield. Here we stocked up with a few supplies, mainly provisions from Mother's pantry. Later we confiscated some old grain sacks for making blinds, somewhat to Keith's disapproval because they were worth five cents each at the local mill.

On May 27, in the late afternoon, we started our ascent of Mt. Mansfield via a two-mile foot trail that led from Smuggler's Notch, where we left our car, to Taft Lodge, a rustic, somewhat rundown log cabin nestled under the Chin (the highest point) of the mountain. Our timing to catch the arrival of the thrushes was nearly perfect. For the last part of our hike we ploughed through deep snow banks. One thrush called questioningly as we approached the cabin. Later, at dusk, one or more called a few times from the dense evergreens surrounding the Chin, but no birds were singing. The next day, the second mild day following a month of protracted cold—cold even for Vermont—several birds called again in the late afternoon; then, in the evening, one burst into a full-throated flight song so characteristic of these birds at dusk. The following day, May 29, as we sloshed our way across the three-mile skyline from the Chin to the Forehead, songs and calls were frequent all along the route. By May 31, with most of the snow melted by warm rains, the evening chorus seemed to have reached its maximum.

On the west side of the Forehead, nestled under a nearly vertical, several-hundred-foot cliff was a new log cabin, Mabel Taylor Butler Lodge, that was ideally located for our studies. We made arrangements with the Burlington Section of the Green Mountain Club to take over as caretakers, which entailed taking care of the cabin, keeping the local trails clear of debris, providing certain services for hikers on the trails, and disposing of nuisance porcupines. Overnight hikers were assessed 25 cents per person per night. The cabin was equipped with four bunks for eight or twelve people and a spacious loft accommodating ten or a dozen more. Hence, twenty people was a crowd, and one night we had thirty-two! (Fortunately for my thrush studies, few people came in June, the black-fly season.) We also sold supplies, mostly canned goods, candy bars, and Kool-Aid. Martha supplemented these with homemade cookies and blueberry pies baked in the stovepipe oven of a wood stove.

Supplies, of course, were not easy to come by. They had to be backpacked up a two-mile trail from the west side of the mountain, or, more conveniently for us, picked up at the summit house hotel, a mile and a half from our cabin. It was a rocky, boulder-strewn but relatively level mile over the skyline, then a nearly vertical half-mile descent to our cabin. The hotel proprietors were very accommodating. They arranged to bring our supplies up the mountain on a delivery truck that made frequent trips to Stowe, the nearest town on that side of the mountain.

Dehydrated foods were uncommon and expensive in those days; canned goods constituted the bulk of our food supplies. These could be supplemented on occasion from Nature's storehouse, mainly blueberries, which were abundant in season, and porcupines. The latter are exceedingly destructive to Long Trail cabins and shelters. They chew their way in through windows and doors or up through the floorboards. A cabin in which porcupines have wintered is a sight to behold. We found the porcupines quite edible in the absence of steaks; the old ones, even with parboiling, were rather tough, stringy, and flavorless, but the younger ones were fairly good. Their livers were a special delicacy; often we were wasteful of resources and ate only the livers. By the end of the summer we almost, but not quite, ran out of porcupines. Once we tried a squirrel stew (I had a collecting gun), but red squirrels, the most carnivorus of the Sciuridae and the only squirrel on the mountain, were not very savory and we didn't try it again.

From our doorstep we had a spectacular view. Nearly all of northwestern Vermont lay stretched out before our wondering eyes—green hills, fertile meadows, winding rivers, and cozy hamlets. And beyond that lay the one-hundred-mile expanse of Lake Champlain, backed up by the Adirondacks of New York. From the summit—Forehead, Nose, and Chin—we could see all this plus the White Mountains of New Hampshire in the east, and sometimes, on the clearest days, parts of Canada in the north. Often at sunset the waters of Lake Champlain shone like a sea of gold. In the mornings great banks of snow-white fog hovered over the valleys below, then rose and dispersed slowly, bathing the mountaintop with mists for hours or even all day. Previous observers of Bicknell's Thrush had noted that it was a bird of the mists, singing more in mist and rain than on clear days. Sometimes we found abandoned nests of previous years still intact with their mossy walls still green. Conifers around the summit were invariably densely covered with gray-green lichens.

The Green Mountains of Vermont extend in a long chain, with lateral extensions, from the Berkshires of Massachusetts to Canada. The 260-mile Long Trail (a part of the Appalachian Trail that in Vermont crosses over to

Mabel Taylor Butler Lodge, Mt. Mansfield, Vermont. A Long Trail lodge where we spent two summers in a study of Bicknell's Gray-cheeked Thrush. © National Geographic Society.

Nest hunting in the spruce and balsam scrub on Mt. Mansfield. © National Geographic Society.

Photographs by Willard R. Culver

46

Nest, young, and adult of bicknell's Gray-cheeked Thrush. © National Geographic Society.

Our Pet "Bicky"—tame, charming, musical. © National Geographic Society.

Photographs by Willard R. Culver

New Hampshire and Maine) threads its way across the summits of all the higher mountains and dips through the valleys connecting successive peaks. The five peaks that exceed 4,000 feet have a true timberline, a treeless, boulder-strewn, wind-swept summit; likewise, some of the thirty peaks that exceed 3,500 feet are bare at the top, a few having been denuded by fires. The other 400 peaks are wooded over the top. A hike along this "footpath through the wilderness," or any portion of it, is a memorable experience.

Mt. Mansfield, the highest (4,393 feet) and most formidable mountain in this chain, has a three-mile stretch of summit from the Forehead to the Chin, mostly bare and wind-swept, but with every available crevice, cranny, and sheltered nook harboring pioneer plants—lichens, mosses, hardy herbaceous plants, and ericaceous shrubs. Wherever they can gain a foot-hold, dense matted stands of conifers—mainly red spruce *(Picea rubra),* balsam *(Abies balsamea),* and dwarfed birches *(Betula papyrifera)*— have taken over; sometimes they are so densely matted that one can walk over the tops of them without sinking through. At lower elevations the trees grow much taller. Below and around our cabin, at 3,000 feet, there were fine stands of spruce and balsam; but above us, where the trail climbed to 4,000 feet, the trees became dwarfed and stunted.

Ground flora consisted of plants often found in bogs a thousand miles further north—common wood-sorrel *(Oxalis montana);* false lily-of-the valley *(Maianthemum canadense);* clintonia or bluebead-lily *(Clintonia borealis);* bunchberry *(Cornus canadensis);* Labrador tea *(Ledum groenlandicum);* creeping snowberry *(Gaultheria hispidula);* and several species of *Vaccinium,* including mountain cranberry *(V. vitis-idaea).* Nearer the summit we found crowberries *(Empetrum nigrum),* clumps of mountain sandwort *(Arenaria groenlandicum),* and three-toothed cinquefoil *(Potentilla tridentata).* In the more boggy areas—as along the numerous rivulets, for instance—were dense stands of Indian poke or false hellebore *(Veratrum viride),* turtlehead *(Chelone glabra),* sharp-leaved aster *(Aster acuminata),* and mountain goldenrod *(Solidago macrophylla).* Spinulose ferns *(Aspidium spinulosum* var. *dilatatum)* grew nearly everywhere, and rock ferns *(Polypodium vulgare)* covered many of the boulders along the trails. Often the ground was carpeted with mosses, chiefly *Sphagnum* in the wetter places and *Calliergon* under the conifers. Both mosses, especially the latter, were used freely in the nests of birds at or near the timberline.

Species of mammals on the mountaintop were few. Porcupines *(Erethizon dorsatum)* and red squirrels *(Tamiasciurus hudsonicus)* were the most conspicuous; the latter, often quite vociferous, were the chief predators on nesting birds. Wood mice *(Peromyscus* sp.) invaded the cabin and became mischievous but charming guests. And we almost made a pet of a red-backed vole *(Clethrionomys gapperi)* that came to supper each evening. Once, while nest hunting, Martha peered over a log and found herself face-to-face with a bobcat *(Lynx rufus)*. In three summers on the mountain I never got a glimpse of one. Occasionally we flushed snowshoe hares *(Lepus americanus)* from the trails, but they were probably more common than our fleeting glimpses of them indicated. Other mammals, of course, occurred at lower elevations.

Summer bird life above 3,000 feet was also severely restricted. Although a total list of Mt. Mansfield birds, including transients and those found in the hardwoods and clearings at the base of the mountain, would number more than one hundred species; less than two dozen occur regularly above 3,000 feet. Perhaps the most common, though not the most conspicuous, were the Blackpoll Warblers. Their soft tinkling song, beginning with a few weak notes and rising to a fine swell, then falling to almost inaudible tones, is hardly noticeable to untrained ears, but it blends in harmoniously among the mist-shrouded evergreens. Nearly every search for a Bicknell's nest disclosed one or more Blackpoll nests tucked inconspicuously among the lower branches of small conifers. Myrtle (Yellow-rumped) Warblers were less common and their more elevated nests harder to find. The only other nesting warbler we found above 3,000 feet was the Canada Warbler. The neat little nest that Martha found, half concealed under the roots of a small tree, is among her unforgettable memories.

The most conspicuous and most vocal of the birds on and around the summit were the White-throated Sparrows and Slate-colored (Dark-eyed) Juncos. The loud incessant trill of the juncos echoed among the boulders and seemed much more musical than when heard during migration in the valleys below. From dawn to dark in June the high sweet quavering whistle of the numerous Whitethroats was seldom lacking. Once I heard one sing eighteen consecutive syllables instead of the usual five or six. The nests of both species seemed well concealed in the crevices among rocks or well camouflaged in mossy banks, yet all too frequently we found them looted by predators.

Another much loved singer, more often heard than seen, was the Winter Wren, whose cascade of melody tumbled like the waterfalls with which it was associated. With the wrens, at least in the more boggy areas, were a few Yellow-bellied Flycatchers, but their spiritless *per-wee* attracted little attention.

Among the taller conifers we often encountered Black-capped Chickadees, but I saw only one Brown-capped or Boreal Chickadee all summer. It is said to be more common in the White Mountains of New Hampshire and in the mountains in eastern Maine. Associated with the chickadees were Red-breasted Nuthatches, Golden-crowned Kinglets, and an occasional Brown Creeper. Once I encountered a family group of creepers. The newly fledged youngsters were having a difficult time clinging to tree trunks with their partially developed rectrices. Musical Purple Finches were also common; roving White-winged Crossbills much less so.

One obliging Ruffed Grouse nested behind our cabin and raised seven young from an eight-egg nest. Occasionally a few hawks were seen flying about distant peaks, but I had poor luck trying to identify them. Peregrine Falcons supposedly nested somewhere on the surrounding cliffs, but I never located an eyrie. Bald Eagles frequented the opposite side of the mountain in Smuggler's Notch, which we seldom visited.

Mt. Mansfield's Thrushes

But our goal was thrushes. Olive-backed (Swainson's) Thrushes inhabited chiefly the areas below 3,000 feet and the Bicknell's Thrushes above that level, but there was some overlap; we found nests of both species both above and below the 3,000 foot contour line. The Olive-backs built bulkier nests with more twigs and fewer mosses, and their larger eggs were a duller blue-green with heavier spotting. I took some notes on Olive-backs, largely for comparative purposes, but I toyed with the idea of returning some summer for further studies. It was never done. Sometimes on still evenings we could hear the songs of Veeries and Hermit Thrushes, and, more rarely, the song of a Wood Thrush, drifting up from the valleys below. Hence, it was possible—though not a common experience—to hear the songs of all five North American woodland thrushes singing more or less simultaneously.

Our quest for nests of Bicknell's Thrush was an exciting challenge. From the literature we had learned that Bicknell's Thrush was reputed to be one of the shyest, rarest, and least known of North American passerine birds. Its choice of the bleakest, most isolated, and inaccessible habitats, and nesting as they did in the most impenetrable tangles, made it difficult to study. Collecting breeding birds posed problems. William Brewster, one of New England's most distinguished early ornithologists, wrote that it was next to impossible to creep within shooting distance of one (Brewster, 1883). "Indeed," he wrote, "the two specimens taken were only secured by snapshots directed almost at random toward some opening in the branches where the flash of a wing betrayed its owners movements." Howell (1901), in seven trips to the summit of Mt. Mansfield, said that although he could hear the birds all around him, "so shy were they that I saw them probably less than a dozen times. . . . A close study of their habits was impossible."

Excursions to the mountains by zoologists for the coveted sets of eggs were also often unsuccessful, sometimes because collectors arrived too late in the season and found only deserted nests or none at all. One successful collector on Seal Island, Nova Scotia, said that the nest was the most difficult to find of any small bird. One female detected carrying nesting material (Tufts, 1909) "dropped her load" on seeing the observer "and silently disappeared in the woods."

After some initial difficulties, however, we found that by sticking with the birds and learning how and where to look for nests, it really was not so difficult. But my second nest discovery (the first nest was soon deserted) reminded me of Tufts' experience on Seal Island. A female carrying nest material dropped it on seeing me, shaking her bill as if to dislodge the last fragment, and flew away. However, she soon reappeared with another load and then dropped that also. Four times this wary bird appeared with nesting material, and four times she dropped it. But on the fourth trip she went close to a partially built nest that I had not noticed before. Thereafter, as soon as I withdrew to a clump of small conifers, she seemed to ignore me and continued to work on the nest unperturbed. Later, observing from a blind, I found this female quite tame and cooperative, and I gleaned much useful information from the nest before it was broken up by predators.

We located twenty nests of Bicknell's Thrush that summer, but seven of them were deserted or empty when found. Thirteen occupied nests were studied in some detail, usually from blinds, and although only four of them were successful in fledging young, we were able to piece together the complete breeding cycle from the initial stages of nest building to the fledging of the young. Keeping two young birds captive—one of them for a full year—gave us additional information. Nesting success (24.4 percent) that summer seemed pathetically low—eleven young fledged from thirteen nests (0.85 young per nest)—but of course one summer's study is not a reliable basis for estimating reproductive success. The full story of our thrush studies is told in a 190-page monograph (Wallace, 1939) and summarized in Bent's *Life Histories of North American Thrushes, Kinglets and Their Allies.*

The song of Bicknell's Thrush has been aptly described by many observers. Structurally it is similar to the song of the Veery, but is distinguishable by an emphatic break a little past the middle of the song. It is introduced by two or three low clucking notes, audible only at close range. The preliminary notes are followed by two to four—usually three—high-pitched, ringing phrases that break usually on the third phrase into several merged climax notes of higher pitch and increased intensity. These notes are held momentarily and then imperceptibly glide into the closing notes, which are not emphasized. Without benefit of sound recording equipment in those days, I described the song as *chook-chook, wee-o, wee-o, wee-o-ti-t-ter-ee,* notes that can be approximated by whistling through closed teeth. During the short breeding season in June, the song is repeated over and over. Often several birds sing at once, until the mountain heights ring with the chiming notes.

Two features of the singing merit special mention. In 1933, I found that Bicknell's Thrushes on Mt. Mansfield had an intensive, ten-to-fifteen-minute period of flight singing at dusk, a phenomenon not previously recorded for these birds. In 1935 they proved to be regular flight singers in the evening. A few minutes after sunset they emerged from concealment, flew from perch to perch or circled in the air, singing on the wing, often several of them simultaneously. They seldom resorted to flight singing at others times of day.

The other peculiar feature was the singing by the females at or on their nests. In nearly every nest studied closely, the females were observed to sing during incubation, hatching, and brooding of the young. Particularly during the hatching process the female sometimes perched on the rim of the nest and sang—in apparent ecstasy—while watching the eggs hatch. Usually the male was not in evidence at such times, but sometimes he visited the female at the nest, occasionally singing in unison with her.

Ann Arbor Again

After amassing these field data in the summer of 1935, we returned to Ann Arbor for a final year at the university. A janitorial job for me in a basement apartment with both of us working at Freeman's (Martha full time) kept the wolf away from our door while I completed my doctoral dissertation. By another fortunate coincidence, one of the department's instructors was on leave that semester and I was allowed to use a desk in his crowded office with the understanding that I would disturb nothing. Since I had few books, I needed only writing space and quiet, which is what I had for the whole semester. Dr. Blanchard, my major professor, was on sabbatical leave, so I was on my own. When he returned, I dumped a nearly completed dissertation on his desk. He was surprised and a little shocked; somehow he had had the impression that I had dropped the whole project.

He looked at it in dismay, read the first few pages, then sized up the bulky manuscript and did the best thing he could have done under the circumstances: before reading it critically himself, he turned the whole thing over to his wife, a good grammarian and experienced editor. Mrs. Blanchard—bless her heart—spent many hours going over the manuscript, ferreting out mistakes and inconsistencies that I didn't know existed. I spent most of another semester revising and getting the manuscript in shape. Then Martha had to retype the whole thing—about three hundred pages.

But the whole project turned out well. It was unanimously approved by my doctoral committee; even sometimes-supercritical Dr. Van Tyne said that it was satisfactory. When finally published in somewhat reduced form three years later, it might have made me famous except for the fact that few people outside New England knew that there was such a thing as the Bicknell's Thrush. Then—the last straw—in the 1957 A.O.U. Check-list, the committee dropped the use of subspecific names. In a sense, then, there is no such thing as a Bicknell's Thrush; it is a geographic race of the Gray-cheeked Thrush. This leaves me in the humiliating position of claiming to be a world authority on a bird not recognized by the A.O.U.

Our apartment life that year had both bright spots and dismal moments. Among the latter was the fact that I tended the furnace (hence we had ample heat), but it was an old relic that had a bad habit of accumulating gas under the top layer of coal, then suddenly exploding, throwing open the furnace door and spreading soot and ashes all over our apartment. Often, after such explosions, we could trace our names on the table in our breakfast nook next to the furnace room. The basement was flooded once during the spell of heavy rains. Mud and water ruined nearly everything—but nearly everything belonged to the landlord, not to us.

One of the bright spots was our precious pet thrush who sang to us all fall, winter, and spring. During the summer we had taken a young thrush from a nest that was doomed to failure. Two of the young had already died, probably from *Protocalliphora* parasites that commonly afflicted young thrushes about halfway through nest life. We nursed the surviving young bird back to good health after removing nearly a hundred eggs of bluebottle flies from his ear cavities—eggs that would soon have hatched into carrion-feeding larvae. He became a charming but short-lived pet. He took daily baths in a dish provided for that purpose. But on his twenty-ninth day, when supper was in progress and before anyone could prevent it, he suddenly plunged into a dish of scalding water on the stove. Though promptly snatched out, it was too late. Death was practically instantaneous, and with a few quick gasps he lay still.

To replace the lost bird we captured a healthy youngster that was fledged from a belated nest. This bird we brought back to Ann Arbor with us. He provided us with incomparable music all year—not the full song of the species, which he presumably had never heard, but a constant flow of thrush-like musical notes, often evoked by hissing steam in hot water pipes, the rattling of dishes in the kitchen, or other sounds. He never learned the complete adult song until we took him back to Mt. Mansfield the following summer and released him.

Washington Revisited

The sequel to this thrush story is that in May 1936 Mrs. Blanchard, who had written an article for *National Geographic Magazine,* decided to drive to Washington to see Gilbert Grosvenor, the editor. She also wanted to visit her widowed mother, who still lived in the old Cobb homestead in Falls Church, Virginia. She invited us to go along to introduce "Bicky" to the celebrities in Washington. Dr. Grosvenor and Dr. Wetmore, assistant secretary of the Smithsonian Institution, were both delighted with the young bird. And Dr. Grosvenor, with some prompting from Mrs. Blanchard, invited me to write a story about our experiences with Bicknell's Thrush on Mt. Mansfield. He would send a photographer to the mountain at the proper time, if we could be there with nests staked out to photograph.

Back in Vermont

Since we were still jobless in spite of applications sent all over the United States, we decided to go back to Mt. Mansfield to find nests for the photographer. I would write the proposed story, and we would spend another summer at Mabel Taylor Butler Lodge. Willard Culver, National Geographic Magazine photographer, visited us twice that summer and got a fine series of pictures. In due time the story was completed, turned in and accepted, but, to my disappointment, it was never published. We never knew why—perhaps it was too "scientific," or too much a condensed version of a thesis; perhaps, some suggested, the pictures should have been in color (they were all black-and-white). However, I was paid royally for my attempt ($300), which more than paid for our first daughter who arrived February 27 the following winter (1937).

There is a final note to our Vermont experiences. One of our letters of application for a job went to the Vermont Fish and Game Service in Montpelier. It seemed rather hopeless because I was neither a hunter nor a fisherman and had had no special experience with game species. A rather casual reply came from Dr. R. P. Hunter, the new director of the Fish and Game Service, suggesting that I drop in to his office sometime, when convenient. I "dropped in" that fall and found that he had written to the University of Michigan for my credentials and for the letters of recommendation (including, I assume, a solid one from C. F. Wells) on file in the placement bureau. After a brief interview he arranged for a meeting of the board of directors to see if they would approve my appointment as a biologist for the Service. It happened just like that! I went to work on October 1, at the magnificent salary of $100.00 a month ($1200 per annum), but at that time we were exceedingly grateful for any steady job.

My nine months with the Service proved to be a useful experience. Although I hobnobbed mostly with state game wardens, some of whom had been former poachers now enlisted as game wardens to track down other poachers, I had a pleasantly varied program both indoors and out. My chief assignment was a pheasant survey to try to determine suitable locations for stocking. But I also had an opportunity to study waterfowl. I started a bird-skin collection for the Service and kept incidental records on all birds seen on my trips. I traveled, usually in company with a game warden, to all fourteen counties in the state, mainly to those that showed some promise for pheasant stocking. Needless to say, the game wardens gave me a liberal education as to their views on fish and game problems.

This part of our story would be incomplete without some comment on our domestic trials. Housing was scarce and expensive in the capital city, but we soon found a spacious, unfurnished third-story apartment over a busy creamery. Six rooms were distributed along a lengthy corridor, a dining nook at one end and the living room at the other, with a kitchen, bathroom, and two bedrooms strung along in between. We used most of our available cash for the first month's rent but had ten dollars left to sustain us until our first paycheck came at the end of the month. But presto! The gas company required a five-dollar deposit to turn on the gas, and the electric company took the other five dollars, leaving us virtually penniless. Most of what furnishings we had, including kitchen utensils, were stored in Ann Arbor. But we had a coffeepot, a wedding gift from a friend. Martha secured a soup bone, and with some vegetables purloined from the farm in Waterbury, she made our daily soup in the bottom of the coffeepot. There was only one light bulb for the six widely separated rooms; after dark we took the bulb with us whenever we went from one room to another. But, by borrowing a bed and certain other necessities from the farm, we survived that first month.

Things went well with work for the Vermont Fish and Game Service. I

55

enjoyed my wide travels throughout scenic Vermont—fall, winter, and spring—although admittedly I was not always at ease with some of the rough-and-ready game wardens. Director Russ Hunter, by academic training an embryologist from Cornell University but an avid sportsman, was an able administrator and friendly counselor. But in June 1937, after nine months with the Service, my work there came to a sudden and unforeseen termination. A private sanctuary, the Pleasant Valley Bird and Wild Flower Sanctuary in Lenox, Massachusetts, in the heart of the Berkshires, was looking for a new "warden"—the old English term for what might better be called a grounds superintendent. One of the trustees of the association, Walter Prichard Eaton, professor of drama at Yale University, had asked his friend Carlton Wells what had become of his Bicknell's Thrush boy. Would he be interested in the job? I was. It paid $1800—$600 more than I was getting in Vermont—and housing on the sanctuary grounds was furnished with all utilities paid by the Association. Dr. Hunter advised me to grab at the opportunity. Although I was due a raise for the coming year, he said, they could not match the terms offered by the sanctuary in Lenox.

References

A.O.U. Check-list of North American Birds. 4th ed., 1931; 5th edition 1957, and 32 supplement, 1973. American Ornithologists' Union.

Baird, S.F. *U.S. Pacific R.R. Surveys,* 9: (1858) p. 217.

Bangs, O. and T.E. Pennard. "Some Critical Notes on Birds." *Bulletin of the Museum of Comparative Zoology,* 63: (1919) p. 30.

Bent, A.C. *Life Histories of North American Thrushes, Kinglets, and Their Allies.* Bulletin 196, (1949) U.S. National Museum, Washington, D.C. ("Bicknell's Thrush," pp. 199–217).

Bicknell, E.P. A sketch of the home of *Hylocichla aliciae bicknelli* Ridgway, with some critical remarks on the allies of the new race. Bulletin Nutt. Ornith. Club 8: (1882) pp. 12–17.

Craighead, J.J., and F.C. Craighead, Jr. *Hawks, Owls and Wildlife.* Stackpole, Harrisburg, Pa., and Wildlife Management Institute, Wash., D.C., 1956.

Davenport, E.B. "Birds observed on Mt. Mansfield and in Stowe Valley in 1902." *Wilson Bulletin* 10: (1903) pp. 77–86.

Howell, A.H. "A Preliminary List of the Summer Birds of Mt. Mansfield, Vermont." *Auk* 18: (1901) pp. 337–347.

Lafresnaye, F. "Habitat ad Bogotam, in Nova Grenada." *Revue Zoologique* 1: (1848) p. 5.

Parkes, K.C. "In Memoriam: Walter Edmond Clyde Todd." *Auk,* 87: (1870) pp. 635–649.

Peters, J.L. *Check-list of Birds of the World.* Cambridge, Massachusetts: Harvard University Press, 1931–1948.

Todd, W.E.C. "The Newfoundland Race of the Gray-cheeked Thrush." *Canadian Field Naturalist,* 72: (1958) pp. 159–161.

_____. *Birds of the Labrador Peninsula and adjacent areas.* A distributional list. Toronto: University of Toronto Press, 1963.

Tufts, H.F. Breeding Notes. Macoun's Catalog of Canadian Birds, Department of Mines, Geological Survey, (1909) pp. 739–740.

Wallace, G.J. "Bicknell's Thrush, Its Taxonomy, Distribution, and Life History." Proceedings Boston Society Natural History, 41(6): (1939) pp. 211–402.

_____. "Vermont's Pheasant Situation." *American Wildlife,* May-June 1940.

CHAPTER 4

Pleasant Valley Sanctuary and the Berkshires

Interviews and Appraisal

MY INTERVIEW FOR the post of warden at Pleasant Valley Sanctuary was an awesome experience. I had an invitation from Miss Mary Parsons, one of the sanctuary's trustees (and, I soon learned, the chief supporter and guiding light of the organization), to come for an interview, to visit the sanctuary, and to be her guest overnight.

I had instructions for getting to Stonover, her home in Lenox. A private drive led through a walled passageway into a large courtyard within which stood a huge stone mansion. My car ground its way noisily through the loose gravel; although I had graduated from a Motel T to a Model A (of 1931 vintage), it looked out of place in a courtyard presumably accustomed to more expensive models. Hesitantly I approached the massive front door and lifted the heavy iron knocker. The door swung open and a tall, gaunt, stony-faced woman eyed me coldly. When I explained that I had an appointment with Miss Parsons, she melted ever so slightly and informed me that Miss Parsons was resting and was not to be disturbed. I was to visit the bird sanctuary first. She summoned a chauffeur—a rotund, jovial, ruddy-faced man who seemed to appear suddenly from nowhere. He gave me directions for finding the sanctuary: up the mountain two miles, a right turn at the top of the steep hill, past a deserted house to the sanctuary, which would be marked by a rustic metal sign over a rail fence.

The scene at the sanctuary was a little frightening, and I considered beating it for home. Cars were parked all along the rail fence, and a large Greyhound Bus had spewed forty or more noisy children all over the place. An old house of brown-stained clapboards—built, I learned later, by a retired officer of the Revolutionary War in the 1790s—stood just beyond the gateway. Beyond that was a red barn with open doors, the scene of most of the bustling activity.

58

The bus with its noisy cargo soon left, however, and things quieted down. The exhausted warden, S. Morris Pell, greeted me cordially, then flopped down on the lawn and said that I was seeing the sanctuary at its worst. Sometimes on weekends in summer (it was a Saturday afternoon in late June) things got pretty hectic, but during much of the year it was usually peaceful and quiet, and in the winter only the most hardy (or foolhardy) attempted the climb up the mountain. He explained his reason for leaving. He was a self-taught naturalist, with little or no academic training in biology, and he wanted to go back to school to get a better foundation for a career in wildlife. The trustees also felt that they needed someone with an academic background. (They made the most of my degrees and apparently instructed sanctuary personnel to address me as "Dr." never "Mr.")

Somewhat reassured by my chat with Morris, I returned to Stonover. I was ushered into a spacious living room and introduced to Miss Parsons, a pleasant, gracious, white-haired lady, actually living fairly simply in the midst of great wealth. The Parsons were a prominent family in the New York social register who had intermarried with the Morgans, New York financiers. Mary, over a long lifetime, had used her social position and inherited wealth in a large number of public-spirited and philanthropic enterprises. The sanctuary, open to the public the year round without charge, was one of her major projects. At her Stonover estate she had spacious gardens that she tended herself; and her delphiniums took many prizes at garden shows. Other enterprises included an elaborate Christmas party with lavish gifts from Macy's in New York for all her employees. There was also a winter lecture series held in her library. Speakers included distinguished guests, such as Harlow Shapley, the noted astronomer from Harvard; Captain Knight and "Ramsey," his tame Golden Eagle; and Robert Cushman Murphy, then curator of birds at the American Museum. And as I had already surmised from my glimpse of the barn museum at the sanctuary, she was a great lover of antiques and colonial furniture.

We had a simple but ample and delicious meal that evening, served by the stony-faced woman who was the only household servant in evidence. That night I had a whole suite of rooms to myself, but I used only one of them.

The following morning I took a closer look at the sanctuary, hiked some of its several miles of trails, and visited more with the Pells. Arrangements had been made for a noon luncheon in the tearoom at the sanctuary, so that I could meet some of the other trustees. The house had a small apartment upstairs—living quarters for the warden; the downstairs was a tearoom and gift shop, well supplied, of course, with antiques. Luncheons and afternoon teas were served here by special arrangements from spring to fall. A Negro cook was engaged to prepare the meals; she was independent and not always

59

reliable (usually late for appointments) but considered indispensable for proper atmosphere.

Miss Parsons particularly wanted me to meet Henry Francis, president of the sanctuary association. She was sure I would love him. He was indeed an amiable, picturesque, white-haired gentleman, a retired president of Berkshire Woolen Company. Formerly a skilled hunter, in his later years he developed a penchant for exploring the countryside, which he knew well, for ferns and orchids for the sanctuary. Later I was to take many trips afield with him to collect botanical specimens. He soon took me aside, however, to explain that he was the sanctuary's president in name only; Miss Parsons really ran things, and I should look to her for guidance. Walter Prichard Eaton, with whom I had had previous correspondence but had never met, also attended the luncheon. Although a professor of drama at Yale, he was a dedicated Berkshirite and had a farm in Sheffield where he and his congenial wife spent summers and as much other time as they could spare from his duties at the university in New Haven.

The luncheon was a pleasant affair. With Miss Parsons looking on approvingly, we chatted amiably about natural history topics—ferns, orchids, snakes, and of course, birds. One of the goals of the sanctuary was to depict as nearly as possible the total fauna and flora of Berkshire County. The idea appealed to me and I volunteered for the position, if they really wanted me; but Miss Parsons said I should talk things over with Mrs. Wallace first. There were certain restrictions and inconveniences for family life at the sanctuary. The tearoom, for instance, was very private, off-limits for children; and laundries would have to be sent out; diapers on a line outdoors were unthinkable. However, despite these not-too-severe restrictions, I started work on July 1, 1937.

The Sanctuary, Early History and Functions

Pleasant Valley Bird and Wild Flower Sanctuary, usually referred to locally as the Bird Sanctuary, was comprised of several tracts of land totalling about three hundred acres at the time I took over. Later several other properties were annexed to it. The two-story frame house, of Post-Revolutionary War vintage and once in near ruins, had been remodeled, using materials salvaged from the old Longfellow home in Pittsfield. The barn had also been extensively repaired, supposedly to serve for a natural history museum, but which actually was largely devoted to a display of antiques and colonial furniture; a few of the items were from a nearby Shaker village. In the basement of the barn was a garage and workshop, part of which I converted to an office. Attached to the barn was a shed and a wintering pen for the Sanctuary ducks and geese.

The grounds included a neatly kept lawn flanked by the remnants of an old orchard and a planted border of fruit-bearing shrubs, mostly *Viburnums (V. opulus, dentatum,* and *cassinoides)*. Bluebird Lane led through an open meadow to Yokun Brook and the Beaver Ponds, then a wooded hillside rose steeply from the 1,220-foot level at Yokun Brook to the top of Lenox Mountain at 1,972 feet, where a fire tower afforded a fine view of the surrounding country. An artificial pond, built with funds donated by Mrs. Pike and thus named Pike's Pond, was stocked with Mallards, Canada Geese, and one mean old Egyptian Goose *(Alopochen aegyptiaca),* an apparent outcast from the other waterfowl.

The Sanctuary had been established in 1929. The first warden was Maurice Broun, who later served so efficiently for so many years at Hawk Mountain. Originally an orphan from the streets of Boston, he had risen to prominence by becoming an assistant to E. H. Forbush, Massachusetts State Ornithologist who was compiling his monumental three-volume work on the *Birds of Massachusetts and Other New England States.* Young Broun had tackled his sanctuary assignment with vigor and enthusiasm. He laid out miles of trails—including a labeled nature trail—built and erected bird houses and feeding shelters, devised a variety of exhibits for the museum, and kept meticulous bird records. And there was a great deal of cleanup work to do, including burying a town dump that was an eyesore on the otherwise beautiful grounds.

When Broun left in 1931, Seward Donaldson, a forester, filled in for a brief interim until Morris Pell came in 1932 to serve a five-year stint. One of Pell's major contributions (there were many others) was the introduction of beavers, at that time extinct in the Berkshires. It took a little doing, but it succeeded admirably—from the Sanctuary's standpoint. A not-so-admirable result, however, was that surplus beavers left the grounds and dammed up road culverts, making general nuisances of themselves. To the Sanctuary, nonetheless, they were a great asset—a major drawing card that attracted many human visitors and afforded habitat for a limited number of water birds in the series of shallow ponds created by the furry engineers.

Things were in good shape when I took over in 1937. My responsibilities and activities during the ensuing four years and eight months were too varied and multitudinous to describe in detail here, but some of the major concerns merit mention. Fortunately, I had a full-time workman to take care of most of the chores around the place. He was also a good amateur carpenter, plumber, and mechanic, who came in handy on many occasions.

During the summer months a museum hostess was engaged to take care of the museum and answer the questions posed by the thousands of visitors. The tearoom was an entirely separate operation for which I had little or no responsibility.

Sanctuary Bird Life

Continuation of the work with birds was, of course, a major enterprise—keeping records, banding birds, building or repairing (and selling) birdhouses and feeders, and, in off seasons at least, working in a little research and writing. I took almost daily morning walks over the grounds, especially during the spring and fall migration periods. (The museum was not open to visitors until 10 A.M., though the grounds were really never closed.) Since the area was an upland farm, mostly heavily wooded with no marshes or large bodies of water, bird life was somewhat limited. Except for the summer resident Spotted Sandpipers and occasional stray Solitary Sandpipers and yellowlegs, there was an almost complete absence of shorebirds, and waterfowl were largely limited to Mallards, Black Ducks, and Wood Ducks—all of which nested on the property, the latter in boxes provided for them. We were elated when a female Hooded Merganser stopped on Pike's Pond and stayed for a month during its fall migration. A similar visit by a Green-winged Teal was another highlight.

But for many land birds the Sanctuary provided nearly ideal habitat. Although our goal of having all the birds of Berkshire County represented at the Sanctuary was, of course, unobtainable with respect to water birds and shorebirds, about 90 percent of the land birds of regular occurrence in the county were recorded in the Sanctuary by 1942; most of the missing were more southern species not ordinarily ranging as far north as Lenox. Warblers were especially well represented; their passage in spring was exciting, and their reappearance in the fall, a challenge in identification. Each year we recorded more than 20 species of warblers on the Sanctuary; I had a maximum of 28 in 1939.

My annual lists for the Sanctuary, not very high by modern standards, ranged from 110 in 1937 (part of a year) to 127 in 1939 and 1940, with a total of 168 for the five-year period. Since then, of course, many new species have been added; by 1950 the list had climbed to 186. In spite of thorough observations by my predecessors, it was still possible to add several species to the Sanctuary list each year, even occasionally recording "firsts" for the county.

Some highlights for me were the discovery of the Sanctuary's first Worm-eating Warbler; the first positive record for an Orange-crowned Warbler in the county; and, with the help of the Bradburn boys (Berkshire summer residents from New Orleans), working out the Golden-wing—Blue-wing—Brewster Warbler complex on the Lone Cedar Trail. Thirty people from four states came to see our Brewster's Warbler. A Saw-whet Owl being mobbed by chickadees at St. Francis Spring in January 1940 was a "lifer" for me. Even more unusual was a puzzling sparrow caught in a banding trap in late November 1940. I kept the bird overnight and called in two local experts on bird identification—Bartlett Hendricks, Curator of Science at the Berkshire Museum in Pittsfield, and S. Waldo Bailey, a well-known local naturalist. We went into a huddle and finally decided the bird was a Clay-colored Sparrow from the midwest (not in our New England bird books), although we debated about the seemingly remote possibility that it might be an immature Chipping Sparrow still in partial juvenal plumage in November.

Some other birds in which we took special pride were the Pileated Woodpeckers in the woods across the road from the cottage, the American Woodcock that performed nightly in spring over our front lawn, the sometimes noisy but usually silent Barred Owls that lived in the woods above Yokun Brook, the Louisiana Waterthrushes that frequented the gurgling waterfall on the hillside, and the musical Winter Wren whose neat little nest was discovered one summer by the Bradburn boys.

Our first breeding bird census was taken in the spring of 1938 and repeated in subsequent years. This census disclosed the Song Sparrow as our leading avian species, with about forty pairs. Catbirds, Veeries, Ovenbirds, Chestnut-sided Warblers, and Common Yellowthroats were also abundant with twenty-five or more pairs of each. Especially welcome for the beauty of their plumage and their songs were the five pairs of Scarlet Tanagers, five pairs of Hermit Thrushes, and six pairs of Rose-breasted Grosbeaks. About seventy species totalling about four hundred pairs were summer residents on the approximately three hundred acres.

One discouraging feature disclosed by these censuses was the failure of so many breeding birds to return in the spring of 1940. The winter of 1939-1940 was extremely severe in the Southern states, with a prolonged freeze that decimated wintering birds. Tree Swallows, bluebirds, phoebes, and other insectivorous species perished in large numbers; often the highways were littered with dead and dying birds. In the spring, eight or ten species that had been more or less regular summer residents at the Sanctuary failed to return, and at least eleven others showed a decline in numbers. For the first time in the eleven-year history of the Sanctuary, no bluebirds returned to our boxes. Of the eight to ten pairs of Tree Swallows occupying our nest boxes in previous years, apparently none returned in 1940; the three pairs that eventually appropriated boxes in late May and June, long after the previous year's territory holders should have returned, were obviously newcomers. Other losses or declines occurred among the phoebes, wrens, Myrtle (Yellow-rumped) Warblers, Northern and Louisiana Waterthrushes, White-throated Sparrows, and Song Sparrows. However, some essentially nonmigratory species, such as woodpeckers, nuthatches, and chickadees, also declined, possibly merely representing a low in their population cycles. Some of the decimated species recovered in 1941 and some did not. The pertinent data have been recorded in a publication in the *Auk* (Wallace, 1943).

Bird banding was carried out somewhat sporadically because of the pressure of other work, but I banded a little over a thousand birds during my years at the Sanctuary. I always subscribed to the philosophy, later adopted by the banding office at Patuxent, that there was limited scientific value in banding spring and fall transients because they seldom produce returns or recoveries; banding large numbers of them seems like a waste of time and bands.

Banding work in the winter, when I had more leisure, did produce interesting results. That first winter I color-banded 74 chickadees (125 during the first three winters). Aluminum color bands were not available from Patuxent in those days, but I obtained celluloid bands from the National Band and Tag Company and made other bands from celluloid dolls. Blue Jays removed such bands, thus thwarting a study I had hoped to make on jays, but chickadees did not. Of the 63 chickadees known to have survived the winter of 1937–1938, 45 were back the following winter, an unusually high return percentage—higher than I obtained the following two winters, by which time the population seemed to have reached a low point in their cycle (see Wallace, 1941a).

Banding disclosed that the Sanctuary's chickadee population was composed of four status groups, similar to those determined for populations of titmice in Europe as recorded by Kenrick (1940). Most individuals (about 80 percent) were permanent (year-round) residents or winter residents, the latter appearing only in winter, although, of course, they may not have been very far away in summer. Seven individuals banded in late fall disappeared soon after banding, but five of them were retrapped in the spring, along with six newcomers, thus indicating a small transient group. The presence of unbanded birds in the summer, after a winter of intensive banding in which all of the wintering chickadees were believed to be banded, denoted a summer resident group.

Several notable longevity records were secured. A chickadee banded by Maurice Broun on January 21, 1931, was present each winter through the winter of 1939 (last observation on April 22), by which time it was nine or more years old. A chickadee banded on December 14, 1931, was last seen in February, 1940, when it was about eight and a half years old. At that time these were the oldest known chickadees, but since then several older age records have been recorded, including one believed to be twelve years and five months old (Kennard, 1975).

Another notable feature in the chickadee populations was the close and more or less permanent association between individuals. The St. Francis Spring group of ten individuals, out in the woods nearly a mile from the cottage, stayed together all winter and rarely mixed with other flocks; in three winters only one of them appeared at the cottage feeders. And of the ten birds that remained together at St. Francis Spring that first winter, nine reappeared at the same station the following winter. Several times I transferred a chickadee from one flock to another—and in one case I took one to Stonover, two miles away—but the displaced birds returned promptly to their former stations and associates.

Perhaps the most spectacular result of the banding work was with Tree Sparrows (Wallace, 1942). Transients banded in the fall soon disappeared and usually were not seen again; but of eight color-banded birds that remained over winter that year, seven were back the following winter from breeding grounds somewhere up in Canada, hundreds of miles away. One Tree Sparrow, banded by Morris Pell, apparently returned for eight successive winters, usually appearing in November and leaving in April.

More remarkable as a longevity record was an eleven-year-old Hairy Woodpecker, banded on January 19, 1939. It reappeared each winter through March of 1949. When I inquired of Alvah Sanborn, my successor at the Sanctuary, about the continued presence of this bird, he wrote that it was still present in the spring of 1949 "with a female." It is reassuring to note that this male woodpecker, one of the oldest known, was still interested in females. Kennard (1975) reports an older record of twelve years and ten months.

Duck banding at the Beaver Pond produced two recoveries: a Black Duck banded on October 13, 1938, was recaptured October 12, 1939, then shot by a hunter on Long Island in November 1939; a Wood Duck banded on October 12, 1938, was recaptured October 14, 1940, and shot in Georgia on December 26, 1940.

Botanical Projects

One of my major assignments at the Sanctuary was a botanical survey. My predecessors were enthusiastic and well-qualified ornithologists, but the trustees felt, rightly, that for a sanctuary that purported to be a wildflower sanctuary, the botanical work had been neglected. One of the aims of the Sanctuary was to have represented every species of tree, shrub, flower, and fern known in Berkshire County. Such a goal seemed realistic except for alpine species on the summit of Mt. Greylock (the highest peak in the state), for certain species in the limestone cobbles in the southern part of the county, and for certain bog plants.

I tackled this challenging assignment eagerly. First came a survey of the plants already growing in the Sanctuary. The first count (1938) disclosed 525 species of trees, shrubs, and flowering plants and 51 additional ferns and fern allies, a number that was increased with further work to 825 species by 1941. My bible for identification was Ralph Hoffmann's very comprehensive *Flora of Berkshire County* (1922) based on his twenty years of exploration in the county. In spite of the thoroughness of his work, I found about ten species that were new to the county (mostly recent introductions) and one that was new for the state, *(Potamogeton Hillii,* possibly brought in with beavers from New York). Needless to say, I encountered difficulties in identifying grasses, sedges, goldenrods, and asters; without the keys in Hoffman's *Flora,* it might have been impossible.

Many of the 825 species were deliberately introduced in the attempt to have the Sanctuary truly depict the flora of the county. By the time I left the Sanctuary, more than three hundred species had been brought in and planted in appropriate places, although, of course, some of them failed to survive. Finding the desired species meant pleasant exploratory trips to remote corners of the county, often in the company of Henry Francis or Waldo Bailey, both local authorities on ferns and orchids and where to find them. In the summer of 1939, a young Harvard University student with a good background in biology, joined our staff, and with the volunteer aid of the Bradburn boys, whom Oliver and the Sanctuary had practically adopted, we made good progress in our planting programs.

One of our major projects was developing a new Fernery near the cottage, an enterprise strongly promoted by Miss Parsons and Mr. Francis. Berkshire County, with its extensive woodlands, ravines, bogs, mountains, and limestone cobbles, was richly endowed with ferns. Eventually we had all forty-three species of Berkshire ferns growing in the Fernery, although some of the limestone forms, in spite of introducing limestone rocks and soil, did not do very well and had to be replaced from time to time. The fern garden proved to be a major attraction for the many visitors who had a special interest in ferns.

Less successful was the attempt to establish a bog garden in a mudhole along the nature trail. Several truckloads of foot-thick sphagnum mats, complete with carnivorous pitcher plants and sundew, orchids, and even small tamaracks and a black spruce, were brought in and laid down on the mud. Some of the plants survived well for a few years; some did not. One of the problems was that unwanted grasses and sedges grew up through the mat, requiring frequent weeding to keep them from taking over. The project floundered and, I think, was abandoned completely when I left the Sanctuary.

The Sanctuary was justly proud of its fields of goldenrods and asters. We tried to help budding botanists with their identification problems by bringing in additional species and planting them along the nature trail. However, most visitors showed little interest in such identification problems—a goldenrod was a goldenrod and an aster an aster—so the project was never completed.

Educational Efforts

The Sanctuary had about ten thousand visitors a year, mostly in the summer months, particularly in August when the Berkshire Symphonic Festival brought in people from far and wide. The guest register for the years from 1937 to 1940 revealed that we had visitors from forty-six states and fourteen foreign countries. Such a flow of visitors required more than trails, a duck pond, and beaver dams to satisfy them. Many merely looked around and asked wonderingly, "Where are the birds? We thought this was a bird sanctuary." We had to explain over and over that this was a wild bird sanctuary, not a zoo. However, we devised all sorts of exhibits. A good beginning had been made by Maurice Broun and continued by Morris Pell. We had electric nature games portraying birds, mammals, flowers, ferns, and animal tracks; wood samples hung in a row from a rack and cut to show bark, cross-sections, and longitudinal sections; a live honeybee colony (one of the most popular exhibits); insect displays; an herbarium; and, of course, the antiques.

By the time I came, however, the natural history section of the barn was full and the antiques prevented further expansion. Miss Parsons' theory was that the colonial exhibits attracted many visitors who could then be converted to nature lovers—a dubious theory at best. No one openly questioned the presence of the antiques during Miss Parsons' day, but after her death in 1940 they became a controversial issue. Eventually they were transferred to another location.

There were almost unlimited opportunities for outdoor exhibits. We never tried to keep birds and mammals in cages—other than the many injured and orphaned animals brought to us from time to time. But we built a turtle pool that housed all the local turtles we could find, had moss-filled terraria for salamanders and frogs, cages for snakes, and an insect shed. These cold-blooded animals were captured in the spring and summer, then released in the fall—except for a champion garter snake that gave birth to a record 73 young (see Wallace, 1938). We failed, however, in our efforts to keep her and some of her young alive over winter in the basement of the barn.

Another educational activity was the conducting of field trips both on and off the Sanctuary. Most hikes were informal free-for-alls, such as Saturday morning bird hikes in spring, but also organized classes were held. One summer I taught a field botany course at the Sanctuary and in the winter had a botany class in the Berkshire Museum in Pittsfield. I was also in considerable demand for local lectures to garden clubs, granges, summer camps, and schools, activities also intended to help promote the Sanctuary.

In 1940, largely, I think, through the collusion of Bart Hendricks with reporter Rex Fall, the *Berkshire Evening Eagle* started a daily column called "Our Berkshires." Five outdoor writers, including Eaton, Hendricks, and me, wrote articles for the five weekdays. For each of us that meant preparing a weekly article for the paper, but after the first year, Bart and I alternated so that we contributed biweekly articles. The column was continued for many years after I left the Sanctuary. (Three of my articles are printed at the end of this chapter as samples of the topics covered.)

Berkshire Bird Life

Studies of bird life at the Sanctuary were gradually expanded until our field of observation included the whole county. In 1940, largely through the initiative and follow-through of Bart Hendricks, we formed the Hoffmann Bird Club, named in honor of Berkshire's noted authority on birds and botany. Thirty-five years later, the Hoffmann Bird Club still functions.

Many trips throughout the county were taken by club members exploring for birds. Bart was working on a *Field List of the Birds of Berkshire County,* and, although a young man then, he soon became recognized as the foremost authority on the birds of that area. He had an amazing grasp of the status and distribution of birds within the county. If I casually mentioned seeing my first House Wren of the season on April 25, he might reply that it was a day earlier or a day later than last year. When I thought I had a new bird, he might add that Waldo Bailey had reported one back in 1929.

In 1941 the *Field List* was published by the Berkshire Museum. The main list, with bar graphs to indicate abundance and seasonal occurrence, included 231 species and subspecies and one hybrid (Brewster's Warbler). A supplementary list of 32 rare or hypothetical forms raised the total to 264, a striking increase over the Faxon and Hoffmann county list of 197 published in 1900. In 1950 Bart came out with a much-expanded booklet entitled *Berkshire Birds,* listing 271 forms. The booklet has not been updated since 1950, but Bart estimates that the number of birds now exceeds 300.

Habitats and their specialties are described in the booklet. Those that I visited most frequently, often in the company of Bart or other members of the Hoffmann Bird Club, are described below.

Most unusual of these habitats was the summit of Mt. Greylock (3,491 feet). It had a small timberline at the top, surrounded by clumps of dwarfed and stunted conifers, which provided a limited habitat for breeding birds not found elsewhere in the state. A few pairs of Bicknell's Gray-cheeked Thrushes and a few Blackpoll Warblers summered around the peak, but, in spite of considerable search, I never found a nest of either species there. (Later, in 1948, two nests of Bicknell's Thrush were found by members of the Hoffmann Bird Club). Just below the summit was one of the most dependable stations I know of for Mourning Warblers. It is uncommon or even rare at most places during migration; I had only one record at the Sanctuary, in late May, 1938. Other nesting specialties we looked for and often found on Greylock were Yellow-bellied and Olive-sided flycatchers, Red-breasted Nuthatches, Golden-crowned Kinglets, Brown Creepers, and roving crossbills.

A less rugged but singularly attractive mountain that I visited frequently both because of its accessibility (it was close to Lenox) and because of its many inviting features was October Mountain. It had spruce and balsam stands sloping down into bogs, beech-maple woodlots, patches of high-bush blueberry (which we used to good advantage), luxuriant beds of ferns, and a great variety of wildflowers. Autumn colors, in a county richly endowed with colorful fall foliage, were at their best on October Mountain. The wild turkeys released there in 1934 and the moose stocked at an earlier date soon disappeared, but upland birds—Winter Wren, Brown Creepers, Red-breasted Nuthatches, Golden-crowned Kinglets, Blue-headed (Solitary) Vireos, and a good assortment of warblers—could usually be found here in summer.

Berkshire is blessed with lakes in highly scenic settings, such as Stock-

69

bridge Bowl, nestled like a glistening jewel between surrounding hills. But the ones I remember best for migrating waterfowl were Lake Pontoosuc and Onota Lake in the Pittsfield area. Bart once wrote that the latter was the best in the county, that "every duck reliably identified in the county, and almost every other water bird, including geese, gulls, terns and shore birds," have been reported there (Hendricks, 1950). Twenty-two species of ducks were seen on the Lake by Bart and Dorothy Snyder in 1946 (Bart, pers. comm.) I still remember seeing all three species of scoters on the lake, a frequent stop-over place on the long migration from their breeding grounds in the far northwest to their winter home off the New England coast. In forty years of birding in inland Michigan, I have only two records each for the White-winged and Surf Scoters, and none for the American (Black) Scoter.

Wood Pond in Lenox was productive in a different way. A shallow pond with reed-grown margins, it was more attractive to puddle ducks—Blacks, Mallards, Green-winged and Blue-winged teal, and Wood Ducks. The marshy shores harbored bitterns, rails, gallinules, and (more rarely) coots. American (Great) Egrets could often be found here in late summer, and the county's only record of Roseate Terns came from this pond.

Less aesthetic, but not to be omitted as a very special place for birding, were the sewer beds in Pittsfield, apparently discovered as a good shorebird spot by Maurice Broun. I took many trips there, alone or with anyone not too highly endowed with olfactory sensitivity. We could sit on the banks of the beds, holding our noses with one hand and our binoculars in the other, and identify "peeps" at close range, trying (sometimes successfully) to pick out a Western Sandpiper or a Baird's. Sometimes we drew a blank, sometimes we were richly rewarded. I have never been a shorebird specialist, but after fifty years of roaming over the earth, I remember the Pittsfield sewer beds as one of the best areas I know of for small shorebirds.

Another special habitat, not for a large variety of birds but for a single species, was Monument Mountain, a steep, rocky escarpment close to the highway in Stockbridge. A pair of Duck Hawks (Peregrine Falcons) nested there regularly in those days. I remember on one ascent of the peak (with baby Sylvia in a pack basket and not liking her confinement), we could see the location of the eyrie but did not attempt closer inspection. But the falcons, now an endangered species throughout the world, have long since been gone.

Still another remarkable habitat, mostly for nonavian features, was Bartholomew's Cobble in the southern part of the county, so aptly described by W.P. Eaton in 1936 and Hal Borland in 1975. Limestone outcrops and an alkaline soil harbor a great variety of wildflowers (493 species) and ferns (52 Pteridophytes catalogued). Some rather special ferns included several spleenworts *(Asplenium),* walking fern *(Camptosaurus rhizophyllus),* purple cliffbrake *(Pellaea atropurpurea),* and a rare hybrid, Scott's spleenwort. We often looted the place (before it was a reservation) for ferns for the Sanctuary—not at all a good conservation practice because most of the lime-loving ferns did not do well in our fern garden. Appropriately, when the Cobble became a nature reservation, Waldo Baily, a great lover of the Cobble, was appointed warden-naturalist of the area. (Waldo literally died with his boots on; he dropped dead of a heart attack while picking up Indian arrowheads on a farm near the Cobble.)

The southern part of the county, including the Cobble, Mt. Everest, Ashby Falls, and Bash-Bish Falls, harbored both birds and plants not found in the central and northern parts of the county. This was one of the few places in the state where Worm-eating Warblers nested. Turkey Vultures, rare then in Massachusetts, could sometimes be seen here. The southern Berkshires also had good places to look for other southern species: White-eyed Vireos (Sheffield), Yellow-breasted Chats (Egremont), Orchard Orioles (Egremont), and Grasshopper Sparrows (Sheffield).

Curtains

But back to the Sanctuary. After Miss Parsons' death in February 1940, following the death of Henry Francis the preceding summer, with war clouds looming ominously, and with heavy taxes imposed on owners of Berkshire's large estates, the Sanctuary came upon lean times. Eventually Stonover was reduced to rubble—a pathetic sight when we revisited it some years later—because the heirs could not afford to maintain it. Percy Morgan, a nephew of Miss Parsons, carried on as Sanctuary president for an interim period; then Dr. Anson Phelps Stokes, a canon of the Washington Cathedral, and former secretary of Yale University, was appointed president in April 1940. He and others worked diligently to keep things running smoothly, but eventually (in 1952) the Massachusetts Audubon Society took over operation of the Sanctuary.

Following Miss Parson's death, my position at the Sanctuary was becoming more and more untenable. The trustees were divided, sometimes sharply, as to the future of the Sanctuary and my role in it. One of the controversial issues was the antiques. Some people, including me, thought that another home should be found for them to permit further development of the natural history museum; others thought that the antiques were

The cottage at Pleasant Valley Sanctuary, Lenox, Massachusetts. Photo by Bartlett Hendricks.

The Barn-Museum in May, 1973. The shadbush *(Amelanchier)* at the left corner of the barn and the spruces at the far right were planted by the author in the late 1930's.

In the mid-sixties a new Trailside Museum largely replaced the functions of the Barn-Museum.

One of the several beaver dams built by the furry engineers after their introduction into the Sanctuary in 1932.

indispensable. Another controversial issue was the tearoom. It was no secret that I had had a covetous eye on its facilities for some time—for a classroom, lecture room, library, and additional exhibits—but taking it over for such purposes at that time would have meant open warfare among the Sanctuary's supporters. (Eventually, but only years after I left, the antiques were removed, the tearoom used for other purposes, and a new trailside museum was built along Bluebird Lane.)

There was also some disagreement as to my role at the Sanctuary. One trustee in particular questioned the need for a naturalist. A hard-headed businessman, he visualized my duty as that of a money-getter. With ten thousand visitors a year (and his eyes gleamed), just a small donation wrung from each one of them would greatly enrich the Sanctuary coffers. Fortunately, the other trustees did not agree; some even questioned that I should have anything to do with the finances of the Sanctuary.

Family life was also becoming more difficult. Keeping our active three- and five-year-old daughters out of mischief (we lived in the small apartment over the tearoom) was almost impossible. And with living costs steadily mounting, we were also encountering financial difficulties. In spite of rising living costs, the director's salary ($1800 per year) remained unchanged from 1929 to 1942. With Miss Parsons' passing we lost many fringe benefits, such as contributions for special projects and season tickets to the Berkshire Symphonic Festival at Tanglewood. I was also getting increasingly involved with duties that required travel: committee meetings, lecturing, and collecting specimens for the Sanctuary—all at my own expense.

But it was mainly World War II that settled matters. The trustees finally decided to put the Sanctuary on a part-time basis (May to October), to rent the Sanctuary cottage for badly needed income, and to give me a leave of absence to work in a local war plant. Several applications for work in war plants, however, failed to produce results (I had neither talents nor training for such work), and trying to find proper housing was discouraging. Hence, we took our terminal winter vacation and returned to Michigan (where Martha's mother, two brothers, and a sister lived) in hope of finding another job.

A ray of hope for a position in the Michigan Department of Conservation developed, but I lacked the residency required by Civil Service, so I took an interim job at the University of Michigan Hospital in Ann Arbor—washing glassware in the pathology laboratory—until the position in the Game Division of the Department of Conservation became available in April. During the War the Sanctuary operated on a part-time basis with Waldo Bailey commuting from Pittsfield (seven miles) to keep the Sanctuary functioning, until Alvah Sanborn was appointed director in 1946, a post he held—miraculously, it seems—for twenty-seven years, much of it under the auspices of the Massachusetts Audubon Society. But I will never regret my nearly five years at the Sanctuary. Although a dead end professionally, it was a memorable, often pleasant, and useful experience.

SAMPLE ESSAYS FROM "OUR BERKSHIRES"
Reprinted with permission from the Berkshire Eagle

Cockroaches

The other day a fat cockroach streaked out of a newly arrived grocery sack and legged it for dear life for the nearest shelter. My wife turned pale but recovered in time to squelch the stowaway just before his disappearing act. Then, lest others had preceded him, the kitchen was turned upside down, and everything (including my supper) was sprayed with pyrethrum and dusted with borax, but no cockroaches dead or alive came to light. My wife gave an exhausted sigh of relief. I pretended to be sympathetic (with my wife, not the roach), though I must confess to some feelings for these much-maligned, longstanding associates of man. They have a sort of right of priority in man's establishments, and their lineage is of ancient vintage.

For the solemn roach in your kitchen—if there is one there—can probably also boast that he had ancestors on the *Mayflower*. He may even be of the very line that looked in on the events in the garden of Eden. As Sutherland appropriately remarks (Lutz, 1921), "Wherever there have been great epoch-making movements of people he has been with them heart and soul, without possessing any particular religious convictions or political ambitions. . . . Man himself is but a creature of the last twenty minutes or so compared with the cockroach, for, from its crevice by the kitchen sink, it can point its antennae to the coal in the hod and say: 'When that was being made my family was already well-established[1]'"

And so it was! Way back in Carboniferous times, millions of years before man or beasts roamed the earth or prehistoric birds took their first gliding lessons, when the comparatively new land was reeking with carbon dioxide and giant cycads, the cockroaches were among the dominant land creatures, perhaps shamefully lording it over their invertebrate allies. But then came the dinosaurs and trod them underfoot, birds arose and found them palatable, and insectivorous mammals made their life miserable. Then in walked man—not a particularly respectable animal to be sure, but one who often left surplus food lying around for hungry roaches. So then and there the roaches pledged themselves to a sort of silent partnership with man, a pledge they have kept in unbroken fidelity ever since. No ship ever set sail for new lands without transporting these stowaway, nonpaying passengers. They watched the building of the pyramids, probably wondering what sort of provender would go into them; they marched with tribes from Asia to help settle Europe; and they have attended kings' banquets and presidential balls, though usually discreetly as uninvited, after-hours guests.

Of course, not all roaches are of this leechlike character. Of the two that appear to be prevalent in the Berkshires, one—the common wood roach—is an independent and respectable citizen, living under bark and stones. The other, the familiar Croton bug, needs no introduction to city people. Probably there are others, at least the Oriental roach and the large American species, but I haven't been given much to prowling around public places on biological investigations. However, they are said to get bigger and better as one goes southward; tropical countries yield upward of a thousand species. It may be some consolation to know that only forty-three of these species have been found in North America north of Mexico.

Cockroach habits as we know them are not especially commendable. They are voracious, cannibalistic, and unsanitary (some more adjectives, please). There is almost nothing short of metal that they won't eat—soap, leather, bookbindings; they have even been known to chew the mucilage from postage stamps. No cockroach is safe prowling around if a larger roach appears on the scene, for the larger soon disposes of the smaller. Their one good deed in the abodes of man is the slaughter of bedbugs in places where the two come together.

I'm practically useless as a cockroach exterminator. I always get to thinking about their ancient lineage, their long association with man, their early origin and subsequent history, and they slip away from me unscathed. But not from my wife!

Violets

Among the 200 or more wildflowers that grace the Berkshires in May, the violets occupy a prominent place. Whether decorating the margin of a cool sylvan spring, lending a delicate touch of color to cold gray rocks and woodland ledges, or trying to be a success on a dump heap, there is a species for almost every conceivable niche, from your doorstep to the remotest swamp or mountaintop. Though by nature preferring seclusive places, to which our native American flora has been crowded by foreign invaders long ago, the violets are a hardy lot and dare to peer innocently up at us from dusty, much-abused roadsides, trampled lawns, and neglected garden corners.

If you are content to call a violet a violet or if you merely distinguish the blues, the whites, and the yellows, you can enjoy and appreciate their quiet beauty in blissful peace. But if you happen to be an individual with a bent for knowing the names of things, the innocent little violets will give you a headache. After eliminating introduced forms, we have left some 23 local species—14 blues, 6 whites, and 3 yellows—some of which are so similar that microscopic examination is necessary to separate them. Moreover, these similar species hybridize rather freely, thus getting their own identity mixed up. And if Nature can't keep her children straight, how can we?

First come the blues. In wet places you can find three of these, the marsh blue *(V. cucullata)* being the most common and differing from its bog-loving neighbors *(V. nephrophylla* and *V. affinis)* chiefly in the terminal knobs on the beard of the lateral petals. (A good hand lens is needed.) In other conditions are many others: *V. latiuscula* around dry woodland ledges, its vernal leaves purple-tinged (that one is easy); *V. papilionacea* and *V. septentrionalis* (two commonly cultivated species) in moist woods or meadows; another easy one *(V. fimbriatula)* with ovate (instead of heart-shaped) fuzzy leaves; and another *(V. sororia)*—not so easy—with typical but somewhat woolly leaves. Two other blue violets in this group help matters by having lobed (instead of heart-shaped) leaves: *(V. triloba,* usually with 3 lobes, and *V. palmata,* with 5 to 9 lobes. Still another violet *(V. Selkirkii)* identifies itself by possessing a giant spur on the lower petal.

All of these blue violets develop flowering scapes separately from the leaf stalks. But two other blue violets *(V. conspersa* and *V. rostrata)* send up their blossoms from the stems of the leaves, a habit they share with the lovely Canada Violet *(V. canadensis),* which is really mostly white but belongs taxonomically with the blues. Many of these blue violets also produce white flowers, frequently in cultivation, occasionally in nature, thus masking their identity and making bad matters worse.

The true white violets are not so bad if you lump together three similar species *(V. pallens, V. blanda,* and *V. incognita),* all of which are known as the sweet white violet and differ from each other for the most part only in the degree of pubescence of the leaves. Remaining then are only *V. renifolia,* with kidney-shaped leaves; *V. lanceolata,* with lanceolate leaves; and the rare *V. primulifolia,* with more or less oblong leaves.

The yellow violets, by a rare nomenclatural coincidence, identify themselves by their common English names—the early or round-leaved form *(v. rotundifolia)*, the downy yellow *(V. pubescens)*, and the smooth yellow *(V. eriocarpa)*.

So there they are—23 of them—sweet innocent little things, all native Americans, strangely prospering in adversity, defying our lack of good conservation, and lending an enlivening touch of color to every landscape they occupy. One of the secrets of their success is that their pretty blossoms are mere show, and children can pick bouquets with little or no harm to nature's supply. The plants are mainly dependent for propagation on tiny root flowers that never open but are fertilized in the bud and produce multitudinous progeny. Most violets also are easy to transplant into home gardens, though under cultivation the species tend to hybridize, exhibiting marked vegetative vigor but impaired fertility.

Call It a Day

Several people have made the well-meaning but, to me, a little alarming suggestion that I write an account of a day's activities at the sanctuary, the idea, of course, being that it would make an interesting story. So it might, possibly, in the good old springtime. But I'm afraid an honest account of a typical winter day might shock some of our venerable trustees, especially those who retire from the Berkshires in winter and expect that work of a highly scientific and educational quality goes on in their absence. So at the risk of embarrassment, I present this picture of a winter day's work. (If you are a trustee, don't read this.)

Came the dawn of this typical winter day, the windows heavily frosted after a cold and blustery night. The first mishap that heralded the long series for the day was a wail of distress from my wife in the kitchen. "George, this water has been on the stove for ten minutes and is still cold. The electricity must be off."

That reminded me that the usually noisy refrigerator had been deathly silent for some time. Inspection showed that it had been defrosting for hours. Lights were checked, and none of them worked. Monkeying with the fuses in the cellar brought no results. No electricity—a not uncommon occurrence where two miles of private line are subject to fallen branches in every storm.

So I proceeded to call a service man, but on lifting the receiver no cheery voice, sweet or otherwise, answered "Number, please." The line was dead.

"Well, let's eat breakfast," my wife said. "I am sorry everything is cold."

"If you don't go to town first thing, the service men will all be out on the lines," she continued, "and we won't have any stove, lights, ice box, water, or telephone till tomorrow or later."

"I'll send Alvah," I said. "I've got a lot to do today and don't want any more interruptions. By the way, where is Alvah? It's after eight and he is never late unless something out of the ordinary happens."

A half-hour later Alvah came puffing in, afoot. He had bucked through drifts for about a mile but had had to give up on the hill. So, armed with shovels and spare links to repair broken chains, we tunneled and bucked the rest of the way in to the sanctuary. By this time the morning was pretty well shot, so Alvah kindly offered to try to get to town to contact Pittsfield Electric, the telephone company, and possibly a snowplow.

Belatedly, I started for the barn. On the way the ducks and geese in the wintering pen greeted me with a loud clamor. "Why you poor things," I muttered. "You weren't watered and fed this morning." So, grabbing a water bucket, I turned on the faucet in the barn. Nothing happened.

"Good grief," I cried, "it's frozen solid." I looked at the thermometer (in my cozy office). It was 26°.

Next I rustled up some wood and built a rousing fire in the stove, but the water didn't give. Finally, after applying torches along the length of the pipe, the water broke through.

By this time it was way past noon. But that didn't matter as far as dinner was concerned. "We will have cold sandwiches and a salad," my wife announced.

"How about a swig of milk to wash down this dry bread?" I asked.

"No," she said firmly. "The milkman didn't make it this morning, and we must save what little milk there is for the children."

By rare good luck (we half expected to be stranded for days) Alvah had rounded up Mr. Welsh, who sent a snowplow to our rescue. This was quickly followed by repairmen from the telephone and electric companies. But now the telephone began to buzz. "It's The Eagle office," my wife called out. "They want to know where your article is for this week."

"Tell them it's practically there," I called back, rummaging hurriedly through my files for some old material that could be patched up quickly, just to get by for this one time.

But now the manuscript had to be taken to Pittsfield. All went well until I struck the main highway, where snowplows, either forgetting or not caring that some people lived in the country, had piled all the snow from the main road into the entrance to our back road. There it was, an insurmountable wall higher than the car.

I had a shovel, to be sure, but it was already three o'clock. So I phoned for help from the nearest house, but the town crews were all out. Next I enlisted nearby help by vague promises of rewards in the hereafter, and in an hour we broke through the wall. As the last shovelful was put away, the road crew arrived—a dozen strong men armed with shovels.

My Pittsfield errands disposed of, the journey homeward began. Everything went fine until I encountered another car, off the road. Typically, a couple of fellows had driven out to see the sanctuary in its winter aspect, but had ended up in the ditch. I helped them push and heave, and pretty soon Alvah came along and added his shoulder to the task. Between the four of us we got the car on the road again.

But now another problem presented itself—three cars on a road plowed out for one-way traffic. So I backed to the main road (a mere half mile) to let the other two cars out, and then started on the homestretch again. More mishaps (new drifts, chains, etc.—there isn't room to write about them) delayed me further, so that supper was waiting when I reached home.

A bowl of warm soup on a winter's night can do wonders, so after supper I began to feel better and sank into an easy chair. "Let's have a fire in the fireplace and pop corn," I suggested. "Just listen to that wind howl. It's lucky we don't have to go anywhere tonight. The road would be impassable by now."

"George," my wife cried out suddenly. "Didn't you have to give another lecture some time soon?"

"Holy smoke!" I groaned, looking at the calendar. "It's tonight! The Egremont Grange. How will I ever make it?"

References

Borland, H. "Rock Garden in a Cow Pasture." *Audubon,* 77(3): (1975) pp. 81–87.

Eaton, W.P. "The Cobble." Reprint from *Wild Flowers of New England.* W.A. Wilde Co., 1936.

Faxon, W. and R. Hoffmann. "Birds of Berkshire County." Massachusetts Faunal Papers on Ornithology, 1: (1900) p. 11.

Forbush, E.H. *Birds of Massachusetts and other New England States.* Boston: Massachusetts Department of Agriculture, 1925–1929.

Hendricks, B. *Field List of the Birds of Berkshire County, Massachusetts.* Pittsfield, Massachusetts: The Berkshire Museum, 1941.

_____. *Berkshire Birds.* Boston: Massachusetts Audubon Society, 1900.

Hoffmann, R. "Flora of Berkshire County, Massachusetts." *Proc. Boston Soc. Nat. Hist.* 36(5): (1922) 171–382.

Kennard, J. H. "Longevity Records of North American Birds." *Bird-Banding* 46: (1975) pp. 55–78.

Kenrick, H. "A Study of Blue Tits by Colour-Ringing." *British Birds,* 33: (1940) p. 307.

Wallace, G.J. "A Garter Snake with a Brood of 73 Young." *Copeia,* (1938).

_____. "Winter Studies of Color-banded Chickadees." *Bird-Banding* 12(2): (1941a) pp. 49-62.

_____. "Summer Bird Life at Pleasant Valley Sanctuary." *Bulletin Massachusetts Audubon Society* 25:(1941b) pp. 87–89.

_____. "Returns and Survival Rate of Wintering Tree Sparrows." *Bird-Banding* 13: (1942) pp. 81–83.

_____. "The 1940 Nesting Population at Pleasant Valley Sanctuary, Lenox, Massachusetts." *Auk* 60: (1943) pp. 403–407.

_____. "Four Seasons of Berkshire Bird Lore." *The Berkshires.* R. Peattie, ed., New York: Vanguard Press, Inc., 1948.

CHAPTER 5

Thirty Years at Michigan State University

Rose Lake

BEFORE TRANSFERRING to Michigan State College in September of 1942, I worked from late April to late September at the Rose Lake Wildlife Experiment Station, a farm-wildlife management area operated by the Game Division of the Michigan Department of Conservation. Beef and dairy cattle, sheep, poultry, and various crops were raised, and a staff of biologists studied farm-game interrelationships and tried to improve conditions for wildlife. At that time the station grounds comprised some 1,600 acres of small woodlots, abandoned and cultivated fields, a shallow lake (Rose Lake) rapidly succeeding to a sedge and cattail marsh, a deep pond (Burke Lake) "poisoned" with rotenone and stocked with trout that summer, and a series of artificial floodings for waterfowl. Durward L. Allen was the biologist in charge and J.P. Linduska was Pittman-Robertson Project Leader. A farm manager supervised farming operations.

For living quarters I was assigned to a small, three-room cottage on the station grounds. It was hardly large enough for a family of four (we moved to a large farmhouse as soon as it was available), but it was in a delightful setting. In the early mornings a Bobwhite perched in a locust tree outside our bedroom window and whistled his musical refrain over and over. Later studies that summer showed that about fifteen pairs inhabited the area in the spring, increased to about seventy-five birds by fall, then were reduced in severe winters to about fifteen pairs again by the following spring. (Rose Lake Annual Report, 1941-1942).

Orioles, grosbeaks, meadowlarks, and vireos also established singing posts in the locust tree by our cottage. A pair of Eastern Bluebirds nested in an old apple tree nearby, and the surrounding fields and their borders harbored a half dozen or more species of sparrows, including the vocally insignificant but much sought-after (by bird listers, at least) Grasshopper and

Henslow's sparrows. A few hundred yards from our doorstep, Vermilion Creek, a sluggish, tree-and-shrub-bordered stream, meandered through woods and fields. It was—and still is—one of the best birding spots on the station grounds.

In addition to my routine pheasant appraisals, one of my major assignments was a study of predatory birds—population surveys, nesting observations, and notes on food habits. During that spring and summer I had under surveillance two nests of Long-eared Owls (the first ever recorded at the station), a Screech Owl nest in a squirrel box, two nests of Marsh Hawks, three of Red-shouldered Hawks, and one of Cooper's Hawks. Red-tails and Broadwings were not found nesting at the station that summer. Six crows' nests (two inactive) was a sharp drop from the fifteen recorded the previous year; we decided that the numerous crows observed included many nonnesting birds. Prey items were collected and analyzed from all of these nests; confining the young in cages at the nest sites toward the end of nest life added to the study materials available, but such procedures were not notably successful.

Prey of the Long-eared Owls, as might be expected, consisted chiefly of mice: *Microtus, Peromyscus,* and a few *Synaptomys.* There were some *Blarina* skulls, one avian skull, and feathers of one or two small passerine birds. Marsh Hawk diet, again as might be expected, was more varied. At first it consisted almost entirely of avian prey, not usually typical of Marsh Hawks. Apparently they were utilizing other birds nesting in or around the marsh—a Virginia Rail, Red-winged Blackbirds and other icterids, and Swamp Sparrows. Four juvenile pheasants ranging in age from one to six weeks were taken. At about nest-leaving time the prey fed to the young changed to young rabbits less than half grown; their age was determined by measurements of the hind feet left at the nest. The surprising scarcity of mice in the diet probably reflected a low in the microtine cycle that summer.

Asynchronous hatching was noted at this Marsh Hawk nest; the eggs hatched intermittently over a ten-day period, resulting in some cannibalism; apparently the youngest sibling was eaten by its nest mates. The female at this nest was particularly aggressive. She often divebombed me when I entered the marsh. I wore a hat for protection, but once she knocked my hat off, then nearly scalped me when I stooped to pick it up. Thereafter I carried a broom over my shoulder. A more friendly acquaintance was a rattlesnake *(Sistrurus catenatus)* that inhabited a brush pile at the edge of the marsh. I usually stopped to greet it en route to the hawk nest and felt a sense of loss when a class from Michigan State College killed it and proudly brought their trophy to the station headquarters.

My identification of raptor prey items was tentative. Later, Joe Linduska sent these and other materials to Patuxent Research Center at Laurel, Maryland, for more detailed analysis and used the data for a doctoral dissertation submitted to Michigan State College (Linduska, 1949). By an odd quirk I was then serving as acting chairman of his doctoral committee; I was to evaluate a thesis that included work I had done under his supervision at Rose Lake!

Always an incurable bird lister, I keep incidental records on all birds seen during my field studies on raptors and often took off-duty walks to look for other birds. Between April 21 and September 22 I recorded 144 species of birds, considerably more than my maximum annual lists (127) at Pleasant Valley Sanctuary. Differences included the greater prevalence of water birds and marsh birds at Rose Lake and the occurrence of more Southern species (e.g., Cardinals, Tufted Titmice, Bobwhite). Sandhill Cranes, always a special feature since several pairs nested in the area, were new for my life list.

Of course, my list of 144 was a partial one (not a full year). Many years later (1975), John Lerg compiled a list of the birds recorded at the station (by then enlarged to 3,334 acres) from 1960 to the mid-1970s. It contained 228 species, not including 14 peripheral species of birds recorded prior to 1960.

My familiarity with the Rose Lake area came in handy after I transferred to the college; throughout my twenty-three years of teaching ornithology classes at East Lansing, Rose Lake was our most frequently visited off-campus area. The great diversity of habitats, mostly readily accessible and without *No Trespassing* signs to annoy us, was a great blessing. However, even at Rose Lake one can get into trouble. Once when we parked by the side of a dirt road where I had seen a Black-billed Cuckoo dash into a thicket, a lady en route to work in the early morning reported us to police as a group of hippies blocking the road. She didn't dare pass us. When the police caught up with us, we were watching Horned Larks in a field. The officers sized up the situation quickly and were as amused as we were. Bird watchers haven't always found the police so sympathetic.

Michigan State University

In the fall of 1942 I learned of a teaching position available in the Department of Zoology at Michigan State College. (The name changed to Michigan State University in 1955). After working in two State Conservation Departments (Vermont and Michigan) and spending nearly five years on a wildlife sanctuary in Massachusetts, where my duties were largely public relations, I felt that college teaching might be more to my liking. Although the work at Rose Lake was pleasant, with congenial working companions, studies primarily concerned with game species were not my cup of tea. Hence, at the beginning of the fall term, I transferred to the college, where I was to remain for thirty years.

The college position was not an immediate bonanza. After six years of postdoctoral experience (1936-1942) in three states, I was starting a new life as a beginning laboratory instructor (at $1800 per year). Then lean times came to the college. The war rapidly drained off most male students not classified as 4-F's, enrollments in zoology dropped off sharply, and staff people not drafted were given other assignments.

But the military program, in a sense, saved the day. AAF and ASTP cadets swarmed onto the campus for instruction in math, physics, English, history, and geography. Even our department head got into the act and taught a math class. Another man on our staff taught physics, and three of us went into the geography program. I learned a lot of geography—that dealing with weather and climates seemed particularly useful. But it wasn't easy. I really burned midnight oil preparing for the next day's assignments. A big boost for our sagging family finances (living costs were rising rapidly) was that Martha, a mathematics major, got in on the math program. After the war she continued teaching in the math department for many years.

Another interesting assignment for me was working on a fish food project with Dr. Peter Tack, ichthyologist. Meat shortages (red points) during the war increased the demand for fish proteins in the human diet. The aim of the project was to encourage utilization of some of the abundant but less popular food fishes such as carp, suckers, burbot, and lake herrings. Biologists caught and dressed the fish, and the Department of Home Economics tried out various recipes on a panel of tasters. We had considerable success with lake herring, but couldn't persuade people to dine on carp, even when the fish came from the then clear waters of Lake St. Clair. Those taken from the polluted Red Cedar River on campus, admittedly, were not very tasty, and the sea lampreys that we tried once were a sickening sight when cooked: they turned to a leaden gray.

The end of the war brought other problems—and some embarrassing inequities. The rush of students back to the campus created a sudden demand for new teachers. New staff personnel, some with no previous teaching experience and even without advanced degrees, were brought in over the heads of experienced staff. My own experience was a case in point. After three years at the college and nine years of postdoctoral experience, I was still an instructor, whereas new and inexperienced staff people were being hired at the assistant professor level. However, some conspicuous inequities were soon rectified. New staff members without Ph.D.'s were usually dismissed if they did not finish work for their degree within three years. Possibly the apparent inequities enhanced my later promotions.

During my first six years at MSC I was virtually a "floater" within the department, on call to fill any need that might arise. Hence, I taught or assisted in a demanding assortment of about twelve different courses. When Burt Ostenson, a vertebrate zoologist, was called into military service, I inherited an economic zoology course he had developed for agricultural students. It was essentially a vertebrate natural history course with emphasis on farm wildlife of economic importance—food fishes, furbearers, birds and their role on the farm, and animal pests. Amphibians and reptiles were included on the theory that farmers should know the potential of such often maligned creatures for good or harm. I enjoyed this assignment, but the course was dropped after a couple years because of a revision in the agricultural curriculum.

Next came a bona fide natural history course developed as the third-term sequence of a year of introductory zoology, but it was out of place as an introductory course and was dropped when a new staff man came to take charge of the first year of zoology.

In response to the need for nature education for elementary school teachers, I developed a course in nature study. This was right up my alley. My years at Pleasant Valley Sanctuary proved useful here, but I was somewhat disappointed in the caliber of the students from elementary education. They informed me in no uncertain terms that they didn't need to know specific details to teach children; they just needed a "general appreciation" of nature. On a field trip for wildflowers, one of the brighter students (a sort of ringleader) remarked that they didn't need to know different kinds of violets, but that they should be able to tell a violet from a geranium. When I gave her a Canada violet *(Viola canadensis)* on a spot test, she called it a geranium!

The postwar flood of wildlife students created a demand for a waterfowl management course. I started one, but it was taken over by Dr. Miles Pirnie, a waterfowl specialist, when he was transferred from the W. K. Kellogg Bird Sanctuary to the campus.

Perhaps my most bizarre assignment during those years was an animal ecology course. Dr. Hunt, our department head, often got so involved in his research on dental caries that he neglected his administrative duties. At the beginning of each new term he would assemble his staff, check enrollment figures, then parcel out teaching duties rather hurriedly. On one occasion he looked at enrollment figures and said, "Hmmm, seventy-five students signed up for Animal Ecology and our ecologist has resigned." He glanced around the room, spied me, and asked, "Wallace, did you ever teach Animal Ecology?" I replied, "No, I've never even had a course in Animal Ecology." "That's fine," he said, "you will learn a lot teaching the course this spring." I did! But perhaps the seventy-five students didn't.

Ornithology Courses

During my first six years at MSC, Professor J.W. Stack taught the ornithology courses, a curriculum that nearly perished during the war years. Although not widely known as an ornithologist, except perhaps for his pioneer work in bird banding, Professor Stack was a popular teacher in a popular course; a poll of former students at one time indicated that ornithology was their best remembered course. During the first postwar rush of students, I assisted Professor Stack on the field trips; then in 1948 he gave up teaching to become the full-time director of the newly organized museum. I inherited the bird courses and kept them until retirement, except for one sabbatical and one consultantship year.

Introductory Ornithology in the spring term was the main course. It had a postwar enrollment of nearly a hundred students, too many to handle efficiently in the field; often, in spite of usually well-qualified graduate assistants, the students didn't get adequate supervision. However, an administrative battle soon developed over the place of wildlife curricula in the university. After some bitter bickering, the wildlife work was removed from zoology, where it originated, and transferred to the College of Agriculture as a new Fisheries and Wildlife Department. Wildlife students were no longer required to take my ornithology; the curricula in the new department covered game birds and waterfowl. For a while there was a decidedly "anti-dickey-bird" attitude fostered by students and staff. Hence I lost about two-thirds of my potential students, including some of the best and some of the worst, the latter, those who were interested only in huntable birds.

However, many wildlife students gradually drifted back into my classes of their own volition, and when Dr. Harold Prince took over the waterfowl work in the 1960's, he made introductory ornithology a prerequisite for his waterfowl students. Enrollment in my class gradually climbed back to about sixty and remained at about that level; it would have gone considerably higher some years but an upper limit had to be set for some lab sections because of lack of laboratory space, always a critical issue in our department.

Needless to say, this class had its ups and downs. Weather in Michigan in spring (the retarding influence of the Great Lakes), transportation problems getting afield, inadequate laboratory facilities, oversized field groups, and the apathy of some students all contributed to the downs, and yet the class was one of my great delights. I enjoyed lecturing to large classes (the ego in me), liked the early-morning field trips in spite of wind, rain, cold, and often indifferent students. And, of course, there were always some outstanding students. Many of the better ones went on for advanced work in ornithology; many who did not still linger in my memory because of their enthusiasm and sharpness in the field.

But my advanced classes and graduate students were my special delight. Advanced classes, with some variations from year to year, included a fall-term systematic ornithology course (birds of the world), a winter-term avian anatomy and physiology course (mainly anatomy), and a spring term for independent field study.

My fall-term systematics course was the one I liked best. It was always a small class of several to a dozen or so well-qualified students. We covered the orders and families of birds of the world from penguins (or ostriches before the change in family sequence) to fringillids. The classification in Van Tyne's and Berger's *Fundamentals of Ornithology* was a useful guide after it became available in 1959. Readings in Gilliard's *Living Birds of the World* (1958) and Austin's *Birds of the World* (1961) were also much used, but (in part for my own review) I liked to spoon-feed the students by going over the complete classification with them in lectures.

We were handicapped at first by our inadequate collection of specimens. The old Walter Barrows' collection of skins that Professor Stack shielded carefully from student use went with him to the museum. That left me with some mounted birds—good, bad, and indifferent—some good but awkward-to-handle Turtox specimens in frames, and a miscellaneous collection—chiefly waterfowl and game birds—that Burt Ostenson had acquired somehow. But these deficiencies were gradually remedied by teaching students in the class how to put up skins. Typically, a few soon became quite skilled in the art; others did not. Among the more skillful was Ted Van Velzen, better known locally as TV, or Channel 6. I think he was disgusted with the condition of our collections, and after leaving Michigan he sent me many beautifully prepared specimens from Oklahoma, Texas, and Alaska. Soon also the museum was transferred from its inadequate quarters in the basement of the auditorium to new facilities in the old library. Dr. Rollin Baker became the director in September 1955. He built up the museum collections rapidly, including a nearly worldwide series of birds.

To cap the climax for this course we always took a trip to the University of Michigan Museum in Ann Arbor, which has one of the largest and best university collections of birds in the country. Van Tyne always welcomed us and—with pardonable pride—usually took us on a personally conducted tour of the museum's facilities—skins, skeletons, and library. When he was not available, his assistant, Dr. Robert Storer, conducted the tour. The trip to Ann Arbor was always a highlight for the students.

The avian anatomy and physiology course in the winter term was less popular but had its bright spots. We used Pettingill's well-known manual (A Laboratory and Field Manual of Ornithology) as a guide for dissection of a pigeon, but we supplemented this with other references on the muscular system, for instance, which was lacking in the earlier editions of Pettingill's text. That class produced three specialists on muscles. Jim Vanden Berge, who went beyond "the call of duty" in working out the musculature of his pigeon, seemed a natural when George Hudson, at Washington State, needed someone to work on ciconiiform musculature. Jim became Hudson's right-hand man and coauthored several important papers with him. Dave Osborne also apparently became intrigued by his initial work on myology and went on for a Ph.D., working on the skin muscles of the Phasianinae. And Wayne Shooks explored the functions of leg musculature in *Coturnix* (see pp. 93, 96).

The spring term course was originally set up as an independent field study, but students going on for advanced degrees could sign up for "investigations," which made my spring course somewhat superfluous. Hence, we changed it to a series of weekend field trips for credit. However, this soon became unmanageable because students who had taken the course previously, other students, and sometimes staff people wanted to join us. Thereafter, it evolved into noncredit weekend trips open to anyone. We went to Erie for winter gulls, to Maple River and Shiawassee National Wildlife Refuge for waterfowl, to Tawas Point for shorebirds, and to northern Michigan for Sharp-tailed Grouse, Bald Eagles, Ospreys, and Kirtland's Warblers. One student told me later—I hadn't realized it at the time—that he took the course three times for credit by signing up for a different number each time.

Needless to say, these outings with students were gala affairs. Incidentally—and perhaps inadvertently—I converted many a student into a bird lister before the American Birding Association (ABA) fanned the flickering flame into a big blaze. I claim I invented the Big Day, not knowing then that other people everywhere were doing it. At Pleasant Valley Sanctuary in Massachusetts in 1939, I had tried a one-day count in May just to see how many birds I could find on the grounds. Conditions

89

were far from ideal (many transients were already gone), and I ended up with only seventy-four species, but by counting up on my fingers the potential species that were missed, I figured a goal of one hundred might be possible. Later, in East Lansing, Bill Overlease (a botany student) and I had an exciting few hours of birding during a good warbler flight. We had about seventy species all told (plus or minus a few countables or noncountables) and realized that we might have reached one hundred with more time and better organization. So we tried it the following spring with another recruit and achieved one hundred and one. Thereafter the Big Day became an annual event.

For local counts we often went to a favorable spot, such as Rose Lake, and bedded down overnight in order to get a good start in the morning. Once we had an overnight group at Rose Lake and an "in-town" group starting out in the morning (some of them stayed in to watch a prize fight on television the preceding evening). We met for a belated breakfast to compare notes. The overnight gang had seventy species, the in-town group, thirty-five! Of course, we counted songs and calls if they could be identified, and they usually could. Once a student accused me of counting a dozen species by voice before he got his head out of his sleeping bag. A more amusing incident took place on an overnight trip in April to the dancing grounds of the Sharp-tailed Grouse. A student with contact lenses put them in a vial of water overnight. In the morning the lenses were frozen solid in ice. He got off to a slow start that morning! Instructors also have their embarrassing moments. Once I identified a squeaking wheel on a boy's tricycle as a Cedar Waxwing!

On overnight outings close to home, Martha often brought our breakfast, and sometimes lunch, out to some designated spot in the field. Her doughnuts for class trips became famous; years later some students seemed to remember the doughnuts better than the birds.

Graduate Students

Among the thousand or more students I had in beginning ornithology, many went on for advanced degrees, some in the Department of Fisheries and Wildlife where I often served on their committees but not as chairman. Others studied in the Department of Zoology, where I served as their major professor. I don't know how many master's degree students survived with me. The university had a Plan A (with a thesis) and a Plan B (without a thesis) for master's students. Many chose the latter, less formidable method.

About twenty of my students, however, elected Plan A and wrote a thesis based on original research. Several who went on for bigger things in ornithology, sometimes by transferring to another university (usually with my approval) merit mention. Robert D. Burns (M.S. 1954) did a master's project on Cardinals at MSU, then went to UCLA for work in physiology but returned to MSU to work with Dr. Braddock for his PH.D. on behavior of kangaroo rats. He continued work with birds, however, first at the University of Oklahoma, then at Kenyon College in Ohio. J. W. Hardy (M.S. 1954) did a summer field study on Least Terns in the Mississippi Valley, then transferred to the University of Kansas and worked on the phylogeny of New World jays for his Ph.D. He is now Curator of Birds at the University of Florida and a Fellow (1971) of the A.O.U. W. John Smith (M.S. 1958) analyzed C.C. Ludwig's voluminous banding records of Herring Gulls in the Great Lakes. Later he went to Harvard to work with Dr. Mayr for his Ph.D. on flycatchers and was partly responsible for the still unpublished flycatcher volume in Peter's *Check-list of Birds of the World*. He is now an Elective Member (1968) of the A.O.U. and an ethologist at the University of Pennsylvania. John L. Zimmerman (M.S. 1959) did a nesting study of Catbirds at MSU, then went to the University of Illinois to work with Dr. Kendeigh on Dickcissels. He is now at Kansas State University and an Elective Member (1969) of the A.O.U. George Fisler (M.S. 1956) studied the morning awakening time of birds in the Red Cedar Woodlot, then went to the University of California at Berkeley for work with mammals under Dr. Alden Miller. Another student, William Armstrong (M.S. 1957), did a project on Long-eared Owls, but went on to veterinarian school and now has his own small animal clinic in Pennsylvania. Jim Lund did a commendable project on Mourning Doves (M.S. 1952) but went into pharmaceutical work later. Others who started with me transferred to Fisheries and Wildlife when work in that department became available. The master's studies that were published later are listed in the references at the end of the chapter.

In my early years at Michigan State, the college was not noted for turning out Ph.D.'s, but in the late '50s and '60s doctorate programs expanded rapidly. Fourteen students finished their Ph.D.s with me. These are categorized briefly in chronological order in the following paragraphs and their dissertation title or published paper listed in the references at the end of this chapter.

J. P. Linduska, then biologist at the Rose Lake Wildlife Experiment Station but formerly a graduate assistant at MSC, returned in 1949 to finish work on his Ph.D. Actually he was Professor Stack's student, but since he made good I like to claim him. Prof. Stack had a demanding assignment on a Presidential Committee at that time and turned Joe over to me. Later, Linduska went on to an important post in the U.S. Fish and Wildlife Service, spent ten years as an ecologist with Remington Arms, and then became Vice-President for Science for the National Audubon Society.

Lester E. Eyer (1954) was my first bona fide Ph.D. He took a leave from Alma College, where he was head of the biology department, and came to MSU where he made a study of two sharply contrasting grackle populations, one in a marsh and one in campus conifers. He retired from Alma College in 1977 and I had the pleasure of participating in his retirement party.

William Pielou (1957), also commuting from Alma, did his research on Tufted Titmice in the campus woodlots. He is now at Furman University, Greenville, South Carolina.

John H. Mehner (1958) studied robins both at Pittsburgh, where he was engaged in high school teaching, and at MSU during the summers of 1954–1957. His East Lansing study was nearly terminated in disaster when the initiation of a Dutch elm disease control program threatened to eliminate his robins. All his campus nests failed in the last year of his study (1957) and only scattered individuals could be found on the North Campus. John is (or was until recently) Head of Biology at Mary Baldwin College in Staunton, Virginia.

Ralph A. MacMullan (1960), like Joe Linduska, was hardly mine, but I like to claim him. After many years with the Michigan Department of Conservation, he returned to MSU to complete work he had started many years earlier on his Ph.D. He preferred to remain in the Department of Zoology rather than to transfer to the new Department of Fisheries and Wildlife. Later he became the dynamic director of the Michigan Department of Conservation, but he died prematurely in his late 50's in 1972. Like me, he got involved in the pesticide controversy and had many staunch supporters but also a predictable number of severe critics.

Richard F. Bernard (1963), a graduate of the University of Maine, came to Michigan State for advanced work but soon went into military service in Germany. He returned to MSU, and, on a grant from the U.S. Fish and Wildlife Service, he undertook the difficult and costly task of analyzing the many dead birds found on campus following the use of DDT fo. control of Dutch elm disease. There were still denials from agricultural, chemical, and administrative officials that DDT was responsible for bird deaths, but Dick's meticulous analyses (under supervision of Dr. E. J. Benne in Biochemistry) and feeding experiments with sparrows almost (but not quite) laid such denials to rest—and possibly kept me from being discharged from the university for insisting that DDT was causing avian mortality. Dick is now at Quinnipiac College, Hamden, Connecticut.

Ernest A. Boykins (1964), from Alcorn A. and M. in Mississippi, continued the work started by Bernard. With aid from a grant from the National Science Foundation, he analyzed soil samples, earthworms, and robins, thus tracing the buildup or magnification in food chains from soils to higher vertebrates. Ernie returned to Alcorn A and M after completing his work at MSU. Later he became president of Mississippi Valley State College at Itta Bena, Mississippi.

David T. Kee (1964) did a project on color preferences in domestic fowl and Japanese quail *(Coturnix)*. He also served as an able assistant in my ornithology classes, and, I am happy to report, patterned his ornithology courses at Northeast Louisiana College after the ones he had taken with me at MSU.

Harold D. Mahan (1964) came from Central Michigan University at Mount Pleasant where he did his field work on the effects of the environment on growth, development, and temperature regulation in nestling phoebes. He returned to CMU after completing his work at MSU, taught classes in ornithology, ecology, and animal behavior, and became director of CMU's Center for Cultural and Natural History. Today he is Director of the Cleveland Museum of Natural History.

Robert L. Fleming II (1967), son of missionaries in India and Nepal where the Fleming family spent many years, came to Michigan State for graduate work. He did a master's project (1962) on the comparative syringeal musculature in three subfamilies of Nepalese babblers (Timaliidae). Then he returned to India, where he made a distributional and ecological study of the birds of Mussoorie, India. He now lives in Kathmandu, Nepal, where he conducts tours for visiting naturalists and has coauthored a book with his father on *The Birds of Nepal.*

David R. Osborne (1968) worked on skin muscles in the Phasianinae. Earlier (1963) he obtained his M.S. on work done at the MSU Biological Station at Gull Lake. He teaches zoology, including an ornithology course, at Miami University in Oxford, Ohio.

Gordon L. Kirkland, Jr. (1969) made comparative population studies in three different woodlots, two on campus and one at Rose Lake. He is now a professor of zoology at Shippensburg State College in Pennsylvania, curator of the vertebrate museum, and a Research Associate in Mammalogy at the Carnegie Museum in Pittsburgh.

Wayne Shooks (1970) also got indoctrinated in my avian anatomy course

517 Ann Street, our home for 30 years. Severely restricted for space in front and at the sides, but in the tree-filled backyard we recorded 74 species of birds in the 13-year period from 1958 to 1970.

First snowfall in the MSU horticultural gardens. My office window looked out over scenes like this.

Preparing a Virginia Rail specimen. Putting up birdskins is one of the time-consuming activities of curators of study collections.

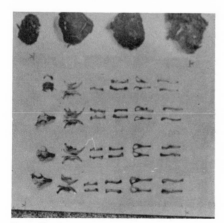

Barn Owl pellets and the bones of four mice taken from the largest pellet.

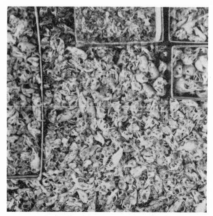

Skulls of mice (92%), shrews (7%), and birds (1%) taken from Barn Owl pellets.

and continued work on the functional anatomy of the hind limb in Japanese quail *(Coturnix)* for his Ph.D. He was one of the unfortunates who graduated at the wrong time. He left high school teaching to get a Ph.D. in hope of future employment in a university, then went back to high school teaching because the market for Ph.D.'s in zoology was virtually closed.

Paul Bradfield (1972), on a grant from the U.S. Fish and Wildlife Service, did another robin study, trying to determine the effects of DDT on robins after methoxychlor replaced DDT in campus spraying. He is now at Bay de Noc Community College at Escanaba, Michigan.

Two other special students merit mention. In 1952 Jukka Koskimies of Helsinki, Finland, came to MSU for a post-doctoral year. Although he enrolled in my advanced ornithology courses, he was so well informed on Old World birds that he was at times practically an assistant. In 1961, Ramish Naik, of the University of Baroda, India, came to MSU for further work with birds, a requirement for fulfillment of his Ph.D. in India. I had served as a foreign referee to evaluate his dissertation. He returned to the University of Baroda, his alma mater, where he is a professor of zoology, doing research on myology and metabolism in birds. He also is editor of the newly established Indian journal *Pavo*.

Social Life

Our social life with students outside of class merits brief mention. At least once each year, usually in the fall, we held a party for my graduate students and their wives—a fun evening with bird guessing games and refreshments. Sometimes we had send-off parties for newly fledged Ph.D.'s; these, however, didn't always materialize because students often left the campus before finishing. In a different category were Thanksgiving dinners for students who couldn't go home for the holidays. Often these were foreign students. Such get-togethers were gala celebrations, sometimes mixing contrasting cultures and competing religions. At least fourteen foreign countries on five continents were represented at one time or another in parties at our house. Sometimes we took in foreign students until they could find other housing. One from Nigeria, not familiar with snow, once shovelled our walk for us, then proceeded to remove all the snow from the lawn and pile it in the driveway!

Research

My own research and writings at MSU resulted in a variety of publications—an ornithology text (now in its third edition), a number of chapters in other books, many encyclopedia bird biographies, bulletins, and articles for various journals and magazines.

My first major research project at MSU was on Barn Owls. The results have been published in a sixty-one-page bulletin by the Michigan Agricultural Experiment Station, but the bulletin has long been out of print, hence some of the pertinent data are repeated here.

The owls had a roost in a pine grove adjacent to the football stadium, nested once (unsuccessfully) on Beaumont Tower on campus, and inhabited an abandoned barn next to Dr. Hunt's house. He thought the owls provided a good opportunity for study because there was some question about their food habits in relation to poultry and pigeons. I collected 2,200 pellets over a three-year period and analyzed them for contents. No poultry or game bird remains were found in the 6,815 prey animals identified. They consisted of 5,791 (85%) meadow voles *(Microtus pennsylvanicus);* 308 (4.5%) deer mice *(Peromyscus,* nearly all *bairdii)*; 80 (1.2%) jumping mice *(Zapus hudsonius);* 37 (0.5%) house mice *(Mus musculus);* and 23 (0.3%) bog lemmings *(Synaptomys cooperi)* for a total of 91.5 percent mice. Three species of shrews *(Blarina brevicauda, Sorex cinereus,* and *Cryptotis parva)* accounted for 7.0 percent of the prey (444 individuals, mostly *Blarina).* Birds amounted to 1.07 percent of the prey: 50 House Sparrows, 15 Starlings, 2 Savannah Sparrows, 1 Song Sparrow, 3 unidentified passerines and parts of 2 pigeon squabs. Other items included 6 rats *(Rattus norvegicus),* 4 star-nosed moles *(Condylura cristata),* 2 prairie moles *(Scalopus aquaticus)*, 2 juvenile cottontail rabbits *(Sylvilagus floridanus)*, and a least weasel *(Mustela rixosa),* the latter apparently the first record for Ingham County.

One surprising habit of the Barn Owls was their storage of excess prey at or near the nest site. In the fall of 1946 I found a collection of 189 mice and one shrew on the barn floor under a roost frequented by one of the adults. Eighty-six of the dried-up carcasses had been beheaded, and there were 9 detached skulls. The mouse-hoarding habit continued in the spring. On March 2, the nest box contained one egg and 13 mice; on March 7, there were 4 eggs and 64 mice; and on March 10, there were 6 eggs and 80 mice. Eventually the entire supply vanished, but their disposal was a mystery. Some, but certainly not all of them, were probably fed to the young after the eggs hatched.

The owls in the barn laid three successive clutches of seven eggs each in an almost continuous laying cycle, but my study terminated suddenly when a local resident shot the female at the nest site on the theory that the owls were catching the pigeons that he wanted to shoot. Actually the owls and pigeons apparently lived together harmoniously; once they nested more or less simultaneously in adjacent boxes. Fragments of two pigeon squabs found in the prey may have been carrion. One of the young owls banded at the nest was taken in Alabama the following winter, another was shot nearby.

Another early project, more interesting from the attendant circumstances than from any profound results, was a brief survey of the summer birds at Gratiot Lake in Keweenaw County in the Upper Peninsula. Professor Noblet, head of forestry at Michigan Tech at Houghton in the U.P., somehow (I'm vague about the details now) needed some credits, I think for a master's degree, to get a promotion at his school. He came to Michigan State and got me to approve a paper he had done in Minnesota for Dr. Gustav Swanson. It was a good paper; I approved it, and he was grateful. He had built cabins—a hobby of his—in several areas, including one at Gratiot Lake. I was welcome to use them at anytime, he said. I think he was a little surprised when Martha and I and our cocker spaniel showed up on his doorstep one evening the following summer. But he more than lived up to his word. He took us to his cabin, a well-constructed lodge in a beautiful setting accessible only by boat. He left us his boat and motor and a well-stocked pantry in the lodge, with the stipulation that we replenish the groceries we used.

We spent a delightful week in early July in the lodge overlooking the lake. A pair of Bald Eagles had a nest in a big pine behind the cabin, a pair of Pileated Woodpeckers frequented the adjacent hillside, and a pair of Black-backed Three-toed Woodpeckers had just vacated a nest in a white cedar stub in front of the cabin. In the week of prowling around in the woods, we found a Bay-breasted Warbler feeding an unidentified young bird, the second indication of breeding in Michigan; a Yellow-billed Cuckoo's nest, the first for the Keweenaw Peninsula; and a Ruby-crowned Kinglet's nest, another first, although the nest was soon deserted. Yellow-bellied Flycatchers inhabited a nearby bog, but we didn't find a nest. We saw a female Pine Grosbeak several times but no male and no indication of breeding. And our young cocker spaniel found her first porcupine. Relieving her of the quills pained us as much as the dog, I think.

My involvement with various aspects of Michigan ornithology during my thirty years at Michigan State resulted in many other, mostly minor, publications. But in the late 1950's and the 1960's I became so concerned with the effects of pesticides on birds that much of my research work and that of some of my students dealt with those issues (see References at end of chapter). Understandably, my involvement with pesticides made me unpopular among some segments of the college community, but I also had staunch supporters, including Congressman John Dingell, who intervened in my behalf when there were threats of my dismissal because I had testified on his committee in Washington, D.C.

Another time-consuming activity for nearly all ornithologists is participation in both professional and popular scientific societies. I have been a member of more than forty ornithological, natural history, conservation, and environmental organizations. Except for attending meetings and serving on various committees, my role in most of these societies has been minor. The chief exception is the Michigan Audubon Society, one of the largest, most active, and best organized of the state societies. I have served on the Board of Directors or advisory committee for more than thirty years, was editor of their quarterly journal, the *Jack-pine Warbler,* for six years, bird survey editor for five years, and book review editor for nine years (since 1969). My years of service in the Michigan Audubon Society culminated in a "Certificate of Appreciation" presented at the annual meeting in 1976, an award of which I am pardonably proud.

MSU Biological Station

In 1954, after trial summer field stations in various parts of the state, the College established a permanent biological station at the W.K. Kellogg estate on Gull Lake. For the first few years, T. W. Porter, assistant director, taught all the zoology courses, including ornithology. As enrollments increased, however, additional staff members were secured, and I was engaged to teach the bird courses. Opportunities for field work with birds were excellent in the diversified surroundings, but laboratory facilities were largely lacking at first. The class met, when it was necessary to stay indoors, in an invertebrate lab so cluttered up with glassware we could hardly find room to sit down, to say nothing of trying to set up a spot quiz. Sometimes, needing additional space, we overflowed into the adjacent parasitology lab.

Then the J.W. Stack Research Building was finally completed with excellent laboratory facilities for both teaching and research. For a few summers we had a room exclusively for ornithology, and the fine collection of local birds at the Kellogg Bird Sanctuary was transferred to our lab. Things were looking up. Then an ecology course took over the lab and the bird class had to go to the Kellogg Bird Sanctuary several miles distant, an inconvenience for both staff and students who lived at the station and had to commute.

Summer bird life in southern Michigan has its limitations for an identification course seeking a large number of species. We had difficulty getting one hundred species—a common goal—without going quite far afield. Otherwise, however, opportunities for observations were excellent. We could step out of the ornithology lab in the early morning and record twenty to thirty species within an hour or so on the Station grounds and could double that number by wandering into the adjacent fields and woods. Vehicles for transportation further afield were also readily available—a much better arrangement than we had on the main campus in East Lansing. Trips to nearby lakes and marshes, to the Kellogg Forest, and to the Allegan State Game Area (the latter was especially good for a variety of birds) netted many additional species. In late summer we extended our explorations to Lake Michigan for gulls, terns, plovers, and sandpipers. Sometimes, at least with advanced students, we took trips to northern Michigan for northern specialties. All in all, things worked out fairly well for summer bird work.

I had some embarrassing problems at the Station, however. One summer I found I had been replaced by a visiting ornithologist but I hadn't been notified of the change. That happened again a few summers later. In 1966, I decided to go to the International Ornithological Congress in England and notified my department head that I would need a substitute at the Station that summer. He said I had already been replaced. This time the replacement was permanent. I was never asked to come back to the Station.

One of my problems at the Station—inevitably—was the spraying program. The Station grounds were sprayed quite thoroughly with a mixture of DDT and Chlordane once a week. Most of the staff were opposed to the spraying because of the biological studies being conducted, but the director, an economic entomologist and a dedicated spraying devotee, apparently never consulted the staff. We had already recorded (and proven by analyses) heavy mortality to robins and other birds on the East Lansing campus from the use of DDT for Dutch elm disease control, but we had only limited evidence that the less severe dosages used for mosquitos would affect birds seriously. Hence, we made an attempt to determine the effects of the spraying on the birds on the station grounds.

Our findings were not very conclusive. Some predatory and insectivorous birds (e.g., Screech Owls, Eastern Phoebes, and Rough-winged Swallows) soon disappeared from the grounds, but these may have been incidental losses. Other apparent losses were quickly replaced by infiltration from surrounding unsprayed areas. Some incriminating evidence came from a Wood Pewee banded as a juvenile in the summer of 1961. It returned in 1962, presumably from a winter home in South America, but died at the

Station that summer. It had 43.7 ppm of DDT in the brain, probably a lethal dose.

Dave Osborne, who had had considerable experience in analytical work at the Mayo Clinic in Minnesota, made some analyses of soil, foliage, bark, berries, earthworms, eggs, and birds. Soils from lawns exposed to sunlight had very little DDT; presumably it had been converted to DDE and was not recoverable by the Schecter-Haller method we were using then for analyses. But soil under shrubs, foliage, and fruit did have considerable residues—up to 1,388 ppm on Juneberry *(Amelanchier)* leaves. All earthworms *(Helodrilus)* analyzed had levels believed to be sublethal to robins. The robins analyzed also had sublethal levels (2.94-22.0 ppm) in the brain; they were feeding heavily on fruit of a tall luxurious mulberry tree that was usually sprayed only on the lower branches. One White-breasted Nuthatch found dead had a lethal 137.0 ppm of DDT in the brain, but probably had been foraging in the bark of sprayed elms. (Some diseased elms were sprayed, but of course they died anyway.)

A Barn Swallow egg that failed to hatch in a five-egg nest had 2.70 ppm of DDT; a Brown Thrasher egg had 7.85 ppm; and three robin eggs had 11.30–15.20 ppm. Hence the effects of the spraying program on birds, although incriminating in some cases, were somewhat inconclusive.

Last Days

As a prelude to my pending retirement in 1972, my graduate students arranged for a send-off party for me. Somehow I never got wind of the coming event. My daughter Sylvia flew in from Texas and was cached away (with granddaughter Sandy) until the evening program. I was presented with a telescope. We had always depended on a department scope for class trips, and sometimes none was available. Martha was given a set of bird glasses in appreciation for her many contributions to the welfare of my students. And then there was the usual sheath of appreciative letters from colleagues and former graduate students. Of course they said nice things about me; the student who collected the letters said he threw out those that didn't.

Various citations followed. Carlton Wells had been asked to comment on my early days as a student at the University of Michigan; then several of my graduate students offered appropriate comments. There was one embarrassing event, however. In classes I had often mentioned that my Scotch father usually sold his hens' eggs and fed his children on guineafowl eggs which, according to my version, turned a sickly unappetizing bluish purple

101

when boiled. Students had managed to purchase some guineafowl eggs from a breeder down state, boiled them, and asked me to open one. The albumen was clear white and the yolk a rich yellow, not a sickly purple as I had claimed.

In a later chapter I describe the gradual termination of my duties at MSU and some continuing ornithological activities during my retirement years.

References

Armstrong, W.H. "Nesting and Food Habits of the Long-eared Owl in Michigan." Michigan State Univ. Museum Publications Biological Series 1(2): (1938) pp. 63-96.

Austin, O.L., Jr. *Birds of the World*. New York: Golden Press, 1961.

Bernard R.F. "Studies on the Effects of DDT on Birds." Michigan State Univ. Museum Publications Biological Series 2(3): (1963) pp. 161-191.

_____ and G.J. Wallace. "DDT in Michigan Birds." *Jack-Pine Warbler* 45: (1967) pp. 11-17.

Boykins, E.A. "DDT Residues in the Food Chain of Birds." Unpubl. Ph.D. dissertation, Michigan State University, 1964.

Bradfield, P.L. "Robin Population Changes and Pesticide Transformations after Methoxychlor Replaces DDT for Control of Dutch Elm Disease." Unpubl. Ph.D. dissertation, Michigan State University, 1972.

Burns, R.D. "A History of the Entry of the Cardinal into Michigan." *Jack-Pine Warbler* 36(1): (1958) pp. 19-21.

Eyer, L.E. "A Life History Study of the Bronzed Grackle, *Quiscalus quiscula versicolor Vieillot*." Unpubl. Ph.D. dissertation, Michigan State University, 1954.

Fisler, G.F. "Variation in the Morning Awakening Time of Some Birds in South-central Michigan." *Condor* 69: (1962) pp. 184-198.

Fleming, R.L. Jr. "The Birds of Mussoorie, U.P., India—A Distributional and Ecological Study." Unpubl. Ph.D. dissertation, Michigan State University, 1967.

Fleming, R.L. Sr.; R.L. Fleming, Jr.; and L.S. Bangdel. *Birds of Nepal*. Bombay, India: Vakil Press, 1976.

Gilliard, E.T. *Living Birds of the World*. Garden City, New York: Doubleday & Co., 1958.

Hardy, J.W. "The Least Tern in the Mississippi Valley." Michigan State Univ. Museum Publications Biological Series 1(1): (1957) pp. 1-60.

_____. "Studies in Behavior and Phylogeny of Certain New World Jays (Garrulinae)." Univ. Kansas Science Bulletin 42: (1961) pp. 13-49.

Kee, D.T. "Natural Color Preferences of the Domestic Chicken and European Quail." Unpubl. Ph.D. dissertation, Michigan State University, 1964.

Kirkland, G.L. Jr. "Avian Utilization of Small Woodlots in Southeastern Michigan." Unpubl. Ph.D. dissertation, Michigan State University, 1969.

Lerg, J.M. "Birds of Rose Lake." Wildl. Div. Report No. 2698, Michigan Department of Natural Resources, 1975.

Linduska, J.P. "Predator-prey Relationships at Rose Lake: Ecology and Land-use Relationships of Small Mammals on a Michigan Farm." Ph.D. dissertation, Michigan State University, 1949.

MacMullan, R.A. "A Population Survey of the Ring-necked Pheasant in Michigan." Unpubl. Ph.D. dissertation, Michigan State University, 1960.

_____. "The Case against Hard Pesticides." *Michigan Conservation,* Michigan Department of Conservation, 1968.

Mahan, H.D. "The Effects of the Environment on Growth, Development and Temperature Regulation in Nestling Eastern Phoebes." Unpubl. Ph.D. dissertation, Michigan State University, 1964.

Mehner, J.F. "Studies on the Life History of the Robin" (*Turdas migratorius* Linnaeus). Unpubl. Ph.D. dissertation, Michigan State University, 1958.

_____ and G.J. Wallace. "Robin Populations and Insecticides." *Atlantic Naturalist* 14(1): (1959) pp. 4-9.

Osborne, D.R. "DDT Residues in a Mosquito Control Program at the Kellogg Biological Station." Unpubl. M.S. thesis, Michigan State University, 1963.

_____. "The Functional Anatomy of the Skin Muscles in Phasianinae." Unpubl. Ph.D. dissertation, Michigan State University, 1968.

Pettingill, O.S., Jr. "A Laboratory and Field Manual of Ornithology," 3rd ed. Burgess Publishing Company, Minneapolis, Minn. (Retitled "Ornithology in Laboratory and Field" in 4th edition, 1970) 1956.

Pielou, W.P. "A Life History Study of the Tufted Titmouse, *Parus bicolor* Linnaeus." Unpubl. Ph.D. dissertation, Michigan State University, 1957.

Rose Lake Wildlife Experiment Station, 3rd annual report, 1941-42. Game Div., Dept. Cons., Lansing. (Predatory birds pp. 139)146.)

Shooks, W.V. "Leg Muscles and Their Function; A Comparative Study in Coturnix and Bobwhite." Unpubl. Ph.D. dissertation, Michigan State University, 1970.

Smith, W.J. "Movements of Michigan Herring Gulls." *Bird Banding* 30(2): (1959) pp. 69-104.

Van Tyne, J.V. and A.J. Berger. *Fundamentals of Ornithology.* New York, N.Y.: Wiley, 1959.

Wallace, G.J. "The Barn Owl in Michigan." Michigan State College Agricultural Experiment Station Technical Bulletin 208: (1948) pp. 1–61.

_____. "Some Summer Birds of Keweenaw County, Michigan." *Jack-Pine Warbler* 27: (1949) pp. 139–147.

_____, W.P. Nickell, and R.F. Bernard. "Bird Mortality in the Dutch Elm Disease Program." Cranbrook Institute Science Bull. 41: (1961) pp. 1–43.

_____, A.G. Etter, and D.R. Osborne. "Spring Mortality of Birds following Fall Spraying of Elms." *Massachusetts Audubon* 48(3): (1964) pp. 116–120.

Zimmerman, J.L. "Nesting Study of the Catbird in Southern Michigan." *Jack-Pine Warbler,* 41: (1963) pp. 142–160.

CHAPTER 6

Michigan Bird Life

MICHIGAN, LIKE forty-nine other states, claims to have many advantages for bird life, and some of the claims are valid. Michigan covers a wide range of latitude, from 41°45'N. to 47°25'N., or beyond 48° if Isle Royale is included. This is a south-north spread of 430 miles, or more than 600 miles by road from Toledo to Copper Harbor at the tip of the Keweenaw Peninsula. Some twenty to thirty species of birds, depending on what and how you count, are largely restricted to the southern five tiers of counties, and about forty species reach their southernmost breeding limits in the northern parts of the state, north of the Saginaw Bay-Muskegon line that effectively separates northern and southern Michigan. This affords a great diversity for the state's bird life.

Michigan is hemmed in by four of the five Great Lakes and has more than 3,000 miles of shore line, if all the bays and inlets are included. The open waters of the lakes harbor loons, far-out gulls, and sea ducks; and the beaches afford habitats for many shorebirds. Michigan has no real mountains, however; the so-called Porcupine Mountains are only 2,023 feet above sea level and only 1,421 feet above the level of Lake Superior. Otherwise, a great variety of habitats is available—sand dunes, remnants of prairies, abandoned and cultivated fields, woodlots (large and small) of oak-hickory, beech-maple, and pine. Two National Wildlife Refuges (Shiawassee and Seney) and many state parks and state game areas afford both attractive habitats and some protection for birds. Most of the state parks, however, are overcrowded, noisy, inadequately financed, and subject to severe vandalism; a person camping overnight in a state park in hope of getting an early start on morning birding may be in for a harrowing experience.

Past History

Michigan has a long and somewhat complicated history detailing its bird life. Published observations date back to 1669-1670 when Father Marquette wandered widely over much of the state. He described the abundance of wild pigeons, eagles, and ravens. It is a sad commentary on the changes since his day that the Passenger Pigeon is extinct; the Bald Eagle is an endangered species; and the ravens, once widespread, are now largely confined to a few areas in the Upper Peninsula. In 1702, in a report to the King of France, Antoine Cadillac, who founded Detroit and was later in charge of the frontier post at Mackinac, described additional birds, some of which can be readily identifed by his sometimes vague descriptions.

But the first real list of Michigan birds was in 1839, when Dr. Abram Sager, a zoologist at the University of Michigan, published a list of 164 species observed in southeastern Michigan. Later observers added to the list. Then in 1879, Dr. Morris Gibbs of Kalamazoo published the first annotated list of Michigan birds. It included 309 forms (species and sub-species), but apparently some inclusions were based on hearsay evidence and later writers considered many of the records dubious for one reason or another. (See Cook, 1893; Barrows, 1912; Wood, 1951; for further data.)

Then, before the turn of the century, two ornithologists at Michigan Agricultural College in East Lansing began compiling bird records. Professor A.J. Cook, who has written that he taught "large classes" in ornithology for twenty-six years, was commissioned by the State Board of Agriculture to prepare a list of Michigan birds. (Cook was an entomologist in the Department of Zoology when the two departments were together; later a quarrel between the two department heads caused a permanent separation of the departments.) Cook's first list, published in April 1893, contained an amazing 332 "species" (increased to 336 "species" in a second edition in September 1893). But this list also was subjected to critical scrutiny by later authorities. Apparently some Wisconsin and Indiana birds were included because it was believed that they must also occur in Michigan. Other inclusions were based on dubious reports, and some birds for which specimens may well have existed could not be located in later years. The lists of 332 and 336 included some subspecies.

Then Walter Barrows, also at MAC, revised Cook's list, threw out 30 species he considered questionable and added 20 new ones, a loss of 10 from the earlier list. Although Cook's *Birds of Michigan* was a comprehensive bulletin (Bull. 94) of 148 pages, Barrows' *Michigan Bird Life* (1912) was a substantial book of 822 pages, with technical descriptions of birds, their distribution and status, life histories, and habits. The accounts of food habits were meticulously detailed, as might be expected in an agricultural school. Barrows' work is still the only book on Michigan birds that covers all aspects of Michigan bird life. It was reprinted without change (after Barrows' death) in 1932 and for many years sold for $2.00. Now out of print, it is a book dealer's bonanza.

J.W. Stack followed Barrows as ornithologist at the college. He was reputed to be working on a two-volume revision of Barrows' book, but it never saw the light. I doubt it was very far along at the time of Stack's death in 1954.

Then the center for ornithology moved back to the University of Michigan, where a new and magnificent museum building afforded unrivaled facilities for ornithology. Norman A. Wood was the curator of birds for many years. He spent sixty years collecting and studying Michigan birds, and at the time of his death, in 1943, he had a manuscript nearly ready to go to press. It was edited, corrected, and slightly revised by Mr. Wood's successor, Dr. J. Van Tyne, and finally published as Wood's *Birds of Michigan* in 1951, an eight-year delay. The book (559 pages) gives the status and detailed distributional data of all Michigan birds accepted for the list—309 species and 334 forms. For inclusion in the list at least one specimen had to be preserved in a museum. This deleted many birds recorded by Cook and Barrows, because presumed specimens could not be found or because the records were considered unsatisfactory. Wood and Van Tyne excluded 19 of Barrows' birds but added 24 new ones.

But 309 species was rock bottom, based entirely on known speicmens in collections, and so the Michigan bird list could only climb upward thereafter, which it did rapidly. In 1959, two years after Van Tyne's death, Dale Zimmerman brought out a revised checklist (Van Tyne had published an earlier checklist in 1938 and was working on a revision). It listed 326 species (356 forms), still 10 fewer than Cook's list of 336 "species" in 1893. However, by now sight records were becoming more acceptable, and recognizable photographs were likewise considered authentic proof of occurrence. Zimmerman, using rigid standards, listed 13 sight records that he considered authentic, though they were not included in his main list of 326; later nearly all of the 13 were collected or photographed.

In 1966, Harrison Tordoff published a supplement to the Zimmerman—Van Tyne checklist, adding 18 new species that had been collected or photographed, raising the total to 344 species (or 346 if the American Flamingo and Bar-headed Goose are included; see below). Tordoff also

106

considered that five sight records were unquestionable but couldn't be included in the main list until specimens were collected or photographed. As yet there is no official new checklist, but quite a few species have been added since 1966. As of 1978 (this writing) I suspect that the number of Michigan birds, based on unquestionable records, is close to 370. The American Birding Associtaion (ABA), which has compiled a list of "seeable" birds for each state, has rounded off Michigan's list to 350 species (excludes extinct, extirpated and some "accidental" birds.)

Whether or not to accept certain records poses some sticky problems. There is no question about the occurrence of the American Flamingo in Michigan, but there is a question of how the several that have been recorded got here—escape from zoos, escape from tourists from Florida, or release by tourists when they discovered it was illegal to import flamingos without a permit. In 1962 a Bar-headed Goose (an Asiatic species) appeared with Canadian Geese at the Shiawassee Wildlife Refuge. It remained for a month—March 20 to April 24 (but left the day before I went to see it). One—possibly the same individual—was reported earlier that year at refuges in Illinois and Wisconsin. The suspicion still lingers that the goose may have escaped from captivity; many people have waterfowl breeding permits. Even more suspect is a Barnacle Goose reported by Ed and Ann Boyes in May 1965 in Mackinac County.

The Carolina Paroquet (Parakeet) was included on some early lists on the basis of past historical records (and specimens in Indiana and Illinois) but apparently a Michigan specimen has never been verified (Schorger, 1965; McKinley, 1977). A mounted Whooping Crane in a roadside museum in Cassopolis has no label and may not have come from Michigan; the likelihood of collecting one now in Michigan is remote. A western Band-tailed Pigeon visiting a feeding station in Niles from December 24 to January 22, 1967-1968, and a subtropical Ground Dove banded by Kay Petts at Alpena, September 5, 1966, also pose questions as to their origins.

Other peculiar quirks in the state records include the Glossy Ibis that was on some earlier lists on the basis of a seemingly authentic specimen. But in 1938, Van Tyne reidentified the bird as a White-faced Ibis, thus deleting the former and adding the latter to the state list. The ink was hardly dry, however, when a real Glossy Ibis was collected on Saginaw Bay. Cory's Bittern was on Wood's 1943 list; it is now regarded as a color phase of the Least Bittern. The Anhinga also was on some earlier lists on the basis of a specimen from the St. Mary's River in the Upper Peninsula, but Van Tyne did a little sleuthing and found that the bird was taken on the Ontario side of the river. Ontario can claim it, Michigan can not.

Birding in Michigan

More pertinent for present-day bird watchers is not the total number of birds recorded in Michigan in the past three hundred years, but which ones occur here now and where can they be found. Past records include about 100 species that are rare stragglers. For many years the Michigan Audubon Society has conducted seasonal bird surveys in the state and published the results in their quarterly journal, *The Jack-pine Warbler*. The state's annual lists, compiled from the reports of all observers, commonly run to about 270 species, which is a good indication of the number of birds that are of more or less regular occurrence in the state. Of course, a few "regulars" get missed; one year no one reported a Long-eared Owl, which is not uncommon but sometimes hard to find. On the other hand, the "regulars" missed are offset by stragglers that show up in certain years—subtropical Scissor-tailed Flycatchers (3 records), Townsend's Solitaires (3 records), and Varied Thrushes (surprisingly frequent winter visitors) from the far West.

Another good criterion of Michigan bird life is the lifetime total of individual observers. In more than forty years of birding in Michigan, I have seen 277 species or about 79 percent of the birds that (supposedly) could have been seen here during that period. At least ten persons have surpassed me, some of them in a much shorter period of time. Roy Smith, of Andrews University in Berrien Springs, has recorded 309 species or 88 percent of the possible total, but his records over the years include many "accidentals" that cannot be recorded every year. Margaret Drake Elliott has recorded 296 species (84 percent) and attributes her high total to the fact she has been birding longer than the rest of us. But she denies having the Passenger Pigeon on her list. Some of the leading listers who have surpassed me are former students of mine—perhaps I taught them too well!

Annual lists are also highly competitive. In 1934, Milton Trautman, now at Columbus, Ohio, reached a record high of 247 species when he was a graduate student at the University of Michigan. Once I accused him of including subspecies in his count (sometimes we did in those days; for instance, Northern and Prairie Horned Larks), but he says he did not. Trautman's record remained unbroken for more than thirty years; he was a poineer in such enterprises. In the 1960's several of my former students, who covered much of the state in their routine duties for the Michigan Department of Conservation, tried repeatedly to top Trautman's record but could not (Ryel, 1964). More recently, however, Trautman's record has been broken several times. Annual leaders, of course, fluctuate from year to year; again Roy Smith seems to be the current record holder with 287 species in 1973, a stupendous effort of covering the most productive areas repeatedly. My own annual record is a meager 215 in 1965, but I have a good excuse; during the spring months, when you need to be all over the state, I was largely tied down in the Lansing area teaching students how to find and identify birds.

Perhaps more pertinent information for beginning birders and for visitors seeking new birds is where the best birding spots are. For, although most birds are somewhat uniformly distributed over the whole state, there are nevertheless certain areas of concentration, preferred lanes of travel during migration, and special places where the rarer or more localized birds can be found. Michigan Audubon Society's *Enjoying Birds in Michigan* (3rd revised edition) gives helpful clues on where to find birds in Michigan. Pettingill's *Guide to Bird Finding East of the Mississippi* (2nd edition) gives detailed directions for finding such places.

The following account of some of the better birding areas in Michigan is probably biased in the selection of those I know best or have visited most often. One of the most productive of these is Monroe County in southeastern Michigan. Quite a few new species have been added to the state list by explorations along the western shores of Lake Erie. The area is quite phenomenal in winter; a Christmas bird count there in 1972 yielded 88 species. Greater Black-backed Gulls are quite regular in winter, and Glaucous Gulls, Iceland Gulls, and Black-legged Kittiwakes have been recorded there. The first Michigan specimens of Franklin's Gull (western), Laughing Gull (eastern), and Little Gull (European) were taken in Monroe County. Barn Owls, once much more widespread over southern Michigan, are now found chiefly—often only—in Monroe County. Jaegers (Long-tailed and Parasitic), Glossy Ibis, Hudsonian Godwit, and a Ruff also have been recorded there. Cattle Egrets, Louisiana Herons, and Yellow-crowned Night Herons apparently invaded the area in the 1960's. Erie Marsh, in the vicinity of Consumers Power sewage pools, is not the most aesthetic place for birding, but it has been very productive.

Vying with Monroe County and possibly exceeding it in the number of specialities is Berrien County in the southwestern part of the state, where exceedingly active members of the Oronoko Bird Club, led by Roy Smith and Walter Booth, have reported many surprising discoveries. Their Christmas counts usually lead the state; high counts are achieved because of favorable habitats for water birds and for winter lingerers that should have gone south and because of a large and well-organized group of observers widely scattered over the allowable fifteen-mile diameter circle. On

December 16, 1973, the club finally achieved their coveted goal of one hundred species.

The Lake Michigan shoreline in Berrien County has yielded most of the rare gulls, jaegers, and kittiwakes reported for Monroe County. In 1968, Walter Booth reported the first Heermann's Gull in Michigan. Equally surprising are some of the land birds: a Black Vulture, Groove-billed Ani, Black-billed Magpie, Yellow-throated and Audubon's (Yellow-rumped) warblers, and a Summer Tanager.

Another special area in southwestern Michigan is Warren Woods, a small stand of nearly virgin hardwoods situated on a bluff overlooking the Galien River. Along the river banks is the home of a pair or more of Louisiana Waterthrushes, perhaps the most dependable spot for this species in the state. On the bluff above the river are Hooded Warblers, Cerulean Warblers, and Acadian Flycatchers. Grand Mere Woods is another good birding spot, with a curious overlapping of southern Blue-gray Gnatcatchers and White-eyed Vireos with northern warblers, like the Canada and Black-throated Blue.

The most complete bird records for any area in the state come from the Detroit region (Kelley et al, 1963). Over the ten-year period from 1945 to 1954, the Bird Survey Committee of the Detroit Audubon Society compiled and published annual surveys based on tens of thousands of observations each year. In the eight county "Detroit region," including five counties in Michigan and three in Ontario, 290 species were reported, of which 147 were known to nest in the area. In the eleven-year period from 1955 to 1965, 19 new species were added to the list, making a total of 309. Highlights in these comprehensive surveys are too numerous to chronicle here. (The records were updated again in 1978, raising the total to 337, including three hybrids—Kelley, 1978.)

The Lansing area, my stamping grounds for thirty years, is not noted for any specialties, but there are a number of good birding places. My favorite, as already indicated in the preceding chapter, was Rose Lake Wildlife Experiment Station, with its 3,334 acres of greatly diversified terrain. Other oft-used areas, mostly because of their accessibility, were the campus woodlots. The Red Cedar Woodlot, now threatened by developments, was one of the best areas for spring warblers. The Sanford and Baker Woodlots deteriorated rapidly in the 1950's and 1960's from overuse, encroachment by buildings, and use of pesticides. A campus marsh—the haunts of grebes, bitterns, coots, rails, and marsh wrens—is now Spartan Village. Aboretum Park and Scott's Woods, both within a few miles of the campus, were also useful, the former for its many songbirds, the latter for its wintering

110

Carolina Wrens and spring warblers. In 1966, Woldumar, a 160-acre plot of land operated by the Nature Way Association of Lansing, became available for bird watchers. Old fields, a brook, a marsh, woodlots, and an artificial pond make it attractive for birds.

Another location in the interior of the state, not remarkable for any particular specialties but because it has been worked over so thoroughly by staff ornithologists and students at Central Michigan University is the Mount Pleasant area. Cuthbert's *The Birds of Isabella County, Michigan* (1962) describes the bird life in the county and gives an annotated list of the 226 species recorded there prior to 1962. (A revised edition is being prepared.)

One of the best places in the state for shorebirds as well as for migratory songbirds is Tawas Point, now a state park with camping facilities and fewer birds than formerly; the campgrounds took out some of the best habitat for songbirds. After a battle by conservationists, most of the point, with its beaches for shorebirds, was saved, but high water in recent years has reduced the mudflats. In 1954 a group of us recorded 18 species of shorebirds on the point in a few hours of observation, but we have never been that lucky since. Warbler flights are sometimes spectacular; except for some of the more southern species (and rare stragglers), I have seen all of the Michigan warblers on the point. A Brant in 1959 and a Snowy Egret in 1964 (it showed us its golden slippers) were highlights.

On the western side of the state, along the Lake Michigan shoreline, there are also good beaches for birds. It was on the rocky shore near Muskegon that Michigan's first Purple Sandpipers were discovered; they returned during several subsequent winters and were a great attraction for birders. Bald Eagles and Piping Plovers formerly nested in Muskegon State Park, and Pileated Woodpeckers occurred along the Muskegon River, one of the southernmost stations for these northern birds.

Perhaps the most distinctive habitats in Michigan are the jack-pine plains in the north-central part of the state, the home of Michigan's unique bird, the Kirtland's Warbler. Discovered nesting in Oscoda County in 1903 by Norman A. Wood, it has since been found breeding in twelve counties; all nests discovered to date have been within sixty miles of the one found in 1903 (Mayfield, 1960). Complete censuses over all known and suspected habitats in 1951 and 1961 disclosed about five hundred pairs, the world's total population. Ten years later, in spite of protection and some management measures, the population showed a sixty percent decline to about two hundred pairs. The 1974 count disclosed another discouraging drop of 23 percent to only 167 pairs. Some recovery was recorded in 1975,

1976, and 1977 but the 1978 census showed a decline of 10 percent from the 219 males counted in 1977 to 197 in 1978.

A Kirtland's Warbler Advisory Committee, composed of state and Federal personnel and environmental specialists, has been studying management procedures to try to preserve the dwindling remnant. Cutting, burning, and planting are among the measures used to perpetuate jack-pine habitats in the right stage of development. The warblers inhabit nearly homogeneous stands of small jack pine, 6 to 16 feet high with branches close to the ground; hence, when the forest becomes too mature, the birds disappear. Controlled burning has been found to be a most reliable method for jack-pine regeneration; high heat is needed to unseal the resin bonds that hold the seeds in the cones. Cowbird control has been another successful experiment; warbler reproduction has been high when cowbirds are removed, and almost nil when they are allowed to remain. Studies are also being made on the only known wintering grounds in the Bahamas to determine if as yet unknown factors are decimating the populations there.

Kirtland's Warblers have few nesting associates in the impoverished jack-pine plains—bluebirds, cowbirds, Vesper Sparrows, Chipping Sparrows, Brown Thrashers, Rufous-sided Towhees, and Hermit Thrushes are among the most common. In some of the areas Upland Sandpipers, Prairie Warblers, and Clay-colored Sparrows occur. Lincoln's Sparrows, a rare summer resident anywhere in Michigan, have been found nesting on several of the tracts.

Close to former Kirtland's Warbler nesting areas on Fletcher Road is a state game area with a good colony of Sharp-tailed Grouse, a choice place for bird watchers to gather at dawn to watch the spectacular dances of these birds. Formerly the Greater Prairie Chicken could also be found nearby, sometimes intermingling and hybridizing with the Sharp-tails, but they have now disappeared from nearly all of Michigan except for a small colony near McBain in northeast Osceola County, where the Department of Natural Resources, with funds donated by concerned conservationists, has set aside an area to try to save the dwindling remnant (Ammann, 1957).

Two other places in the northern Lower Peninsula that are often visited by bird watchers are the Dead Stream area (Michelson's) and the Hartwick Pines State Park. The former is a flooding noted for its nesting Ospreys, Great Blue Herons, and, formerly at least, Bald Eagles. The Hartwick Pines, one of Michigan's last stands of virgin pines, are more noted for their majestic beauty than for concentrations of birds, but some northern species such as Winter Wrens, Brown Creepers, Golden-crowned Kinglets, Solitary Vireos, and Pileated Woodpeckers are found there in summer. For many years a pair of Bald Eagles nested in a dead snag in the park; when the tree collapsed, the birds moved to an alternate nest in the park. Then one of the pair was killed, and the lone survivor frequented the next site for another year or so. A pair of Goshawks also nested along the Scenic Trail in the park for several years.

Farther north, in Cheboygan County, is the site of the University of Michigan Biological Station at Douglas Lake. Lakes, marshes, bogs, aspen woodlands in all stages of succession to pine, and mature beech-maple stands afford a wide variety of habitats for birds. Observers from the Station, covering much of Cheboygan and Emmet counties, have recorded 251 species of birds (Pettingill, 1974). Waugoshance Point in Wilderness State Park, as well as Cecil Bay en route to the park, and Duncan Bay further east are good places for shorebirds at times. Piping Plovers, on Michigan's and Wisconsin's endangered species lists, formerly nested regularly in the park.

The Upper Peninsula of Michigan has many special areas for birds. Some, like the Spruce Grouse, Gray Jay, Common Ravens, Boreal Chickadees, Three-toed Woodpeckers, and several northern warblers are largely confined to the Upper Peninsula during the nesting season. Some of the better areas, or the ones with which I am most familiar, are mentioned here.

Seney National Wildlife Refuge, some 91,000 acres taken over by the Federal Government for a refuge when a big land boom for agricultural development failed, is a good spot. A series of impoundments with a good water supply has created a haven for waterfowl. A major project here has been on the rearing and restocking of Canada Geese. Many nesting geese throughout the state had their origin at Seney, but the ponds are also attractive to both breeding and migratory ducks. In 1948 there were about eight eyries of Bald Eagles on the refuge, but these have dwindled to one or two; one nest tree was struck by lightning and the sitting bird was electrocuted. Sandhill Cranes nest on the refuge. Rarer birds sometimes seen include the Spruce Grouse, Yellow Rail, and Le Conte's Sparrow.

Two of my favorite spots in the eastern Upper Peninsula are Tahquamenon Falls and Whitefish Point. In 1946, Martha and I camped overnight near the falls on September 12, our twelfth anniversary, In the morning our tent was covered with hoar frost, but it was a beautifully clear day and we had a delightful drive and walk along the old dirt road (now paved) leading to the falls. A male Spruce Grouse, his red eyebrows blazing, walked leisurely across our path, apparently unperturbed. Several Boreal Chickadees, the first I had seen in Michigan, entertained us. Gray-cheeked

Kirtland's Warbler (male). An endangered species found breeding only in a few counties in northern Michigan. Photo by Robert Harrington, Michigan Department of Natural Resources.

Kirtland's Warbler habitat among the jack pines near Grayling. White cloth marks the side of an abandoned nest.

White birches along the shores of Lake Superior on Whitefish Point.

Hand-held Barred Owl netted and banded on the Point, where more than 400 owls, including 18 Barred Owls (a "threatened" species in Michigan), have been captured in nets.

and Swainson's thrushes, a Philadelphia Vireo, and a good assortment of warblers and sparrows, especially Whitethroats, were active along the trail. Now a large parking lot, a store, and a well-beaten path offer many conveniences and facilities for visitors, but I have never seen as many birds at the falls since our 1946 visit.

Whitefish Point, a scrub-covered peninsula jutting out into Lake Superior beyond the village of Paradise, is in truth a paradise for bird watchers. In 1958, on another anniversary, Martha and I spent several days, September 12 to 17, in the area. We recorded seventy species of birds on or near the point, including fifteen warblers (Wallace, 1960). For shelter one night we crawled into an old boathouse on the point. The wind howled and waves lapped against the posts supporting the boathouse, but, miraculously it seemed, it held fast. I collected several birds, (while Martha collected agates); some of the Horned Larks, as I suspected, proved to be the Hoyt's subspecies (*Eremophila alpestris hoytii*), the earliest fall record for Michigan. Another surprising find was a Blue-gray Gnatcatcher, seen on several different days; at that time (1958) these were the northernmost records for this southern species. Hawk flights, said to be spectacular in the spring, were not spectacular that fall; about forty Red-tails going over on September 13 were the only groups observed. Back in 1921, more than two thousand hawks from Whitefish Point were turned in for bounties; in 1920, one man alone got 563 birds, 60 in one day (Tyrrell, 1934). Fortunately, the bounty was repealed in 1922, thus making the continued slaughter of hawks unprofitable.

In spring Warren Lamb and his assistants from Port Huron and banders from the Ontario Bird Banding Association operate a banding station on the point. Of chief interest in their activities is the banding of large numbers of owls caught in nets during the night. In the period from 1966 to 1971, the Ontario group banded 231 Long-eared Owls, 117 Saw-whet Owls, 60 Boreal Owls, and 1 Great Gray Owl (Kelley, 1972). In spite of several trips to the point, I have never seen a Great Gray Owl or a Boreal Owl there or elsewhere in Michigan.

At the western end of the Upper Peninsula are several areas of special interest: the privately owned Huron Mountain Tract (the site of the ill-fated wolf releases in 1974—hunters promptly disposed of the wolves), the Keweenaw Peninsula, and the Porcupine Mountains. Percival Dodge (1961) has published a list of the 219 birds observed in the Huron Mountain area. My observations of birds in the Keweenaw peninsula were described in the preceding chapter; a note of additional interest is that on October 6, 1971, I found my first Michigan Harris's Sparrows at Fort Wilkins State Park at the tip of the peninsula. By some quirk of fate or punishment from the gods, I have never been to the Porcupine Mountains when it wasn't raining. It is said to be a good place for birds and—even in the rain—has some beautiful vistas, such as Mirror Lake, Carp River, and several spectacular waterfalls.

The Marquette region has been quite thoroughly explored by members of the Marquette County Audubon Club and staff people at Northern Michigan University. Their Christmas counts often disclose waterfowl not commonly recorded elsewhere in the state as well as a surprising sprinkling of wintering American Robins, Mockingbirds and Cardinals. Michigan's first Purple Gallinule (a southern species) was found at Grand Marais, May 10, 1964. A Painted Bunting at Marquette, closely observed at a window feeder, might still be unbelievable if colored movies and slides had not recorded the unprecedented event (Ilnicky, 1968).

It may seem inappropriate to include Point Pelee, Ontario, in a discussion of Michigan birds, but it has been visited so frequently by Michiganders that we consider it a part of our heritage. The Detroit Bird Survey Committee includes the park in their coverage. My classes from MSU and the Lansing Audubon Society have taken many trips there. Hence this brief account of some of our trips to the park is appended here.

Birding on Point Pelee

Reprinted with minor revisions from the Jack-Pine Warbler, *34: (1956) pp. 6 – 9.*

For nearly a century, Point Pelee, a nine-mile peninsula jutting into Lake Erie from Ontario's southernmost mainland, has been one of North America's most heralded spots for observing birds during spring migration. Though Dr. Brodie collected birds there as early as 1879 (Taverner and Swales, 1907), discovery of the unique birding opportunities on the point is usually credited to W.E. Saunders, a pharmacist-ornithologist from London, Ontario (Taverner, 1944). He visited the point in 1882 and in subsequent years guided many parties of ornithologists over the area (Wood, 1910).

Point Pelee really came into its own in the early 1900's, when Saunders showed the locale to members of the Great Lakes Ornithological Club. The full history of these early expeditions to the point by Canadian, Michigan, and Ohio ornithologists has been duly chronicled by Taverner and Swales (1907-1908). Their accumulative list of 209 species, with copious notes on many of the records, stands as a monument to their ambitious field work during that decade. Dedication of Point Pelee as a Canadian National Park in 1918, and subsequent increase of its recreational facilities, have made the park more and more accessible to both birders and tourists, until at the present time [1950's] it has more than 200,000 visitors annually. Unfortunately, such heavy use threatens to destroy the unique natural features of the park and to defeat the purpose for which it was set aside (Gunn and Mosby, 1952).

We made our first trip to Pelee in 1950 and were so intrigued with our initial success that the event has become an annual affair. Invariably we go on Friday evening of the first or second weekend in May, in time to bed down in some favorable spot for an early start of intensive birding on Saturday morning. Usually the party consists of one or two staff men with one or two carloads of advanced students, some of whom have made the trip nearly every year. Thus there is always a nucleus of experienced and reasonably reliable veterans at the game, plus a fringe of promising "tenderfeet" just getting broken in. Perhaps needless to say, the excursion is a rather strenuous affair, starting with the first peep of a bird in the early morning (often after a relatively sleepless night) and continuing until we give up and give out sometime in the late afternoon.

Our daily lists on the six successive spring trips (two early October counts were not very successful) have run from a low of 105 species in 1951 to 147 in 1953. Rapid-fire listing of this sort necessarily poses problems in identification ethics, but we feel that our records are reasonably reliable. Invariably, however, we end up with a few debatable items on or off the list—perhaps a bird seen only by a newer "untrusted" member of the group, or a bird on whose identification there was not unanimous agreement.

The following tabulation records the dates, hours of observation, number of observers, and number of species seen on each of these May-day counts:

Year	Day	Hrs. of obs.	No. of obs.	Total species
1950	May 7	5 a.m. to 2 p.m.	6	124
1951	May 13	4 a.m. to 3 p.m.	10	105
1952	May 10	4 a.m. to 4 p.m.	10	136
1953	May 9	3 a.m. to 3:45 p.m.	12	147
1954	May 8	4:30 a.m. to 4 p.m.	9	118
1955	May 14	4:30 a.m. to 5 p.m.	10	127
		Total species for 6 trips		189

Our first trip on May 6-7, 1950, was somewhat experimental since none of us had visited Point Pelee before. We thought May 7 would be too early for a maximum list, but it proved to be nearly ideal. Six of us (three of whom were not particularly ardent birders) recorded 124 species in about nine hours of observation. We were amazed at the large numbers of certain species and the ease with which they could be observed. The morning was cool and windy, the birds perhaps tired after a flight across the lake, for we found tree-top species perched in low bushes or even resting on the ground. Often four or five Eastern Kingbirds, for instance, would be together in a small bush and could be approached closely before they flushed. The big show, as has been the case in subsequent years, was of small land birds, for though quite a few marsh and water birds can be added to one's list in the relatively inaccessible five square miles of marsh near the entrance of the park, we have never found anything very spectacular there.

Imbued with our success in 1950, we planned on a bigger and better expedition in 1951, but we were doomed to disappointment. It was a beautiful day, about the best we have seen on Pelee, and 10 of us, all enthusiastic birders, worked 11 hours looking for birds, but rounded up only 105 species. My own list totaled only 95, compared to 120 the year before when I had missed only four of the 124 recorded by the group.

May 10 of the following year, however, was really a red-letter day. Though we actually recorded more species in 1953, I believe the numbers of individuals, particularly of warblers and fringillids, was greater in 1952. The day had inauspicious beginnings. It had rained most of the night, and we had spent a miserable time under a picnic shelter, but awoke (?) about 4 A.M. to a chorus of frogs, rails, coots, and red-wings in the nearby marsh. After rapidly recording a few marsh birds, we drove slowly toward the point, which usually affords the best waves of small birds. Birds scattered before us in incredible numbers—flycatchers, thrushes, tanagers, grosbeaks, and warblers. It was nothing to see a half dozen or more species of warblers in one tree, but they passed on so rapidly it was impossible to check them all. It was exasperating also to check 20-30 warblers in quick succession with binoculars only to find that all of them were of species already on our list.

Another unusual feature on this trip, not duplicated before or since, was an abundance of sparrows (10 species) hopping about the sparse vegetation on the sandy beaches, where one would ordinarily expect to find only the Savannah Sparrow. Hundreds of them flushed before us, mostly Whitethroats and Whitecrowns to be sure, but with a generous sprinkling of such rarities as Le Conte's, Clay-colored, and Lincoln's sparrows.

May 9, 1953, was another banner day. My impression was that there were smaller numbers, but perhaps a greater variety of birds than on the preceding year. Twelve of us, working partly together but often scattering widely and then rejoining, recorded a total of 147 species. (My own list was only 122—a probable sign of senescense, as I had missed 25 of the birds seen by others). Other parties on the point that day, from Toronto and New York, also reported record lists.

Apparently we reached our peak in 1953, for May 8, 1954, was decidedly a letdown. Ten of us worked diligently (but with waning enthusiasm when we recognized that it was going to be an off day) for nearly 12 hours but could round up only 118 species. Other parties on the point that day also reported low numbers. Observers who tried again the following weekend did no better. Bill Gunn, Toronto naturalist stationed on the point through most of May, reported that the season as a whole was singularly poor with no spectacular waves and only a few minor ones during the whole month (Gunn, 1954).

May 14, 1955, was largely a repetition of 1954's unenviable experience. This time we worked in two entirely independent teams, thus attaining a creditable total of 127 species, but one group had only 109 and the other 106. Both lists, also, were swelled by a visit to a notable shorebird concentration just outside the park, where we added seven species of plovers and sandpipers and one duck. With the exception of a lone Hudsonian Curlew in 1950, the park itself has never produced any shorebirds of particular interest.

Thus in our six May trips to Pelee we have had three mediocre days (it is never really poor) and three that seem quite phenomenal. In spite of the gamble involved—often one could see as many or more birds at home—we recommend the trip to those who like to do their birding in this way. The event need not be as exhaustive as we usually made it. We were amused one year by several elderly ladies who had brought folding chairs and were sitting comfortably in a strategic place, with Peterson guides in their laps and binoculars in hand, leisurely watching the birds working their way up the beach. We never went back to check their results, but wondered if they did not do nearly as well as those of us who were tearing frantically over the landscape trying to ferret out the last bird.

There is hardly space here to comment on the many specialties we have observed on Point Pelee. These have, for the most part, been duly recorded by more meticulous observers in appropriate places, such as in *Audubon Field Notes,* and in the *Detroit Bird Survey.* But for people from central

Michigan it affords a good opportunity to see southern species that we seldom see at home. The Orchard Oriole and Yellow-breasted Chat, for instance, are Pelee notables that seldom fail us; often they seem quite common. On three of our trips we have recorded the Bewick's Wren, while the Carolina Wren is even more dependable. A Mockingbird in 1953 and a Summer Tanager in 1954 were other southern specialties found on the point.

Warbler hunting is notably good in some years, as in 1952 and 1953, and equally poor in others. We have seen all the warblers on the Michigan Audubon Society checklist except the Kirtland's, Hooded, and, perhaps surprisingly, the Mourning, all of which have been recorded there by other observers. The lake itself supports great flocks of Red-breasted Mergansers, gulls (3 species), and usually cormorants, but not much else. The five square miles of intriguing-looking but relatively inaccessible marsh usually yields a few ardeids, ducks, rails, marsh wrens, etc., but nothing really unexpected. The big show, as heretofore indicated, is in the frequent waves of small land birds that make observations so exciting.

Since the 1950's, our trips to Pelee have been less frequent and, for the most part, less successful. More recently the Lansing Audubon Society has made the excursion to Pelee an integral part of their field trip schedule. In 1973, George Stirrett, a park naturalist for the Canadian National Park Service for many years, published four booklets, one for each season of the year, on the birds of Point Pelee National Park. Combining all the known records up to 1973, he produced a list of 163 species for winter, 303 for spring, 195 for summer, and 272 for fall, with a grand total of 326 species. Forty of these were put in a hypothetical list.

Since our early visits to the park many improvements and conveniences for visitors have been installed: a long boardwalk and observation platforms in the formerly inaccessible marsh, a visitors' center providing literature and information on birding areas, a nature trail through the heart of the park; a lunch stand with snacks for coffee breaks for weary observers; and a campground with facilities for tents and trailers. In 1975 the American Birding Association held its annual meeting on Point Pelee, May 23 to May 25, when more than 300 of the country's top birders assembled at one of the most heralded birding spots in North America.

References

American Birding Association (ABA). *Birding,* a bi-monthly magazine, 1969-1977.

Ammann, G.A. *The Prairie Grouse of Michigan.* Lansing, Michigan: Game Division, Department of Conservation, 1957.

Barrows, W.B. 1912. *Michigan Bird Life.* Special Bulletin Department of Zoology and Physiology, Michigan Agricultural College, East Lansing. (reprinted in 1932).

Cook, A.J. 1893. *Birds of Michigan.* Bulletin 94, Michigan Agricultural College, East Lansing.

Cuthbert, N.L. *The Birds of Isabella County, Michigan.* Ann Arbor, Michigan: Edward Brothers, Inc., 1962.

Dodge, P. "Birds of the Huron Mountains, Marquette County, Michigan." *Jack-pine Warbler,* 39: (1961), pp. 3-33.

Gunn, W.H.H. 1954. "Pelee letter, May 1954." Bulletin Federal Ontario Naturalists 65:35-38.

_____ and H.S. Mosby. "Preserve or playground." *Wilson Bulletin.* 64: (1952) pp. 57-60.

Ilnicky, N.J. "First Painted Bunting Record in Michigan." *Jack-pine Warbler,* 46: (1968) p. 72.

Kelley, Alice. "Birds of Southeastern Michigan and Southwestern Ontario." Cranbrook Institute of Science, 1978.

Kelley, A.H., D.S. Middleton, and W.P. Nickell. "Birds of the Detroit-Windsor Area: A Ten-year Survey." Bulletin 45, Cranbrook Institute of Science, 1963.

_____ and J.O.L. Roberts. "Spring Migration of Owls at Whitefish Point." *Jack-Pine Warbler,* 49: (1971) pp. 65-70.

Mayfield, H. *The Kirtland's Warbler.* Bull. 40, Cranbrook Inst. Sci., Bloomfield Hills, Michigan: 1960.

McKinley, D. "The Carolina Parakeet in Michigan: A Review." *Jack-Pine Warbler* 55: (1977) pp. 2-4.

Michigan Audubon Society: the Jack-Pine Warbler, 1945-1977; Seasonal Records, Michigan Bird Surveys, Christmas Bird Counts.

Pettingill, O.S. "Jr. Ornithology at the University of Michigan Biological Station and the Birds of the Region." Special Publication No. 1; Kalamazoo Nature Center, Kalamazoo, Michigan, 1974.

Ryel, L.A. "The Michigan Bird Listing Record, a Second Look." *Jack-Pine Warbler* 42: (1964) pp. 310-311.

Schorger, A.W. "The Carolina Parakeet in Michigan." *Wilson Bull.* 75: (1963) p. 276.

Stirrett, G.M. 1973. "The Birds of Point Pelee National Park: Spring, Summer, Autumn, Winter" (4 bulletins). Ottawa.

Taverner, P.A. "Memories of William Edwin Saunders, 1861-1943." *Auk* 61: (1944) pp. 345-351.

_____ and B.H. Swales. "The Birds of Point Pelee." *Wilson Bulletin* 19: (1907-1908) pp. 37-54, 82-99, 133-153; 20:79-96, 107-129.

Tordoff, H.B. "Additions to the Birds of Michigan." *Jack-Pine Warbler,* 44: (1966) pp. 2-7.

Tyrrell, W.B. "Bird Notes from Whitefish Point." *Auk* 51: (1934) pp. 21-26.

Wallace, G.J. "Birding on Point Pelee." *Jack-Pine Warbler* 34:(1956) pp. 6-9.

——————. "The 1958 Fall Migration at Whitefish Point." *Jack-Pine Warbler* 38: (1960) pp. 140-144.

Wood, N.A. "Bird Migration at Point Pelee, Ontario, in the fall of 1909." *Wilson Bull.* 22: (1910) pp. 63-78.

—————— *The Birds of Michigan.* Miscellaneous Publications, Museum of Zoology, University of Michigan, No. 75, 1951.

Zimmerman, D.A. and J. Van Tyne. "A Distributional Check-list of the Birds of Michigan." Occ. Papers, Museum of Zoology University of Michigan, No. 608, 1959.

CHAPTER 7

Bird Watching: East, West, and South

PRIOR TO 1951, most of my observations on birds were limited to three Eastern states: Vermont, Massachusetts, and Michigan. Exceptions included brief explorations around Washington, D.C., and Falls Church, Virginia, in late May 1936; field trips at A.O.U. meetings in South Carolina in October 1937; a three-week winter vacation in Florida in 1940; and other A.O.U. or Wilson Ornithological Society meetings in West Virginia, Wisconsin, Illinois, and Iowa in the years between 1946 and 1951. All of these excursions yielded new birds for me, especially the ones to Virginia, West Virginia, South Carolina, and Florida.

Westward Ho

Because of my limited geographical experience thus far, I looked forward eagerly to our long-planned family vacation to the Western states in 1951. On a five-week camping trip, from August 4 to September 8, we toured through or into all of the contiguous states west of the 100th meridian, except North Dakota and Nebraska. We had two teen-age daughters, two pup tents, a Coleman stove, and a nearly new Fraser car—a much maligned post-war Kaiser-Fraser model manufactured at Willow Run and hence dubbed by a wag as a "Willit Run." But it performed nobly for us. It averaged 23 miles per gallon (when gas was 12 to 15 cents per gallon), and our total repair bill for the five-thousand mile trip was 35 cents (speedometer cable trouble in the Tetons). It also boasted a capacious trunk for baggage.

We all weathered the strenuous trip in good shape. On four nights we were forced into motels by heavy rains or lack of campgrounds at the right place, and on two nights we stayed with relatives. Otherwise, we camped along the way, usually in the National Parks, but sometimes, of necessity, almost anywhere along the roadside. Although it was essentially a family camping trip, I was, of course, always looking for birds, especially in the mornings while Martha was preparing breakfast. August is far from ideal for bird watching, but I managed to record 183 species on the trip, 69 of which were new for me.

On our first evening, a boat trip across Lake Michigan from Ludington to Manitowac, Wisconsin, was delightfully relaxing after our frantic day of preparations. A thousand or so gulls, Herrings and Ring-bills, and a few Spotted Sandpipers were the only birds I recorded. Late that night we set up camp in Lincoln Park, Wisconsin—a dismal beginning for our planned itinerary, because a gang of hoodlums was having a noisy carousal in the park most of the night.

In the morning we took a boat trip through the Wisconsin Dells. Many Cliff Swallow nests, mostly deserted in August, were plastered along the walls of the ledges. The Dells are noted for their nesting swallows, though they are not as highly publicized as the famous Capistrano Cliff Swallows in California. The remainder of the day, spent in travel, was a little discouraging; we ran into heavy rains and reluctantly put up in a motel in Minnesota, thus admitting defeat on our second night.

But on the next day, August 6, things looked brighter. Near Chamberlain, South Dakota, we flushed my first Lark Buntings. Then a handsome male Blue Grosbeak nearly caused me to lose control of the car. In the Badlands the next day we encountered more new birds: a Swainson's Hawk, characteristically perched on a telephone pole and displaying its identifying breast band; a family of Mountain Bluebirds, adult and mottled young; and a Rock Wren, somehow finding a home in those bleak and impoverished surroundings. And at our lunch stop in an almost treeless city park in Kadoka, a Western Kingbird greeted us.

More Western birds showed up in Custer State Park: a Red-shafted Flicker (now considered conspecific with our Eastern Yellow-shafted Flicker); many Western Wood Pewees, readily distinguishable from the Eastern species by their conspicuously different nasal song; and several Audubon's Warblers, counterpart of our Eastern Myrtle Warblers and now merged with them as Yellow-rumped Warblers.

Some sightseeing, of course, intermingled with my birding activities. We visited a Dinosaur Park, where five huge dinosaur models were on display; inspected a neatly kept reptile house where trained personnel explained the live exhibits; and gazed in awesome wonder at the Mt. Rushmore Memorial, the massive stone-carved faces of four of our greatest presidents—

Washington, Jefferson, Lincoln, and Teddy Roosevelt. We had superb views of the Black Hills all around us, and the girls capitalized on an opportunity to feed a tame bighorn sheep beside the road.

We camped that night in eastern Wyoming, near the base of Devils Tower, a massive pillar of volcanic rock towering more than 1,000 feet above the nearby Belle Fourche River. At the prairie dog village at the base of the tower twelve-year-old Myra tried with patient desperation to get pictures with her dime-store Kodak. Mostly she got shots of heads peeking out of holes or tails disappearing into burrows. With one sweep of my glasses I counted 104 prairie dogs; and there may have been as many more underground—one colony, at least, spared from the widespread poisoning campaigns so prevalent then and since in the Western states.

On August 9, we toured leisurely across the broad expanse of Wyoming, over the rugged Big Horn Mountains with their hairpin curves, steep canyons and rocky cliffs, and on to Shoshone Forest campground for the night. En route we saw Spotted Towhees, more or less distinct from our Eastern Rufous-sided Towhees. Black-billed Magpies and Violet-green Swallows were quite common. A Townsend's Solitaire perched momentarily on a rocky crag, then flew from rock to rock as it uttered its plaintive calls.

For the next three days we camped in Yellowstone National Park, where we were entertained by bears, watched geysers, and hiked and toured over parts of the 3,472 square miles of the huge park. I added seven new species of birds to my list. The most conspicuous were the Steller's Jays and Canada (Gray) Jays, which, along with occasional Clark's Nutcrackers, shared our meals with us. Martha accuses me of nearly causing a wreck by stopping suddenly on a sharp curve to watch my first Western Tanager. She had another hair-raising experience of a different nature. While the girls and I were off on an unsuccessful fishing expedition, a black bear came to supervise supper arrangements. The bear leaned over one edge of the table while Martha was cooking spaghetti and hamburgers at the other end. Banging on a pan to frighten the bear away only seemed to serve as a dinner bell. Fortunately the couple in a neighboring tent came to the rescue and helped drive the animal away. During the night we heard a shot ring out and wondered if a park ranger had disposed of another nuisance bear.

Yellowstone, as millions of Americans have found, has many attractions, including 10,000 geysers. We watched Old Faithful spout off four times, viewed other equally impressive hot springs, and were saddened by the distracting coins and litter in Morning Glory Pool. We saw many elk—both bulls and cows—as well as moose, antelope, a distant coyote that Myra

126

discovered for us, and, of course, the comical golden-mantled ground squirrels, pikas, and marmots. A special trip to a remote part of the park to look for Trumpeter Swans was unsuccessful; I had to go to Alaska years later to see my first Trumpeters. We did find 11 Barrow's Goldeneyes on another pond and saw 5 huge Osprey nests atop rocky crags around various waterfalls.

Of course we had to take in the Tetons just south of Yellowstone. We camped there one night, walked the well-labelled Nature Trail, and hiked up to Hidden Falls, where I saw my first Dipper or Water Ouzel, appropriately beside a tumbling waterfall. It bounced from rock to rock and plunged repeatedly into the rushing torrent. Several times we saw it emerge with food and go to a partially concealed crevice in the rocks, presumably to feed its young.

Birdwise, the most rewarding place on the whole trip was Bear River National Wildlife Refuge in Utah. In a few hours of observation I recorded 55 species of birds, not a remarkable list but impressive because of high numbers and for spectacular views of birds I had never seen before. All the way from Wisconsin westward I had looked expectantly for Yellow-headed Blackbirds, but saw none until we reached Bear River. White Pelicans, White-faced Ibis, Avocets, Black-necked Stilts, and Wilson's Phalaropes were well represented. There were large flocks of teal, apparently mostly Cinnamon Teal but hard to distinguish in their late summer plumage. Western Grebes, Long-billed Curlews, and Short-eared Owls were also welcome additions to my list.

A diversion from the exciting birding at Bear River, especially for the girls, was a visit to Salt Lake City, where we tried to swim in the heavy bouyant waters of Salt Lake and imbibed enough salt brine to cause hardening of the arteries. We browsed around Temple Square, gazed with awesome respect at the majestic Temple (open only to worthy Mormons), attended an organ recital in the Mormon Tabernacle, and viewed the famous monument to the gulls erected by appreciative Mormons after a visitation of gulls cleared the grain fields of a plague of crickets (*Anabrus simplex*) and saved the Mormons from threatened starvation. I wanted to check on the identity of the gulls, which G.M. Allen, in his *Birds and their Attributes* (1925), had recorded as Franklin's Gulls. The gull on the stone statue was unidentifiable, but two museum specimens, labelled as the gulls that saved the Mormons, were California Gulls. Franklin's Gulls are widespread in the Western states, but it was a visitation of thousands of California Gulls, which breed in the interior but winter on the Pacific Coast, that wiped out the crickets.

Our route from Salt Lake City took us north through fertile green and amber fields backed up by the Wasatch Range, which forms the western wall of the Rockies. Then we veered westward across southern Idaho into eastern Oregon. That summer a serious drought had struck that part of the country. Hundreds of jack rabbits littered the highway, many crushed and mangled on the pavement; many others were seen dashing across the road, presumably headed for the nearest water. Birds were scarce on this part of our journey, but near Declo, Idaho, when Martha was driving and I was napping, she woke me and said she had seen an owl perched on a fence. "Probably a Burrowing Owl," I exclaimed, "let's go back." We did and it was! We hadn't seen any in prairie dog village at Devil's Tower.

Drought conditions also prevailed in interior Oregon; everything looked parched and dry, and the sultry heat was intense until we finally reached the cool evergreen forests of Mt. Hood, where we camped for the night. The drive next day around Oregon's most spectacular mountain, towering majestically in a steep cone over the fertile Willamette Valley, was a welcome relief from the previous day's heat. We stopped along the scenic Columbia River Drive to see Bonneville Dam and its fish ladders, by means of which salmon bypass the dam on their ascent of the river for their spawning grounds. Then, at the insistence of the girls, we crossed a bridge into Washington just long enough to say we had been in another state.

Bird life picked up again on the Oregon coast. At Devil's Punch Bowl we saw Pigeon Guillemots, Common Murres, and a Black Turnstone. At Devil's Hole State Park I discovered two Wrentits, a peculiarly localized Oregon-California species formerly assigned to the family Chamaeidae as its sole member. But now it is believed to be a New World representative of the babblers (Timaliidae), whose other 263 species are confined to the tropics of the Old World.

In contrast to other parts of Oregon, we encountered rough and stormy weather along the coast; both the cold and the rocky beaches prevented Sylvia, a proficient synchronized swimmer, from taking a plunge. In the park where we camped overnight, I had an odd experience. Early in the morning, on my way to the beach to look for birds, I found a woman lying beside the path. She was covered with a wet coat and I thought she was dead. I called Martha, who managed to arouse the woman from an apparent drunken stupor. She got up slowly, muttering incomprehensible words, and walked away.

Further down the coast we stopped at Sea Lion Caves. The rocks were splattered with sprawling California sea lions and their well-grown pups. Hundreds of cormorants, both Pelagic and Brandt's, perched on the surrounding rocks. Two Wandering Tattlers nearby were squabbling over a salamander that one of them had fished out of a pool in the rocks.

We spent most of the next day at beautiful Crater Lake, a deep volcanic crater filled with clear blue water and rimmed around on all sides by high steep walls. Wizard's Island protruded ominously out of the water. That afternoon we listened to an informative lecture by the park naturalist, Don Farner, a well-known figure in American ornithololgy. That evening, by invitation, I went along on a collecting trip for frogs with Don and another park naturalist. (They were looking for—but didn't find—a rare *Ascaphus*.) The next morning our car, tents, and the whole campground were white with heavy frost.

California, obviously, has much too much to be seen in the six days we spent in the state. We camped the first night among the coastal redwoods, in perhaps the best campsite of the trip. Soft sequoia needles formed a thick carpet on the ground (we had no air mattresses), giant stumps walled us in, and showers with hot water were available. Luxuriant ferns, reminiscent of Carboniferous cycads, flower-bordered pathways, and stately trees were everywhere. Other highlights in California were Yosemite, Kings Canyon, and Sequoia national parks. We spent a day or more in each. In Yosemite we witnessed the major tourist attractions: Yosemite Falls, reduced to a mere trickle in August; Bridalveil Falls, still flowing generously; El Capitan's huge granite extrusion, rising up 3,600 feet; and Half Dome, the gigantic slab of granite projecting against the skyline. Kings Canyon, with the continent's deepest canyon, and Sequoia, with the world's largest and (almost) oldest trees (3,000 or more years) wound up our sightseeing in the state.

Bird life in California in late August was not at its best, but I added ten new birds to my list. Notables were the abundant Red Phalaropes at Arcata; Acorn Woodpeckers, Plain Titmice, and Western Bluebirds at Altaville; Mountain Quail dashing across the road in Yosemite; and a White-headed Woodpecker in Sequoia.

On August 28, we reluctantly left California's magnificent parks, exiting via Bakersfield and its smelly oil wells. To avoid the intense diurnal heat, we crossed the Mohave Desert at night. Attempts to get a little sleep beside the road were frustrated by rain, so we drove on to Las Vegas, arriving there at 4:00 A.M. Even at that hour, the city was ablaze with lights, and the gambling casinos were going full blast. Although we were low on cash, we didn't attempt to enrich our coffers by playing the machines; after a brief survey of the scene we drove on to Lake Mead for an early breakfast under the red sandstone cliffs.

Zion National Park and Bryce Canyon, in southwestern Utah, were our next stops. Both were incredibly beautiful, the bright colorful spires of eroded sandstone jutting skyward in fantastic columns. Bryce in particular was breathtaking in pink splendor. Bird life, as might be expected in the scanty vegetation available, was scarce, but Allen's and Calliope hummingbirds found the colorful canyon flowers attractive.

Grand Canyon, of course, was a must on our itinerary. The trip from Utah's southwestern deserts took us through green fields and pastures backed up by wooded hills and evergreen forests. We stayed that night at Bright Angel Camp on the North Rim. Small flocks of Gray-headed Juncos and five deer came to breakfast the next morning. Sylvia and Myra went off on a little excursion of their own and came back in breathless excitement. They had seen a skunk in a tree—at least it had a white tail, they said in answer to my doubting query. Then it suddenly dawned on me: it must be (and was) the rare and localized Kaibab squirrel, an endangered species restricted to the North Rim of the Grand Canyon; another similar form, the Abert's or tassel-eared squirrel, inhabits the South Rim.

We found the South Rim quite different from the North Rim. It was more barren, with scrub junipers instead of tall trees, but with even more spectacular views, and, inevitably, more commercialization. Words cannot describe the scene: the world's mightiest gorge, cut a mile deep by the Colorado River. One observer commented that the view "belittles one's ego but expands the soul." John Burroughs called it "the world's most wonderful spectacle, ever-changing, alive with a million moods." And Teddy Roosevelt's oft-quoted classic, unheeded by would-be dam builders: "Leave it as it is, you cannot improve on it, the ages have been at work on it, and man can only mar it."

Time was running out, so after a fascinating tour of the ancient Indian cliff dwellings and palaces at Mesa Verde in southwestern Colorado, I was ready to take the shortest route home. But no! The girls had to see Carlsbad Caverns in southern New Mexico, hundreds of miles out of our way, and then go home by way of Fort Worth, Texas (more mileage), to see their cousins. That way they could add two more states to their list. I grumbled but lost and have never regretted it. Carlsbad Caverns, perhaps the most spectacular stalactite and stalagmite limestone formations in the world, were among the highlights of our trip. We took the guided tour down into the caverns' remote recesses, had lunch in the Big Room, and gazed in speechless awe at other underground features. The previous evening we had witnessed the emergence of thousands of Mexican free-tail bats (*Tadarida mexicana*) from the cave. We also watched an opportunist Great Horned

Owl perched on a dead branch above the cave's entrance, picking off bats as they emerged. The owl would plunge into the swirling mass, grasp a bat, then return to its perch for a leisurely meal. The owl made a dozen sallies while we watched. He missed on several attempts but caught about eight bats before retreating from the scene.

Then came the long drive to Fort Worth where my sister Alice lived with two daughters close to the ages of our two girls. En route I counted some 17 Scissor-tailed Flycatchers and found a Ladder-backed Woodpecker at our breakfast stop in a park in Mineral Wells. I had the whole family alerted to watch for a Roadrunner, but we saw none; my first Roadrunner came much later on a Christmas bird count in Fort Worth. But my list now totalled 183 species, of which 69 were new for me. However, the "lumpers" have been active since 1951, and I stand to lose about six of the new birds by their demotion to subspecific status.

The rest of the trip was relatively uneventful. After a pleasant couple days with my sister and her family, we headed north on September 6 and arrived home two days later, in time for the girls' school next day.

Florida Bird Life

Although I have traveled to all of the states, including Alaska and Hawaii, and have done at least a little birding in each, three often-visited Southern states—Florida, Texas, and Arizona—are particularly important for having many special birds not found in the other states. Of these, Florida has the longest ornithological history. In 1832, John James Audubon took a six-week cruise around the peninsula of Florida and visited the Dry Tortugas off the Gulf Coast. Many of his paintings, such as the Magnificent Frigatebird, White-crowned Pigeon, and Sandwich Tern (the latter first discovered by Audubon), were done in the Florida Keys in 1832. Actually Mark Catesby preceded Audubon by more than one hundred years, but it is not known how many of the birds described in his *The Natural History of Carolina, Florida and the Bahama Islands* were seen in Florida.

Florida indeed is a paradise for bird watchers. The ABA credits the state with 420 "seeable" birds (excluding extinct and extirpated birds and those not recorded in the state since 1920). Florida is a must for anyone aspiring to membership in the "600 Club" and a must for anyone wanting to get acquainted with a good sample of American birds.

Certain geographic and physiographic features make Florida unique. Among these are the 120-mile chain of islands (the Keys) in a true tropical zone, more than 3,000 miles of coastline, the vast everglades with their hammocks and rivers of sawgrass, and salt marshes, inland lakes, prairies, and pinelands. A mild winter climate with abundant sunshine makes the state a winter haven for both tourists and bird watchers.

Florida's bird life has been well documented. In 1932, A.H. Howell published *Florida Bird Life,* a large book with detailed accounts of all the birds known to have occurred in the state up to that time (435 forms—species and subspecies). In 1954, Alexander Sprunt, Jr., published a revised and updated version of Howell's work, adding 74 new birds. Since then remarkable progress has been made in chronicling the bird life of the state. The articles covering Florida in *Audubon's Field Notes* (1947–1970) and in *American Birds* since 1970 have always been noteworthy. Those written for so many years by Henry Stevenson are particularly discerning analyses.

Florida has for many years been especially popular for Christmas bird counts. Those engineered so effectively by the late Allan Cruickshank at Cocoa for nearly twenty years have often led the nation in the number of species tallied. The Cocoa marathon, well organized as to parties and the areas to be covered, has several times exceeded 200 species in a one-day count. Florida, of course, is the winter home for many northern birds as well as for northern tourists. It is also on heavily traveled migration routes for spring and fall transients. Many birds wintering in the West Indies or passing through the islands en route to or from South America, take off from the mainland in the fall or land along the east coast in spring. Many other birds traverse the whole peninsula en route to or from more southern wintering grounds. Still others take the shortcut across the Gulf of Mexico between Yucatan and the Gulf Coast of Florida or take the longer 500-mile trans-Gulf route from Central America to the panhandle of northwestern Florida.

My total Florida bird list of 171 species, based on seven trips to the state, is, in a sense, a miserable showing; it is only 41 percent of the possible total. However, most of my visits were for short periods in winter, another in sultry August. I have never been in the state during the migration seasons, and none of the seven trips was exclusively for birds. Nevertheless, the short list includes many of the rare or localized species for which the state is noted. Many of those not seen are common northern birds that also occur in Florida; for example, I have never seen a goldfinch in Florida and have seen only five of Michigan's 18 or more sparrows there.

Our first—and in some respects, most memorable—trip to Florida was a 1940 February-March vacation from Pleasant Valley Sanctuary in Lenox, Massachusetts. Myra, then only seven months old, had been suffering from severe ear infections that winter, and her doctor suggested that a little Florida sunshine might be beneficial for the whole family. We agreed! Unfortunately, I lost or mislaid the bird records compiled on that trip, but I can vividly recall some of the places visited and some of the birds seen.

The area around Lake Okeechobee, as I recall, was the most productive. At that time Alexander Sprunt, Jr., was leading Audubon tours in the area, and although we couldn't join his group because of the children, he kindly informed us of the routes he usually took and what we might see going on our own. I believe we saw all of the herons and egrets that occur in Florida—except the Cattle Egret, which didn't appear in the U.S. until 1952, and the rare Reddish Egret, which I saw much later in the Everglades in 1963. Brown Pelicans, Anhingas, Wood Storks, Glossy Ibis, White Ibis, Black Vultures, plovers, sandpipers, Black-necked Stilts, Laughing Gulls, several terns, Ground Doves, Fish Crows, Boat-tailed Grackles, and, of course, Loggerhead Shrikes and Mockingbirds were quite common, although I am not sure that all of these were seen at Lake Okeechobee at that time. Shorebirds were more common along the Atlantic Coast. But a severe storm of near-hurricane proportions hit us on the Gulf Coast at Fort Myers and curtailed birding activities there.

One memorable find at Lake Okeechobee was a Crested Caracara feeding on a dead bobcat along the highway. We passed that way several times, and by nightfall the bobcat had been pretty well disposed of. Somewhere, I think near Okeechobee, we found a few Florida Jays, now considered a localized race of the more common Scrub Jays in the Southwestern states. Once widespread in the oak scrub regions of Florida, it has declined severely with the clearing of the land and is now so restricted that it is considered endangered (Woolfenden, 1973).

Of course we visited many of the tourist attractions in the state, all of them less crowded in 1940. Bok Tower, Cypress Gardens, Palm Springs, Miami Beach, Wakulla Springs (where I saw my first Limpkin), and Rare Bird Farm, were among the highlights. We drove across the Tamiami Trail twice, along the border of the everglades seven years before the Everglades National Park was established. We started out on the 120-mile road across the Keys, but our tires, as well as our pocketbooks, were getting thin, so we turned back, leaving the wonders of the Keys for a later trip.

August 13 to 16, 1963, the A.O.U. held its 81st Annual Meeting at the University of Florida in Gainesville—a charming setting for nature lovers. An alligator pond on campus, threatened repeatedly, of course, by developers, but still more or less undisturbed, furnished nocturnal music—the bellowing of alligators, the croaking of frogs, and the voices of marsh

Boardwalk in National Audubon Society's Corkscrew Swamp Sanctuary in Florida, the home of alligators, Wood Storks, Limpkins, and the largest stand of bald cypress in North America.

By contrast with Corkscrew Swamp, bird life in the Arizona deserts is severely restricted in terms of density of birds per acre, but desert species are of special interest because of their unique adaptations.

Plain Chachalaca, a part of the "welcoming committee" at Santa Ana Wildlife Refuge in Texas. In the United States this neotropical gallinaceous bird is limited to the Rio Grande basin.

birds. Less musical to my ears was the roar of a spray truck going past our open dorm windows and fogging for mosquitos.

One of the several field trips held in conjunction with the meetings took us to a pine woodland where we found Brown-headed Nuthatches and Red-cockaded Woodpeckers, the latter an endangered species dependent on old pines infested with red heart (*Fomes pini*), which cleanup squads strive to eliminate. At our lunch stop in a park, a graceful Swallow-tailed Kite flew over, to the delight of northern delegates.

After the meetings, Martha and I went on to Everglades National Park and stayed in the luxurious facilities at Vermilion. Here I saw my first Reddish Egrets and Roseate Spoonbills, both thrilling sights. The vast expanse of sawgrass, the many trails we tramped, the alligators, drying pools teeming with shorebirds, and colorful giant grasshoppers are indelible memories.

At the park we met an enthusiastic birder who was bubbling over with excitement. A Blue-gray Tanager, the white-shouldered variety from South America, had been discovered in Hollywood, a few miles north of Miami. It was the first record for the States and she had seen the bird. She gave us specific directions for finding it—the name of the street and number of the house, even the name of the tree where the bird came to feed between 3 and 4 P.M. each day. I had seen many Blue-gray Tanagers in Colombia, where they are common, but it seemed worthwhile to try to see one in Florida on our homeward trek. At about 3 P.M. we found the street, the house, and the tree, but no tanager. We walked around the block slowly, looking in all likely places, then came back to the original spot. At a little after three an unmistakable Blue-gray Tanager, with whitish shoulder patches, came winging into the tree and started to partake of the fruit.

We returned to Florida in 1966 during our between-terms vacation from MSU, March 18 to 25. This trip was primarily for a visit with Martha's brother and sister, who had retired from positions in Michigan and New York and were living in Port Charlotte. I did a little birding each day, visited National Audubon Society's Corkscrew Swamp Sanctuary, and took another look at Everglades National Park. A find at Port Charlotte was a pair of Burrowing Owls in a sandy field beside the much-traveled road to the beach. So secretive were they that no one we met knew of their presence. Apparently there were several occupied burrows, but in another year or two new developments in the area eliminated the owls.

March was too early for several birds I wanted to see, such as the Mangrove Cuckoo and Black-whiskered Vireo. We also looked in vain for the Cape Sable Sparrow in a place where it was supposed to occur; in 1966 the place was a rubbish pile. Neither could we find any Dusky Seaside Sparrows on Merritt Island, and my standard of ethics, while not as high as that of some bird listers, nevertheless prevented me from counting a possible Black Rail I glimpsed darting into concealment. However, we did see a flock of thirty or more Fulvous Tree (Whistling) Ducks on the island.

Our return visit to the Everglades in 1966 was less productive than the one in 1963. Stormy weather with high winds limited observations on birds. The visit to Corkscrew Swamp, however, was highly rewarding. Although I didn't find any new birds, hiking the boardwalks among giant Bald Cypress trees and luxuriant ferns, viewing the dwindling colony of Wood Storks, seeing Pileated and Red-cockaded Woodpeckers, and noting the many wintering or transient passerines made the visit there well worthwhile. On another visit in 1970 we saw and photographed the rare, snail-eating Limpkin as it perched accommodatingly on the rails of the boardwalk.

Painted Buntings had eluded me on my previous trips to Florida and other Southern states. Allan Cruickshank, with whom I had corresponded, practically promised me one if I would come to his house in Rockledge. A phone call to Allan to forestall a possibly fruitless bunting chase reassured me. While answering the phone he was looking out the window and could see a male and a female Painted Bunting at his feeder. They were still there, along with Indigo Buntings, when Martha and I arrived. We had a brief but pleasant visit with Allan and his wife, Helen, at their home in Rockledge.

On none of our several recent visits to Florida (primarily social) have I been to Miami at the right time to see the exotic Spotted-breasted Orioles, Red-whiskered Bulbuls, Smooth-billed Anis, and the other escaped "convicts" (Monk Parakeets, for example) that occur there. But I may make it yet; three of Martha's sisters and two brothers moved to Florida after retirement, although one couple decided they didn't like Florida and moved back to Michigan.

Texas

Except for Alaska, Texas is by far our largest state and has the highest bird list. The ABA credits Texas with 550 "currently countable" species, 30 more than runner-up California. The reasons are quite obvious. Texas has nearly everything—a humid Gulf Coast and coastal islands for water birds; the Austin-Edwards plateau, the only summer home of the Golden-cheeked Warbler; arid Western deserts and chapparal plains; the Chisos Mountains, the only U.S. breeding grounds of the Colima Warbler; the Big Thicket, possibly the last stand of the Ivory-billed Woodpecker; Aransas National Wildlife Refuge, until recently the only winter home of the surviving wild Whooping Cranes; and the Rio Grande Valley, which has a dozen or so "Mexican" species that occur nowhere else in the U.S. The state also includes heavily used migratory pathways for birds passing to and from Mexico and the Americas. And, of course, most Northern species make it to Texas at one time or another. Texas, like Florida, is a must for ambitious bird listers.

In spite of nine trips to Texas, mainly to visit a sister living in Fort Worth and a daughter and family in Nacogdoches, my Texas bird list is worse than that for Florida—215 species or 39 percent of the possible total. However, I have seen most of the state's specialties—except for the possibly extinct Ivory-billed Woodpecker and some severely localized birds in the southwestern part of the state, where I have not been.

During a between-term break in late March 1968, we did some birding in both Fort Worth and Nacogdoches, then took a more extended trip to Rockport, where Connie Hagar has done such a fantastic job of recording birds and helping visiting bird watchers find them. Then we went on to Aransas to see the Whooping Cranes. My five-day March list totalled 116 species, including about 30 esentially non-Michigan birds (rarely or never seen in Michigan).

On this 1968 trip I kept detailed notes. On March 16, en route from Texarkana to Fort Worth, I recorded 16 species along the roadside, all common Michigan birds except for the numerous Mockingbirds and Loggerhead Shrikes. At Forth Worth, with some good help from sister Alice I added 22 more species; including the Ladder-backed Woodpecker, Bewick's Wren, and numerous Lark Sparrows. At Nacogdoches we found Carolina Chickadees and Carolina Wrens, quite common at my daughter's home.

On March 19, Martha, Sylvia, and I drove to Port Lavaca where we put up for the night. By driving slowly and making frequent stops, especially around Rockport (too early for heavy migrations), we added 36 more birds to my list, including some essentially non-Michigan species, such as Eared Grebes, White Pelicans, Cattle Egrets, Black Vultures, Snowy and Wilson's plovers, Willets, Black Skimmers, Laughing Gulls, and Royal Terns. The next day, mostly at Aransas Wildlife Refuge, we extended the list to its final 116. Of special interest to me were the Louisiana Herons, Reddish Egrets, Mottled Ducks, Wild Turkeys (30 or more at Aransas), Marbled Godwits, Long-billed Curlews, Avocets, Black-necked Stilts, Sandwich Terns, Gull-billed Terns, Scissor-tailed Flycatchers, and, finally, the long-anticipated Whooping Cranes.

Seeing the cranes took a little doing. The park ranger in charge at Aransas directed us to the most likely spot for finding them. We climbed the observation tower and strained our eyes in all directions but saw no cranes. We tried hard to make out some distant white spots as cranes but decided that they were White Pelicans. Back at headquarters we expressed our disappointment. The ranger wasn't surprised; the cranes hadn't been seen there for several days and were probably gone from the refuge. *Then* he told us there were still some on the Intracoastal Waterway bordering the refuge. A tour boat, *The Whooping Crane,* was taking visitors to see the cranes—at $5.00 per person. But we put one over on the boatman; Sylvia was several months pregnant and we didn't pay for the hidden passenger. My first Whooping Crane cost $15, but we saw 23, which at that time was exactly half of the world's population of wild birds, so the cost per bird was only 65 cents.

Our next visit to Texas, April 29 to May 6, 1974, after my retirement, was deliberately planned for the most favorable time for birding in Texas. Like all birders, I wanted to get to the Rio Grande Valley, one of the most heralded spots in the country for seeing unusual birds. Lane (1972) lists 82 "specialties of the Rio Grande Country," not commonly found outside the valley in the U.S.

On April 30 at Nacogdoches, I looked up Dean Fisher, ornithologist at Stephen F. Austin University and one of the current leaders in world listing—more than 4000 species on his world list, a high total achieved in part by his years in Australia. He played truant from his classes (sent his students to the library) and took me birding. In a few hours that morning, thanks to Dean's sharp eyes and discriminating ears, we recorded 73 species of birds. We made a special effort to run down the usually elusive Swainson's Warbler, one of the few North American warblers I had never seen.* We were eminently successful. The bird posed for us and displayed itself in good view repeatedly, not ordinarily a characteristic of this bird of the dense undergrowth. Dean also had a Bachman's Sparrow more or less pinned down, a rare sparrow that I had seen only once, at Jackson's Mill in West Virginia in 1950.

Highlight of our 1974 trip was a visit to the Rio Grande Valley. We more or less followed the itinerary outlined in Lane's *A Birder's Guide to the Rio Grande Valley of Texas.* We checked recommended places at Brownsville, Laguna Beach, Santa Ana Wildlife Refuge, Bentsen State Park, and Falcon Dam, but lack of time prevented extending the trip the two hundred or more miles to Big Bend National Park. We arrived in Brownsville in the early evening of May 1, got lost several times, then drove along the thicket-bordered levees of the Rio Grande. Shorebirds were numerous, among them several Hudsonian Godwits, a rare or uncommon species that had always eluded me in Michigan and elsewhere. It was on the U.S. endangered species list until large flocks of migrants and sizable breeding populations were discovered along the shores of Hudson Bay (see Hagar, 1966). The raucous din emanating from the dense thickets I assumed was produced by Chachalacas, but—exasperatingly—it was getting dark and I couldn't see them. I need not have worried; the next day, at Santa Ana, several very vocal Chachalacas came to greet us at the refuge headquarters. We slept that night in our Opel station wagon at Laguna Beach. In the morning we saw many plovers and sandpipers along the shore, but nothing new. On our return to Brownsville we somehow overlooked the opportunity to see Cassin's and Botteri's Sparrows in the old fields along the way, but we did see several White-tailed Kites hovering over the meadows.

---

*On a hurried trip for the wedding of a niece in Houston in late May 1978, sister Alice took us to Meridian State Park for the highly coveted Golden-cheeked Warbler. We saw several.

Santa Ana is one of the most promising spots in the U.S. for bird watchers wanting to add new and unusual species to their lists. Much of the Rio Grande Valley has been spoiled for birders by agricultural and other developments, but 2,000 acres of subtropical forests have been preserved in the Santa Ana Wildlife Refuge. Migration of warblers and other passerines across the Rio Grande in late April and early May is supposed to be fantastic; we had timed our trip to coincide with this period but were doomed to some disappointment. Almost unbelieveably, we didn't see a single warbler in our two days along the Rio Grande. Hot sultry weather was our undoing. However, I was less interested in observing the spectacular migrations than in seeing the resident birds: I don't need to go to Texas to see Michigan warblers. Birds were relatively inactive, especially during midday, but we did see many of the specialties we had come to see; 11 were new for my life list, 21 new for my North American list.

When we reached the refuge, noisy Chachalacas served as the welcoming committee. Lichtenstein's Orioles (we missed the Hooded and Black-headed Orioles—they hadn't been seen there recently) and Green Jays, as well as White-fronted Doves, Tropical Kingbirds, Kiskadee Flycatchers, and Weid's Crested Flycatchers were present, though mostly inconspicuous. It took some patience and repeated observations of flowers, mostly by Martha, before the Buff-bellied Hummingbird appeared.

We went to Bentsen State Park too late in the day for favorable birding. But that evening we toured the roads in our car to flush the numerous Pauraques along the roadside; we could see their red eyes glowing in the dim light—and then see their shadowy forms fluttering away. We set up an evening vigil at the telephone pole where an Elf Owl was said to reside. Another birder from Ontario, with more patience than I have, did most of the watching and waiting. He said the owl might suddenly emerge from its hole, disappear for the night, then reappear in the morning momentarily for a quick disappearance into the telephone pole again. His vigil was successful. The owl emerged at its appointed time, perched in a nearby tree and called softly; then another owl, presumably its mate, came and perched beside it. In spite of the dim light, we had good views of the two birds.

At Falcon Dam the next day we added a few more of the specialities for which that area is noted. There were two sizes of cormorants at the dam. We concluded, perhaps not too ethically, that the smaller ones were Olivaceous Cormorants. We found a pair of the impressively large Ringed Kingfishers along a stream, but the little Green Kingfisher eluded us. In an oak grove along the river I found an Acorn Woodpecker and a Golden-fronted Woodpecker, both surprises to me as I thought they were more

Western in distribution. It was here also that we finally found an Olive Sparrow, more like a towhee than a sparrow. We had looked in vain for one at Santa Ana and at Bentsen.

On the way back to Nacogdoches via Sinton we wanted to stop for a visit with Clarence Cottam, director of Welder Wildlife Foundation, but we couldn't spare the time. He had invited us to stop whenever we had a chance. The chance, unknown to me then, had already slipped away. Clarence had died on March 30 of that year of a previously undetected cancer. He was 75 years old. It was the end of the long and distinguished career of one of America's most eminent and likable wildlife biologists.

Southeastern Arizona

Southeastern Arizona, like the Rio Grande Valley and south Florida, is justly famous for its bird life. It also has many specialties, and its mild and pleasant winter weather makes it attractive for visiting birders. However, the intense late spring and summer heat discourage birding at the only time when some late arrivals are present. The region is extremely arid much of the year; deserts, high plateaus, canyons, rocky outcrops, and scant vegetation characterize much of the area. But the several rivers, flowing in all directions, have lush vegetation along their borders. High mountains rising to more than 9,000 feet have coniferous forests at the higher elevations.

In spite of the apparent barrenness of the arid lands, the region is singularly attractive to birds. The area known as southeastern Arizona has 265 species of birds, about 30 of which are basically Mexican species that spill over into the Southwest, some of which are found only in southeastern Arizona. Lane's (1965) *A Birdwatcher's Guide to Southeastern Arizona* is virtually a must for birders visiting the area. It tells when and where to go for the most-wanted birds. And in addition to a complete annotated list of birds, it describes eight "loops" that can be taken for the most fruitful observations. For a more detailed classic, or for armchair reading, one should consult Brandt's *Arizona and its Bird Life: A Naturalist's Adventures with the Nesting Birds on the Deserts, Grasslands, Foothills, and Mountains of Southeastern Arizona* (1951).

I have rarely taken trips to distant states strictly for birding purposes; most of my quests for birds have been in conjunction with or incidental to other activities—ornithological meetings, family vacations, or visiting relatives who live in good birding areas. But our trip to southeastern Arizona was an exception. During our between-terms period in March 1967,

I suggested rather suddenly, "Let's go to Arizona to see birds." And Martha responded, "O.K., let's go." I called Santa Rita Lodge in Madera Canyon, a noted lodging place for birders, and, miraculously, they still had one vacancy. We boarded the first available plane and in almost no time were in Tucson. In spite of—perhaps because of—lack of preparation (sometimes we plan elaborately for trips—then are not ready when the time comes), the excursion was one of the most delightful that we have ever taken. Everything seemed to go our way.

At the airport in Tucson we rented a Hertz car—expensive but virtually indispensable for our purposes. Moreover—a pleasant surprise—I was given a professor's discount on the car. The forty-mile drive to our lodge in Madera Canyon was a memorable one. Musical House Finches were warbling at the airport parking lot. Wintering White-crowned Sparrows and Lark Buntings lined the roadside, several Gambel's Quail (my first) scurried for cover, and Pyrrhuloxias perched on shrubs along the way. We made frequent stops along a back road. One of the most rewarding was at Florida Canyon where (then or later) we saw Ash-throated Flycatchers, Verdins, Cactus Wrens, thrashers (Bendire's, Crissals, and Curve-billed), Phainopeplas, and Lucy's Warblers. A Bridled Titmouse greeted us on our arrival at the lodge.

The lodge had comfortable and attractive living units, each with a small kitchenette. A dining room restaurant was available for those not wishing to prepare meals. A long wire with hummingbird cups suspended from it was strung along outside the picture windows. March was too early for most trochilids, but Broad-billed Hummingbirds were back and came to the feeders quite regularly. Before we left, a Rivoli's Hummingbird appeared.

Hiking around Madera Canyon during the next day or two we saw Red-shafted (Common) Flickers, Arizona Woodpeckers, Black Phoebes, Mexican Jays, Canyon and Rock wrens, three vireos (Bell's, Gray, and Hutton's), Black-throated Gray Warblers, Painted Redstarts, Green-tailed and Brown towhees, Gray-headed and Mexican (Yellow-eyed) juncos, and four new sparrows (Black-chinned, Black-throated, Rufous-crowned, and Rufous-winged).

A side trip one day to Patagonia, Sonoita Creek, and Nogales (on the Mexican border) added other birds: Gila Woodpeckers, Cassin's Kingbirds, Vermilion Flycatchers, Black-tailed Gnatcatchers, and Scott's Orioles. Lovely Sonoita Creek, repeatedly threatened by developers, was finally rescued in a campaign by concerned conservationists and established as a sanctuary. Because of my attachment to the area I was glad to contribute a little when an appeal for funds reached me in faraway Michigan.

In late April 1969, the Wilson Ornithological Society and the Cooper Ornithological Society held a joint meeting in Tucson. This afforded another opportunity to see Arizona birds. Inca Doves were common on the University of Arizona campus, a beautiful Red-faced Warbler showed up in Madera Canyon, and a pair of Black Hawks and a pair of Gray Hawks, not seen on our earlier trip, were found nesting along Sonoita Creek. Two more flycatchers (Weid's Crested and Olivaceous), presumably not yet returned from winter quarters when we were there in March 1967, were present on this later trip.

Southeastern Arizona, like most other good birding areas I have visited in various parts of the world, is a place I would like to revisit. Even in late April we couldn't find the rare and extremely localized (in the U.S.) Rose-throated Becard and Coppery-tailed Trogon, or several of the late-arriving hummingbirds and flycatchers.

References

Allen, G.M. *Birds and Their Attributes.* Boston: Marshall Jones, 1925.

American Birds. 1971—. Bimonthly published by the National Audubon Society.

Audubon Field Notes. 1947-1970. Predecessor of *American Birds.*

Brandt, H. *Arizona and its Bird Life: A Naturalist's Adventures with the Nesting Birds on the Deserts, Grasslands, Foothills, and Mountains of Southeastern Arizona.* The Bird Research Foundation, Cleveland, Ohio. 1951.

Catesby, M. 1731-1743, *The Natural History of Carolina, Florida and the Bahama Islands.* 2 volumes., London.

Hagar, J.A. "Nesting of the Hudsonian Godwit at Churchill, Manitoba." *Living Bird,* 5: (1966) pp. 5–43.

Howell, A.H. *Florida Bird Life.* New York: Coward-McCann, 1932.

Lane, J.A. "A Birdwatcher's Guide to Southeastern Arizona." A 46-page booklet distributed by L & P Photography, Santa Ana, California, 1965.

_____. "A Birder's Guide to the Rio Grande Valley of Texas." A 72-page booklet distributed by L & P Photography, Sacramento, California, 1971.

National Geographic Society. *America's Wonderlands: The National Parks* (1959) and *Wild Animals of North America* (1960).

Oberholser, H.C. *The Bird Life of Texas.* Austin, Texas: University of Texas Press, 1974.

Peterson, R.T. *A Field Guide to the Birds of Texas.* Boston: Houghton Mifflin, 1963.

Pettingill, O.S. Jr. *A Guide to Bird Finding East of the Mississippi,* 2nd ed. New York: Oxford University Press, 1977.

_____. *A Guide to Bird Finding West of the Mississippi.* New York: Oxford University Press, 1953.

Sprunt, A. Jr. *Florida Birdlife.* New York: Coward-McCann, 1954.

Woolfenden, G.E. "Nesting and Survival in a Population of Florida Scrub Jays." *Living Bird* 12:(1973) pp. 25-49.

CHAPTER 8

Alaska and the Pacific Northwest

The A.O.U. Meetings

JUNE 18 TO 23, 1968, the A.O.U. held its 86th Stated Meeting at the University of Alaska at College, Alaska. Attending this particular meeting had a high priority for me, in spite of the fact that Alaska, at that time, was considered foreign travel by MSU and not reimbursable by the University. As a boy, strongly influenced by adventure stories of the Arctic by Jack London and James Oliver Curwood, I had dreamed of going to Alaska. Attending these meetings, then, was to be the fulfillment of a long-cherished dream. In conjunction with the meetings, Martha and I spent nearly a month in Alaska and the Pacific Northwest, from June 13 to July 8.

Getting so conservative a body as the A.O.U. so far afield must have taken great persuasion. For many years, beginning in 1884, the A.O.U. had held its annual meetings in Eastern cities—Boston, New York, Philadelphia, and Washington, repeated year after year with monotonous regularity. Most Easterners frowned on expanding Westward. But even before the turn of the century the A.O.U. had a large membership in the Western states and in Canada. Eventually the Executive Council bowed to the inevitable and held its meetings in other parts of the continent. My own first A.O.U. convention was in Toronto in 1935, and since then I have been to meetings in South Carolina, Florida, Louisiana, Colorado, Nebraska, Sasketchewan, and Seattle, Washington. But also, of course, in Boston, New York, Philadelphia, and Washington, D.C.

Nevertheless, even in 1968 there were doubts about getting an adequate turnout for a meeting in Alaska. To explore the possibility the secretary of the union canvassed a sizable sample of the membership. The results, I understand, were overwhelmingly in favor of Alaska; the alternative was Los Angeles. But there did prove to be some disadvantages to meeting in

145

Alaska. For one thing, few Easterners showed up. In fact, we had more representatives from East Lansing, Michigan, than the combined total from Boston, New York, Philadelphia, and Washington.

Another disadvantage—not counted as a disadvantage by most of us—was that interior Alaska in summer, with its long days (20 hours or more of daylight) and warm temperatures (up to 80°F by midday when we were there) was a delightful place to be. Considering the large turnout for the conference, the indoor paper sessions were not as well attended as they might have been. Many delegates, especially newcomers to Alaska, were out in the field. On the final day of the paper sessions, the local committee had arranged for a sternwheeler riverboat excursion down the Chena and Tanana rivers. It was primarily for the ladies, but many men went along. In fact, I had intended to go until I discovered that I was on the program that morning. I'm still wondering if the poor attendance for my paper was because so many delegates went on the sternwheeler boat trip or because they had heard me sound off before, beginning in 1935, and decided to forego that part of the program.

Actually the University of Alaska was an excellent place to meet. Most delegates were housed in Moore Hall, a plush dormitory with modern facilities. Two well-equipped campus buildings were used for the paper sessions, and the University Museum had many attractive exhibits. One unfortunate incident, however, marred the arrangements. A few days before the meetings the University Dining Commons, where we were to have obtained our meals and where the Annual Banquet was to have been held, had a disastrous fire. That left three choices for meals: an over-crowded, so-so cafeteria with seemingly exorbitant prices, finding transportation to downtown Fairbanks (few people had cars) or fasting. Remembering that Lord Mayor of Cork had lived forty-five days without eating, Martha and I decided to fast, at least by spells. One welcome break came at the President's Reception. Bounteous refreshments were available—king salmon, king crab, tasty sandwiches, and other goodies, and no apparent restrictions on repeats. I was faring well until I noticed one of the hostesses, the wife of a former acquaintance of mine at MSU, eyeing me suspiciously as a chronic repeater.

Since the sun comes up at about 3 A.M. in central Alaska in June, there was ample time for local birding before the paper sessions at 9 A.M. White-crowned Sparrows seemed to be everywhere; their sweet wheezy whistles could be heard throughout the day and night. When we heard one singing at 2 A.M., we didn't know if it was a bird that hadn't retired for the night or one that was just arousing. The nest of a Common Redpoll was located in a low bush along the path leading from our dorm to the meeting house. A Hammond's Flycatcher, best identified by the fact that local people said it was the only summer resident *Empidonax* on campus, had an active nest in a birch tree near our dorm. Bohemian Waxwings, which I had seen only three times in Michigan, were a welcome sighting.

Several organized field trips with local leaders took us to nearby off-campus areas before the morning paper sessions. Highlights for me were the Arctic Loons in full breeding plumage; Varied Thrushes, with their surprisingly high-pitched eerie whistles; and Townsend's Warblers, so similar to our Eastern Black-throated Green Warblers. Seeing Gray Jays, Rusty Blackbirds, Pine Grosbeaks, Lincoln's Sparrows, and Fox Sparrows on their breeding grounds was also a thrilling experience.

Three major excursions, preceding and following the regular meetings, were also sponsored by the A.O.U. But since we had arrived on June 14, the day before the meetings began, Martha and I joined a bus tour to Matanuska Valley to see the seventy-pound cabbages and the luscious strawberries for which the valley is famous. But the seventy-pound cabbages were nearer seven ounces when we saw them, and the strawberries were far from ripe. Here we learned of the sorry plight of homesteaders who had once immigrated to Alaska in the hope of finding a profitable and comfortable living in a new land. Lush fields of forage testified to the productive capacity of the land, but the settlers soon found that the growing season was too short to produce enough forage to sustain livestock over the long hard winter. Feed had to be imported from the lower states at great cost. We saw many run-down and abandoned homesteads. But we also saw many well-kept homes of the settlers who stayed and found other employment; we visited an attractively designed experimental farm, backed up by the snow-capped Matanuska Range; and had lunch at Finger Lake, whose fingers sprawled out in various directions and whose blue waters were encircled by high mountains with jagged peaks.

The Aleutians

The first of the scheduled A.O.U. excursions took us out into the Aleutians, with our first stop at Cold Bay, headquarters of Izembek National Wildlife Refuge on Unimak Island. Cold Bay is well named. A cold barren treeless landscape nearly encircling the bay, it is the home of Whistling Swans, Northern Phalaropes, and many other water birds. Here an incident gratifying to an aging professor occurred. When our plane landed, a pretty girl in a red jacket emerged from seemingly nowhere to greet us and said, "Hello, Dr. Wallace. Do you remember me? I was in your ornithology class a few years ago." She had married the assistant refuge manager, who served as one of our guides on the island.

Among the ornithological highlights for most of us were the numerous Rock Sandpipers, an Asiatic species that has spread over parts of the Aleutians. They posed—though not too accommodatingly—for the many photographers trying to get pictures. The Northern Phalaropes were also new for me. Except for a wing-injured transient that we had kept in the ornithology lab at MSU for a few days, I had always missed them on their rare spring and fall migrations through Michigan. The captive bird would eat flies floating on a pan of water but would not probe for wiggling pieces of earthworms in the bottom of the pan. We concluded that phalaropes glean insects from the surface of the water but do not probe for animal life below the surface.

At Cold Bay passerine birds seemed scarce. In three summers of banding, Edgar Bailey (1974) captured only 21 species, and three species—Savannah Sparrows, Yellow Warblers, and Common Redpolls—made up about 70 percent of the total. The redpolls were the only passerine birds that remained over winter.

From Cold Bay our plane took us to Umnak Island, where half of our passengers deplaned while the rest of us went on to St. Paul in the Pribilofs. Accommodations at both Umnak and St. Paul were inadequate for our large party, so a shuttle service had to be arranged. Those of us going on to St. Paul were treated to spectacular scenes en route—the bird cliffs below us on St. George, teeming with white spots that we were told were mostly kittiwakes; a sprawling group of sea lions basking on the shores below; and a large swirling black mass that I thought was an oil spill until we were informed that it was a flock of Slender-billed Shearwaters, a species that nests only on Bass Strait off the coast of Australia, but spends its non-nesting season in the North Pacific.

We deplaned at St. Paul, a picturesque, mist-shrouded hamlet where the sun seldom shines. Inhabitants of the village, many of them true Aleuts, are mainly employed by the U.S. Fish and Wildlife Service for work in the fur seal colonies. The native children were shy, but by offering them cookies, Martha enticed three of them to pose for pictures. We had been advised in advance that accommodations here as well as at Umnak would "not be fancy" but would be "adequate." They were just barely that. One reward at the men's quarters was a Snow Bunting in full song posed on the roof of the shelter and a trio of Oldsquaws on a puddle behind the building.

During the evening, after an "adequate" meal at the "hotel," we visited the bird cliffs. Even at 10 P.M. it was light enough for some photography, and I secured a good shot of my first Red-faced Cormorants, rarest of the six North American species, as they perched on the edge of the cliff with mist-covered but light-reflecting waters for a background. Crevices in the cliffs were teeming with Fulmars; Black-legged and Red-legged kittiwakes; Common and Thick-billed murres; Least, Crested, and Parakeet auklets; Horned and Tufted puffins; and, out over the water, Harlequin Ducks and Glaucous-winged and Mew gulls. Wildflowers in considerable variety found footholds in the grass-and-sedge-grown spaces between the rocks.

The next morning we visited the fur seal colonies, one of the most spectacular mammalian scenes I have ever witnessed—belligerent bulls, placid cows with calves, and yearlings sprawled all over the rocks. Fortunately, this was during the nonbutchering season. Harvesting the seals, although carefully controlled by wildlife officials, is said to be a bloody carnage and a sickening scene to the fainthearted. The bulls guarding their harems can be very dangerous. One of our party, veteran birder Stuart Keith, got too close—an angry bull lunged at Keith and tore an ugly gash in his leg that required thirty stitches. He stuck with us, however, even on the arduous trip to Nome and St. Lawrence, but he was in severe pain at times and under heavy sedation.

Later that morning we explored Webster Lake and its bordering fields. Common Teal (the European form) and several shorebirds, including a Red Phalarope and a lone Wandering Tattler, were found here. Lapland Longspurs in full flight song and Gray-crowned Rosy Finches made the air over the fields ring with their melodious refrains. We found a nest of the finches in an old shed in the field.

Then we went back to Umnak Island, changing places with the group that had been stationed there the previous night. During the long evening there was time to do more exploring. A jeep took some of us to a distant point, the driver promising to come back and pick us up at a designated time. He didn't—and gave mechanical failure in the jeep as the reason. But we spent several enjoyable hours on the point. Pigeon Guillemots and Common Eiders were new, but the other water birds, including hundreds of Harlequin Ducks and Oldsquaws, were repeats of what we had seen at Cold Bay and St. Paul. It was here that I found the surprisingly large Giant Song Sparrow (*Melospiza melodia maxima*), really a giant compared to our Eastern subspecies. Disintegrating quonset huts and military hardware, remnants of World War II occupancy, were evident everywhere, but tall lupines (*Lupinus arcticus*), beach peas (*Lathyrus maritimus*), and other herbaceous growth were doing their best to conceal the ugly scars left by man.

The next morning, after a nearly sleepless night in a room where a dozen or so of us were crowded together in tight quarters, station vehicles took us out on the tundra. Again our driver failed to come back for us at the designated time, and we hiked the two miles back to headquarters in the rain. Nevertheless, our brief stay on the tundra was a delightful experience. Lush grasses, sedges, and colorful wildflowers, thriving in the damp maritime climate, carpeted the ground. A singing Winter Wren seemed out of place in a steep gulley that had no trees and no shrubs except dwarf willows (*Salix spp.*) only a few inches high. The slopes and crest of the ravine, however, were covered with a fantastic array of flowers: narcissus-flowered anemones *(Anemone narcissiflora),* villous cinquefoil *(Potentilla villosa),* nagoonberry *(Rubus stellatus),* and purple orchids *(Orchis aristata).* Even in the rain—really more of a heavy mist than a rain—they were magnificent.

Nome

Our next major expedition, on June 22 to 24, following the meetings at College, took us to Nome and St. Lawrence Island. Nome proved to be a run-down town, a relic of more prosperous gold-mining days; probably it would have failed to survive were it not for a substantial tourist business in the summer months. A bit of possible family history came to light in Nome. A sign on one of the shops in Main Street (if a dirt lane can be called a street) prominently advertised "Wallace Liquors." I recalled that when I was a boy Dad used to tell of a distant relative who had joined the gold rush to California in 1848. We all dreamed that he would come back someday, loaded with gold. But he never came back; so far as I know he was never heard from again. Could it be, I mused, that he went on to Alaska, found it more profitable to sell booze to the gold miners than to pan for gold himself, and established a family business there?

Our two days of birding around Nome were more productive than in any other part of Alaska. Dr. Brina Kessel, biologist at the University of Alaska and chairperson of the local committee for the meetings, was our field leader. She knew where to go and what to look for, and even had some specialties practically staked out for us. She was knowledgeable, enthusiastic, indefatigable, and always in good humor in spite of some inevitable mishaps.

Our first day took us out on the tundra. Our bus driver had his difficulties. En route someone yelled, "Stop, stop! A Snowy Owl!" We piled out of the bus to watch an extraordinary light-phase Rough-legged Hawk hovering over a cliff. Later someone found a nest, but only the most ad-

150

venturous climbed the cliff for closer inspection. Further on, at the end of the road, I think, the bus driver was instructed to turn around. He tried, but instead he got the bus hopelessly mired in the soft turf. He had plenty of advice from the passengers, but none of the suggestions worked—except to send back to Nome for a derrick.

In the meantime we were turned loose for several hours of rewarding bird watching. We saw all three species of jaegers—the world's total—and found nests of the Long-tailed Jaeger and the Parasitic Jaeger. A Pomarine Jaeger, a chance visitor in that area, obligingly flew by to complete the jaeger roster. Golden Plovers, those amazing transcontinental migrants that winter in southern South America, were quite common; several of their nests with their astonishingly large eggs were found. A pair of much agitated Whimbrels hovered around a presumed nest site, but we didn't find the nest. A Western Sandpiper's nest was just fledging young. One of the agile youngsters was captured and probably became the most photographed Western Sandpiper in the world.

Other finds on the tundra that day included Arctic and Red-throated loons on a small pond, several Short-eared Owls, a lone Snowy Owl perched on a hummock, and numerous Lapland Longspurs and occasional Snow Buntings hovering overhead. Here I was finally satisfied with the identification of Hoary Redpolls cavorting along the edge of a snowbank; the ones I thought I had seen earlier in Anchorage now seemed questionable. Orange-crowned Warblers were the most common of the New World warblers (parulids) seen; the Arctic Warbler, an Old World sylviid, also occurred here.

We arrived back at our hotel that night, tired and hungry. It was the night of the Midnight Sun Festival, a show featuring costumed natives, Eskimo dances, and blanket-tossing. We will never know what we missed. We forfeited the opportunity in favor of a belated supper and a little sleep before the next busy day of birding.

We were off again early next morning for another long day of adventures around Nome. It seems traditional in Alaska to put in long days in summer, with a minimum of sleep, then to catch up during the long winter nights. In fact, there is much "moonlighting" in Alaska. A taxi driver in Anchorage told us he worked for the government from eight to five, then drove a taxi off and on until midnight. Then he rubbed it in by disclosing that he was making more money than university professors. However, he probably needed to; living costs were high in Alaska and presumably his taxi business was slack in the winter.

On this second day in Nome, Brina guided us to the presumed nest site of a White Wagtail, then one of the few known nesting records of this Old World motacillid in Alaska. We watched adults carrying food into an abandoned dredge in a lagoon, but no one waded out to the partially submerged structure to observe the actual nest. A nest of Yellow Wagtails, another Old World species now fairly well established in Alaska, was found along the grass-and-sedge-grown borders of a pond.

At Safety Lagoon later in the day we found more waterfowl, including good numbers of Whistling Swans, but all were repeats of earlier observations. On a scrub-covered hillside we looked for an Old World Bluethroat reported to have been seen there. Roger Peterson wanted to find it in order to add another species to his North American list, but our search was in vain. Wildflowers covered the borders of the lagoon. One of the most attractive was a lousewort (*Pedicularis lanata*) with profuse rose-colored blossoms, but white-flowered primroses (*Primula borealis* and *P. parviflora*), and small-flowered anemones (*Anemone parviflora*) decorated the fields like small white daisies.

From Safety Lagoon it was a long trek to another area where a Gyrfalcon and a Golden Eagle were known to be nesting. En route, the bus flushed two Willow Ptarmigans, the only ones I saw in Alaska. One of them then perched accommodatingly on a sand bar where we could view it from the bus. The strenuous climb to the Gyrfalcon nest site was rewarded by good views of the nest and two young on a ledge below us. A young man studying the food habits of the hawks was lowered on ropes to the actual nest site, and a young bird was hauled up for all to admire and photograph. The adults, seemingly unperturbed, were hovering around in the far distance and didn't come in for an attack as Gyrfalcons sometimes do. The Golden Eagle nest, containing a partially grown young on an adjacent ledge, was more accessible, and the evening light was nearly perfect for photography. But alas, I checked the light, distance, and focus and then tried to click the shutter. No more unexposed film!

St. Lawrence Island

Next on our agenda was the long-anticipated excursion to St. Lawrence Island, a remote rocky outpost in the Bering Sea, closer to Siberia than to Alaska. I had viewed this trip, mistakenly as it turned out, as a sort of climax to our Alaskan adventure. We assembled at the airport early (Bering Sea Daylight time) but were informed that it was snowing on the island and that our plane couldn't land. We fiddled around impatiently at the airport several hours before getting clearance for flying. After landing on the island we found the bay clogged with ice, could see the mist-covered nesting ledges across the bay, and were met by a reception line of colorfully costumed natives wanting their pictures taken for a price.

Access to the cliffs for most of us was achieved by walking a mile or more on loose gravel in which our feet slipped back nearly a foot for every foot gained. The boulders strewn around the base of the cliffs were teeming with alcids, some perched on rocks, some milling around in the air, and unknown numbers hidden in crevices among the rocks where we could hear them growling. Frequently one would shoot out of its hiding place and whistle past our ears like a bullet. Natives are very skillful at capturing the emerging auklets in hand nets. We met one man with a whole sackful of Crested Auklets, the largest and hence most-coveted species. We wondered at the need of some conservation measures to protect the birds but concluded that snaring auklets had been going on for hundreds—perhaps thousands—of years, yet the birds were still abundant. Bédard (1969) estimated the total number of Least and Crested auklets on the island at 1,527,000.

My brief observation of the alcids (auklets, puffins, murres, and guillemots) on the island was indeed exciting but added no new species to my Alaskan list because all had been seen earlier at St. Paul or elsewhere. My only new bird on St. Lawrence was a not-too-certain Emperor Goose winging its way past at some distance. Brina Kessel had given us a list of 126 species known to occur on the island, 28 of which would have been new for me, but 20 of these are quite rare (mostly strays from the Old World), having been recorded on the island less than six times in the past sixty years.

Mt. McKinley National Park

The A.O.U. also sponsored a shorter field trip to Mt. McKinley National Park, but it coincided with the Nome–St. Lawrence excursion. Naturally Martha and I chose the more extensive (and more expensive) trip, then went to Mt. McKinley later. After our arrival at the park we found that most A.O.U. members had already been there, were still there, or were planning to come later. The park was well patronized by delegates from the convention.

We had mixed feelings about our accommodations at the park hotel. The setting was magnificent; the view from the spacious front porch was breathtaking. But the crowded interior, with its gift shops and souvenirs, was all too like hotels in New York and Chicago. We ate expensive meals (at least one a day) in the commodious dining room; usually we selected king

President's reception at the A.O.U. meeting in College, Alaska. Dr. and Mrs. S. C. Kendeigh in center foreground, Dr. A. Wetmore (white-haired man in left background), Dr. and Mrs. Peter Stettenheim seated on steps.

Fur seals at St. Paul in the Pribilofs.

Red-faced Cormorants, adult (left) and immature, photographed at about 10 p.m. North America's rarest cormorant.

Nest and eggs (full clutch) of Long-tailed Jaegers on the tundra near Nome, Alaska.

Nest and eggs of Parasitic Jaegers on the tundra near Nome, Alaska.

Gyrfalcon eyrie near Nome. Climber was making a study of Gyrfalcons in Alaska.

The most photographed Gyrfalcon in the world.

salmon, for us the choicest (and cheapest) item on the menu. Our small room looked out on a backyard where the kitchen help were wont to assemble for noisy nightly rendezvous.

On our first full day in the park we went on the twelve-hour bus tour to Wonder Lake at the far extremity of the park, some ninety miles from the hotel. Views, when we could see any, were spectacular, but it rained much of the day, and clouds (typically we were told) covered Mt. McKinley, permitting us only occasional glimpses. Two days later we tried the eight-hour tour to Eielson Interpretive Center which, when weather permits, affords one of the best views of Mt. McKinley. We were fortunate this time—a perfect day with blue skies, the Alaskan Range in full view nearly encircling us, and superb views of Mt. McKinley—the dominant feature in the range. Once, as I watched, a Golden Eagle floated past the snow-clad peak; so absorbed was I in watching it that I forgot to take a picture; even with my telephoto lens it would have been only a silhouette, but that would have added a nice touch.

Bird life at times was fairly conspicuous, but I found no new species for my Alaskan list and actually saw only 29 of the 132 species that Adolph Murie, research biologist in the park for many years, has recorded in the park. I tried hard to make out Gray-headed Chickadees, a rare local specialty, but decided the ones I saw were actually immature Boreal Chickadees. The most spectacular wildlife scenes in the park, however, were the big game animals. On one trip Martha kept a count of the caribou visible from the bus (which stopped when such scenes were available). She tallied over 80, mostly in small and widely scattered groups. Dall sheep dotted the hillsides or perched on rocky crags. Parka ground squirrels unhesitantly came to lunch, unlike the more timid marmots. A red fox that had its den in a field bordering the roadside came to meet our bus, a routine daily procedure, according to our driver. And in a boggy area of tamaracks and balsams, Martha and I found a cow moose with two calves.

Numerous well-kept hiking trails threaded their way to many points in the park. We hiked several of them, including a climb to Mt. Healy that afforded spectacular views of the surrounding country. On Mt. Healy I found a Water Pipit feeding young and saw an immature Wheatear; lower down, near the base of the mountain, the nest of a Swainson's Thrush with a record five young was a pleasant surprise. But the big show on the trail to Mt. Healy and on the trails around the hotel was the abundance of colorful wildflowers: dwarf fireweed (*Epilobium latifolium*), nagoonberry (*Rubus arcticus*), mountain cranberry (*Vaccinium vitis-idaea*), chiming bells (*Mertensia paniculata*), mountain avens (*Dryas integrifolia*), Norwegian

156

cinquefoil (*Potentilla norvegica*), alpine shooting star (*Dodocatheon frigidum*), meadow bistort (*Polygonum bistorta*), parrya (*Parrya nudicaulis*), rosewort (*Sedum roseum*), bluebells (*Campanula rotundifolia*), and many others. Martha took the initiative in flower identification and had a list of 68 Alaskan species largely worked out from Heller's *Wild Flowers of Alaska* (1966).

After leaving Mt. McKinley, we returned to Fairbanks for a brief visit with Jim Greiner and his family. Jim, a former graduate student of mine at MSU, had left Michigan rather suddenly before finishing his master's thesis on the effects of pesticides on the campus mallards. I rediscovered him, at the time of the conference, in the wilds of Alaska near Fairbanks where he had built himself a splendid log cabin lodge with modern facilities. An ardent hunter and fisherman, he fed us royally with mooseburgers and king salmon from his well-stocked larder. From his dining room window we could look out over a vast expanse of wilderness, with Mt. McKinley in the far background.

The Yukon and the Inland Passage

The next stop on our itinerary was at Whitehorse, where we indulged in a leisurely cruise up the Yukon River. Both of us had contracted severe colds. So we were glad to relax in the sun on the upper deck of the boat, to take in the superb views, and to watch the limited bird life that came into view—a Common Loon and four Surf Scoters on the water, and a Townsend's Solitaire on a ledge by the riverbank. In picturesque Miles Canyon, Bank Swallows had numerous nesting holes in the banks. A loudspeaker on the boat announced that the birds were Cliff Swallows. When I told our hostess that they were really Bank Swallows, she said she knew it—she had been so informed by other passengers—but the tape had not been corrected. To confuse the issue, a few Cliff Swallows were present, and we noted some of their gourd-shaped nests plastered to the walls of the canyon.

A ride on the railway from Whitehorse to Skagway was our next adventure. We had thought the trip would prove something extra special but were somewhat deflated on reaching home to learn that nearly everyone who visits Alaska takes the same journey. Nonetheless, it was a delightful excursion along the shores of beautiful Bennett Lake, along the old Yukon Trail used by prospectors for gold, through deep canyons with waterfalls, past towering peaks and coniferous forests. At a halfway point we stopped at a wayside restaurant where a bounteous lunch was all set up for us. We were herded into one half of the spacious dining room and wondered why the other half, also all set up, was left vacant. The reason was soon obvious: the northbound train arrived and disgorged its passengers into the other half of the dining room. On a high bluff outside the restaurant stood a picturesque church, established in 1899 by a Presbyterian minister for the gold miners using the Yukon Trail. But gold strikes failed to materialize here, and the church was abandoned.

At Skagway, the terminus of the railway, our reverses set in. The Wickersham Ferry on which we had reservations for our Inland Passage voyage to Vancouver, British Columbia, was not in dock. We had to put up overnight in a local hotel, in the poorest and most expensive accommodations we had anywhere in Alaska. Next morning the boat was still not available for boarding, and we loafed around the boat dock impatiently along with many other equally irritated passengers. My only consolation was watching sixty or more Northwestern Crows, a new species for me, although they are probably conspecific with our Common Crow and may have to be culled from my list.

Eventually the Wickersham came in, and, after more confusion and delays, we were finally on board. It was a beautiful reconditioned Swedish vessel that had been held up for repairs. Our stateroom was luxurious, and the meals on board were sumptuous. Views, as everywhere in Alaska, were superb. Numerous Bald Eagles—both adults and immatures—and a flock of fifty or more White-winged Scoters were the only new birds for my Alaskan list.

The Pacific Northwest

Then further mishaps set in. The Wickersham failed to make connections with the British Columbia ferry on which we had reservations. Again we were stranded, along with many other annoyed passengers, for an overnight in Prince Rupert. No ferry was available the next day, but some of us managed to get out by plane for our destination in Vancouver. A ferry at Vancouver took us to Victoria, on Vancouver Island. Victoria was a delightful city. Bright flowers in hanging baskets lined the streets and decorated the lampposts in the heart of the city. I wanted to see the island's famous Skylarks, imported from England in 1902 or 1903 and now well established on the island. We rented a car with another couple who said they were bird lovers, but as it turned out they had no interest in Skylarks and drove too fast to identify "little brown jobs" along the way.

The highlight of our stay in Victoria was a visit to Butchart Gardens, perhaps the most famous gardens in North America. An old quarry that had left ugly rubble all over the stripped landscape had been transformed at great cost into magnificent gardens. No signs of previous excavations were visible; the whole thirty acres had been planted with trees, shrubs, and flowers, much to the enjoyment of the millions of tourists who visit the gardens.

In Vancouver, British Columbia, the next night we had reservations at Park Royal Hotel, an attractive cottage with old English charm and lovely flower gardens. The Capilano River flowed by, and there was a wooded path lined with luxuriant ferns and alive with singing birds. Vaux's Swift, the smaller, darker version of our Eastern Chimney Swifts, was the only new bird for my life list.

The next day's flight to Seattle, Chicago, and home ended our memorable trip to Alaska and the Pacific Northwest. My Alaskan bird list totalled only 125 with 15 mostly unexciting species added in British Columbia, a far cry from the 321 recorded by Gabrielson and Lincoln in their *Birds of Alaska* or the 380 credited to British Columbia by the ABA. But 26 species were new for my life list, 36 were new for my North American list, and 21 others were birds rarely if ever seen in Michigan.

Three years later, when the A.O.U. held its Annual Meeting at the University of Washington in Seattle in 1971, I had other opportunities for birding in the Pacific Northwest. The indoor sessions on August 30 to September 3 were preceded by a pelagic trip forty miles out to sea and followed by two concurrent field trips, one of them (the one I chose) to Mt. Rainier National Park.

Some opportunity for birding on and around the university campus was possible before and after the daily paper sessions. Few campuses I have visited are so attractively designed and maintained as the one at the University of Washington. By some miracle a woodland path on the main campus has survived. But the spacious flood plain bordering Lake Washington, below the high bluff on which the campus buildings are situated, was not faring so well. It was being developed for additional parking and other facilities. Bird life on campus and along the meandering channel leading to the lake was interesting but not at its best in late August and early September; the only non-Michigan birds I recorded were the Band-tailed Pigeons and Steller's Jays.

The pelagic bird trip, in spite of—perhaps to some extent because of—the stormy weather was truly exciting. We assembled in the evening at Westport, where I had reservations at the Coho Motel. Several who didn't have reservations piled in with me and slept all over the place. In the early morning we were off to sea. I was assigned to *Three Deuces;* other delegates boarded *Playboy* or another launch. The small vessels pitched and tossed on the turbulent waters. Some passengers got seasick, but I didn't have time for that because the birds were so exciting. Thousands of Sooty Shearwaters (one estimate—not mine—was 50,000) were floating on the water or soaring overhead. Three species of cormorants (Brandt's, Double-crested, and Pelagic) perched on pilings in the bay. Seven species of gulls, including the rare Sabine's Gull, were observed. Fork-tailed Petrels, a half dozen or so, and several Leach's Petrels, were new for me. I had missed the former that some people had seen in Alaska and, unlike most Eastern birders, I have never visited the well-known Leach's Petrel breeding colonies off the New England coast. We also saw six species of alcids: the Marbled Murrelet, Cassin's Auklet, and Rhinoceros Auklet were new for me. Our guides, Dennis Paulsen and Terence Wahl, were exceedingly sharp. They could spot a bird far out over the water and identify it before I could even see it, but fortunately for seabird novices like me, most of the birds eventually came in to closer range.

One of the goals of this pelagic trip was to find the New Zealand Shearwater and Black-footed Albatross, both of which had been found recently in the area. We found both, five of the former and two of the latter. All three launches surrounded the birds and hemmed them in for close views. Fair numbers of Pink-footed Shearwaters were also present. Several Surfbirds, found along the mile-long, boulder-strewn, treacherous breakwater on shore, capped the climax for me—eight new birds for my life list. Although the Surfbirds nest in Mt. McKinley National Park in Alaska, we didn't have time when there to scale the high peaks where they nest.

The post-session trip to Mt. Rainier turned out to be more of a sight-seeing tour than a birding expedition. In spite of the fickle weather—alternate clearing and clouds—the glimpses of snow-capped peaks and glaciers and the Alpine meadows decked with wildflowers were breathtaking. Blue Grouse—seven of them—were the only new birds for me, but I thrilled again at seeing Dippers along the mountain streams, just where they should be seen, and I enjoyed watching and photographing the Clark's Nutcrackers being fed at the lodge.

My Washington bird list, for August 28 to September 3, at Seattle, Westport, and Mt. Rainier, totalled 75. The ABA credits Washington with 390 species, Oregon with 400, and British Columbia with 380. Obviously I need to return to the Pacific Northwest sometime.

References

Bailey, E.P. "Passerine Diversity, Relative Abundance, and Migration at Cold Bay, Alaska." *Bird-Banding,* 45: (1974) pp. 145-151.

Bédard, J. "The Nesting of the Crested, Least, and Parakeet Auklets on St. Lawrence Island, Alaska." *Condor,* 71: (1969) pp. 386-398.

Gabrielson, I.N., and S. G. Jewett. *Birds of the Pacific Northwest.* 1970. Dover reprint of the *Birds of Oregon* (1940) by the same authors.

Gabrielson, I.N., and F.C. Lincoln. *Birds of Alaska.* Harrisburg, Pennsylvania: Stackpole, and the Wildlife Management Institute, Wash., D.C., 1959.

Heller, C. *Wild Flowers of Alaska.* Copyright 1966.

Murie, A. *Birds of Mount McKinley National Park, Alaska.* Mount McKinley Natural History Association, 1963.

CHAPTER 9

Colombian Sabbatical

Preparations

MOST NATURALISTS dream of visiting the tropics—that mythical paradise of colorful birds, gay butterflies, and lush tropical vegetation. My dream became a reality in 1955 when I planned for a sabbatical year in some neotropical country. Possibilities included Mexico, any Central American country, Panama (Smithsonian's Barro Colorado Biological Station), Colombia, Venezuela, Ecuador, and, less seriously, any of several other South American countries. But a round of inquiries and letters to selected places in most of these countries produced mostly negative and disappointing results. Latin Americans are noted for not answering letters; if they do, the letters are usually belated, polite, and give little or no pertinent information. A response from a biological station in Venezuela, for instance, came nearly a year late, tendered me a cordial welcome to come, but answered none of my questions about costs, facilities, and opportunities for study there.

Two notable exceptions merit mention. James Zetek, former resident manager of the Barro Colorado Biological Station in Panama, answered my exploratory inquiry in great detail and sent me reports and literature about the station, its facilities, and the prospects for research on the island. But two dilemmas developed. None of the neotropical thrushes I wanted to study occurred on the island, and costs without some sort of grant were prohibitive. However, Mr. Zetek suggested a promising alternative. Popayán, Colombia, he said, might be a good locale for the desired thrushes, and two ornithologists stationed there might prove helpful.

His suggestion bore fruit. Mr. M.A. Carriker, Jr., a veteran American collector who had spent much of his adult life in the American tropics and was then living, by choice, in Popayán became an unstinting correspondent

162

and adviser. He left no stone unturned in apprising us of the pros and cons of settling in Popayán, not glossing over the disadvantages. Indeed, his last letter, received the day before we embarked for Colombia, advised us not to come. The political revolution in that country, he wrote, was making living there increasingly difficult and hazardous. In fact, he was considering returning to Costa Rica, a more stable country politically and one of his former favorite stations.

Planning for a sabbatical included making out an application for—and justifying—a leave of absence. At that time MSU usually approved of and sometimes even encouraged staff people to take a leave, either a half year at full pay (seldom granted) or, preferably, a full year at half pay. Such a sabbatical could be granted after seven years of "meritorius service" at the institution. Understandably, it was as easy—perhaps easier—to get a leave if one's services had not been especially "meritorious." My superiors urged me to go.

Sabbaticals were also encumbered, at that time, by an outdated rule that one could not have an additional source of funds, even from a research grant, to help defray expenses. I wanted to apply for a research grant equal to the amount I would lose by being on half salary. My request was denied at first, but Dean Combs acknowledged that the old rule seemed antiquated, and President Hannah, to whom the request eventually went, said he would not raise any question should I apply for a grant. However, of the several granting agencies contacted, only the National Science Foundation showed any interest in my project. NSF approved my research proposal for studying neotropical thrushes but suggested that it would be better as a three-year project. That was impossible, of course, since I was taking only a one-year leave. Also, NSF funds for fiscal year 1955-1956 were not available, and I was asked to reapply for the following year. (After my return from Colombia and completion of my research there, NSF was still asking if I wanted to reapply for the following year.)

In my application for a sabbatical, I submitted a threefold proposal: (1) I needed a first-hand acquaintance with tropical birds to improve my teaching: I was teaching a "Birds of the World" course and had had no experience with foreign birds in the field; (2) I wanted to do some research on neotropical thrushes, which was the basis of the proposal for a grant from NSF; (3) We needed specimens of South American birds for our university collections, which at that time were woefully deficient in foreign birds.

Anyone planning to visit a foreign country knows that many advance preparations are necessary—visas, passports, health cards requiring costly and time-consuming shots and inoculations, and the need for more knowledge about the country to be visited. None of us, for instance, could speak Spanish, the almost universal language in Colombia. Mr. Carriker had advised us that a speaking knowledge of Spanish would be necessary; almost no one in Popayán, he said, spoke English. We studied Spanish grammar diligently, listened to Spanish records almost endlessly, and tried to converse with each other in Spanish. Then, on reaching Popayán, we found to our chagrin that the Colombians didn't understand our brand of Spanish, nor we theirs. I never did learn to speak the language; I hobnobbed chiefly with Mr. Carriker and with the Swedish director of the natural history museum in Popayán, Mr. Kjell Von Sneidern, who spoke some English. But Martha learned enough Spanish to shop in the markets, to barter and dicker over prices, and to try to uphold our social responsibilities with our new neighbors. The girls did even better. On our arrival in Popayán they were taken in tow by several charming young girls who spoke little or no English and who took them on tours of the town. They learned to communicate rapidly.

Our greatest initial difficulty was in securing visas. Letters to the Colombian consuls in Washington and Chicago went unanswered. Telephone calls were received politely and reassuringly but were non-committal. Then, shockingly, the day before our scheduled departure, our visas were denied for no apparent reason. Frantic calls to our congressman in Washington started things humming. He put pressure on officials in Washington, and we soon had a wire to go to Chicago immediately to pick up our visas at the office that had refused them the day before. But my passport, needed for the visa, was in Washington, where it had been sent to get an Ecuadorian visa. It came back at 10:00 A.M. on August 31. I caught a noon flight to Chicago and procured the coveted Colombian visa without further difficulty. Meanwhile, Martha and the girls, with the volunteer help of neighbors, were frantically doing the last-minute packing. One of the neighbors offered the use of a pickup truck for transporting our cumbersome baggage to the railroad station for transit to New York. We had had to cancel our reservations on the Grace Line's fifty-two-passenger cargo vessel, the Santa Luisa, but got reinstated—unfortunately in separated staterooms, which posed difficulties in getting together for meals and for visits on deck.

We were fortunate in housing arrangements both at home and in Colombia. We rented our house in East Lansing to a visiting German mathematics professor at MSU. He came with his family the day after we left for Colombia and vacated the house a few days before our return in

August the following year. Procuring suitable housing in Popayán was attended by annoying delays and ludicrous but often amusing requirements. But for housing in Popayán, it was better than average and at about half the price we were receiving for renting our home in East Lansing.

We were well aware of the need for pictorial mementos of our trip. I never had much use for a camera until 1968, more than ten years after our sojourn in Colombia. But Martha had had a dime-store Kodak for many years. It took good black-and-white pictures, but we wanted color slides of our trip. In the confusion of planning, packing, and leaving, we didn't get around to doing anything about photographic equipment until reaching New York, where we purchased a Voightlander at Willoughbys. Martha studied its use diligently in the interval between boarding the boat and setting sail the next morning, then started snapping pictures as soon as the boat took off at dawn. We joke about her first attempt—a badly underexposed picture of the Statue of Liberty in New York Harbor in the dim early morning light. But she improved rapidly and the eight hundred color slides depicting our adventures in Colombia are among the most prized possessions of our sabbatical year.

The Voyage

We were off at dawn on September 2 for our first experience on the ocean. The Santa Luisa, with its Spanish-speaking crew, was a small vessel with small and crowded staterooms, a bathtub-sized swimming pool, and space on deck for a few games or lounging in the sun. I had to share a stateroom with a veterinarian from Peru who had spent a year at the University of Illinois and whose baggage hardly left standing room in our small double-bunk stateroom. Fortunately, he could speak a little English. Martha bunked with a lady from Chile who spoke no English. The girls managed to get a stateroom together.

As anyone who has sailed the seas on pleasure cruises knows, the meals en route are superb. We had a jovial but absent-minded waiter who was very accommodating but inefficient. We seldom got what we ordered but always had plenty. Once he brought me a full platter of pancakes but no butter; when I asked for butter he brought me oodles of it but took away the syrup. Often he removed food before we had had a chance to sample it.

Naturally I was on the alert for sea birds and spent many mostly futile hours on deck scanning the waters. After we left the numerous gulls and terns in New York Harbor, the open expanse of the Atlantic was virtually birdless until we passed close to Cuba on September 6. Then, like

Columbus, we noticed land birds out at sea, but, like Columbus, we usually couldn't identify them. Once, however, a Yellow Warbler, and a few minutes later a Black-and-white Warbler, came close enough to be identified. Several other warblers and a few flycatchers went unidentified. The next day (September 7) small groups of swallows, including several distinguishable Barn Swallows destined for a winter home in South America, cruised around the boat.

When we entered the Panama Canal on September 8, birding picked up considerably. Brown Pelicans hovered around the boat or perched on the piers. Magnificent Frigatebirds sailed majestically high over the waters, and many vultures, mostly Blacks but an occasional Turkey Vulture, were very conspicuous.

We docked briefly at Cristobal to visit the neighboring city of Colón. The open markets with strips of darkening meat infested with flies were nauseating but intriguing. Squalid huts with dirty half-naked children lined the streets, but a little farther on were attractive Spanish-type homes, well-dressed school children, and well-kept gardens ablaze with flowers. Here I had a chance to see my first really new birds. Smooth-billed Anis and Tropical Mockingbirds were all over town. Tropical Kingbirds—perhaps the flycatchers seen earlier from the boat—and Gray-breasted Martins perched on wires. However, our stay ashore was cut short; Myra was feeling sick, so we hurried back to the boat. Perhaps the market had been too much for her.

Back on the Santa Luisa we sailed across Gatun Lake in the canal. I gazed wistfully at an attractive structure perched on a high bluff overlooking the lake. It was one of the Barro Colorado laboratories where Frank M. Chapman was inspired to write *My Tropical Air Castle*. The lake itself was a shining jewel, its blue waters dotted with tree-clad islets created by construction of the canal. Olivaceous Cormorants and Little Blue Herons perched on stumps and snags. The numerous swifts flying about I decided were Swallow-tailed or Cayenne swifts (*Panyptila cayennensis*), whose nests, I learned later, are long sleeve-like tubes made of the feathery tufts of thousands of plant seeds glued together with saliva and fastened to the side of a building or tree trunk (Haverschmidt, 1958). Building time is said to take six months.

The open waters of the Pacific off the west coast of Colombia, as on the Atlantic, were almost birdless. An exciting exception was the appearance of four, then five, six, and finally eight shearwaters that spent much of the day around the boat, becoming invisible as they dipped into the troughs between the waves, then reappearing, their long curved wings extended, rarely flapping as they sheared over the waves. I couldn't identify them then (there are 56 species of shearwaters), but years later, after much browsing in books, study of distribution, and elimination, I decided they must have been Pink-footed Shearwaters *(Puffinus creatopus)*.

The major event of the day for us, however, was the disembarking of some passengers at Panama, so that we were able to persuade the ship's purser (it took considerable persuasion) to give Martha and me a stateroom together. It was roomier and more comfortable than the ones we had been in, and it gave us an opportunity to assemble and reorganize our baggage in preparation for the dreaded morrow.

The Santa Luisa pulled quietly into Buenaventura Bay during the night and docked until morning. Martha and I didn't sleep that night; we were deeply concerned, even a little frightened, about the landing. We had heard grim rumors about stolen baggage, hold-ups by banditos, and the repercussions of the political revolution. Carriker's last letter advising us not to come weighed heavily on my mind.

One worry was my collecting gun. I had written to various officials in and out of Colombia long in advance for the required gun permit but had received no replies about it. Dr. VanTyne, and others in the know, had advised me to take the gun anyway and bribe or bluff my way through customs. It would be simple, they said. But, of course, the revolution in Colombia altered matters. A Colombian official in Chicago looked blank— I thought a little alarmed—when I asked about the gun. He stared at me, then left the room without a word and didn't return. Another official at the Grace Lines' office in New York also was perturbed. The gun would be confiscated, he said, and my visa revoked. But another official said no, that the gun would merely be held at customs until I could get a permit. That proved to be the case—almost. The gun was whisked away at customs, but a polite inspector told me the weapon would be held until I could establish residence in Popayán, get a permit, and then return for the gun.

To digress a bit, it took months of paper work and cost far more than the gun was worth to get a permit. In February, with the paper work finally completed, we returned to Buenaventura on an exciting two-day family expedition by train and car. But, not surprisingly, the gun couldn't be found. A letter (a cover-up, an American official said) stated that the gun had been sent to Bogotá. That proved to be the case. I flew to Bogotá and spent two days running down and reclaiming the gun—on February 14, five months after our landing in Colombia. But the three days in Bogotá were well spent. I visited the university's Instituto de Ciencias Naturales, examined their ornithological collections, and met Dr. Borrero, the curator.

Back on the boat we had our last breakfast, under considerable nervous tension, while various officials came aboard, checked visas, passports, and various papers before we could disembark. Then Negro carriers swarmed aboard, gathered up baggage in carts, and wheeled it away. We watched with misgivings, fearing we might never see it again. But the Grace Lines had an agent assigned to help with disembarkation details. He assured us everything was all right; our baggage was being taken to customs for inspection.

Inspection was a farce, even a little amusing. The air had cleared a little by this time; everyone was polite and cordial. Some bystanders whistled at the girls but made no further moves. Everything had to be opened for inspection—boxes, crates, suitcases, even Myra's violin case. A smiling Negro lad laboriously undid the parcels while a poker-faced inspector stood around. He glanced casually at the opened packages, then signaled the boys to do them up again.

The other details through customs went fairly smoothly. Our heavy baggage had to be shipped separately to Popayán. We were afraid we might never see it again, but we did; it actually arrived in Popayán six days later and everything was there. We tried to arrange for passage to Cali and Popayán by bus, but while I was negotiating, a navy lad who had spent a year at the University of Miami and could speak English engaged in conversation with the girls. He was delivering a car to a navy lieutenant in Bogotá and offered to take us to Cali, about halfway to Popayán, for half the price of bus fare. Moreover, he was going right away. It seemed like a good deal, and it really was.

We had some misgivings at first. After his taking a drink of something I couldn't identify, we set off in a cloud of dust. He scattered chickens and small children from the road with repeated blasts of the horn, chattering amiably all the time. It was a wild ride, but he negotiated sharp curves, avoided obstacles and puddles with such dexterity that I decided he was really a good driver. It was supposed to be a five-to-six hour drive to Cali; he made it in four hours.

The scenery en route—when we could pause to look at it—was spectacular, part of it through the Western Andes. We counted about fifty waterfalls along the way, some of them flooding portions of the road. Most of the hills had been debrushed, and cattle grazed on the steep slopes, but some of the higher peaks were clothed with dense vegetation, presumably harboring toucans, tanagers, motmots, and other specialties I longed to see.

In Cali our accommodating young driver went to some trouble to locate a suitable hotel for us. His first stop was at a luxurious hotel way beyond our meager means. Next try was the "New Yorker," but the management wouldn't take us because we couldn't speak Spanish. Hotel Europa took us in, at 16 pesos per person per day, including meals, a reasonable price considering the favorable rate of exchange for American dollars.

We called the vice-consul at the American embassy in Cali about some further arrangements. He wanted to meet us; he had a boy who was planning to go to MSU that fall. He picked us up at the hotel and took us to visit the Shepherds, an American family from East Lansing who were living in Cali, where Mr. Shepherd was engaged in the Point-4 agricultural program from MSU. Next day, a day of leisure before going on to Popayán, we visited the Shepherds again, went to an American church service, toured the city in the afternoon, and stayed overnight with our congenial hosts, thus saving another hotel bill.

Our scheduled flight for Popayán the next day was cancelled because of foul weather. The best we could arrange was to go by train (autoferro) the next day. We imposed upon the Shepherds again for overnight accommodations. The four-to-five-hour trip to Popayán was a fascinating experience in a new and strange country. The landscape in the intermontane Cauca Valley was quite different from that in the more rugged Western Andes through which we had passed a few days earlier. Steep slopes—some wooded, some largely bare and badly eroded—with cut banks of red clay and steep hillsides with grazing cattle and horses were evident all along the way. The train made frequent stops at way stations where small crowds, mostly barefooted and ill clad, tried to sell their wares to passengers. It was a chilly, drizzly day, and most of the train windows were open. We were hardly prepared for such cool weather in a tropical country.

Mr. Carriker and his Colombian wife met us at the station. We hadn't been able to inform them just when and how we would arrive, so they had met every plane and train arriving during the past two days. Meeting them was fortunate; we had no place to go and didn't know what to do first. Young boys swarmed all over us, clawing at our baggage to carry it for us, but we didn't know where. Then Mr. Carriker took charge of things. He parceled out coins to selected individuals who took our baggage to waiting taxis. Americans can rarely get away with carrying their own baggage; the boys even wanted to carry Martha's purse, but she clung to it tightly. We were whisked away by taxi to Hotel Victoria, where Carriker had made arrangements for us to stay until a house he had located for us was available.

Hotel Victoria was a quaint and somewhat antiquated facility, operated by a Jewish couple who had fled from Germany during World War II. Our accommodations were adequate, and the meals good—Carriker said the best in town. We had our first meal on the porch or balcony overlooking a courtyard with trees and shrubs. I hoped to see some exotic bird in the well-planted patio while we were dining. I finally spied a bird lurking in the shrubbery—a common pigeon!

We stayed at the hotel for a week, amid pleasant surroundings and congenial company, including some American visitors. But it was a serious drain on our pocketbooks. Daily or more often we went to inspect the progress on our house; it had been left in bad shape, and its plaster walls were being repainted and other renovations made. Our first visit to the house was discouraging. A live rat ran out the front door when we opened it, and a dead one lay on the kitchen floor. The house was infested with large Oriental cockroaches. It had been stripped bare by the previous occupants. All the light bulbs and most of the fixtures, including the transformer for the functionless doorbell, were gone. Workmen were cleaning up the place, but their progress was slow. Eventually we moved in before the house was ready; it seemed to be the only way. Much to the consternation of the Colombian workers, we grabbed mops and cloths and put some finishing touches on the job. Americans weren't supposed to do things like that, but we got away with it. As housing goes in Popayán, we soon learned that our accommodations were luxurious compared to the rows of squalid huts in which the poorer people lived. The girls had separate bedrooms for the first time in their lives, and there was a spacious living room-dining room complex, a room that served as my office, a tile-floor bathroom with a cold shower, and a miserable kitchen space. Then there was the customary patio in back with crude laundry facilities and a rather dismal maid's room that we rarely used. After some initial adjustments, we learned to like our new home.

Initial Birding

During the interval from our arrival in Buenaventura on September 10, to our arrival in Popayán on September 13, I had little opportunity to look for birds. I was anxious to learn as much as possible about all the local birds and to locate some thrushes for more detailed studies. I had had tantilizing glimpses of unidentified birds while we were speeding from Buenaventura to Cali by car and, more leisurely, by autoferro from Cali to Popayán. The Central Plaza in Cali was alive with bird songs, mainly from the abundant Andean, or Rufous-collared, Sparrows *(Zonotrichia ruficollis)*. The parks and even some streets in Cali harbored numerous Ruddy Ground Doves

(Columbigallina talpacoti), and in a few minutes of leisure at Shepherds, I located an unmistakable Blue-black Grassquit *(Volatina jacarina)*. These grassquits proved to be common around Popayán. The males perch on tufts of grass or low shrubs, hop up into the air, deliver a weak ecstatic song, then flutter down to their perches again, repeating the performance at frequent intervals. One observer said a field full of grassquits hopping up and down resembled popcorn in a popper.

During our enforced seven-day stay at Hotel Victoria, I took daily morning walks to the outskirts of town, not a great distance in any direction from the centrally located hotel. At that time Popayán had a population of nearly 45,000 people, but they were jammed into a relatively small space in crowded quarters. Getting up at dawn was no problem. Church bells from several nearby churches started clanging before dawn, a weird unmusical din that woke us all up. There were few birds around the densely clustered houses, but a well-kept Central Plaza of flowering trees and shrubs harbored a few species of hummingbirds, flycatchers, and tanagers. The outskirts of town, with fields, pastures, and wooded gullies had a much greater variety of species.

Some of the better finds on these brief excursions around town included Squirrel Cuckoos *(Piaya cayana)*, long-tailed harmoniously colored, nearly crow-sized birds that clambored around in trees like squirrels; Vermilion Flycatchers *(Pyrocephalus rubinus)* found feeding young at a nest, although it was not their usual nesting season; numerous Blue-and-white Swallows *(Atticora cyanoleuca)*, much like our Tree Swallows but with a black vent; Yellow-faced Grassquits *(Tiaris olivacea)*, flaring out their bright yellow facial tufts of feathers when they sang their ridiculously weak song; and numerous, mostly unidentifiable hummingbirds feeding on flowers wherever the latter could be found. Tanagers were my special delight. Eventually I was able to identify 24 of the 117 species that occur in Colombia, not a very good showing, but I had transportation difficulties in getting around to different habitats. And in the spring, when we did have an old Willys jeep, I was tied down with my nesting studies of the local thrushes.

Of course I had difficulty identifying birds in the field. At that time there were no field guides to Colombian birds; de Schauensee's illustrated *Guide to the Birds of South America* was published much later. I found Blake's *Birds of Mexico* (1953) useful for approximate identification (some species the same, others closely related) and found Eisenmann's *The Species of Middle American Birds* (1955) useful for pinning down distribution more closely. But my bible was Carriker's (or Von Sneidern's) copy of de

Schauensee's *Birds of Colombia,* an unillustrated two- or three-volume (depending on the binding) distributional work designed for keying out specimens in the hand. Helpful also was the Universidad del Cauca's collection of bird skins originally housed in miserable crowded quarters but moved in January to more spacious facilities in the engineering building. I took notes on birds seen in the field, then tried to find a like specimen in the collection. In another building there was an excellent collection of mounted birds, skillfully prepared by Von Sneidern. But the room with the mounts was seldom open; when it was, I found the entrance guarded by a dog lying on the floor. I sneaked cautiously past the dog several times before I discovered, to my embarrassment, that it was one of Von Sneidern's mounted specimens!

Odd as it may seem, Carriker and Von Sneidern were not much help in identifying birds in the field. They were collectors, and like all pre-Griscom or pre-Peterson ornithologists, they scoffed at the idea of identifying birds in the field by sight. However, Carriker, who was (jutifiably) a little vain about his knowledge of Colombian birds and their distribution, could be tricked into revealing identifications. If I casually and tactfully mentioned seeing a blue-and-yellow tanager in a certain place, he would pause a moment, then say it would have to be such and such a species—the only tanager of that description that occurs at that elevation at this season of the year.

My quest for thrushes that fall was disappointing. I had the preconceived notion that tropical birds nested pretty much the year around, regardless of seasons. Ideally then, I could start my field research in the fall. Three thrushes proved to be reasonably common around Popayán, and two or three others were somewhat marginal, but none showed any indications of nesting in the fall. They sang irregularly, sometimes frequently, apparently on loosely defended territories, but I found no nests in spite of much search. Von Sneidern suggested that they might nest during the December-January dry season. However, there really was no December-January dry season in Popayán in 1955-1956. It rained almost every day during that period. Some local people said it was unusual; others said it just wasn't raining as much or as hard as it did in October and November.

Even the abundant and ubiquitous Andean Sparrow, with an almost constant output of song on territory from September to June, made only a few, mostly abortive, attempts at nesting in the fall. In 1958, Alden Miller found that Andean Sparrows in the vicinity of Cali had two complete nesting cycles, one in the late fall or early winter and another in the spring; but such was not the case in Popayán in the fall of 1955. John Davis, working in Peru, and Larry Wolf in Costa Rica, also found that fall nesting of Andean Sparrows was not characteristic in their areas of study.

To digress a bit, I found the Andean Sparrow the most abundant and widespread bird in Colombia, at elevations from 2,000 feet to 11,000 feet, in a great variety of habitats. In the Central Plaza (0.7 acres) I could count fifty or more birds (not in flocks) feeding or singing. They appeared to be nonnesting birds congregating in the park from the surrounding treeless streets and clustered shops and houses. They were also abundant in fields, pastures, coffee and banana plantations, along fencerows, and in wooded gullies. They were in almost constant song from a little before dawn at 6 A.M. until darkness fell abruptly at 6 P.M. Decline of song in June appeared to be related to post-nesting molt. The short sweet song was repeated at six-second intervals, or about ten times per minute, when the birds were singing steadily. Louise de Kiriline (Lawrence) has recorded the output of a Red-eyed Vireo in Ontario as 22,197 songs in one day, probably outdoing my Colombian sparrows, but the vireo's season of song is short (three months or less), whereas the Popayán sparrows sang persistently for ten months or more.

Fortunately for my bird walks, our house was located on the outskirts of the village within a couple blocks of an attractive though often badly littered park with flowering trees and a sluggish stream. Between September 15 and June 12, I recorded 51 species on this approximately one-acre plot. Fifteen of these were Michigan birds wintering in or passing through Popayán. Somehow I got a thrill out of finding Common Nighthawks, Yellow-billed Cuckoos, Eastern Kingbirds, Great Crested Flycatchers, Eastern Wood Pewees, Swainson's Thrushes, and seven species of Michigan warblers all in this small park. Spotted Sandpipers were frequent along the stream in the park; one was observed there on April 21, later than some of the first arrivals in the Northern states.

Warblers were common throughout the Cauca Valley all winter. I found 10 Michigan species in and around Popayán, some of them seen almost daily (Wallace, 1958). Of interest also were the late departure dates for several wintering birds—a lone Solitary Sandpiper and three Greater Yellowlegs and an Eastern Kingbird on May 9, and a Yellow-billed Cuckoo on May 24. Other species, notably Barn Swallows, Bobolinks, several sandpipers, and Common Nighthawks, were transients at Popayán, passing through in the fall for more southern winter quarters in southern South America.

In the tradition of the North American Christmas bird counts, we tried one in Popayán on December 26. Two students from the university wanted to join us, but it was raining at 5:30 A.M., the time set for the beginning of the count, and the students, not surprisingly, did not show up. The rain stopped temporarily at 6 A.M., so Martha and I took a pre-breakfast count in nearby Mosquera Park, recording 20 of the 20-30 or so species that could usually be found there. After a brief breakfast snack to fortify us, and finding the students still missing, we went further afield into more varied habitats and added 23 more species but missed a half dozen or so that should have been present. By 11 A.M., however, it was raining again, so we returned home for the old jeep we had purchased in late November. We headed for the Cauca River by a route where I had previously seen Fork-tailed Flycatchers. They were still there, 17 of them, perched on wires and posts and flying about in the rain with their long graceful banners trailing behind them. Along the Cauca River we added more species, bringing our morning total to 56 without benefit of any fish-eating birds, because sulphur pollution from a nearby volcano makes the river uninhabitable for fish.

By now it was raining so heavily it was useless to try to use glasses for treetop birds, so we merely drove around, visiting likely places for additional birds. Many suspects couldn't be found. One of our routes was blocked off by a fence a local farmer had built across the road. My best woods within the required 15-mile diameter circle was inaccessible; the two-pole bridge I usually used to cross a river was under water. The government farm where I knew we could find Blue-black Grassquits was closed. By now darkness was falling rapidly, so we called it quits with 64 species for the total count, much better than we ever did in a one-party count in East Lansing but below the record numbers usually found by larger counting groups in some southern Michigan areas. A post-mortem calculation indicated that we had missed about 10 fairly common species and perhaps 10 or more irregulars. Of course, the potential in Colombia is far higher, perhaps the greatest in the world, but not in any one habitat. To get a record list one would have to visit widely separated and relatively inaccessible areas in the Eastern Andes, the Western Andes, the tropical lowlands, and the ocean coasts.

Life in Popayán

Living in Popayán proved to be a challenge—often frustrating, sometimes hilarious, always interesting. One of the frustrations was the difficulty in getting simple things done. It was always *"mañana"*—try again tomorrow. Once when I tried to pay our light bill I was told to come back *mañana*; they weren't ready to receive payment. At another time we found a man with a ladder at our house; he was shutting off our electricity because, he said, we hadn't paid our light bill. He was right; we guessed that a delivery boy had tossed the bill over the fence (nobody in Popayán had mailboxes) and that the wind had blown it away. Electricity was not very dependable; often it was turned off for repairs, sometimes for days at a time. On such occasions we had to use candles for light after 6 P.M.; we suspected a candle concession of having something to do with the frequent failure of electricity. We had good running water—when it would run. Often our water was shut off, but not for long periods.

The difficulty of getting things done was well illustrated by our attempts to get a dripping faucet replaced. Our landlady promised to get it fixed *"pronto,"* but several reminders over the days failed to get any action. Finally a man did come to repair something, but he didn't know what. When we showed him the leaking faucet, he nodded knowingly and disappeared. We never saw him again. Finally a real plumber came. He checked the kitchen sink and informed us that we needed a new faucet—which we knew all along. He wanted some money for a new faucet. We had misgivings, fearing we would never see him again. However, he did return quite promptly with a new faucet. It didn't fit, so he had to make another trip (by bicycle) to the local hardware store. The next faucet did fit—after a fashion. It still leaked a little, but water was cheap in Popayán and we learned to put up with it. Looking at it on the more cheerful side, however, our total bill for several service men, their trips to and from, their labor, and the new faucet came to only a few pesos—most of that for the faucet.

Even more frustrating but sometimes amusing were our experiences in buying a car. In November, after considerable shopping around, we bought a used (very used) Willys jeep or station wagon with a 4-wheel drive. The car dealer, Hernado Grueso, was a friendly and probably trustworthy man, but he was not very efficient. The car needed a few minor repairs, he said, guaranteed before delivery. We checked on its progress daily or more often, but it was never quite ready. I delayed matters some by finding things on the car that didn't work. Finally Mr. Grueso announced triumphantly that the car was ready. I couldn't start it, he couldn't start it, his mechanic couldn't start it. Finally we got it going by pushing it with another car. Strange as it may seem, we rarely had any further troubles getting the car started.

But we had infinite delays in getting the car properly registered and the title transferred. A vast and incredible amount of paper work had to be done, signatures secured, fingerprinting done, et cetera ad infinitum. We visited the *automotores* at least eight times, once with Mr. Grueso who was also getting impatient, before getting the necessary signatures. It was always

"Come back *mañana.*" Mr. Carriker, who was getting a Land Rover at about the same time, laughed at us. From long experience he knew how to do things and how to handle people in Colombia. He did! He never bothered to get his car registered.

Our social life in Popayán was a rich and rewarding experience. Most Colombians are friendly and sociable. We had an endless stream of visitors dropping in without advance warning because almost nobody had telephones. When Americans appeared in town—a frequent occurrence— our Colombian friends would bring them to see us. Often they had to sit on a trunk, a box, or the floor, but they didn't seem to mind. I found one disadvantage in our visits to the homes of some of the elite; I couldn't stand either the strong wine or the *aguardiente* they usually served.

Colombians dearly love parades and fiestas. It seems that some sort of a festival was going on all the time. Schools, post offices, banks, and business establishments were often closed for holidays. There was the "Day for the Whites," when people plastered themselves (and others) with flour; the "Day for the Blacks," when everyone tried to blacken their friends with shoe polish; the "Parade for the Prisoners," when people carried huge kettles of food on stretchers through the streets and school children carried paper sacks of goodies for inmates of the jails. The parades and marching bands were very colorful, with a remarkable array of bright costumes. Often the festivals had some religious significance that we didn't understand. Sometimes the participants couldn't explain what it was all about—it was just something they had always done.

The celebrations reach their climax with *Semana Santa,* a week-long Easter procession noted throughout the world for its splendor. It is said to be second only to the one in Seville, Spain. Thousands of visitors come every year to Popayán from all over the world to witness the amazing spectacle. The main *Semana Santa* is followed by a *Chiquita Semana Santa,* when little tots emulate the adults by carrying miniature *pasos* (platforms bearing statues and carried on the shoulders) through the streets. People claim that it never rains during *Semana Santa* week, that no one gets drunk (which is traditional in other celebrations), and that people vie for (and pay for) the honor of carrying the *pasos.* Some have collapsed from exhaustion and even died while carrying the heavy pasos, some of which weigh over a ton and are carried on the shoulders of eight men.

We celebrated Thanksgiving and Christmas in Popayán. For the former we bought a scrawny hen that proved so skinny when plucked that we had to supplement it with a meat loaf for our four Thanksgiving guests. Christmas was more auspicious. Some friends helped us get a free Christmas tree from a government farm, the girls made Christmas decorations, and we shopped all over town for appropriate gifts with a Colombian flavor. One of mine was a handsome machete in a sheath. I really splurged for Martha. I bought a beautiful potted lily with eleven blossoms—for one peso (about 25 cents at the time)! Martha made me a desk of scrap lumber covered with gray plastic and a drying rack for my birds. Preparations for Christmas involved creating an appropriate Christmas card for our friends in the States. Martha and the girls composed the following poem (I put in or took out a few commas) which still serves as a reminder of our days in Colombia.

OUR CHRISTMAS POEM—1955

We dreamed a dream a year ago—
When all the streets were filled with snow—
Of a sunny southland far away
Where George could work and all could play.

For George was bent on tropic thrushes,
But also birds of reeds and rushes,
And tanagers of red and blue
(He likes the señoritas too).

On September 1 we left our home,
Part of this wide world to roam.
We came by train and ship and car
To Popayán, Colombia, afar.

Where homes are close and streets are narrow,
Where a man's hat is called *sombrero,*
Where on her head a woman may
Carry wood, a basket, or a tray.

Where many folks do not have shoes,
And four Americans are news.
Where we hear Spanish every day
And try to speak in the same way.

The houses all have patios
Where many a kind of flower grows.
The parks and plazas, if you please,
Have flowers even on the trees.

The folks are friendly here, we've found;
And eager to show us all around.
They love fiestas and parades,
And almost everyone has maids.

The market is another tale
Where there are fruits and vegetables for sale.
Queer things we've never seen before—
And Martha's always trying more.

There are chickens tied up by their feet,
And dealers in small stalls sell meat.
Indians leave their mountain cares
And come to town to sell their wares.

In Popayán the rain pours down,
The sky is dark, the clouds abound.
At other times the sun is bright,
The sky is blue, and clouds are white.

A volcano stands not far away;
The name of it is *Puracé*.
Sometimes its ashes here it throws,
And then the people say, "It snows."

Nestled in the hills of green
Grass-thatched shacks are often seen.
Few roads cut gashes in these hills,
But those that do provide some thrills!

This land to us is very new,
And each of us has work to do.
We meet new friends and learn new skills,
(And it's George who pays the bills.)

Myra and Sylvia to a *Colegio* go
And now are learning Español.
Martha helps to teach them too
(Which gives her something else to do).

We like so much the chance we stand
To make new friends in this strange land,
And as Christmastime draws near
We think of other friends so dear.

So at the end we say to you
(And note it's in Español too):
   ¡FELIZ NAVIDAD y
   PROSPERO AÑO NUEVO!
   —George, Martha, Sylvia, and Myra

The market in Popayan was a fascinating but sometimes nauseating place—a fantastic display of meats, fruits, vegetables, pottery, and flowers. Martha shopped every day for perishable foods (we had no refrigeration). Prices were low for most native products. Americans trying to live like Americans in Colombia found food prices in the stores very high, but we learned to enjoy, even relish, the cheaper native produce. Tree-ripened bananas were delicious *(muy sabrosa)* and very economical buys, as were papayas, platanas, lulus, and many other fruits and vegetables.

The girls' schooling suffered during our year in Colombia, but there were compensations. Sylvia, valedictorian in her East Lansing high school class, with eighteen advance credits from Michigan State University, was considered ineligible for enrollment in the Universidad del Cauca. She would have had to take another year of high school (Colegio) to catch up with her Colombian classmates. She ended up teaching English (without pay) in the university, but she could not enroll in courses there. Martha, a mathematics instructor at MSU, taught Sylvia three math courses, which she later wrote off with departmental exams at MSU. (Her scores on these three exams were 99, 98, and 97, a credit to both mother and daughter.)

Myra, a high school junior at East Lansing, fared no better. None of the courses available in the Colegio (Colombian history, etc.) would give credit at East Lansing High School. Both the girls took informal, noncredit classes in dancing, Colombian cooking, and similar activities. Myra also taught English in this nonsectarian school. She took correspondence courses under Martha's supervision and completed her year's work on time. Thus both girls were able to keep up with their classmates at home.

As Protestants in a strongly Catholic country, we were apprehensive about religion. In fact, we suspected that our Protestant status was a factor in the original denial of a visa. Protestant missionaries were being barred from Colombia but often got in as teachers or educators. I may have been "suspect" as an educator. Protestants at that time were often persecuted, and their churches burned, but we had no trouble of this sort during our year in Colombia. Sometimes we visited the Catholic churches, truly ornate and beautiful edifices, especially in the interior. More often we attended a small, not very well-known Protestant mission church near the outskirts of town. I didn't get much out of the sermons in Spanish, but the singing of hymns, even without an organ, was superb; many Colombians have marvelous voices.

Excursions afield

After the purchase of our car in November, we were able to take trips into the surrounding country. Usually we took along one or more university students as guides on the trips; they loved such expeditions. Several of our favorite places merit some description.

The only near-original woodlot I found around Popayán was a tract of woods along the Rio Blanca, 10 kilometers north of town. I visited it frequently after purchasing our jeep. The only access I found to the woods was to cross the river on two poles or trees that had been felled across the stream. Here I saw my first and only Green Kingfisher (*Chloroceryle americana)*, collected my only Green Jay *(Cyanocorax yncas)*, and could usually find Blue-crowned Motmots (*Momotus momota*). Once I watched one of the latter perched on a branch over a stream as it swung its racquet tail back and forth like a pendulum and looked down occasionally to inspect it. Several species of woodhewers (Dendrocolaptidae) occurred here. In the spring my best two solitaire nests were found in this woods.

A more extended trip, taken several times, took us 40 or more kilometers east to Puracé, the sulphur mines, and on up to the Paramo above 10,000 feet. The quaint village of Puracé is situated near the base of an active volcano also called Puracé. Often we saw fumes and smoke issuing from its crater; once it erupted and spewed a grayish ash over the streets of Popayán. People called it "snow." Once, egged on by a geology instructor in the university, I climbed partway up the volcano but experienced breathing difficulties above 11,000 feet. Also, I had reason to be apprehensive about a possible eruption. Years earlier 17 students attempting to scale the peak lost their lives when the volcano erupted. They are commemorated by an attractive but sobering memorial in a cemetery in Popayán.

Beyond the village of Puracé were the sulphur mines, somewhat reminiscent of the pools and geysers in Yellowstone. Steam and warm water gushed up in little sulphurous pools. Sylvia dabbled her feet in the warm water. Supposedly one can bathe or go swimming in the larger pools, but the yellowish, smelly waters didn't appeal to us. More interesting biologically was the high Paramo beyond the springs. Gnarled and stunted trees and shrubs, fantastically festooned with colorful lichens, grew in such dense mats that sometimes we could walk over the top of them. A small cold lake, Laguna San Rafael, with its pristine waters, harbored a few waterfowl, but the only ones we identified were the Colombian form of the American Coot (*Fulica americana colombiana*).

Our favorite trip, both for birds and scenery, was to the cloud forest on Munchique in the Western Andes. Although only about 60 kilometers from Popayan, it was a several-hour journey even under optimum conditions, which seldom occurred. Negotiating the mud-filled Main Street in El Tambo was one obstacle; washed-out roads were others. Our first trip there was January 2 to 4, having been postponed until the three students who organized the trip for us were free to go because of their New Year's holiday. We were reluctant to go at that time, because MSU was playing UCLA in the Rose Bowl and we wanted to listen on the radio. As it turned out, the electricity was off (again) in Popayán, so we couldn't have used our radio anyway. And our hosts at a *finca* (farm) on Munchique had a battery-operated radio over which we got snatches of the game. The boys rooted for UCLA to tease us, then helped celebrate MSU's victory by sending up a sky rocket.

The cloud forest on Munchique is fantastic; everything is so saturated in mist that mosses and lichens grow on fence posts, transforming them into objects of incredible beauty. Epiphytes, including beautiful orchids, decorated the trees. On clear days one can see the Pacific Ocean from the mountaintop, but in two trips to Munchique we didn't have any clear days. It rained and rained, not a deluge but a steady drenching drizzle. The December rainfall that year was 19.3 inches, with only three rainless days in the month. Even with a 4-wheel drive we got hopelessly mired crossing a wet field. We sent for help, and several men from the *finca* came to the rescue with picks and shovels. They surveyed the situation, shrugged, and suggested we wait for the July to August dry season. Then we all set to work by filling the deep ruts with stones and pushing the car ahead by inches.

Bird life in the cloud forest is fantastic but difficult to observe. At times the jungle was weirdly silent, then there would be a flurry of wings and voices in the treetops for a few exciting moments, then ominous silence again. Ten of the birds we identified I had not seen in Popayán. The boys, who had air guns and a borrowed shotgun (an illegal possession) collected one or two specimens of each species for me. Other birds went unidentified. Choice specimens collected included an Emerald Toucanet *(Aulacorhynchus prasinus)*, a pair of Green-and-black Fruit-eaters *(Pipreola riefferii)*, two rare Barred Fruit-eaters *(P. arcuata)*, Blue-and-black Tanagers (*Tangara vassorii*—a dazzlingly blue-plumaged bird), two Hooded Mountain Tanagers (*Buthraupis montana*), and a Collared Inca (*Coeligena torquata*—one of the largest and handsomest of the hummingbirds).

We returned to Munchique briefly June 14 to 15, thrilled again at the spectacular scenery in the rain and mist, and collected several more birds: a Grass-green Tanager (*Chlornis riefferii*), which, as the name implies, was a beautiful, almost startlingly grass green; a White-billed or Mountain Cacique *(Archiplanus leucoramphus)*, which is a large blackbird with bright-yellow wing patches; a Yellow-eared Paroquet (*Ognorhynchus icterotis*), which is one of the larger and more spectacular parrots of the rainforest; and a male and a female Blue-capped Conebill *(Conirostrum albifrons)*, which is one of the honey-creepers (Coerebidae) that taxonomists are not sure how to classify. Getting the latter illustrates my prowess as a collector. I shot at the male and missed (not unusual for me); then under the tree I discovered a wounded female that I had hit without seeing it. Alvaro Tomás, a traveling companion, collected the male.

In sharp contrast to the cold, wet, high cloud forest on Munchique, we found Patía Valley, a hundred or so kilometers south of Popayán, hot and dry. We made several trips to the area, the most productive one a three-day affair in early February in company with three of our frequent traveling companions—Alvaro Tomás, Victor Gomez, and Jamie Valencia. Alvaro had arranged for us to camp in a road house built originally by his father for road crews. We tried to sleep on the board floor but found it pretty hard and uncomfortable. Always something of a clown, Alvaro cooked us a weird Swedish concoction that was barely edible and shot a Guiana or Buff-necked Ibis (*Theristicus caudatus*) to supplement our meager rations. I don't recommend ibis, however prepared, as a steady diet.

Our roadhouse headquarters, near the confluence of the Guachicono and Patía rivers, was in different country than any we had seen previously, with different people (mainly Negroes living in bamboo huts caulked with dung) and different birds. All three of our companions had guns of a sort (I didn't have one at that time) and collected 26 birds for me. In that hot country I couldn't save the birds for later skinning, so we set up a table in a corridor in the roadhouse, where a group of curious observers, including men, boys, and a woman nursing a baby, gathered to watch the skinning process. One young boy looked on in silence for a while, then disappeared momentarily and brought back a beautiful Black-throated Euphonia (*Tanagra musica*) that he got with a slingshot. Next day we met a man with a sackful of pigeons; he gave me a Cauca Pale-vented Pigeon (*Columba cayennensis*) that I coveted.

Other avian trophies on this trip included another ibis, three other pigeons or doves, two parrots (different species), a hummingbird (*Amazilia saucerrottei*), a large woodpecker (*Phloeoceastes melanoleucus*), three flycatchers, four fringillids, and nine more tanagers. Along a clear stream bed where we lunched and drank the questionable water, we found a small colony of Crested Oropendolas (*Psarocolius decumanus*), their long pendulous nests suspended from the upper branches of a tall tree.

Sight records in a tropical country are risky, but I was sure about a pair of Black-bellied Tree (Whistling) Ducks *(Dendrocygna autumnalis)* flushed from a pond along a back road. In a reedy marsh I spied a Sun Bittern (*Eurypyga helias*), a gruiform oddity so distinctive that it is put in a separate family (Eurypygidae) by itself.

Nesting Studies

During the winter and spring of 1956, we went on many other collecting or sightseeing trips, the latter usually winning out because I am a poor collector (reluctant and hesitant about shooting a bird that I might not need), and more interested in studying living birds. My main efforts in March, April, and May were concentrated on nesting studies of thrushes. These have been published in some detail in an MSU Museum bulletin (Wallace, 1965) and need only a few comments here.

Three thrushes—the Black-billed Robin (*Turdus ignobilis*), the Andean or Gray-crowned Solitaire *(Myadestes ralloides)*, and the Orange-billed Nightingale Thrush (*Catharus aurantiirostris*) were available for study in Popayán. The Great Thrush *(Turdus fuscater)*, a large blackish robinlike bird, was a frequent visitor but nested only at higher elevations, where it was abundant. I found no nests of this species on frequent trips out of town, but three nestlings of different ages found by Oscar La Torre and Roberto Ayerbe on Ayerbe's *finca* were brought to me for keeping. They didn't do well in captivity. The youngest died on the second day, perhaps from an internal injury. Another survived five days but had difficulty swallowing food, apparently due to a canker (trichomoniasis?) in its throat. The other nestling survived 13 days but contracted wryneck (torticollis). I suspected that all three birds might have been affected by insecticides used in the potato fields where they were captured.

Turdus ignobilis was the common "robin" in Popayán, much like our American Robin in general habits but less colorful (a drab brownish bird with no bright feathers), less musical (it sang its spiritless robinlike song infrequently), and much more wary and unapproachable. I found six occupied and many deserted nests of this species, the first a freshly built but empty nest on February 29 that had two eggs (the full complement) on

183

Our home in Popayán, Colombia. Our next door neighbors play with ring toss that Myra made for them.

Leticia Mosquera, culinary artist, with a fruit bowl made from a papaya. One of our closest Colombian friends, Leticia is from one of Popayán's leading families.

"Cathy," our pet Orange-billed Nightingale Thrush—tame, friendly, charming.

Hill country and mountains near Popayán. Puracé, volcanic peak barely visible in the background, erupted several times while we were there.

Mist-shrouded Munchique, one of our choice collecting spots, the haunts of many cloud-forest birds.

March 3. On May 25, I found a freshly built nest that was soon deserted. Only one of the six occupied nests was successful in fledging its two young; four nests were robbed or deserted in the egg stage; in the other nest the young disappeared before fledging. Small boys were among the predators robbing bird nests in Popayán.

Observations on the Andean Solitaire were more rewarding. Although uncommon around Popayán, a few pairs lived in the more heavily wooded areas on the outskirts of town. They were difficult to observe except at a known nest site and sang infrequently even while attending nests. But the song had a remarkable quality, the best, I thought, of any I heard in Colombia. The song was a leisurely refrain of about three low-toned, bell-like notes repeated at infrequent intervals. Rich and melodious, it had a strangely eerie and ventriloquistic effect, so that a singing bird perched motionless in a tree or shrub was hard to locate.

I had four active nests under observation, all of them well-concealed mossy structures tucked into crevices in banks. One, a beautiful nest with two young, was some distance from town and not revisited, so its fate was not known. All of the other nests were unsuccessful. One was broken up in the early egg stage, the nest torn out of its emplacement and feathers of the incubating adult strewn about. In another nest the half-grown young disappeared without a trace. (I suspected a Green Jay seen near the nest a little earlier.) The remaining nest was followed through to near completion. The adults were quite tame and permitted close observations without a blind. Putting up a blind would have been a risky venture; someone might be wearing it the next day. Within a day or two of fledging, Martha observed a weasel approaching the nest. She drove the weasel away, but we suspected it would be back, so we rescued one of the young and took it home for further observations. The other young bird (there were only two) was left in the nest, but it was gone when I returned the next morning.

The young captive, a male, did not thrive in captivity, but he learned to sing a little at about 16 days of age and continued "warbling" off and on (not the true solitaire song) until the time of his demise. He had an insatiable appetite for fruit; when about 31 days of age he consumed 57 blackberries (approximately his own weight), then we ran out of blackberries and substituted pieces of orange, banana, bread, cheese, and meat. He always preferred fruit, which suggests that Andean Solitaires are primarily fruit eaters. But the young bird had problems, perhaps from an unbalanced diet of fruit, which went through him without complete digestion. He developed a type of paralysis (rickets?) in his legs, sores about the face and head, and considerable defeatherization. So I made a study skin of him after keeping him for 37 days.

186

Most of my spring studies, however, were concentrated on *Catharus,* the Orange-billed Nightingale Thrush. It was fairly common in partially wooded ravines, horse and cattle pastures, along fence rows and brushy hillsides. Apparent pairs, or at least singing males, were on territory throughout the year, hence they were usually easy to locate. In spite of occasional outbursts of song at irregular intervals during the day, they showed no signs of nesting until spring. I had 10 nests under observation in March, April, and May. Nesting data are too detailed to chronicle here (see references). Suffice it to say that I had detailed data on nests, eggs, incubation, development of the young, fledging and some post-nest observations. The song, so often repeated in spring (I had a count of 333 songs between 8:30 A.M. and 9:30 A.M. at nest 7) is of an inferior quality for a thrush—an explosive, unmusical, three-to-five syllable warble.

As in the case of the young solitaire, I kept a fledgling *Catharus* ("Cathy") in captivity for post-nest observations on growth, development, and behavior. Unlike the solitaire, Cathy proved to be a charming and lovable pet—tame, friendly, musical, and mischievous. Often he perched on my head or shoulders while I was working at my desk. Sometimes he slept in my hair. When we had visitors he would fly from one head to another, sometimes leaving a little token as he departed. Some visitors were delighted, others annoyed. We kept Cathy for 92 days, then released him when we left Popayán. I needed to make a study skin of him, but the Wallace womenfolk voted it down in no uncertain terms. So I carried him out to a wooded hillside where there had been a successful nest and released him.

We had other pets around most of the year. Nighthawks were common fall transients in Popayán, where they perched on low buildings and in trees by day and made tempting targets for boys with slingshots. Several were brought to me, the capturers anticipating a reward. But Carriker had warned me not to pay boys for specimens, else I would be bombarded with birds I didn't want. However, the nighthawks soon left for more southern wintering grounds, and, inexplicably, didn't come back through Popayán in the spring. Injured nighthawks that I tried to care for did not make good pets.

A more intriguing captive was an unidentified rail that was picked up, apparently flightless, on a street in Popayán and brought to us for keeping. It was a small, Sora-sized, beautifully plumaged brown-and-gray rail. We got together with Carriker and Von Sneidern to identify it and decided it was a Colombian Crake (*Neocrex erythrops colombianus*), a rare form not previously taken in Popayán and only a few times in other parts of Colombia. Carriker and Von Sneidern coveted it for a specimen, but we

187

wanted to keep it for a while at least. We gave it free rein in the enclosed patio, where it skulked around the potted plants, usually hiding but sometimes running about in the open. It was fairly tame, ate well, and could be handled a little. But the inevitable happened, as Carriker had predicted. It disappeared on the fifth day, probably having recovered its power of flight and taken off in an almost vertical ascent out of the patio. The "rat" theory of its demise seemed illogical; there was no trace of a stray feather anywhere in the patio.

But our most endearing pet was a young owl, a fluffy ball of feathers brought to us on March 16. Oscar, who found it, said it had fallen out of a church tower in a cemetery. Even Carriker couldn't identify it and suggested we try to keep it until after its postjuvenal molt, when it could probably be identifed. As the days went by, however, its sprouting ear tufts and soft whinnying led me to believe it was a Colombian or Costa Rican Screech Owl *(Otus choliba luctisonus)*, which it eventually proved to be. Like most young owls, it snapped and bit at first, lying on its back and clawing at us with its feet. But it soon quieted down, ate well, developed rapidly, and made a most charming and amusing guest in our house until our departure from Popayán on July 20, when we gave the bird back to Oscar.

The little owl had many adventures. We tethered him (an assumed male) out in the patio on a long string to give him some freedom. On March 26, after we had had him 10 days, he escaped, string and all. The whole neighborhood turned out to look for him, and someone finally spied him atop a utility pole, the string dangling down but far out of reach. We borrowed a ladder, and I was able to retrieve him. After that he frequently perched on the roof of our patio, especially on moonlit nights, but with the string securely attached. We all loved him, but he was Sylvia's special pet, sitting in her lap or on her shoulder while she studied her math lessons on the patio.

Feeding him was no problem. We bought meat daily at the market, and "Buho" usually came to inspect the contents of the market basket when we returned. I also fed him carcasses of the birds I was skinning out for my collection. But most of all, he relished the big Oriental cockroaches. He would pounce on one in a stately, dignified manner, hold it up in one foot while he nibbled at it the way one would eat a banana. We soon ran out of cockroaches in our house and enlisted eager neighborhood children to collect them from other sources.

More Expeditions

Because my nesting studies terminated in late May, we were free to take longer, overnight trips in June and July, leaving neighbors to take care of our pets. One of the longer trips took us to Pasto, a quaint and picturesque village near the Colombian-Ecuadorian border. We had an Ecuadorian visa and wanted to visit Quito, but our Colombian visa was for one entry only. Had we gone into Ecuador, we might not be allowed back into Colombia.

Southern Colombia contains much rugged, picturesque country with superb views, but some roads were almost impassible and even frightening. One of them, a one-way road carved on the side of a precipitous mountain, had a sheer drop-off of several hundred feet—and no guardrail.

One memorable event on this trip was a visit to Lago de la Cocha, a cold, high-altitude body of water stocked with trout. We stayed in a luxurious Swiss-type hotel that night, had a four-course fish-and-chicken dinner, enjoyed an amiable chat with other guests around a roaring fire, slept in cold beds supplied with hot water bottles, and the next morning went for a boat ride on the crystal-clear lake.

But our longest and most eventful trip was a six-day journey to the Eastern Andes—to Garzon, Gigante, Altamira, and Florencia. The first day took us across the Central Andes—Puracé and the high Paramo—then down, down by curving narrow passages to flatter country and better roads to Garzon and Gigante, where I did a little birding and collecting the next morning. I got nice specimens of the Boat-billed Flycatcher (*Megarynchus pitangua*), Chestnut-capped Warbler (*Basileuterus delattrii*), and the Red-breasted Starling (*Leistes militaris*).

At Altamira that evening we saw a sign that read: *Florencia 100K*. It was still daylight, so we decided to go on to Florencia, presumably a two- or three-hour drive up over the mountain and down the other side. A lady from whom we got some water for the leaking radiator said the road was *bueno*. How wrong we were! We reached Florencia the next morning after more than 12 hours on the road. The "good" road soon deteriorated into a deep muddy gully with a drop-off on one side so steep we couldn't see the bottom in the dusk. Soon we were stuck in the mud where truck wheel tracks were too deep for our small car. We extricated the car by building up the ruts with dirt. Further on we came to a big lumber truck parked in the middle of the road. The driver was in a drunken stupor. Shining lights on him, blasting on the horn, and shaking him failed to arouse him, so we settled down in our jeep to try for a little sleep before morning; the girls kept one-hour vigils while I tried to sleep. In a couple hours a patrol car with six or eight men, most of them "under the influence," came along. They couldn't rouse the truck driver either, but they bolstered him up in the seat and one of the more sober men took the wheel and backed the truck into an open space so that we could pass. Then on we went in the mud and rain, around sharp curves, up and down steep grades until we met two more trucks hopelessly mired side by side in the road. Apparently one truck had tried to pass another one already stuck and couldn't make it. Again the road crew came to the rescue, and after much good-natured bantering while working with shovels, they extricated one truck and pulled out the other one by towing it. (It didn't look possible to me.) Five other trucks and buses had been held up behind the other two.

Then on for more trouble. By now the radiator was leaking so badly we had to fill it constantly from roadside puddles. Then I stalled the car in trying to pass another truck, and the car wouldn't start again. A soldier from the truck tried unsuccessfully to fix the battery cable. They pushed us until the motor started and thereafter we parked only on downgrades while filling the radiator. The first man we met on the outskirts of Florencia at about 7:00 A.M. to ask for the nearest garage turned out to be the garage owner. He soldered our radiator, fixed the battery cable, and repaired a tire for 30 pesos (about $8).

In spite of our mishaps and a mostly sleepless night, we had a pleasant stay in Florencia, eating, sleeping, sightseeing, and birding. I secured several more specimens. The most interesting was a Black-capped Mocking-thrush *(Donacobius atricapillus)*, a peculiar Mimidae with cheek pouches that Von Sneidern told me later were used for singing (I didn't hear one singing).

Next morning we were off again at 5:00 A.M. for the return trip up and over the mountain. We had apprehensions, for we had been warned it had been raining for fifteen days and that we might run into landslides. We did! Twenty-eight kilometers out of Florencia, at about 6:30 A.M., we found two trucks held up by a landslide. One had been there since 5:00 P.M. the preceding evening, the other since 4:00 A.M. One man had the right idea—he was fast asleep under his truck; others were playing cards. In an hour or so a bulldozer came along and cleared out enough rubble so that we could pass. But in another 9 kilometers we encountered another landslide. Men were shoveling and preparing to blast out a big rock with dynamite. Of course I looked for birds while waiting, but we were in a gully with steep hillsides covered with almost impenetrable tangles. I did manage to collect a pair of Fulvous-bellied, or Brown, Jacamars *(Brachygalba lugubris)* that were hawking insects over the road.

After the blast, which was only partially successful, we managed to get past this landslide but soon met another. This was a longer hold-up with at least 14 trucks and buses waiting to get untangled. Fortunately there was a rest stop and restaurant at this location, so we had a leisurely lunch, and I collected a beautiful Little Black Woodpecker *(Melanerpes cruentatus)*.

Then we proceeded without further delays, although it looked as if there had been a dozen other landslides already cleared away. We took shelter that night at a dismal-looking hotel in Pitalito, but it had a spacious and not uncomfortable room for the four of us for only 4 pesos. I did a little more collecting near Pitalito en route to St. Augustine to view the famous archeological wonders in that park. One choice trophy was a Wagler's Paroquet *(Aratinga wagleri),* a red-fronted parrot that is fairly common in the lower elevations in Colombia. Another was a Wattled Jacana *(Jacana jacana),* a polyandrous species in which the female foists housekeeping duties onto her several males.

Finally we reached home in Popayán after an arduous, adventurous six-day trip to the Eastern Andes. Cathy and Buho seemed glad to see us; Von Sneidern had looked in on them daily or oftener to see that they had food and water.

With my field studies on thrushes terminated in late May and our various excursions south, east, and west over by mid-July (not all chronicled here), it was time to plan for the trip home. Getting out of Colombia proved almost as difficult as getting in. A variety of permits had to be secured, papers signed by key officials who were rarely available, more finger-printing and checking of police records. Our accumulation of possessions that couldn't be shipped or taken with us had to be disposed of. Some items we were able to sell, others we gave to friends, neighbors, or needy people. We sold the old Willys jeep (more papers, signatures, and red tape) for almost as much as we had paid for it. It had served us reasonably well; we hope the new owner got many more kilometers out of it. Our baggage had to be sorted for different methods of shipment or transport. Getting it out of Colombia proved to be complicated, time-consuming, and annoying.

One concern was getting my valuable ornithological collections through customs. I had 220 bird skins (127 species), plus a few nests, eggs, and preserved specimens. Mr. Carriker had warned me, from his long years of experience, that I might have difficulty clearing the specimens through customs, not in Colombia (collecting permits were not required there), but at the port of entry in the United States, whether it was Miami or New York. He suggested the latter because experienced curators at the American Museum of Natural History could be contacted to help with importation problems. (However, the specimens went through Miami without difficulty.

An official at customs there said I should have a form to fill out, listing all the specimens, but the required forms were not available, so he let us pass.)

With our car now disposed of, we had to depend on friends to tote our baggage and us to various destinations. They really came to our rescue on several occasions. We had decided to take the slow and leisurely trip by boat down the Magdalena River to Barranquilla on the Caribbean coast. Friends advised us to "try it once, for the novelty of it, but never twice." We agreed after trying it: it was an interesting but slow and somewhat tedious method of transportation.

We took a plane from Popayán, where a group of friends assembled at the airport to see us off. We flew via Cali to Medellin, where we imposed on our good friends the Pettigroves, an MSU couple living in Medellin, for accommodations. They treated us royally, met us at the airport, and took us and our cumbersome baggage to their home overnight. Then they took us to an evening church supper with an abundance of American foods. Next day we toured the city, and visited orchid gardens on the outskirts of town. Then our hosts put up with us for another night. In the morning they transported us and our baggage (it took two trips in their small car) to the railroad station for a train that would take us to Porta Berria to catch the afternoon boat for Baranquilla.

We had apprehensions about the train ride. We heard that bandits had held up the train recently and killed an American engineer. But the American consul said that the rumor was untrue and that we would be safe. We did know that bandits were a problem in many parts of the country. They plundered prosperous *fincas,* held up buses and trains, and were a law unto themselves. But they usually avoided conflicts with Americans; we never encountered any bandits during our year in Colombia. The train ride to Porta Berria got us there safely after passing through greatly varied and often spectacular country.

At Porta Berria we had more difficulties. The paddle wheel steamer, the *Monserrata,* was not in dock as scheduled. One rumor (apparently the correct one) was that the boat was stuck on a sand bar upstream and might not be in till evening or even the next day. We waited and waited and finally put up overnight in a miserable structure called a hotel. Our baggage was left at the *Naviera* where a boy, who made friends with the girls, said that he slept there overnight and that he would keep watch of our baggage. Our chief difficulty was in getting our baggage aboard when the boat finally came in at about noon. "Vultures" swarmed over our baggage and wanted to carry it aboard in spite of our insistence that we could handle it ourselves. We wrangled and dickered with them, but they wouldn't set a price, they said, until after the luggage was on board. It turned out that they wanted to be paid by the number of parcels, including small items, which would have been exorbitant for our twenty-three parcels. After more wrangling a couple of the would-be carriers stalked away, muttering "stupid Americanos." We tipped the man who finally helped us 5 pesos, which the boy at the office told us was more or less a standard price of such services.

Once aboard we made ourselves at home. We had two small but reasonably comfortable staterooms. There was a small lunchroom and lounging chairs on deck (first come, first served). Meals were bounteous and well balanced at first, but the food deteriorated rapidly thereafter. The boat was behind schedule and perhaps running low on supplies. It anchored offshore on two nights, posting guards to keep bandits from coming aboard (as had happened in the past). But on the third night, in deeper water nearing the mouth of the river, we made up some lost time.

Of course, I watched for birds from the deck but didn't see many and couldn't identify some of those glimpsed along the shore. Among the more spectacular sights were the frequent groups of Blue-and-yellow Macaws *(Ara ararauna)*—big, beautiful, long-tailed parrots—that flew leisurely around the boat or along the shore. Another rewarding sight was a white-headed, black-bodied bird perched on a dead branch of a tree that had fallen into the river. I puzzled over its identity until it flew from its perch and snapped up an insect, a performance repeated at frequent intervals. It was a White-headed Marsh Tyrant *(Arundinicola leucocephala),* one of the confusing 149 species of tyrant flycatchers in Colombia. Flycatchers seem to fill all possible niches in Colombia; a Serpophaga *(S. cinerea)* hops along stones in brooks like a sandpiper; the Pied Water-tyrant *(Fluvicola pica)* perches on exposed plants in marshes like Red-winged Blackbirds; a handsome chestnut-bellied, black-backed, chat-like bird with conspicuous white lores I tried repeatedly to identify as a thrush until I finally collected one and found it to be a Chat-tyrant *(Ochthoeca cinnamomeiventris);* and a small titlike bird with a little topknot proved to be a Tufted Tit-tyrant *(Spizitornis parulus).* Then there are the *Todirostrums* or tody-flycatchers, a dozen or more species that build neat little enclosed nests suspended from a low branch. At the mouth of the Magdalena, as we approached the city of Barranquilla, we noted several Everglade Kites *(Rostrhamus sociabilis)* cruising over a marsh like melanistic Marsh Hawks.

At Barranquilla, confusion prevailed. The Avianca was closed, the Grace Line's office was closed, and at the hacienda the important officials we needed to see were gone. Our health cards needed checking and our police record card (good for only twenty-four hours) was supposed to be renewed.

Our reservations for the plane to Miami hadn't been confirmed in spite of advance notices. We had to wire Miami for confirmation, and it was past time for the plane to depart; the fact that it was an hour late saved the day. Even then the accommodating pilot held up the flight a few minutes while I scrambled on board—I had been detained by three baggage porters looking for their tips. There was no time for baggage inspection, perhaps fortunately; we wondered for a while if it even got put on board.

The flight over the Caribbean was pleasant and relaxing, with a brief stop at Montego Bay in Jamaica. We were served a sumptuous meal of American food on board, but I ate too much or else the sudden conversion to American food was too much for me; I had an upset stomach that lasted for the next three days.

Of course we had complications getting the rest of the way home. Even in America the best-laid travel plans can go awry. One ironical event: Martha guarded her camera closely during our year in Colombia, having been advised that it would probably be the first thing to be stolen. She relaxed vigilance a little in Miami—and someone stole the camera.

Except for Sylvia, who had to catch the first bus to Michigan, we were in no hurry. We had to go through New York City to pick up our heavy baggage that had been sent from Cali and Buenaventura to New York. We spent a couple of days sightseeing around Miami, and a couple more days in New York, where Dick Manville, a former colleague of mine at MSU, met us at the station, put us up overnight, and helped us with the ordeal of getting around in New York.

We finally arrived home in East Lansing on August 4—in the rain, an unnecessary reminder of the almost endless rains in Popayán. Our German tenants, the Meixners, had left things in spic-and-span condition—except that days later we found a crude makeshift bomb that the boys had cached away in the basement. It had been ingeniously contrived of nails, bolts, and other items; a knowledgeable neighbor thought that it might actually go off if ignited.

Our Colombian adventures were over. Often we think of them and sometimes review our slides. We have kept in contact with a few of our Colombian friends; some have visited us in East Lansing. We have often yearned to return to Colombia sometime, but we know that it is out of the question now, at least as a family. Once we planned to write a book, each of us contributing some portion of it, but this ambition also has faded. Hence, this chapter stands as our only written record of that Colombian adventure.

The following Christmas we composed another poem, a reminder to us and to our friends of our year in Colombia.

CHRISTMAS POEM—1956

For some of you this tale is new—
For others 'twill be volume two—
Of things we saw on every hand
While living in a foreign land.

Christmas there is strange indeed,
For firecrackers take the lead
Until the very day before,
And after Christmas there are more.

A *pesebre* is a manger scene
With shepherds, flocks, and pastures green.
Chirimia bands play in the street;
Nochebuenas are a treat.

From Popayán as our home base
We took short trips to many a place.
We crossed the lofty *Paramo*
And saw volcanos capped with snow.

One day we climbed a mountain high
That reached into the misty sky;
The road was muddy, narrow, steep;
But we went up in our green jeep.

'Twas January—the second day—
Three college boys showed us the way.
There in the jungle at the end of the road
We were warmly welcomed at their friend's abode.

From there we went out to explore
The jungle with its wondrous lore.
And in the evening with great glee
Heard MSU's Bowl victory.

We sloshed around on jungle trails,
Collecting birds and swapping tales;
And, when hunting grew too slack,
Drank *café tinto* in a native's shack.

Great quietness lends cathedral awe,
A beauty that we felt and saw.

195

Rare birds, tall trees, and brilliant flowers
Made minutes of our too few hours.

In contrast to our mountain high,
Patía Valley's hot and dry.
Through it the Guachicono flows
Where half-clad natives wash their clothes.

Here we found still different birds,
Some too beautiful for words.
We cooked an ibis for our meat
But found it pretty tough to eat.

In March the birds began to nest,
And then for George there was no rest.
Martha also looked for birds
But was afraid of Brahma herds.

Sometimes our house was like a zoo,
For we had pets to care for too.
For birds we kept an open door
With neighbors always bringing more.

Our pets, the town, its friendly people,
Our lovely view of Belen's steeple,
The hills beyond—all are keys
To a treasure book of memories.
But spring and summer faded fast;
Our days in Popayán soon passed.
We took a plane, a train, a boat—
That river trip now seems remote.

Another plane, another day,
Brought us back to the U.S.A.
Then we traveled east and traveled west
and back to the place that we love best.

It's home and school and church and friends
And this is where our story ends.
We'd like to make our wishes clear—

Have a

MERRY CHRISTMAS

and a

HAPPY NEW YEAR!

The Wallaces—George, Martha, Sylvia, and Myra.

––––––––––––––

References

Blake, E.R. *Birds of Mexico.* Chicago: University Chicago Press, 1953.

Chapman, F.M. *My Tropical Air Castle.* New York: Appleton, 1929.

Davis, J. "Breeding and Molt Schedules of the Rufous-collared Sparrow in Coastal Peru." *Condor,* 73: (1971) pp. 127-146.

de Kiriline, L. "The Voluble Singer of the Treetops." *Audubon Magazine,* 56: (1954) pp. 109-111.

de Schauensee, R.M. "Birds of Colombia." *Caldasia,* 5, Nos. 22-26, 1948-1952.

Eisenmann, E. "The Species of Middle American Birds." Transactions Linnean Society, New York, 1955.

Haverschmidt, F. "Notes on the Breeding Habits of *Panyptila cayennensis.*" *Auk,* 75: (1958) pp. 121-130.

Miller, A.H. "Response to Experimental Light Increments by Andean Sparrows from an Equatorial Area." *Condor,* 61: (1959) pp. 344-347.

––––––––––––––."Molt Cycles in Equatorial Andean Sparrows." *Condor,* 63: (1961) pp. 143-161.

Wallace, G.J. "A Colombian Christmas Bird Count." *Jack-Pine Warbler,* 14: (1956) pp. 23-26.

––––––––––––––. "Notes on North American Migrants in Colombia." *Auk,* 75: (1958) pp. 178-182.

––––––––––––––. "Studies on Neotropical Thrushes in Colombia." Publications Michigan State University Museum, Biological Series 3(1) (1965) pp. 1-47.

Wolf, L.L. "Breeding and Molting Period in a Costa Rican Population of the Andean Sparrow." *Condor,* 71: (1967) pp. 212-219.

197

CHAPTER 10

Northwestern Europe and the Scottish Cruise

OUR EXPERIENCE with European birds stems chiefly from two visits to Europe, one in 1964 to Germany and England, when Myra and her family were living in Birmingham; the other in 1966 for the meetings of the International Council for Bird Preservation (ICBP), in Cambridge, and the International Ornithological Congress (IOC), in Oxford. The IOC meetings were preceded by a cruise of the Scottish Bird Islands and included a midweek excursion to Slimbridge, England, where the Wildfowl Trust maintains the largest collection of living waterfowl in the world.

Northwestern Europe, 1964

While teaching at MSU's Kellogg Biological Station at Gull Lake, in the summer of 1964, I came home one weekend to find Martha bursting with excitement. Myra was going to have a baby. For once I said the right thing. With hardly a moment's hesitation I replied, "You better go over right away to supervise the happy event, and I will join you as soon as summer school is over." Martha's grateful response: "I was hoping you would say that." She flew to England as soon as she could get ready and I joined her in London a month or so later.

Getting together in London threatened to be another Evangeline tragedy. Martha was not at the airport as she had promised. In London, passengers do not remain at the airport but are scuttled by bus to a waiting station some distance away. Martha wasn't there either, and I visualized a never-ending quest for her somewhere in England. But by a curious coincidence I happened to see Mr. Biraben, a long-time resident of the London area who had once been a neighbor of ours in East Lansing. After a cordial greeting he assured me I was in the right place—the only place—to meet my family.

No doubt they had been delayed, he said, in one of London's frequent traffic jams. This proved to be the case, and in due time Martha, Myra, Jim, their daughter Tanya, and the new baby, Tasha, appeared for a joyous reunion.

Somehow Mr. Biraben managed to cram all of us and our baggage into his small car and took us on a long and exciting ride through London's narrow crowded streets to the Bonnington Hotel, where we had reservations. En route we got a highly informative narrative about London and the pros and cons of living there.

Even in the confusion of getting around in London, I was watching for birds. I wanted to see some of the birds so highly lauded by the early British poets and naturalists. But you've probably guessed it—my first birds in London were Starlings, House Sparrows, and Common Pigeons. But the next day (August 15) we picnicked in one of London's busy but well-groomed parks. Here, hopping along the greensward, were numerous Blackbirds *(Turdus merula)*, quite obviously not blackbirds in the American concept, but typical dark "robins." A few large handsome Wood Pigeons *(Columba palumbus)*, a pest in rural England, mingled with the numerous Common Pigeons *(C. livia)*, I thought I could distinguish a few Stock Doves *(C. oenas)* by the lack of the white rump patch supposedly characteristic of Common Pigeons, but in cities the white rump of the latter is often obscured by soot.

Later we visited St. James Park in downtown London, where semiwild and captive water birds abound. European Wigeons *(Anas penelope)*, Pochards *(Aythya ferina)*, Shelducks *(Tadorna tadorna)*, and European Coots *(Fulica atra)* were among those I assumed to be at least semiwild. Common, or Mew, Gulls *(Larus canus)* and Black-headed Gulls *(L. ridibundus)*, which proved to be so common throughout Northwestern Europe, were new for me.

But we did more sightseeing than birding during the several days we remained in London. We rode in the "tube" all over the city; Jim was adept at figuring out how we could get the longest rides for the least money. It was a novel experience for all of us. We visited and thoroughly enjoyed many of the well-known tourist attractions: for instance, a Sunday service in Westminster Church; picnics in the parks; the Changing of the Guard; and the seething crowds and flocks of pigeons in Trafalgar Square. The abundance and tameness of the pigeons amazed me. Some Britishers would banish the pigeons that desecrate monuments and perhaps transmit ornithosis. But Mr. Biraben expressed the sentiment of many when he said it would be a national disgrace to harm Britain's beloved pigeons.

Interlude in Germany

On August 17, Myra and her family returned to their home in Birmingham, while Martha and I went to visit friends in Germany before returning to England. We crossed the generally stormy English Channel and wondered how swimmers dared to challenge its foreboding waters. We watched the white cliffs of Dover slowly receding in the distance. We came into Ostende, Belgium, at dusk. Next morning we were awakened before daybreak by noisy Jackdaws *(Corvus monedula)* in the church belfry across the street from our upper floor hotel room. Then a tourist bus with a bilingual hostess aboard to point out and explain various attractions en route took us through Belgium into Germany.

Birding was largely out of the question on the long ride through Belgium and Germany, but I did recognize the Lapwings *(Vanellus vanellus)* that proved so conspicuous in the fields and pastures of northwestern Europe; in some countries their large eggs are still harvested for food, but under strict regulation. Easily recognized also were the House Martins *(Delichon urbica)*, blue-black swallows with a conspicuous white rump. Associated with the martins were numerous Barn Swallows *(Hirundo rustica)*, one of the most widely distributed passerine birds in the world. I have seen them on all continents except Australia, where they are replaced by the almost identical Welcome Swallow *(H. neoxena)*.

In Germany we traveled along parts of the historic river Rhine, through industrial Aachen, through Stuttgart with its massive old buildings flanking the frightfully narrow streets; then on to Munich, where Dr. Hildegarde Maschlanka met us at the bus station. She had been one of our post-war correspondents; Martha had participated in the program of sending packages to needy ornithologists in Europe. We wondered how she recognized us, having never seen us before, but she quickly singled us out in the seething mob assembled at the station. We were her guests for a couple of days at the Max Planck Institute for Animal Physiology where she was employed.

Dr. Konrad Lorenz, eccentric Nobel Prize Winner and director of this institute, was away, but I had met him in 1954 at an A.O.U. meeting in Madison, Wisconsin, where he had captivated his American audience. A paper on the scratching behavior of towhees, for instance, had been followed by some discussion and some disagreement about the exact nature of the performance. Dr. Lorenz jumped out into the aisle and said, "Let me show you how they really do it." He put on a sidesplitting demonstration of how towhees really scratch.

Dr. Maschlanka was a charming hostess. That first evening Martha and I found candy boxes under our pillows. My chocolates were spiked, apparently a tradition in Germany, so I helped Martha consume hers. Next morning Dr. Maschlanka took us on a tour of the institute, explained its functions, introduced us to some of the staff, who in turn tried to explain their research projects (in German) and helped us identify some of the local birds. We were able to identify 18 species, including 5 of the 12 titmice that occur in northwestern Europe. Titmice (Paridae), which include our familiar chickadees, are predominantly Old World species; more than 50 of the 65 species occur in the Old World compared to only 14 in the New World. We also singled out European Robins *(Erithacus rubecula),* quite unlike our American Robins; European Nuthatches *(Sitta europaea),* a striking combination of our White-breasted and Red-breasted forms; Chaffinches *(Fringilla coelebs),* harmoniously colored and popular European songsters; and more soberly clad Greenfinches *(Chloris chloris).*

Dr. Maschlanka also took us to the Bavarian Alps, through quaint villages such as Garmish, whose houses were attractively decorated with murals and window boxes of bright flowers. And all around us were jagged mountain peaks sharply etched against the sky. We hiked up a wide, well-traveled trail to a well-patronized restaurant where we had a bounteous dinner on a porch overlooking spectacular mountain views. Cruising around the peaks were many European Swifts *(Apus apus),* a bird I especially wanted to see because Jukka Koskimies, a Finn who had done some post-doctorate work at Michigan State, had written a classic monograph on the species for his Ph.D. Bavaria is also the locale where all of the known specimens of the Jurassic fossil Archaeopteryx have been found. Although I thought about the possibility, we didn't do any digging.

From Munich we went to Marburg for a visit with Dr. Heinz Ludtke, another post-war correspondent we tried to help after the devastating war that had disrupted so many German families. He and his wife and four children had faced difficult times during and after the war, but now he had a new post in animal physiology at the University of Marburg and had a new home of which he was justifiably proud. He really laid out the red carpet for us. (A few years earlier, in another setting, he had entertained Sylvia and her girl friend on their bicycle trip through Europe.) On a tour of the city, we saw many fine centuries-old buildings, and in the surrounding country, many productive farms. Driving through the Black Forest was a revelation; I marveled that it had survived two World Wars and the industrial expansion. I added a few birds to my growing list, among them the Common Buzzard *(Buteo buteo),* a close relative of our Red-tailed Hawk,

201

and a questionable Eagle Owl *(Bubo bubo)* seen winging its way across a field at dusk.

Back in England

From Marburg we returned to England for an extended stay with Myra and her family in Birmingham. This two-year sojourn in Birmingham resulted from Jim's dream of becoming a minister in the Church of England and of being a gardener on an English estate. The church ambition did not materialize because his training there would have required remaining in England to serve the Church indefinitely; and a gardner's position, secured by placing an ad in the *London Times,* proved impractical because the owner of the estate was impossible to satisfy. Hence Jim settled for a job in a small parts factory outside Birmingham. Part of his assignment was to pick up and deliver women workers to the factory. He also organized a bible-study class which the women attended during their noon hour. Both Myra and Jim cherish memories of their life in England.

In Myra's backyard I got better acquainted with the blackbirds, robins, and titmice seen earlier in Germany. The English Robin, still in nearly full song in August, baffled me. Again and again I ran down a "new" song, only to find that it was another Robin. Song Thrushes *(Turdus ericetorum)* and Mistle Thrushes *(T. viscivorus)* occurred there, but it was past their season of song. I didn't even see a Mistle Thrush, but Martha had seen them there earlier in the summer. Another delightful but shy and seclusive English bird is the Dunnock or Hedge Sparrow *(Prunella modularis),* a soberly clad sparrowlike bird, with a slender bill and a sprightly song. It builds a beautiful mossy nest to cradle its four eggs. It belongs to a small Old World family (Prunellidae) of 11 species, one of which *(P. montanella)* has been recorded in Alaska.

During our stay in Birmingham we rented a car. All six of us managed to squeeze into the small vehicle for an extended trip through northern England and part of Scotland. Our first overnight was at the huge Croft Hotel in Ambleside, in the famous Wordsworth lake country, which was England's most scenic landscape before its hedgerows were demolished to make way for more intensive agriculture. Now farmers are regretting their haste in eliminating the hedges that protected soils from erosion and sheltered useful wildlife.

We spent a day or two exploring in Northern England. Here I saw my first European wren, which the British proudly call *The Wren,* as if there were no others. There are 63 species in the Americas; one of them, our

Winter Wren *(Troglodytes troglodytes),* has spread over the Alaskan land corridor into much of Asia and Europe and even into North Africa. At the hotel, one sang for us, and I heard others at Carlisle (our next stop) and in Scotland, but their somewhat abbreviated songs didn't measure up to the musical outpourings of Winter Wrens in northern Michigan bogs or of those on Mt. Mansfield in Vermont.

At Ambleside and in the surrounding country we also noted European Jays *(Garrulus glandarius),* a little larger but less brightly marked than our Blue Jays; Rooks *(Corvus frugilegus),* hardly distinguishable from our crows except by their calls and (at close range) the bare facial pattern; Linnets *(Carduelis cannabina),* much like our California House Finches; and Bullfinches *(Pyrrhula pyrrhula),* large handsome birds that are serious economic pests because of their destructive debudding of fruit trees in commercial orchards.

In Scotland, Sterling was a must. A monument to Sir William Wallace, renowned Scottish chief, is one of its prominent features. I can't claim direct descent from Sir William because he left no offspring; he was too busy mowing down Englishmen with his 75-pound claymore. Like Robert the Bruce, who also has a monument erected in his honor in Sterling, Wallace is still a national hero, even commemorated by present generations of Englishmen whose forefathers finally captured him and dragged him behind a horse through the streets of London as a public example of a villain and a traitor.

Of course we climbed the woodland path up the hill on which the monument stands. And true to my nationality, I tried to get in free because of a presumed relationship to Sir William, but the ticket collector countered by saying I should pay more, perhaps make an extra contribution for upkeep of the monument.

Our next stop was at St. Andrews, whose impressive university buildings reminded me that Thomas H. Osgood, former head of physics and later dean at MSU, had received some of his early training here. We went down to the coast, even dabbled our feet in the water, but the cold rough waves didn't prove very inviting. Bathing at the seashore is not a popular pastime in Scotland. However, Common Eiders *(Somateria mollisima),* European Oystercatchers *(Haematopus ostralegus),* and Redshanks *(Tringa totanus)* did find the beaches and waters attractive for foraging. Rock Pipits *(Anthus spinoletta),* actually the same species as our Water Pipits in the States, inhabited the rocky outcrops along the coast.

From the coast at St. Andrews we traveled inland into the Scottish Highlands, where we paused to listen to a musical group playing bagpipes beside the road for a handout. Jim did most of the driving; he was used to English cars with the steering wheel on the righthand side. When I took over for a spell, I burned out the clutch by my awkward manipulation of the shift. We seemed hopelessly stranded out in the desolate barrens, but fortunately we found good accommodations in a bed-and-breakfast place at the top of the next hill.

It took a day or so to get the clutch fixed, but this gave me an opportunity for leisurely strolls over Scottish hills of heather. Birds seemed abundant, at least in the morning hours, but most of them were species already observed in Germany and England. Titmice were especially prominent and included a thrilling sight of about 20 Long-tailed Tits *(Aegithalos caudatus)* perched on wires and flying from perch to perch. Tree Pipits *(Anthus trivialis)*, Meadow Pipits *(A. pratensis)*, and Pied Wagtails *(Motacilla alba)* were also quite common. Reed Buntings *(Emberiza schoeniclus)*, numerous in a rocky, stubble-grown field, and several Twites *(Carduelis flavirostris)*, associated with the buntings, were new for me. In a boggy spot dotted with tamaracks I flushed a snipe, but it proved to be our American species *(Capella gallinago)*.

We stopped for a brief visit at the Speir School in Beith, south of Glasgow. The school was founded by one of Jim's distant ancestors. We walked over the school grounds (no new birds), inspected the classrooms and library, and Jim talked with one of the administrators about the origin and past history of the school. It had been started by Mrs. Robert Speir, (Jim's great, great, great grandmother) in memory of her son John, who is commemorated by a statue in the hall of the school. Then we drove back into northern England where we parted company, Myra and family returning to Birmingham with the car while Martha and I took a train to Middlebrough on the east coast to pay our respects to Don Spratt and his family.

Meeting Don several years earlier in East Lansing was one of those curious coincidences. I received a call one day from a government chemist from England who was attending some chemistry meetings at MSU. He was tired of sitting in Chemistry meetings, he said (I didn't blame him), and wondered if anyone was available to show him some American birds. I was available and we had a pleasant afternoon looking for birds. It was mid-August, so we didn't do too well, but Don consoled me by saying we did as well as we could have in England at that time of year. He knew water birds quite well; a few were the same species as, or quite similar to, those in England, but most of the passerine birds were new to him. He was delighted, as other European visitors have been, with our Cardinals, which have no counterpart in Europe. He urged us (Martha served him tea and light refreshments) to visit him in England sometime to see their English birds. Now was our chance.

Don and a birding friend of his took us to an estuary famous for its birds of passage, especially shorebirds. But it proved to be the wrong day, as is often my fate with shorebirds. Several flocks of Shelducks on and over the water were some consolation; the ones seen earlier in St. James Park in London may have been planted birds. And I finally saw a Skylark *(Alauda arvensis),* but it was September, way past its season of song, so I had no opportunity to evaluate the high praise lavished on it by Shakespeare, Wordsworth, and Shelley.

On the following day Don and his companion took us to the Farne Islands, a notable bird refuge off the northeast coast of England near the Scottish border. Again it was the wrong day; most of the sea birds for which the refuge is noted—puffins, guillemots, gannets, shags, and kittiwakes— were through nesting, although some of them, especially kittiwakes and shags, still roosted on the ledges. We inspected some of the puffin and rabbit burrows that honeycombed parts of the islands, but the puffins were out to sea. Inspection of the historic islands, their ancient stone buildings in ruins, and the boat trip to and from the islands were novel experiences. Actually I recorded 45 species of birds on the long day's trip, but most of them were birds that had been seen elsewhere.

One bird found on the return trip merits mention. I wanted to acquire a few European specimens to bring back to MSU, but since I had no permit or authorization for collecting, I was constantly on the alert for possible road kills to salvage. Such kills, however, proved to be rare at that time in England. Roads were narrow, full of curves, and cars move more slowly than in the States. Don had an antiquated jalopy (converted from a former hearse). He brought it to a halt slowly by shifting to lower gears before using the brake. When I finally noted a bird fluttering helplessly beside the road (it had been hit by the car ahead of us), I asked Don to stop. He did— in another 100 yards or so—and I ran back hurriedly to pick up the prize. It was a young House Sparrow!

Back in Birmingham again, Myra made arrangements for me to meet Dr. W. B. Yapp, ornithologist-physiologist at the University of Birmingham. Author of several books on birds, at that time he was doing some research in the Wyre Forest, the only really mature forest left in the Midlands. We had a pleasant lunch together but did not go afield. He showed me his office-lab setup and explained some physiological experiments he was conducting. It seemed odd to me that he had so few books around, but he said he preferred to go to the library, where it was quiet and he would be undisturbed, for his reading and reference work.

Myra also contacted Derek Thomas, a preparatory school physics teacher who was a dedicated bird watcher. I showed him a list of English birds I had not seen and he knew immediately which ones could be found easily, others that were probables or possibles, and some that did not occur locally at that time of year (mid-September). Derek, like many "amateur" bird watchers, was almost infallible at quick identification. We recorded 46 species of birds that morning, 10 of which were on my *desiderata* list.

Our first stop was at the Bittell Reservoirs where Derek said we could find Great Crested Grebes *(Podiceps cristata)* and Little Grebes or Dabchicks *(P. (ruficollis)*. We counted a dozen or so of the former, some still in breeding plumage, a bird that became well known through Julian Huxley's detailed courtship and behavior studies on it in 1914. An equal number of Dabchicks, plump little birds with chestnut-colored heads when still in breeding plumage, were associated with the larger grebes. There were also many Gray Herons *(Ardea cinerea),* similar to and possibly conspecific with our Great Blue Herons. We counted 11 of them in one place and saw others elsewhere. Ducks, mostly Mallards, were numerous, but there were many Common Teal *(Anas crecca),* now considered conspecific with our Green-winged Teal, and some Tufted Ducks *(Anas fuligula)*, There were also many shorebirds, three of which—Little Ringed Plover *(Charadrius dubius),* Little Stint *(Calidris minuta)*, and Common Sandpiper *(Tringa hypoleucos)*—were new to me. The Little Stint is one of the several sandpipers that have a unique nesting schedule; the female lays two sets of eggs, the male taking charge of one set while the female cares for the other.

Leaving the reservoirs and the water birds we went afield and found Whinchats *(Saxicola rubetra)*, soberly clad, warblerlike thrushes; Yellow Wagtails *(Motacilla flava)*, an Old World bird that has invaded Alaska; and a Lesser Spotted Woodpecker *(Dendrocopus minor)* that Derek said was quite rare in the Midlands. I had seen the Great Spotted Woodpecker *(D. major)* earlier in northern England and found the Middle Spotted Woodpecker *(D. medius)* two years later in Switzerland. These names—Great Spotted, Lesser Spotted, and Middle Spotted—intrigued me.

The next day Derek took us to the Wyre Forest in hope of finding a European Dipper *(Cinclus cinclus),* an unusual bird in the Midlands but one that I was particularly eager to see. With some difficulty we found one, characteristically bobbing along from rock to rock in a swift-flowing stream. Compared to our rather drab Dipper in the Rockies, it was a handsome bird with its clear white cheek patch and chocolate brown head.

Other birds, except for some quite vocal titmice and an occasional nuthatch, seemed strangely scarce in the forest, perhaps because it was getting late in the day.

Aboard the Mauretania

Our brief but eventful visit to northwestern Europe terminated in mid-September. We boarded the *Mauretania* at Southhampton on September 15 and set sail on the leisurely journey home. Between the substantial meals, a delightful feature of most cruises, I spent much time on deck to look for sea birds, but after leaving the gulls in and around the English Channel, we noted few birds on the open ocean. A few shearwaters that I presumed to be Cory's *(Puffinus diomedia)* came into view occasionally, as did some of the smaller Manx Shearwaters *(P. puffinus),* which breed abundantly on islands in the British Isles. A few more readily identified Sooty Shearwaters *(P. griseus)* appeared at times, and several jaegers, believed to be Pomarines *(Stercorarius pomarinus)*, flew past the ship. Other uncertainties included small groups of petrels (Mother Carey's chickens), presumed to be Wilson's Storm Petrels *(Oceanites oceanicus).*

But birding improved on the afternoon of the fourth day, somewhere in the mid-Atlantic. At first a few stragglers, then a flock of about three hundred Greater Shearwaters *(Puffinus gravis)* came skimming over the water, followed by a hundred or so more, then smaller groups during the rest of the afternoon and the next day. We couldn't identify all of them for sure, but the majority, perhaps all of those in the mid-Atlantic, were Greaters, radiating far out at sea from their only known nesting grounds on the Tristan de Cunha Islands, where millions breed.

Thus ended our first trek to Europe, a pleasant combination of sightseeing, visiting with family and friends, and seeing many birds both new and old. According to my notes I had recorded 108 species in Europe and about 7 more (including the doubtfuls) on the Atlantic crossing. Of the 108 seen in Europe, 80 were new for me and 28 were North American birds that also occur in Europe.

Northwestern Europe—1966

Our second excursion to Europe was primarily to attend the International Ornithological Congress in Oxford. The congress meetings were preceded by those of the International Council for Bird Preservation and the Scottish Bird Islands Study Cruise. However, we had long dreamed of visiting

Switzerland sometime and of vacationing in the Swiss Alps, a desire given additional stimulus when Sylvia returned from her bicycle trip through Switzerland and showed us slides of attractive cottages nestled in the mountains. Hence, we arranged for a week in Switzerland before going on to the meetings in England and Scotland.

Our trans-Atlantic flight was marred by annoying delays and a disrupted schedule. We had reservations for a direct, nonstop flight from New York to Geneva, but our plane from Detroit to New York was nearly two hours late and the plane for Geneva had already departed. A later flight to Geneva was full and, exasperatingly, our baggage did not come in on our plane from Detroit. Someone suggested—perhaps facetiously—that it might have been returned to East Lansing as unclaimed baggage and would be waiting for us on our porch when we returned from Europe. But later in the evening I chanced to spy a porter wheeling a load of baggage to the lost baggage room. It included our luggage, which had come in on a later flight from Detroit.

Meanwhile, airport officials were trying valiantly to reschedule stranded passengers on substitute flights. Eventually Northwest booked us on a BOAC 11:00 P.M. flight to London via Prestwick, Scotland; then we could take our chances on catching a plane from London to Geneva. In due time we almost took off on a BOAC flight. The plane taxied down the runway—bumpity-bumpity-bump. It had a flat tire and the brakes were defective, so we returned to the terminal for transfer to another plane.

Another long delay. Stranded passengers were amusing: some paced the floor impatiently; some sprawled out on sofas or the floor in hope of getting a few winks; others were munching snacks, writing cards to friends about their troubles, or reading. Most were taking the situation philosophically. Finally we boarded a plane at 2:30 A.M., but it didn't take off until after 3:00 A.M. As we were settling down for a long overdue nap, dinner was announced. Dinner at 4 A.M.? Of course, we had it coming and it was really welcome. Then breakfast was served at 7:30 A.M. as we were approaching Scotland. After an hour's delay in Prestwick we were off for London—and had another snack en route. By some miracle there were no delays or baggage problems in London. We caught a flight to Geneva right away, without reservations, and had another meal en route.

Switzerland

In Geneva things went smoothly. We boarded a train that took us to Berne. The train traveled a highly scenic route, along the shores of beautiful (but I learned later highly polluted) Lake Geneva, through green valleys dotted with grazing cattle, and past placid lakes framed by rugged mountains. Although we were twelve hours behind schedule, our reservations at Hotel Savoy in Berne had not been cancelled. We were ready for a little rest.

In Berne I tried to do a little birding, but conditions in the city were not favorable. Many swifts, both the Common Swifts, seen on our previous trip to Europe and Alpine Swifts *(Apus melba)* circled around the city buildings. A small but attractive, neatly groomed Botanical Garden was within walking distance from our hotel, but it was not open during my early morning visit, and later in the day the birds there were not very active. Titmice, as over much of Europe, were fairly common—Great Tits, Blue Tits, and Coal Tits. Other repeats from earlier experiences were Wood Pigeons, Blackbirds, Wrens, Robins, Chaffinches, and Greenfinches. In other parts of the city, while we were sightseeing or shopping (in Berne's modern malls), we saw Black Redstarts *(Phoenicurus ochruros)* and Blackcaps *(Sylvia atricapilla)*. In the animal park (Tierpark) we discovered our first Middle-spotted Woodpecker *(Dendrocopus medius)* and our first Short-toed Tree Creeper *(Certhia brachydactyla)*.

One goal on our trip to Switzerland was to find the Tolcsvais, a family that had fled their native Hungary and found refuge in Switzerland. Martha had corresponded with them for some time, then lost track of them until a friend of Myra's later located them in Berne. They had left a note for us at the hotel. Then one of the boys came for us and took us to their home on the outskirts of the city. Mr. Tolcsvai, an artist, taught art in a local school. Mrs. Tolcsvai gave me a precious memento—a small painting of a Redstart *(Phoenicurus phoenicurus)* and a Whitethroat *(Sylvia communis)* enclosed in the same frame. It had belonged to her father, a former president of the Hungarian Ornithological Society.

During our visit with the Tolcsvais, we learned more about their hardships during and following World War II and their flight at night to Switzerland. Now they seemed to be comfortably established in Berne. They helped us formulate plans for spending a few days in a chalet in the Swiss Alps. They knew of a possible place—the Pension Bellevue at Heiligenschwende—not far from Berne.

The pension proved to be just what we were looking for—an attractive, not too luxurious facility on beautiful Lake Thun, almost completely hemmed in by high snowcapped peaks. We had two rooms—an odd arrangement, it seemed—with separate entrances from a corridor in front but which communicated at the back by means of a balcony overlooking the lake. It was so cold and rainy during our brief stay there that we took the feather tick from one bed and added it to the bed in the other room, then used one room for sleeping and the balcony and the other room for sitting.

One or both of us took frequent short excursions afield to look for birds, but showers often sent us scurrying for cover. Birds were quite active in the brief periods of sunshine between showers, but the number of species at that altitude was small. In a one-hour midforenoon inspection of the grounds that first day, I recorded 14 species and added only 3 more on a longer three-hour jaunt through the woods in the afternoon. Next morning it was raining at dawn (4:30 A.M.), but it cleared a little by 7 A.M., so I managed a short pre-breakfast hike and a longer post-breakfast hike, then got rained out again in the afternoon. We fared no better on the third morning, our last day at the pension. But in spite of mostly dismal weather, our brief stay at the pension was enjoyable. The views from our balcony, even in the rain, were breathtaking: high mountains bathed in mist and clouds that opened up at times to reveal glimpses of snowcapped peaks.

My bird list at the pension (parts of three days) totaled only 31 species and only 49 for our eight days in Switzerland, but there were some exciting finds. A pair of Yellowhammers *(Emberiza citrinella),* a species missed on our first trip to Europe, was feeding in the driveway of the pension when we arrived; the male sang frequently from the roof of the building. Along a woodland path I found a small flock of Goldcrests *(Regulus regulus)* accompanied by several of the nearly identical Firecrests *(R. ignicapillus),* both Old World species much like our Golden-crowned Kinglets. From our balcony one rainy afternoon we identified a Red-backed Shrike *(Lanius collurio)* perched on a wire. It dropped to the ground, caught an insect or small mammal, and went to a nest of young in a nearby thicket. And on a morning walk in a pasture I found a small group of Fieldfares *(Turdus pilaris),* handsome, gray-headed, spotted-breasted "robins."

Before we left Switzerland, the Tolcsvais persuaded us to visit Luzerne, to walk through the famous five-hundred-year-old bridge with its 111 history-depicting murals, and to ascend Mt. Pilatus in a cable car. The latter was thrilling, our car skimming high over the landscape below. I wondered if the cables would hold. Do they ever break and spill passengers down onto the rocks below? Views from the cable car and from the summit encompassed a vast wilderness; the only flaws, as in our ski slopes in the Rockies, were the ugly gashes carved through the forest to permit access. I wanted to see a few alpine birds on the summit, but the only ones seen were a hundred or more Alpine Choughs *(Coracia graculus),* red-legged, yellow-billed corvids so pampered by tourists that they feed out of the hand.

Thus ended our eight-day sojourn in scenic Switzerland, a few new birds recorded, our dream of staying in a Swiss chalet fulfilled, and our visit with the Tolcsvai family achieved.

The International Council for Bird Preservation (July 11 to 14)

The meetings of the ICBP in Cambridge were attended by delegates (contributing members) from 28 participating nations. Fifteen topics were listed on the agenda; some of those receiving the most critical attention and discussion were: Oil Pollution at Sea, the Effects of Toxic Chemicals on Bird Life, Protection of Birds of Prey as a World-wide Problem, Dangers of Bird Ringing and Use of Nylon Nets, Threatened Species of Birds, and Modern Agricultural Development.

Although one whole session was devoted to toxic chemicals, the use and misuse of pesticides seemed to creep into most of the other sessions. Delegates from several foreign nations pointed an accusing finger at the United States for exporting to their countries large quantities of pesticides for uses no longer legal in our country. In contrast, Great Britain and several other European nations were years ahead of the United States in banning or restricting the use of aldrin, dieldrin, and phosphorus, formerly widely used in seed dressings. A precipitous decline of Golden Eagles in Scotland prompted the ban on the use of dieldrin in sheep dips. Sweden realized the dangers of mercury poisoning long before it came to the attention of wildlife administrators in this country. Israel, plagued with outbreaks of rodents in its intensively managed agricultural areas, had used thallium sulphate so heavily that birds of prey were virtually exterminated by secondary poisoning. Then a ban on thallium sulphate because of its dangers to human life permitted new and worse outbreaks of rodents, since there were no raptors to control them.

Mist nets, so useful for ringing (banding) studies, were being used illegally in many countries for catching birds for food or for the pet trade. The fear was expressed that if widespread use of mist nets was adopted in the developing countries, it could have a devastating effect on birds in those fragile environments. Restrictions in the use of nets and stricter control in their sale were called for.

There were several pessimistic reports on rare and endangered species. Everywhere, it seemed, birds of prey in particular, but also fish-eating and insectivorous birds, and seed-eaters in countries using toxic chemicals for seed dressings, were in serious trouble. Colonel Jack Vincent, ICBP liason officer, circulated a list of 318 species and subspecies of birds that he felt

211

Bavarian Alps, near the site where all known specimens of the Jurassic fossil *Archaeopteryx* have been found.

Lake Thun, Switzerland, as viewed from our Pension balcony at Heiligenschwende.

Mist-bathed St. Kilda, one of the "stacks" circumnavigated on our Scottish cruise. It is the breeding site for 30–40,000 gannets.

Nest ledges at Marwick Head in the Orkneys, where dense concentrations of sea birds find sanctuary.

Gulls following our cruise ship for handouts.

Nene or Hawaiian Goose at Slimbridge, England. Offspring of captive birds are flown to Hawaii for restocking.

were facing critical conditions. Every year, he said, more species had to be added to the critical list, whereas only rarely could a species be removed from the list because of recovery. And at that time, before "recovery teams" were set up in various nations, very little was being done to resolve the problems.

Two pleasant interludes interrupted the paper sessions. One was a guided tour of the centuries-old colleges in Cambridge, followed by a reception "on the green". One host at the reception remarked that the grass had not been trampled on by so many feet in the past six hundred years. At the end of our tour, I pulled a real boner. Our guide held out her hand toward me and I shook it cordially, then noted, to my acute embarrassment, that other people were placing coins in her outstretched hand.

The other diversion was a bus trip to the Royal Society for the Protection of Birds. The headquarters, or lodge, was a magnificent old castle. We inspected its facilities, had tea, and strolled over a part of the 104-acre estate. Guides explained the functions and activities of the society.

Each morning before the paper sessions started I took walks to look for new birds. Around the Arms Hotel where we stayed birds were numerous on the lawns and in the hedges. In the Botanical Gardens nearby, Moorhens (gallinules) ran over the lawns and among the flower beds like chickens. Titmice (4 species) were especially conspicuous, and Robins, Blackbirds, Song Thrushes, Wrens, Dunnocks, and Chaffinches were common. Along the thicket-fringed Gam River, I had a chance to work out some of England's confusing species of sylviids or Old World warblers—Blackcaps, Whitethroats, and Reed and Sedge warblers *(Acrocephalus scirpaceus* and *A. schoenobaenus)* carrying food for their young. Other sylviids (there are 398 species), including the nearly identical Willow Warbler *(Phylloscopus trochilus)* and Chiffchaff *(P. collybita)*, were seen in other parts of England.

The Scottish Bird Islands Study Cruise (July 16–22, 1966)

The trip from Cambridge to Edinburgh for the Scottish cruise involved a long, uncomfortable ride in an overcrowded train. For much of the way we had to stand up between cars (for fresh air) or sit at a table piled high with empty ale cans: a troop of soldiers was en route to a training camp in Inverness in northern Scotland. We had reservations for the night at the Country House, which proved to be a rundown hotel with creaking board floors, poor beds, and antiquated plumbing. But early the next morning, sans breakfast because coffee shops were not open, we were off for a pleasant two-to-three-hour bus trip through picturesque Scottish countryside to Greenock, where we boarded the *M.S. Devonia* for a seven-day, 1,200 mile cruise around the perimeter of Scotland. For one who has spent much of his life observing land birds, this cruise proved to be one of the outstanding events of my ornithological career.

The *M. S. Devonia* was a 12,796 ton British India educational cruise ship manned by an Indian crew. They served us a welcome coffee snack as soon as we were on board, doubly welcome because we had had no breakfast. More than nine hundred passengers from thirty-seven different countries were on board, including two hundred Americans and delegates from all of the European countries. Some of the "elite" passengers had cabins, but the rest of us were sorted into groups under colored flags and assigned to dormitories, the men separated from the women at opposite ends of the ship, which posed problems for husbands and wives getting together for meals or for observations on deck. Meals were served cafeteria-style in four shifts, and the red, pink, yellow, and gray card holders were rotated daily. Meals were substantial and pleasant, get-acquainted affairs, but somewhat hurried. When pink card holders were on the first shift, for instance, the red card holders standing in line were understandably impatient for the "pinks" to vacate the tables promptly.

The whole cruise had been superbly organized by the Scottish Ornithologists' Club, with many months of planning at weekly and sometimes daily meetings of the staff. Dr. W. J. Eggeling was chairman and cruise leader, George Waterston and his wife Irene (secretary of the club) were responsible for working out the minute details, and James Fisher, said to have been the originator of the cruise idea, was a leading commentator. Several other commentators made frequent announcements over a loudspeaker from the bridge. They notified passengers of special birds appearing on the right or the left and described the geological and ecological features of the islands being passed. Commentaries from the bridge were in English, but they were then translated into German and French for the benefit of German and French passengers. (Ornithologists from thirty or more other nations had to figure things out for themselves.)

Arrangements had been made for evening programs given by fourteen lecturers and commentators. Several documentary movies were also shown. For a part of one evening's entertainment some concert singers were ferried in from the Shetlands, then transported back to the island after the performance. Hence, we were well taken care of but could not attend all of the programs because of crowded conditions or overlapping events.

Gulls of several species, abundant in the harbor at Greenock, followed us throughout much of the cruise. Lesser Black-backed Gulls *(Larus fuscus),* prevalent in the harbor, were largely replaced by Great Blackbacks *(L. marinus)* further out at sea. Herring Gulls *(L. argentatus)* often came aboard to be hand-fed at the rail, but the Common, or Mew, Gulls *(L. canus)* and the Black-headed Gulls *(L. ridibundus)* were more aloof. Kittiwakes *(Rissa tridactyla)* were also more abundant around the remoter islands and nested in great concentrations on some of the cliffs.

Circumnavigating Ailsa Craig, the first of the bird islands we passed, was a novel experience. Large rocks, or stacks, rose several hundred feet out of the sea, their steep slopes capped like snow with thousands of Gannets *(Sula bassana),* one of the six largest gannetries in the world. Mingled with the Gannets were numerous but less conspicuous Razorbills *(Alca torda)* and Guillemots *(Uria aalge)* or Common Murres, as Americans call them.

Most of the next day (Sunday) was spent ashore on the Isle of Rhum, a 26,400 acre nature reserve, largely devoid of trees except for several plantings. We assembled at Kimlock Castle, a massive magnificent structure built by Mrs. Bullough in 1900 but eventually turned over to the nature conservatory for a sanctuary. Here we were divided into excursion groups, some exploring the castle with its periodic furniture, historic paintings, fantastic baths, mechanical organ, and observation tower on the roof, while others went afield. The most hardy and adventurous people scaled a 2,500 foot peak to view the nesting burrows of the island's several thousand pairs of Manx Shearwaters *(Puffinus puffinus).* A few sleepy incubating or brooding birds were hauled out of their burrows to be held in the hand. I wanted to go on this strenuous hike, but I was having trouble with leg cramps and had to join a more leisurely jaunt on more level terrain. I was partially rewarded that evening, however, when hundreds—perhaps thousands—of the shearwaters came skimming over the waters of the bay.

The Manx Shearwater, it will be recalled by many, made history when Rosario Mazzeo, a former personnel director of the Boston Symphony Orchestra, on a concert tour in England, was persuaded by R. M. Lockley to take two shearwaters from a nesting burrow on Skokholm, Wales, back to Boston with him by plane. The surviving shearwater (one died) was released in the Boston Harbor and was back in its nest burrow 12 1/2 days later, having traveled 3,200 miles at an average rate of more than 250 miles per day. And presumably the bird did some wandering rather than pursuing the shortest course.

Other compensations on Rhum included a family of Common Eiders *(Somateria mollissima)* swimming around in the bay, European Oystercatchers *(Haematopus ostralegus)* and a Eurasian Curlew *(Numenius arquata)* feeding on the mud flats, and a dozen or so car.ion-feeding Eurasian (Hooded) Crows *(Corvus corone cornix)*. Then the climax—a Black Guillemot *(Cepphus grylle)*, my first, flew over.

Some land birds occur on the island, especially in and around the plantations near the castle—Robins, Song Thrushes, Winter Wrens, Dunnocks, and Chaffinches. Another first for me was a Gray Wagtail *(Motacilla cinerea)*, a handsome male perched on stones in a brook and flitting about in search of food. (The other wagtails, the Pied and Yellow—*M. alba* and *M. flava*—were seen elsewhere.) Another prize was a beautiful male Stonechat *(Saxicola torquata)*, perched on a fence along an old road.

On the following day we circumnavigated St. Kilda, huge rocky stacks protruding five hundred or more feet out of the water and featuring incredible numbers of sea birds. St. Kilda is the British home of the Fulmar *(Fulmarus glacialis)*, one of the world's largest populations. It also harbors the world's largest gannetry, 30,000 to 40,000 birds. And the comical Puffins *(Fratercula arctica)*, Martha's favorite sea bird, were everywhere. James Fisher estimated their numbers at St. Kilda as 1 to 3 million. Puffins have regained their numbers from a previous low when a local priest declared the fishy birds permissible for Catholics to eat on Friday; hence the Puffins were nearly exterminated before their nesting islands became sanctuaries.

The next day we passed numerous islands, some of them so shrouded with mist that neither birds nor landscapes were visible. Then we circled around Foula, home for nine hundred pairs of Great Skuas *(Catharacta skua)*—another superlative, the largest colony in the northern hemisphere. One of the 37 hardy people living on the bleak island waved to us as we passed.

Another ornithological highlight of the cruise: the following day we docked briefly at Lerwick, in the Shetlands, and unloaded 600 women and elderly or less active men for a day of shopping and sightseeing on the island. Martha made the most of it; she bought some hand-knit woolen goods and engaged an elderly woman whose home she visited to knit sweaters and tams for our grandchildren, Tanya and Tasha, for Christmas. The rest of us, 250 supposedly physically fit men went on to try for a landing on Noss, never before attempted by a ship the size of the *Devonia*. I wasn't physically fit, as my underpinning was still bothering me, but I didn't let on. We had been warned that it might be a difficult landing, even impossible if strong winds prevailed. Then there was the gloomy prospect of sudden cancellation under adverse conditions; or, if a storm threatened while we were ashore, a warning blast from the ship's siren would call us back. Literally months of preparation had gone into the building of a floating dock by means of which agile-footed passengers could scramble ashore.

As it turned out the landing was perfect. The waters were calm and we were relayed in small boats to the improvised dock from which we scampered ashore with hardly a wet foot. We spent several glorious hours on the island. Many terns, both Common and Arctic *(Sterna hirundo* and *S. paradisaea),* were milling around the landing site. I had difficulty, as nearly everyone does, distinguishing the Common Terns with their black-tipped red bills from the Arctic Terns with their all-red bills and their more deeply forked tails. We found nests of both the Great Skua and Arctic Skua or (to Americans) Parasitic Jaegers *(Stercorarius parasiticus).* It was getting late in the season, but we found a two-egg nest of a Great Skua, perhaps deserted, and another active nest with one egg just hatching and one chick still in the nest. Two jaegers, typically aggressive in defending their nests divebombed me and brushed through my hair but didn't draw blood (as sometimes happens). Skylarks were numerous on and over the moors, some still singing, but probably the songs were not full strength, or else they just didn't measure up to their reputed quality.

At the far end of the island we came to the famous bird cliffs of Noss, with closer views of colonies of sea birds than we had seen at other islands. Martha had our only camera on the tour in the Shetlands, so I got no pictures, but at our next stop in the Orkneys we climbed up the steep incline to Marwick Head and once again got marvelous views, as well as photographs, of birds on the nesting ledges.

We spent most of the next day in the Orkneys. We disembarked in relays at Kirkwall; then half of the passengers (450) took a morning bus tour of the island and the other half went in the afternoon. We drove past prosperous-looking farms with waving fields of grain, viewed with awe the prehistoric ruins (the Standing Stones of Stennes, their origin still largely unsolved), and shopped for woolens and native handicraft in Kirkwall.

The visit to the Orkneys was our last stop before final disembarking in Leith (and Edinburgh), but we sailed at close range around three famous bird islands along the east coast of Scotland. The most northern of these, Fair Isle, is the site of an active bird observatory where scientific studies of bird migration are being carried out. The idea for the observatory was largely dreamed up by George Waterston and a companion while they were prisoners of war in a German camp during World War II. Waterston bought the island in 1948, then it was taken over by the National Trust for Scotland in 1954. Now the formerly largely uninhabited island is being resettled, a hostel with modern facilities accommodates many visiting bird watchers, scientists, and tourists. Revitalized craftspeople sell knitwear and other handmade goods to visitors.

Toward the end of our cruise we passed by another bird observatory on the Isle of May, an island noted for its wealth of bird life ever since 1508 when James IV visited the island to "schut at fowlis with the culveryn." Now the cliff dwellers—shags, kittiwakes, and alcids—are fully protected, and an amazing number of migrants, including Scandivanian birds en route to England and the Continent, visit the island. More than 250 species of birds, including breeding birds, birds of passage, and winter residents, have been recorded on the island.

Our last big event of the cruise was the circumnavigation of Bass Rock, another well-known gannetry from which the Gannet *Morus bassana* received its name. Bass Rock was made famous by Bryan Nelson, who spent three years on the rock studying the Gannets, with his wife as "field assistant, cook, secretary, companion, and critic" (Bryan's words).

On July 22 we sailed into Leith, where 600 of our passengers disembarked; the remaining 300, destined for the IOC meetings in Oxford, remained on board overnight. The next day was spent in Edinburgh, where we were royally entertained by various officials sponsoring the cruise. In the morning many of us visited the Edinburgh Zoo, which has one of the finest exhibits of penguins in the world. I remembered an MSU lecture program that showed pictures of the penguins being let out for a promenade up one street and around the block for their daily constitutional, then returning to their confinement. They seemed much at home in the zoo; some were sliding down a sluiceway and plunging into a pool below, others were just standing around. Three King Penguins stood motionless under a rocky ledge with their backs to us. They reminded me of bad boys standing in a corner for punishment, but actually they were brooding eggs or young.

In the afternoon we took a tour of the city, were well entertained by our hilarious story-telling bus driver, saw many of the historic sights of the city, and then returned to the club headquarters for a reception and evening of entertainment.

All in all, the cruise was an outstanding success, and the many planners who worked so long and diligently on it are to be congratulated. Fortunately, the weather, which can be miserable in that part of Britain—even by British standards—cooperated fully; otherwise the bars, lounge, and recreation facilities on the boat would have been jammed to capacity. Many passengers spent much of their time on deck sunning, visiting, and watching for birds. Hats off to the SOC and its heroic staff!

All too soon it was time to leave Scotland for the IOC meetings in Oxford. Confusion prevailed at Edinburgh's Waverly Station, in spite of two years of struggle on the part of the SOC to arrange for a special night train with sleepers to transport us to Oxford. Martha and I managed to secure a berth, but some others did not and wandered about the train during the night, knocking on doors to try to find a place to sleep.

The International Ornithological Congress (July 24 to 30)

The night train from Edinburgh brought us into Oxford early Sunday morning in time for a breakfast snack that had been arranged for us. Delegates were assigned to rooms in the various colleges. Martha and I were housed in Jesus College, but I (and other men) had to go downstairs, across one end of a courtyard, and into the basement of another building for washrooms.

After the delightful week-long cruise around the Scottish Bird Islands, the meetings of the congress seemed something of a letdown. Those held at Cornell University in 1962 (the congress meets every four years), I thought, were better and more efficiently organized. Morning sessions at Oxford, Monday through Saturday (except for Wednesday, which was an all-day excursion), were devoted to plenary sessions with twenty invited speakers, noted authorities from a dozen or more different countries, presenting papers on original research or reviews of special topics. Most of the papers were interesting and informative but not outstanding; often they were simply reviews of the work done in a particular field. However, the plenary morning sessions were perhaps the best part of the paper programs.

The afternoon meetings were impossible. They were divided into six concurrent sessions in different buildings widely scattered over the campus. One had a choice of sitting through any one of the six concurrent sessions on a given afternoon, with one or more of the papers in a foreign language, or of dashing from place to place in hope (often futile) of getting in on a desired report. Moreover, my leg cramps had become so severe by now (my problem proved to be varicose veins, remedied when I reached home) that I had difficulty walking from one building to another. Most of the papers I was able to attend were less than stimulating. Probably I was biased—a notable case of sour grapes?—because my proposed paper on DDT in birds, based on nearly ten years of research, was rejected by the program committee. The reason soon became apparent. Among the more than one hundred papers listed, only one (Wingate on the endangered Bermuda Petrel) dealt with conservation and only one (another was canceled) on pesticides. Several of Britain's distinguished workers on toxic chemicals were present but did not report on their research. Even as late as 1966, reports on the effects of pesticides were unaccountably unpopular at ornithological meetings, and some journals would not publish such papers.

The film sessions, held every evening Monday through Friday, included 34 listed movies, but there were two concurrent showings in different buildings, so that a person could see only half of the films. The pictures were outstanding; I never cease to marvel at the photographic perfection some have attained in filming birds. On the screen we saw birds from all over the world: Ostriches in Africa, birds of paradise in New Guinea, Lyrebirds in Australia, albatrosses on Midway, Galapagos finches, flamingos in the high Andes, and many outstanding European and American films.

Wednesday (the 27th) was set aside for excursions, with several choices available. Most of us elected to go to Slimbridge to see the Wildfowl Trust's outstanding collection of waterfowl. To accommodate all who wanted to go, we were divided into two parties. One group went directly to Slimbridge for a three-hour tour of the grounds, the other group visited other points of interest en route and went to Slimbridge in the afternoon. Some "en route" points of interest included Winston Churchill's estate, a veritable museum of treasures; Berkeley Castle, famous for its historical collections; and Stonehenge.

The visit at the Wildfowl Trust was the chief ornithological attraction. Sir Peter Scott and his staff have assembled there the world's largest collection of living wildfowl; only 21 of the 156 known species were lacking. Research projects were explained by staff members. Their eminently successful effort in raising Nenes (Hawaiian Geese) for restocking were described. From the original three geese acquired by the trust, hundreds of progeny have been raised; by 1966 about 90 had been flown to some of the remoter islands of Hawaii to replenish the nearly extinct native supply there.

Another plus for the congress was the opportunity to meet so many ornithologists from other parts of the world. A colleague of mine at MSU told me not to feel slighted if he ignored me at the meetings: he wanted to spend his time visiting with foreign ornithologists. I am usually something of a recluse at meetings (I attend the paper sessions rather than hobnob with people in the halls), but the sessions in Britain (the I.C.B.P., I.O.U. and Scottish cruise) provided extraordinary opportunities for meeting colleagues. On the congress membership list I checked the names of 83 foreign ornithologists from 30 different countries whom I met or at least had some association with.

My birding afield suffered at Oxford for lack of time, my locomotor difficulties, and the absence of good birding spots within walking distance of the campus. The visit at Slimbridge, of course, was an exception—a display of most of the world's waterfowl—but birders consider it unethical to include captive or restrained birds on their life lists. My total list of wild birds for three weeks (July 2 to 23) spent in Switzerland, England, and Scotland in 1966 was only 104 species, 18 of which were new (not recorded in 1964). The total for the two visits to northwestern Europe was 137, not a very good showing compared to Britain's all-time list of 424 species (Fisher, 1947). But it did include a good representation of birds characteristic of northwestern Europe. I was a little disappointed, however, not to see or hear a Nightingale, Britain's highly regarded songster (but which John Burroughs said didn't measure up to the Hermit Thrushes in the Catskills). But the Nightingale barely reaches southern England and its season of song is short, so the chances of hearing one sing as late as July, I was told, were quite slim.

References

Fisher, J. *The Birds of Britain.* London: Collins, 1947.

Huxley, J.S. "The Courtship Habits of the Great Crested Grebe." London: Proceedings Zoological Society, 1914, pp. 491–562.

Koskimies, J. "The Life of the Swift, *Micropus apus* (L), in Relation to Weather." *Ann. Acad. Scient. Fennicae* 4, Helsinki, 15: (1950) pp. 1–151.

Mazzeo, R. "Homing of the Manx Shearwater." *Auk,* 70: (1953) pp. 200-201.

Nelson, B. "The Breeding Biology of the Gannet *Sula bassana* on the Bass Rock, Scotland." *Ibis,* 108: (1966) pp. 584–626.

Peterson, R.T; G. Mountfort; and P.A.D. Hollom. *A Field Guide to the Birds of Britain and Europe.* Boston: Houghton Mifflin, 1954.

Wurster, C.F., Jr., and D.B. Wingate. "DDT Residues and Declining Reproduction in the Bermuda Petrel." *Science,* 159: (1968) pp. 979-981.

Yapp, W.B. *Birds and Woods.* London, New York: Oxford University Press, 1962.

———. *The Life and Organization of Birds.* London: Edward Arnold Ltd., 1970.

CHAPTER 11

India, Nepal, and Ceylon

I HAD GOOD REASON—or, at least, good excuse—for wanting to go to India. India led all foreign countries except Canada in the number of students enrolled at Michigan State University. As a pre-medical enrolling officer and laboratory instructor, I had had only minor responsibilities with most of these students, but four of them took my advanced ornithology (Birds of the World) course and knew more about the birds of that part of Asia than I did.

Hence, it was not too difficult to persuade the administration that I ought to go to India to learn more about birds in that part of the world. My teaching duties that winter term in 1969 were light: a small class of advanced students in an avian anatomy and physiology course. By timely coincidence, I had a graduate student, Wayne Shooks, working on his doctorate in avian anatomy. He took over the class for me during my four-week absence. (On my return I gave the students a final exam over the material covered by Mr. Shooks. They did so well on the exam that I was actually a little embarrassed. Perhaps Wayne should have been teaching the course in the first place!)

Two of the students from India merit special mention. One was R. M. Naik, who had just finished his doctorate at the University of Baroda in India under the guidance of Dr. J. C. George, coauthor of the George and Berger text *Avian Myology*. Naik had worked on the histology of the pectoral muscles in birds. I had served as "foreign referee" (a requirement for Indian doctorate students, I believe) on Naik's committee. I was of little or no help to him on histology or myology problems, but was, I hope, of some assistance in editing the dissertation. I was offered 100 rupees for the assignment. Not having the slightest notion then of the value of a rupee, I had visions of being able to retire on that amount. It turned out to be twenty-five dollars—minus certain deductions required by the Indian government. Dr. Naik (Ram, as we called him, because we couldn't pronounce his full first name) spent a year with us at MSU. He was a congenial companion for other ornithology students and a help to me in my Birds of the World course.

The other special student was Robert Fleming, Jr., an American who had spent much of his life in India. His father was on the staff of a mission school in North India, but he was also a competent ornithologist and botanist who, with his son, collected specimens for American museums, particularly the Field Museum in Chicago. Mrs. Fleming (Dr. Bethel) was a medical missionary who had dedicated her life to ministering to needy Indian, and later Nepalese, people.

Young Bob came to Michigan State to work under me for advanced degrees: his masters' on the *Comparative Myology of the Syrinx in the Avian Family Timaliidae* (1962), based on material collected by his father in Nepal; and his Ph.D. on *The Birds of Mussoorie, U.P., India: A Distributional and Ecological Study* (1967), carried out in India after his return to that country. Over the years we became well acquainted with the Flemings. We had met the parents (Bob and Bethel) at the International Ornithological Congress in Oxford, England, in 1966. Bob, Jr., served as our guide while we were in Nepal, and Martha visited Dr. Bethel's Nepalese clinics in Pharping and Chapagaon. Later, father and son collaborated in producing *Birds of Nepal* (1976), which I helped edit. Grace Nies Fletcher tells the story of the remarkable family in her book, *The Fabulous Flemings of Kathmandu* (1964).

For our trip to India, Nepal, and Ceylon, we joined a tour group visiting wildlife sanctuaries in those countries. Joining a well-organized tour is often the best way of seeing the most with the least effort and least expense; let the tour leaders work out the annoying travel details.

An additional incentive in our case was that Harold Peters, an old friend, was the tour leader. Harold is a versatile zoologist. In his early years he worked on the ectoparasites of birds for his M.S. degree (1926) at Ohio State University. He was an entomologist with the U.S. Bureau of Entomology and a biologist with the Fish and Wildlife Service until his "retirement." Then he served as a pesticide adviser for the National Audubon Society. He retired again and became Executive Director of the Farmington River Watershed Association in Connecticut. Somewhere in between he found time to coauthor the Peters and Burleigh book on the *Birds of Newfoundland* (1951). In addition, over the past decade he has been conducting ornithological safaris all over the world for several travel agencies.

Harold and I became acquainted when we were both involved in pesticide studies. We cried on one another's shoulders on several occasions. I had been in trouble in Michigan for insisting that campus robins were dying of DDT, and Harold had had trouble with a mattress firm for saying that he wouldn't want to sleep on a dieldrin-impregnated mattress.

On Our Way

As with our trip to Switzerland, our flight to India in late January was not without mishaps. At the Kennedy Airport in New York we watched the baggage carrier go around and around. My large suitcase, containing all my belongings except carry-on luggage (which, fortunately, included my binoculars and camera) was missing. Apparently it had been left on the plane and gone on to Baltimore. At least it didn't show up in New York that evening. Harried officials tried to help, took detailed notes on everything I could remember as being in the suitcase (even the color of the neckties), and promised to send it on (if found) to one of our stops in Amsterdam, Athens, Beirut, or New Delhi. (I recovered it four days later in New Delhi.)

During our brief stop in Amsterdam, rain confined us to the spacious terminal until our plane left for Athens. We flew over much rugged terrain in south central Europe and northern Greece—the highest mountains still covered with snow in January—and deplaned in Athens in the rain. We were supposed to remain in Athens long enough for a cursory inspection of the city's ancient ruins and for me to find a new bird or two (I had never been in southern Europe before), but we had arrived in a storm—the worst weather, one native said, that he had ever seen there. So we were willingly herded into a waiting room with a snack bar and souvenirs to await transit to Beirut.

We landed in Beirut in the rain and were bused to the Hotel Riviera. Martha and I had a luxurious room with a balcony overlooking the stormy Mediterranean, where the breaking waves dashed high on the rocky shore. Next morning I tried unsuccessfully to do a little birding along the wet and flooded streets. Somehow my rubbers had been separated; I had one, but the other was in my lost suitcase. I got wet feet—the rubberless foot wetter than the other.

We spent the rest of the day on a tour of the city, a trip to Dog River to see its ancient ruins in the forenoon, and a jaunt to Byblos in the afternoon. A scheduled visit to the University of Beirut that I especially looked forward to proved largely useless because of rain. However, the rain let up long enough for our visit to Byblos, the oldest continuously inhabited city in the world. The excavations, still incomplete, and the story of the buried city were amazing revelations. Both Martha and I had cameras on this trip, so Eastman made a good profit that afternoon.

Our last stop in Beirut was at a rug factory, where some of our party ordered Oriental rugs to be shipped home, but the several hundred-dollar price tag on most of them (greatly reduced, we were told!) was too much for me. The free coffee was also too much—it was so thick and strong I couldn't drink it.

India

Then an overnight flight took us to New Delhi, bypassing Teheran where the runways were reported to be glazed with ice. We landed in New Delhi before dawn. *It wasn't raining.* In fact, we encountered very little rain on all the rest of our trip.

The long fast ride from the airport to Hotel Ashoka in the early dawn was exciting as well as exasperating. Birds seemed to be everywhere as they flushed out ahead of the speeding car. The numerous crows had to be House Crows *(Corvus splendens),* one of India's most abundant birds and one of the few that can eke out a living in congested cities. They are so bold and fearless that they sometimes enter open windows and snatch food and even silverware from tables. The equally abundant smaller dark brown birds were Common, or Indian, Mynas *(Acridotheres tristis).* The long-tailed parrotlike birds streaming across the road proved to be Rose-ringed Parakeets *(Psittacula krameri),* and the hawks soaring overhead proved to be Black Kites *(Milvus migrans),* India's most common raptor.

At the hotel, before and after our tours of the city, I managed to sneak in a little birding around the well-planted lawns and gardens. My bird list, which eventually totalled 265 species, is too lengthy to mention each species as seen, hence I have relegated all but the more impressive finds to an annotated list at the end of this chapter. Best find for me at the hotel was a Hoopoe *(Upupa epops),* a bird so odd that it is placed in a family (Upupidae) by itself.

In the gardens I also found my first Tailor Birds *(Orthotomus sutorius),* plain-looking sylviids that build their nests of one or more leaves sewed together with plant fibers to form a pensile cup lined with grasses. On the hotel grounds were three of the Old World's 110 species of bulbuls (Pycnonotidae): the Red-vented *(Pycnonotus cafer)*, White-cheeked *(P. leucogenys),* and Red-whiskered *(P. jocosus).* The last has been widely transplanted into other lands, including Florida. More spectacular was an Indian Tree-Pie *(Dendrocitta vagabunda),* a handsome, long-tailed, jaylike corvid. (We saw the other species, the Himalayan Tree-Pie, later in the hill country of Nepal.)

Birding around Delhi was somewhat incidental and piecemeal. Our time was spent in tours of the city and a visit to Agra (Taj Mahal) before we went on our first big birding spree to Keoladeo Ghana Sanctuary at Bharatpur on January 26. India was celebrating Independence Day in New Delhi. It was said to be just a rehearsal that first morning, but it exceeded—at least in sheer numbers—anything we had seen in Colombia. A mob of thousands of people gathered around the ornate administration buildings to watch the processions—marching bands, soldiers in spic-and-span uniforms, nurses in immaculate white, students in special costumes, and the inevitable elephants. Amid all that glittering splendor, people seemed unmindful that the thousands of ill-clad, presumably homeless people not attending the ceremonies were on the verge of starvation.

I missed the afternoon tour. Word came that my lost suitcase was at the airport. Retrieving it proved to be a frustrating ordeal. One car and driver had to be diverted from the tour to take me to the airport. Some twenty or more persons got involved; forms had to be filled out, more than a dozen signatures secured, and then when I started to pick up my bag from the others I was restrained. Someone had to pick it out and hand it to me (for a good tip). The reason cited for so much red tape was that it gave some employment to needy people.

Next morning we toured the sights in and around New Delhi, but the several attractions visited are somewhat mixed up in my mind. The first was an inspection of Humayan's Tomb, where a snake-charmer exhibited his presumably defanged cobra for photographers for a fee. Then an English-speaking guide recited the history of the tomb, but it was largely lost on me; I was more interested in the Dusky Crag Martins *(Hirundo concolor)* squabbling with House Sparrows over nesting or roosting crevices in an archway and with the House Swifts *(Apus affinis)* soaring overhead.

Then we visited some ancient ruins that included a twelfth-century tower (Quitb Minar) with lookouts that had been barricaded to prevent suicidal people from jumping off the high platforms. Another attraction was a long row of craft shops where workers, including a nine-year-old boy learning his father's trade, demonstrated their skills. And while viewing these truly impressive sights, I discovered my first Little Brown Dove *(Streptopelia senegalensis)* nesting along a briar-covered fence, a Brahminy Myna *(Sturnus pagodarum)* perched on one of the towers, and a Fire-breasted Flowerpecker *(Dicaeum ignipectus)* in a tree amid the ruins.

Another highly worthwhile sight that morning was Birla Temple, one of the most ornate structures I have ever seen. Many people, the women in beautiful saris blowing in the breeze, were milling around on the spacious plaza. We had to take our shoes off to enter the interior of the temple.

That afternoon we flew to Agra to see the Taj Mahal, truly one of the seven man-made wonders of the world. Our guide told us the amazing story: A reigning monarch started to build that magnificent edifice as a memorial to his wife, but he was imprisoned by his son before the building was completed. The father died in prison.

On the well-kept lawn in front of the Taj Mahal we watched a group of Jungle Babblers *(Turdoides striatus)*, often, but not invariably, sorting themselves into groups of seven (hence the local name "seven sisters"). On the mud flats behind the Taj Mahal was a good assortment of stilts and plovers, apparently unconcerned by the human skeleton that had washed ashore nearby.

Before dawn the next day we were off on the thirty-mile jaunt to Keoladeo Ghana Sanctuary at Bharatpur, one of the finest wildlife sanctuaries in India, if not in the world. As soon as it was light enough to identify the shadowy forms visible along the way, we stopped occasionally to watch the numerous storks, ibises, and doves. A Peacock *(Pavo cristata)*, assumed to be a wild bird, was easily identifiable in a roadside field. At one place a dense cluster of White-backed Vultures *(Gyps bengalensis)* was feeding on an animal carcass, now stripped to the bones. We were amused to see a man standing in the shallow water with the vultures while brushing his teeth with a stick. Later Dr. Aggarwahl, an Indian on the zoology staff at MSU, told me that some people in India use acacia sticks *(Asadirachta indica,* the toothbrush tree) frayed at the end for cleaning their teeth. Judging by the whiteness of some of the teeth we saw, that method may well have merit—as effective as Close-up or Crest.

Inside the gates at the sanctuary was a rest house where we paused for refreshments and met Salim Ali, India's 80-year-old dean of ornithologists, coauthor (with S. Dillon Ripley) of the ten-volume *Handbook of the Birds of India and Pakistan.* An active bird-banding program, initiated by H. Elliott McClure, a transplanted American who had worked with Harold Peters on Mourning Dove investigations, was in progress. A Wryneck *(Jynx torquilla)*, a Golden-backed Woodpecker *(Dinopium benghalense)*, and a Bluethroat *(Erithacus svecicus)* had been captured in the nets and were banded and released after we had had a chance to examine and photograph them.

Then V.S. Saxena, divisional forest officer at Bharatpur, led us over the jeep trails through several thousand acres of shallow ponds that harbor enormous concentrations of both breeding and visiting water birds—herons, storks, ibises, ducks and geese, cranes, rails, and kingfishers. Some wooded spots and the acacia-bordered impoundments provided homes for many songbirds. My list for that one morning totaled some 90 species of birds, and I missed quite a few that Mr. Saxena tried to point out for us. With his years of experience on the sanctuary he knew what to expect and could identify birds almost unerringly, without glasses, at distances beyond my field of recognition.

Particularly impressive sights were the concentrations of Sarus Cranes *(Grus antigone)* and a surprising showing (47, my notes said) of the rare and endangered Siberian Crane *(G. leucogeranus)*. Intermingled with cranes were egrets (3 species), herons (3 species), cormorants (2 species), large flocks of Graylag Geese *(Anser anser)*, eight species of ducks (including four "American" forms), and kingfishers (3 species). We examined a large rookery of Painted Storks *(Ibis leucocephalus),* a part of the two to three thousand pairs that nest in the sanctuary and are said to consume one hundred or so tons of fish during the nesting season. During our visit in January, the nests were largely abandoned, but a few adults and many immatures perched in the white-washed acacia trees. A special treat for me (because of my special interest in thrushes) was a close view of a Magpie-Robin *(Copsychus saularis),* a favorite cage bird in many parts of the world because of its superior song and handsome black-and-white plumage. Even with the expert help of Mr. Saxena, however, I got frustrated trying to identify and remember the various babblers, bulbuls, warblers, chats, and flycatchers seen along the trails.

Mammals, except for domesticated cattle and buffaloes, are not conspicuous at Bharatpur, but we did see black bucks *(Antilope cervicarpa),* Sambhar deer *(Cervus unicolor),* and spotted deer *(Axis axis).* Many smaller mammals occur on the sanctuary, but they are more secretive and often nocturnal, and so more difficult to observe. Unfortunately, large numbers of cattle and buffaloes belonging to the native farmers of Bharatpur (who have grazing privileges in the sanctuary) are greatly overgrazing the area, to the detriment of wildlife.

With some reluctance, understandably, we left the sanctuary in late afternoon to return to Agra and New Delhi. Our route took us through crowded villages still celebrating Independence Day. The streets were jammed with people, afoot or on bicycles, as well as with pigs, cattle, and assorted animals. Nonetheless, our drivers sped through the crowds with constant use of the horn while people merely moved nonchalantly aside and, miraculously, it seems, no one got hit. En route to Agra we stopped briefly to view the ruins and the well-kept gardens at the famous Walled City of Fatepur Sikri, a deserted city said to have been abandoned when the water supply failed. The ruling monarch had had three wives—a Hindu, a Moslem, and a Christian, but (wisely) he housed them separately.

Nepal

Next day (January 27) we went to Kathmandu, Nepal, for five days of birding and sightseeing in that country. We stayed at Hotel Annapurna, a very pleasant and comfortable facility operated by an Irish manager. With the able guidance of young Bob Fleming, Nepal provided the best birding of our whole trip, although it was spread out over several days instead of being concentrated into a few hours as at Keoladeo Ghana. My total list for Nepal was 113 species, a small showing compared to the nearly 800 that the Flemings have recorded in their *Birds of Nepal,* but our birding was limited to one full day and three half days during the Nepalese winter.

Three afternoons were spent touring the fascinating ancient villas around Kathmandu, Patan (Durbar Square), and Chapagaon. Ornate temples, palaces, Buddhist shrines, and other impressive edifices dominated the scenes. Narrow, dusty, cobblestone streets, lined by rather dismal shops, thronged with people young and old, mostly ill clad, but cheerful and friendly. Cattle, pigs, chickens, and monkeys also roamed the streets. We shopped, chatted with natives (some could speak English), and viewed with awe the magnificent buildings, some of which dated back several hundred years.

On our first evening in Kathmandu, Harold, Martha, and I visited the Flemings in their home. They surprised us with a good assortment of both Nepalese and American foods, including pumpkin pie a la mode and a delicious drink that proved to be Tang. Then they brought out their latest collection of Nepalese birds, beautifully prepared specimens, some quite rare, awaiting shipment to the Field Museum in Chicago.

On our first morning afield, young Bob led us up to Kakani Ridge, where a summit hotel was surrounded by neat cane-thatched huts. We climbed steep grades where the bare, dry hillsides (Nepal has serious erosion problems) were terraced for growing crops during the wetter seasons. A bus stuck in the dirt road blocked our passage for a while, but this gave us an opportunity to look for roadside birds. A Great Himalayan Barbet *(Megalaima virens)* made a spectacular exit from a tree just as a Long-tailed Minivet *(Pericrocotus ethologus)* flew in. Several flocks of Slaty-headed Parakeets *(Psittacula himalayana)* streamed across the road. A Blue

230

Whistling Thrush *(Myiophoneus caeruleus)* and a Rusty-cheeked Scimitar Babbler *(Pomatorhinus erythrogenys)* posed for us in our path, and two Himalayan Tree-pies *(Dendrocitta formosae)* greeted us near the summit house. Later, two Wall Creepers *(Tichodroma muraria),* presumably winter visitors, displayed their red wing patches as they fluttered across the road onto a rocky ledge.

But the most exciting birding came the following day—a full day afield at Godaveri and in the surrounding hills. I recorded 78 species that day (Bob had 88), 45 of which were new for me. First we visited the grounds of a Catholic boys school where a grove of tall trees harbored a Chestnut-bellied Nuthatch *(Sitta castanea)* and a Brown-fronted Pied Woodpecker *(Dendrocopos auriceps).* A Scarlet Minivet *(Pericrocotus flammeus)* complemented the long-tailed species seen the previous day. In the thickets along a fencerow we saw a pair of Common Rose Finches *(Carpodacus erythrinus);* we found the Pink-browed species *(C. rhodochrous)* later at a higher elevation. I am still confused about the four species of laughing thrushes seen (actually babblers in the genus *Garrulax*), elusive birds that dash quickly into concealment and are thus hard to identify in spite of prominent markings; on one of them, the White-crested Laughing Thrush *(G. leucolophus),* I saw only the crest and head as it perched momentarily on an exposed branch before darting into thicker cover. And then there were the smaller babblers (5 species), some seen in full view, others affording only quick glimpses.

At the base of the mountain we stopped at a camp where the Waltners, Bob and his wife, were collecting birds for the University of Kansas, their alma mater. A small table was set up outdoors for skinning out specimens. They set me to work, and I did a hurry-up job on one of their Scarlet Minivets. A beautiful Fire-tailed Sunbird *(Aethopya ignicauda)* and several Red-headed Tits *(Aegithalos concinnus)* came to watch the proceedings. In a brook bed near the camp we found a wounded Spotted Forktail *(Enicurus maculatus)* that had escaped Waltner earlier in the day. (I couldn't catch it either.)

At this point several in our party returned to town, while Harold, the two Bobs, and I proceeded up a steep mountain trail to an abandoned iron mine. We found a dozen or so new birds for our list, among them several Hoary Barwings *(Actinodura nipalensis),* a timaliid that young Bob Fleming said was quite rare, a Striated Green Bulbul *(Pycnonotus striatus)* that posed perfectly for us, and a White-collared Blackbird *(Turdus albocinctus)* high up in a tree but offering a good view. Then I discovered (all by myself) a female Maroon Oriole *(Oriolus traillii)* and caught a glimpse of the handsome male as it flew away. And Bob was kind enough to agree that a large dark hawk I saw flying over the treetops was undoubtedly a Black Eagle *(Ictinaetus malayensis).*

Martha reluctantly forfeited the Godaveri (and one other) birding trip in order to visit Dr. Bethel Fleming's clinics at Pharping and Chapagaon. Some of the patients came to the clinics for routine checkups, but most were suffering, often severely, from a variety of maladies—tuberculosis, elephantiasis, hookworm, badly infected hands or feet, and skin diseases. Some members of our party were so impressed by the work being carried out at the inadequately equipped clinics that they contributed substantially to new and much-needed facilities being planned for Nepal.

Our next trek was to Pokhara, a short flight from Kathmandu. We rode on a cargo plane that had no regular seats; we sat on benches or on baggage. There was no real airport in Pokhara; we simply landed in a grass field, where a group of people had assembled to watch the plane come in. An open market, with a good supply of fruits and vegetables displayed in front of a row of shops, attracted a few unenthusiastic buyers. Squalid huts, carts pulled by cattle, and native carriers with heavy loads of wood or other materials were among the scenes that greeted us. The Annapurna mountains, with jagged towering Fishtail Peak (one of the features we had come to see) were visible at times, but were obscured by clouds most of the day.

At midday we walked leisurely along an old road to look for birds, had a picnic lunch, and then young Bob and I went on to Lake Phewatal where we counted a record nine Great Crested Grebes *(Podiceps cristatus),* two more than Bob's previous high count. Several Pond Herons or Paddybirds *(Ardeola grayii)* also occupied the lake. Other birds seen en route to or from the lake included a Steppe Eagle *(Aquila nipalensis),* an Egyptian Vulture *(Neophron percnopterus),* a Brahminy Kite *(Haliastur indus),* Crimson-breasted Barbets *(Megalaima haemacephala),* a Hair-Crested Drongo *(Dicrurus hottentottus),* a flock of Striated, or Red-rumped, Swallows *(Hirundo daurica),* and several species of flycatchers (Muscicapidae).

On our last day in Nepal, Bob, Harold, and I took a brief morning trip to look for the rare and elusive Spiny Babbler *(Turdoides nipalensis),* once thought extinct but rediscovered in Nepal where the Flemings have found that it is not particularly rare. I didn't see one; Bob heard one chirp and caught a glimpse of it in a thicket before it disappeared completely. There was some consolation for me, however, in seeing a beautiful Himalayan Rubythroat *(Erithacus pectoralis)* hopping along obligingly in the path ahead of us and displaying its black-bordered bright red throat, white forehead, and white-edged tail.

Calcutta

Our trip from Nepal to Kaziranga Wildlife Sanctuary in Assam entailed a brief overnight stop at the Grand Hotel in Calcutta. The hotel really was grand, but it was set in dismal surroundings. The Calcutta we saw then was the most miserable place I have ever seen; nine million people jammed into crowded quarters, many homeless, ill clad, and starving, sleeping in the streets or on doorsteps with or without covering blankets. Wagons patroled the streets at dawn to carry away the dead.

Fortunately, on our return trip from Kaziranga a week later, we had a chance to see Calcutta under more auspicious circumstances. Apparently there was a shortage of rooms in the Grand Hotel that night, so Martha and I were given an ambassador's suite (we assumed at no extra cost) complete with kitchenette, refrigerator, and a conference room that we couldn't use. We spent the next day visiting the better parts of the city: the zoo with its superb exhibits of native birds, the magnificent government administration buildings, and Zain Palace—perhaps the most lavishly ornate structure seen on our whole trip. People here, as at the equally magnificent Birla Temple in Delhi, were not poorly clothed; most men were well dressed and the women wore incredibly beautiful saris. But once again we were impressed by the sharp contrast between the "haves" and the "have nots" and the apparent utter indifference of the former toward the latter.

That evening we took the opportunity to look up David and Mary Lamb, who operated a mission church and school in Calcutta. They had been our guests in East Lansing when Martha was president of the Missionary Society of Peoples Church. Martha had corresponded with the Lambs and with Gordon Liu, whose family fled from China to India, where Gordon continued his education in the Lambs' school. We had sponsored Gordon through Christian Children's Fund and were anxious to meet him in person. Mrs. Lamb took us to "The best Chinese restaurant in the city." Rev. Lamb had another meeting that evening and couldn't accompany us, but we met Gordon Liu, who proved to be a fine young lad who was finishing his schooling in Calcutta and planned to emigrate to Canada with his family as soon as they could manage it.

Kaziranga

Kaziranga Wildlife Sanctuary, in a remote and relatively undisturbed part of Assam, is comprized of 166 square miles of marshy fields, small lakes, and patches of woods. It is one of the last stands of the endangered Indian or one-horned rhinoceros; more than half of the country's total population resides on the sanctuary. Kaziranga is accessible by plane from Calcutta via Gauhati and Jorhat and then by small motor cars the remaining 63 miles to the sanctuary. Narrow roads lead through comparatively prosperous-looking country with tea plantations, military installations, and road construction that give employment to many people. The rest house at the sanctuary is an attractive and reasonably comfortable but not luxurious facility; in fact, we came nearer to "roughing it" here than in any other place on the trip, but I greatly enjoyed the setting. Areas around the lodge could be explored on foot, or for short distances by cars, but travel into the remoter areas is by elephants. We spent three full days and parts of two other days at Kaziranga.

We arrived in mid-afternoon, too late for an extended excursion. So after a tea break, Martha and I strolled over the grounds. We were entertained by several semi-wild monkeys, and we watched the hobbled elephants we were to ride the next morning. Of course we looked for birds but found no new species. After supper we listened for owls and heard two but couldn't identify them.

Meals served at the rest house were bounteous and appealing, but, in spite of our precautions about eating raw vegetables, nearly all of us had digestive upsets of some sort. Fortunately, one of our party, Fred Beecher from Bennington, Vermont, was a pharmacist and had an assortment of remedies on hand for just such emergencies.

Our first full day at Kaziranga was a busy and exciting one. A boy brought tea and cookies to our room at 5:15 A.M. Then we were off for a three-hour pre-breakfast elephant ride. The six elephants were saddled and waiting for us, each with a driver (mahout) who perched astride the elephant's neck and guided it by verbal admonitions, by poking it behind its ear with his feet, and by prodding it with a stick equipped with a sharp metal hook. Each elephant carried two or three passengers plus the mahout. We rode side saddle, of course; an elephant's back is too broad for riding horseback fashion. Climbing aboard was accomplished with the aid of ladders placed beside the kneeling elephants. Blankets for padding, metal bars or ropes for handholds, and footrests made riding safer and more comfortable.

We saw an abundance of game animals on this and subsequent elephant rides: rhinos, many wild buffaloes surrounded by Cattle Egrets, a wild bull elephant that eyed us threateningly from across a protective pond (he pawed the ground but didn't venture into the water), and herds of deer—swamp deer, hog deer, and Sambhars. But birding from the back of an elephant has

234

its drawbacks. It proved almost impossible to keep a bird in view in binoculars from the back of a swaying elephant. We often stopped for viewing and photographing big mammals and some of the larger birds, but an elephant seldom stands perfectly still. Digestive processes, heavings and rumblings in the several stomachs, go on constantly. We flushed many ducks, mostly Mallards, we thought, and one or more species of teal, but seldom were we sure of their identity. However, we could distinguish the grotesque Spot-billed Pelicans *(Pelecanus philippensis);* and at one marsh numerous Indian River Terns *(Sterna aurantia)* and Black-bellied Terns *(S. acuticauda)* circled about us at close range.

Back at the lodge for a late breakfast, I scouted around the premises for birds. Best finds were an extraordinarily brilliant male Verditer Flycatcher *(Muscicapa thalassina),* a female Red-breasted Flycatcher *(M. parva),* and a Blue-throated Barbet *(Megalaima asiatica).*

In the afternoon, saddle sore and with aching bones, we drove leisurely in cars through some woodlands. A proud cock Red Junglefowl *(Gallus gallus),* ancestor of all our domestic strains of chickens, barred our way momentarily, then slipped off into the underbrush. We also flushed a flock of Red Munias *(Estrilda amandava),* mostly females or immatures but including one adult rosy male. En route back to camp in the early dusk, we saw a dozen or so nightjars *(Caprimulgus),* their red eyes glowing in the dim light, but we weren't sure of the species (there were several possibilities).

The next morning's elephant ride—a four-hour jaunt into more rhino country—produced the greatest excitement. Two of our elephants separated from the other four on a supposed shortcut back to camp. As we emerged from dense cane cover at one point we came suddenly upon a rhino guarding her calf. The angered rhino charged my elephant, then veered and attacked the other elephant, opening up three ugly gashes in the animal's flank. We all hung on for dear life; falling off probably would have been fatal. Subsequently there was heated discussion about the incident. An inexperienced mahout was blamed by some for trying to steer his elephant out of the way of the charging rhino, thus exposing the elephant broadside. Had the elephant been made to face the rhino and trumpet a warning (as it did too late), the rhino might not have attacked. At any rate, both elephants were wounded and had to be taken to a veterinarian for repairs. My chief loss, aside from shattered nerves, was the lens from my camera. Somehow it had worked loose and probably dropped into the marsh. I still had a telephoto lens (in another case), but I was seriously handicapped thereafter without the regular lens.

Our last elephant ride the following day, in another unsuccessful attempt to flush a tiger, was more peaceful—and less exciting. But it didn't help matters to learn from a local paper that three woodcutters along the border of the refuge had been trampled to death by a rhino.

A side trip on foot that last day took us to Mikir Village, a settlement of primitive natives back in the hills. The women we saw were small, slender, shy, but full of curiosity. Their cane-thatched, bamboo-frame huts, which we did not enter, looked reasonably neat and well cared for. Women and children peered out at us from partial concealment, but most of them (except some small children) ducked for cover when we tried to photograph them. An elderly bearded chieftain, clad only in a loincloth, apparently presided over the village. The young men were all afield, gathering faggots for firewood or building materials. Unfortunately they have stripped the fields and hillsides of nearly all usable vegetation, leaving the surroundings largely bare and badly eroded.

In spite of difficult birding conditions at Kaziranga, from car, from elephant back, or by searching the virtually treeless hills around Mikir Village, I managed to identify 27 new species of birds. A brushy fencerow and a brook with wooded banks near the rest house were especially productive. Among birds not already mentioned were several yellow-breasted, green-backed Green Pigeons *(Treron phoenicoptera)*; a questionable Jungle Owlet *(Glaucidium radiatum)*, seen fairly closely from elephant back; a Black-naped Green Woodpecker *(Picus canus)* along a wooded path; several Black-headed Orioles *(Oriolus xanthornus);* and a Little Spiderhunter *(Arachnothera longirostris),* feeding on a flowering shrub in front of the rest house on the morning we left. A curious observation was of a Black-headed Yellow Bulbul *(Pycnonotus melanicterus)* that I chanced to see flying into a tree where it was so well camouflaged in the yellow-green leaves that it was difficult to see. I tried to point it out to our sharp-eyed naturalist guide, but even when I designated the branch on which the motionless bird was perched, he couldn't see it. I took a picture and was surprised to discover, when the film was developed, that there were two birds sitting close together, one of which I hadn't seen.

Madras

From Kaziranga we proceeded by car and plane via Calcutta to Madras in southern India. Madras proved to be a pleasanter and more prosperous city than Calcutta, one-fourth the number of people living in twice as much space. There were many fine homes in evidence, including the well-planted estate of Mr. Badshah's nephew, who entertained us lavishly one evening.

Our hotel accommodations were the most luxurious we had in India—a private entrance, an ornate bathroom with large mirrors, a balcony overlooking the gardens, and a spacious living room with a table on which we found a bowl of fruit with a card reading: *compliments of the management.*

We spent most of two days in Madras, visited two famous churches (whose historical significance was largely lost on me), visited Deer Park with its fine collection of deer, peafowl, ducks, and caged birds, and stopped at the Theosophical Society's world headquarters with their impressive gardens, walks, and a wide-spreading banyan tree said to be one of the largest in the world.

In Madras, birding was largely out of the question. In crossing a bridge by car we did see a good assortment of shorebirds on mud flats beside the bridge, but the only birds I recognized were the Black-winged Stilts (not new) and the numerous Brown-headed Gulls *(Larus brunnicephalus)* flying over the river. A disappointment to me was that we could not visit the renowned Vedanthangel Bird Sanctuary with its "ten thousand breeding birds." A severe drought had dried up the marshes and the birds were said to be absent. So the sanctuary was temporarily closed to visitors.

On our return to Madras, after a week in Ceylon, we fared no better birdwise. On a prebreakfast check for birds, Harold and I visited the attractive university campus, which also included a boy's school. Our only new birds were a female Golden Oriole *(Oriolus oriolus)*—a common European bird I had missed in Europe—and a Large Pied Wagtail *(Motacilla maderaspatensis)*, which is usually considered specifically distinct from the wintering European form *(M. alba)*. Later in the day I returned to the campus to photograph the Hoopoes I had seen earlier, but I was surrounded by small boys who bombarded me with questions, wanted their pictures taken (impractical with my telephoto lens), asked to look through my binoculars (but looked at each other instead of birds), and begged me to help them get to the States for further education.

Ceylon

Our week in Ceylon was a mixture of pleasant events, disappointments, and trivial annoyances. En route to Colombo from the airport that first evening, our bus was held up an hour or so by police. We didn't quite comprehend the problem, but apparently our driver lacked a valid permit for the bus he was driving.

I was a little disappointed in Colombo, the capital city where we spent our

Ornithologists looking for birds in the Katana forest in Nepal. Left to right, Harold Peters, Bob Fleming, Jr., Bob Waltner.

Bob Waltner preparing a specimen at his camp in Nepal. Harold Peters and Bob Fleming, Jr. standing at left, Mrs. Waltner and Bob Fleming, Sr. at right.

Rest House at Kaziranga in Assam. Not luxurious quarters but adequate.

Elephant riding in Assam. Loaded and ready to go.

Elephants can go where motor vehicles can not—and are safer, but not entirely safe, from attacks by tigers and rhinos.

first and last days in Ceylon. From glowing accounts I had read in *National Geographic* and from travelogue programs seen at MSU, I had been led to believe that Colombo was a veritable paradise for naturalists. But I found it much like other cities—overpopulated, unattractive shopping districts and many impoverished people. On our drive through the suburbs the next day we saw more attractive housing, with well-kept lawns and gardens, but the grounds were virtually birdless. Even the rice paddies further out of town lacked the usual egrets and Paddybirds. Then it occurred to me, with some chagrin, that colleagues of mine from Michigan State had been sent to Ceylon to promote the use of pesticides for malaria control (perhaps accounting for the overpopulation problem) and to improve rice culture.

But my initial gloom was partially dispelled en route to Kandy. The drive took us up into higher hills where we stopped once to cool off an overheated motor, giving me a chance to find my first White-bellied Drongo *(Dicrurus caerulescens)*. At one point we saw what I took to be vultures circling around in the sky; they proved to be fruit bats that had been flushed from a large roost in a grove of trees. Later we stopped at a tea factory where women were sifting tea leaves and trampling on them with bare feet. And in a tree beside a rushing stream that supplied water to the factory, I discovered a beautiful Golden-fronted Leafbird *(Chloropsis aurifrons)*.

Our accommodations in Kandy proved to be conveniently located. Our second floor balcony overlooked the main street, where we observed a long funeral procession of closely packed people—monks with shaven heads and long yellow gowns, men and women in white robes, and some people in less conventional attire—following an expensive-looking hearse. A high priest had died and all this was his funeral procession.

That evening, again from our balcony, we witnessed a different spectacle. Noisy Jungle Crows *(Corvus macrorhynchus)* by the thousands came streaming into a nocturnal roost in the nearby park. Their clamor outdid the band concert in progress. Their cawing continued, though somewhat subdued, through the night until they dispersed from the roost in the morning.

That morning most of our party were off at 6:30 A.M. for the Royal Botanical Gardens at Peradeniya, said to be (and I agree) among the finest in the world. At the entrance we experienced another minor annoyance. Opening time was 7 A.M. and we were ten minutes early. The gates were open and a man with a watch in hand stood guard. Impatiently we watched him count off the minutes; then at exactly 7 A.M. he let us pass.

But the gardens were well worth the wait: neatly trimmed flower beds and borders, flowering shrubs and trees, a mammoth wide-spreading banyan tree, a long avenue of tall palms, and a fascinating orchid house near a pool of lotus and lilies. Birds were numerous, but those in the tall trees made identification difficult. Still, I identified seven new birds, which, appropriately, included a Thick-billed Flowerpecker *(Dicaeum agile)* and, around the greenhouses, a flock of White-rumped Munias *(Lonchura striata)*. We discovered in the tall trees several noisy Grackles or Hill Mynas *(Gracula religiosa)* and a pair of Koels *(Eudynamys scolopacea),* the male with red eyes and a glossy black plumage, the female a more soberly clad barred brown.

That afternoon we were entertained by a circus of trained elephants. And in the evening the Kandy dancers put on a show for hotel guests. The dancers, especially the men, were gaudily adorned with glittering ornaments. Earlier in the day they had put on a demonstration in an enclosed courtyard for a party of Germans. Harold and I sneaked in uninvited and got several good daylight pictures before we were discovered by the Germans and evicted as intruders.

Next day we took the 94-mile drive to Anuradhapura, where we were lodged two nights in a pleasant rustic rest house located in a large courtyard. En route we stopped at Rock Temple in Dambulla and climbed the long stone stairway leading to the temple on the rocks. Most of our party went inside, but I was tired of taking off my shoes on so many previous occasions and remained outside to watch and photograph the comical monkeys and to look for new birds. Best finds were a Blue-tailed Bee-eater *(Merops philippinus)* and a Loten's Sunbird *(Nectarinia lotenia).* Later, in a Dambulla park, I found a nest attended by a pair of Purple Sunbirds *(N. asiatica).*

Anuradhapura was an ancient town with much history. Two thousand years ago it was the capitol of Ceylon. Monuments, temples, and Buddhist shrines abounded; one large circular building, or stupa, and several smaller ones were surrounded by a high wall in which 150–200 elephant trunks had been carved. That evening Martha and I went frog hunting to find the source of the musical chorus emanating from several puddles. We could see small frogs resembling our spring peepers, but we didn't catch any. Another reward that evening was watching several Crested Tree Swifts *(Hemiprocne longipennis)* circling over and around the rest house. Most taxonomists separate the tree swifts (Hemiprocnidae—3 species) from the other swifts (Apodidae—76 species) because of differences that include unique nesting habits. The tree swifts glue a few sticks to the side of a branch on a tree, a nest so small that the incubating bird sits crosswise on the branch with its brood patch extending over and enveloping the single egg, which is glued to the nest.

Next morning we were off early for Wilpattu National Park, one of

Ceylon's three national parks. But in some respects our experiences there were disappointing. From the park entrance we drove nine miles to the headquarters over a narrow, mostly one-way road covered by a canopy of trees. I sensed that the forest must be teeming with wildlife rarities, but park visitors are not allowed to get out of cars because of possible encounters with dangerous animals, including poisonous snakes. At the headquarters there was no government official to greet us, as there was supposed to be. Harold, somewhat annoyed, finally located a guide (we couldn't go anywhere without one), but he couldn't speak English and was of little help. The facility—a rather crude wood structure—was situated on the shores of a lake where, with binoculars, we could make out several Asian Open-billed Storks *(Anastomus oscitans)* standing in the shallow water and several White-necked Storks *(Ciconia episcopus)* in the distance.

Then we went on a long bus drive through other parts of the park, truly a scenic drive but frustrating to me because we couldn't stop for anything. We even ate our lunch on the bus, although there was a picnic shelter en route. At one point we were allowed to stand beside the bus for viewing some shorebirds on mud flats in the distance, but we were not permitted to approach them for a closer view. However, I could make out two Great Stone Plovers *(Esacus magnirostris)* standing by what appeared to be their nests, with a chick near one of the nests. And Badshah, who wasn't always reliable on identifications, correctly identified two obscure shorebirds as Indian Coursers *(Cursorius coromandelicus)* in winter plumage. This added two more shorebird families (Burhinidae and Glareolidae) to my growing list.

En route to our lodging in Anuradhapura, we made several stops (outside the park) to look for birds. Two plain-looking birds getting webbing from a worm's nest for a possible nest of their own puzzled us for some time. Badshah finally came up with the right answer; they were Tawny-flanked Prinias *(Prinia subflava),* one of the 398 species of sylviids that are so hard to identify. We also added a Pied Crested Cuckoo *(Clamator jacobinus)* and an Indian Plaintive Cuckoo *(Cacomantis merulinus)* to our list.

Our trip back to Colombo from Anuradhapura was a long (more than a hundred miles), pleasant, leisurely drive with several rewarding stops. We had a good driver; unlike some of the drivers we had had earlier in India, he slowed down for pedestrians, for the numerous bicycle riders along the road, and for cattle or other animals. I was able to identify 55 species of birds en route, although only four were new: an Ashy Wood Swallow *(Artamus fuscus),* a Stork-billed Kingfisher *(Pelargopsis capensis),* a Black-winged Kite *(Elanus caeruleus),* and a nondescript lark believed to be a

Lesser Skylark *(Alauda gulgula).* An interesting sight (but not a new bird) was a group of about one hundred Little Grebes (Dabchicks) on a tank beside the road.

Back in Colombo, on our last morning in Ceylon, several of us got out early—too early, as it turned out—to visit a marsh outside the city. We arrived before dawn, too dark to see birds for another half hour or so, but we could hear strange calls issuing from the marsh. As soon as it was light enough, we had a good opportunity to work on some of the hard-to-identify sandpipers and could distinguish Marsh, Wood, and Common sandpipers *(Tringa stagnatalis, T. glareola, T. hypoleucos)* and Greenshanks *(T. nebularia).* More exciting were the Black Bitterns *(Dupetor flavicollis)* seen both perched and in flight, and a female Water Cock or Kora *(Gallicrex cinerea)* watched at close range.

Homeward Bound

Except for another stop in Madras en route home, Ceylon ended our birding ventures. We were off almost nonstop for home via Calcutta, Karachi (Pakistan), Cairo, Athens, Zurich, Amsterdam, and New York. Our brief half-hour stop in Karachi at night enabled us to visit the airport's shopping center. Lack of time (and the late hour) prevented us from trying to look up our Pakistanian friends, the Shamis, who had stayed with us in East Lansing while they were house hunting when Mr. Shami was attending MSU.

In Cairo, Athens, and Zurich we weren't allowed to leave the airports. But we did have a day's layover in Amsterdam, which was having one of its worst cold spells in many years; therefore we didn't venture far from our hotel. In New York an annoying incident showed that foreign countries are not alone in cumbersome red tape. A dour inspector told us our health cards were invalid; mine had had something scratched out (illegal, he said) and Martha's had not been properly stamped when we left Lansing a month earlier. However, there didn't seem to be anything he could do about it except to give us a verbal dressing down, so he (begrudgingly) let us pass.

As after our other travels in foreign countries, it was good to be home again. And as our first participation in an organized tour to a foreign country, it was a highly memorable event. The ornithological rewards, which have proved so useful on so many subsequent occasions, are indicated in the list of birds identified.

References

Ali, Salim. *Indian Hill Birds*. London: Oxford University Press, 1949.

_____. 1964 (7th ed.). *The Book of Indian Birds*. Bombay Nat. Hist. Soc., Bombay.

Ali, Salim, and S.D. Ripley. *Handbook of The Birds of India and Pakistan, together with those of Nepal, Sikkim, Bhutan and Ceylon*. London: Oxford University Press, 1968–1976.

Fleming, R.L. Jr. "The Comparative Myology of the Syrinx in the Avian Family Timaliidae." Unpubl. M.S. Thesis, Michigan State University, 1962.

_____. "The Birds of Mussoorie, U.P., India: A Distributional and Ecological Study." Unpubl. Ph.D. dissertation, Michigan State University, 1967.

Fleming, R.L. Sr.; R.L. Fleming, Jr.; and L.S. Bangdel. *Birds of Nepal, with Reference to Kashmir and Sikkim*. Bombay, India: Vakil Press, 1976.

Fletcher, G.N. *The Fabulous Flemings of Kathmandu: The Story of Two Doctors in Nepal*. New York: E. P. Dutton & Co., 1964.

George, J.C. and A.J. Berger. *Avian Myology*. New York and London: Academic Press, 1966.

Ripley, S.D. II. 1961. *A Synopsis of the Birds of India and Pakistan, together with those of Nepal, Sikkim, Bhutan and Ceylon*. Bombay Nat. Hist. Soc., Bombay, India.

Whistler, H. (4th ed., revised and enlarged by N.B. Kinnear 1963). *Popular Handbook of Indian Birds*. Edinburgh and London: Oliver and Boyd, 1949.

My India, Nepal, and Ceylon Bird List: January 24—February 15, 1969

(Other members of our party—especially our guides—recorded other birds, but I did not include those not seen or verified by me. Nomenclature is from Ali, Flemings, and Ripley.)

Podicipedidae (Grebes)
Great Crested Grebe *(Podiceps cristatus)*. Pokhara, Nepal, Jan. 30; 9 on Lake Phewatal

Little Grebe *(P. ruficollis)*. Anuradhapura, Ceylon, Feb. 12; 100 ± on a tank along the roadside

Pelecanidae (Pelicans)
Spot-billed Pelican *(Pelecanus philippensis)*. Kaziranga, Assam, Feb. 2; Wilpattu, Ceylon, Feb. 11; Colombo, Feb. 12

Phalacrocoracidae (Cormorants)
Great Cormorant *(Phalacrocorax carbo)*. Keoladeo Ghana (Bharatpur), Jan. 26; a few

Indian Shag *(P. fuscicollis)*. Ceylon, Feb. 10–12; many

Little or Pygmy Cormorant *(P. niger)*. Common, or abundant; Keoladeo Ghana, Kaziranga, also in Ceylon

244

Anhingidae (Darters)

Oriental Darter *(Anhinga rufa melanogaster)*. Common; Keoladeo Ghana, Kaziranga, Ceylon. *(melanogaster* may be a distinct species.)

Ardeidae (Herons, Egrets, Bitterns)

Gray Heron *(Ardea cinerea)*. Keoladeo Ghana, Kaziranga, Ceylon; a few at each place

Purple Heron *(A. purpurea)*. Keoladeo Ghana, Kaziranga, Ceylon; a few at each place

Indian Pond Heron or Paddybird *(Ardeola grayii)*. Nearly everywhere in wet areas—rice paddies, ditches, ponds

Cattle Egret *(Bubulcus ibis)*. Abundant nearly everywhere—fields, pastures, marshes; associated with grazing animals

Great Egret *(Egretta alba)*. Common nearly everywhere in wet places

Little Egret *(E. garzetta)*. Common with above species (I never was quite satisfied with the identification of the Intermediate Egret—*E. intermedia.*)

Black-crowned Night Heron *(Nycticorax nycticorax)*. Wilpattu, Ceylon, Feb. 10; flock roosting in trees. (Many around zoo in Calcutta, Feb. 5; probably wild birds.)

Black Bittern *(Dupetor flavicollis)*. Colombo, Ceylon, Feb. 14; one perched and in flight. (3 uncertains in dim light)

Ciconiidae (Storks)

Painted Stork *(Ibis leucocephalus)*. Keoladeo Ghana, Jan. 26, many (2,000–3,000 pairs reported); Wilpattu, Ceylon, Feb. 11

Asian Open-billed Stork *(Anastomus oscitans)*. Wilpattu; several standing in water, with open bills

White-necked Stork *(Ciconia episcopus)*. Wilpattu; several seen

Black-necked Stork *(Xenorhynchus asiaticus)*. Keoladeo Ghana, Jan. 26, a dozen or so seen; Kaziranga, Feb. 12

Greater Adjutant Stork *(Leptoptilos dubius)*. Kaziranga and vicinity (en route), Feb. 1 to 5, common; Wilpattu, Feb. 11

Threskiornithidae (Ibises, Spoonbills)

White or Black-headed Ibis *(Threskiornis melanocephala)* Keoladeo Ghana, Jan. 26, abundant; Wilpattu, Feb. 11

Black or White-shouldered Ibis *(Pseudibis papillosa)*. One seen in flight en route to Keoladeo Ghana, Jan. 26. (Identified by Harold Peters and M.A. Badshah.)

White or Eurasian Spoonbill *(Platalea leucorodia)*. Keoladeo Ghana, Jan. 26, many; Wilpattu, Feb. 11, large flock

Anatidae (Waterfowl)

Graylag Goose *(Anser anser)*. Keoladeo Ghana, Jan. 26; large flocks

Indian Tree-Duck or Lesser Whistling Teal *(Dendrocygna javanica)*. Wilpattu, Feb. 11; Colombo (en route), Feb. 12

Ruddy Shelduck *(Tadorna ferruginea)*. Keoladeo Ghana, Jan. 26; 100 ± seen

Pintail *(Anas acuta)*. Keoladeo Ghana, Jan. 26, common; Kaziranga,

Feb. 2, several flocks

Common Teal *(A. crecca)*. Keoladeo Ghana, Jan. 26, many; Kaziranga, Feb. 2, many; Ceylon, Feb. 12

Spotbill Duck *(A poecilorhyncha)*. Keoladeo Ghana, Jan. 26, common (?); Kaziranga, Feb. 2 to 3, a few (identification questionable)

Mallard *(A. platyrhynchos)*. Kaziranga, Feb. 2, 1 male, several females.

Gadwall *(A. strepera)*. Keoladeo Ghana, Jan. 26, common; Kaziranga, Feb. 2, a few

Eurasian Wigeon *(A. penelope)*. Keoladeo Ghana, Jan. 26, common

Garganey *(A. querquedula)*. Uncertain observations at Keoladeo Ghana, Madras Deer Park (captive) and in Ceylon

Northern Shoveler *(A. clypeata)*. Keoladeo Ghana, Jan. 26; quite common

Cotton Teal *(Nettapus coromandelianus)*. Keoladeo Ghana, Jan. 26, a few (identified by guide); Colombo, Feb. 12 (en route) a few

Accipitridae (Kites, Hawks, Eagles, Vultures, Harriers)

Black-winged Kite *(Elanus caeruleus)*. One in Ceylon, near Colombo, Feb. 12

Pariah or Black Kite *(Milvus migrans)*. Common nearly everywhere (except Ceylon)

Brahminy Kite *(Haliaster indus)*. Pokhara, Nepal, Jan. 30, 1; Kaziranga, Feb. 1 to 5, several; Madras, Feb. 7, 1; Ceylon, Feb. 9 to 14

Common Buzzard *(Buteo buteo)*. Godaveri, Nepal, Jan. 29; occasional thereafter

Crested Hawk-eagle *(Spizaetus cirrhatus)*. Kaziranga, Feb. 4, 1

Tawny Eagle *(Aquila rapax)*. Keoladeo Ghana, Jan. 26, apparently common but hard to identify (Peters, Badshah, and guide)

Steppe Eagle *(A. nipalensis)*. Pokhara, Jan. 30, 1; identified by Fleming

Black Eagle *(Ictinaetus malayensis)*. Godaveri, Jan. 29, soaring over forest; Kaziranga, Feb. 4, 1

Pallas' Fishing Eagle *(Haliaeetus leucoryphus)*. Keoladeo Ghana, Jan. 26, 1 or more; Kaziranga, Feb. 2, nest with young

Indian White-backed Vulture *(Gyps bengalensis)*. Very common (except in Ceylon), flocks in air at many places

Egyptian Vulture *(Neophron percnopterus)*. Quite common, India and Nepal

Hen Harrier *(Circus cyaneus)*. Pokhara, Jan. 30, well marked. (Harriers were seen in several places but not always identified as to species.)

Pale Harrier *(C. macrourus)*. New Delhi, Jan. 25. (Light-colored harrier believed to be this species. Badshah agreed.)

Crested Serpent Eagle *(Spilornis cheela)*. Kaziranga, Feb. 4, 1

Pandionidae (Osprey)

Osprey *(Pandion haliaetus)*. Keoladeo Ghana, Jan. 26, 1 flying over

Falconidae (Falcons)

Eurasian Kestrel *(Falco tinnunculus)*. Chapagaon, Nepal, Jan. 31, 1; Kaziranga, Feb. 2, 1

246

Phasianidae (O.W. Partridges, Junglefowl, Peafowl.)
Gray Partridge *(Francolinus pondicerianus)*. Keoladeo Ghana, Jan. 26, small group spotted and identified by our guide
Red Junglefowl *(Gallus gallus)*. Kaziranga, Feb. 2, in road, male seen further along the road
Ceylon Junglefowl *(Gallus lafayetti)*. Wilpattu, Feb. 11, male in road, 2 females later.
Common Peafowl *(Pavo cristatus)*. Wild male seen in field en route to Keoladeo Ghana, Jan. 26; others in sanctuaries

Gruidae (Cranes)
Sarus Crane *(Grus antigone)*. Keoladeo, Ghana, Jan. 26, 100 ±
Siberian White Crane *(G. leucogeranus)*. Keoladeo Ghana, Jan. 26, a sizable flock and a few strays. Our guide was pleased with the high count (endangered species).

Rallidae (Waterhens, Gallinules, Coot)
White-breasted Waterhen *(Amaurornis phoenicurus)*. Keoladeo Ghana, Jan. 26, 12±; Kaziranga, Feb. 2 to 5, fairly common; Ceylon, Feb. 9 to 14, many, solitary, or in two's
Water Cock or Kora *(Gallicrex cinerea)*. Colombo, Ceylon, Feb. 14; female watched carefully in roadside marsh
Moorhen or C. Gallinule *(Gallinula chloropus)*. Keoladeo Ghana, Jan. 26, many; Kaziranga, Feb. 2 to 5, common
Purple Moorhen *(Porphyrio porphyrio)*. Keoladeo Ghana, Jan. 26, several; Kaziranga, Feb. 4, 2; Feb. 13 and 14, several
Eurasian Coot *(Fulica atra)*. Keoladeo Ghana, Jan. 26, large concentrations; Kaziranga, Feb. 2 to 5, a few

Jacanidae (Jacanas)
Pheasant-tailed Jacana *(Hydrophasianus chirurgus)*. Keoladeo Ghana, Jan. 26, quite common; Kaziranga, Feb. 2 to 5; Ceylon, Feb. 8 to 12, quite a few, most in winter plumage (short tails)
Bronze-winged Jacana *(Metopidius indicus)*. Keoladeo Ghana, Jan. 26, 2 or more; Kaziranga, Feb. 2 to 5, fairly common

Charadriidae (Lapwings, Plovers)
Gray-headed Lapwing *(Vanellus cinereus)*. Keoladeo Ghana, Jan. 26, many; not seen elsewhere
Red-wattled Lapwing *(V. indicus)*. Agra (Taj Mahal), Jan. 25; common at Ghana, Kaziranga, and in Ceylon
Spur-winged Lapwing *(V. spinosus)*. Agra (Taj Mahal), Jan. 25. (Identified by Badshah and Peters.)
American Golden Plover *(Pluvialis dominica)*. Wilpattu, Feb. 11, several
Little Ringed Plover *(Charadrius dubius)*. Agra (Taj Mahal), Jan. 25; also seen at Ghana, Kaziranga, Madras, and Ceylon.

Scolopacidae (Sandpipers *et al.)*
Common Redshank *(Tringa totanus)*. Keoladeo Ghana, Jan. 26, apparently common but I couldn't check red legs on all of them

Marsh Sandpiper *(T. stagnatilis)*. Ceylon, Feb. 14, recorded for sure only in a marsh near Colombo

Greenshank *(T. nebularia)*. Keoladeo Ghana, Jan. 26, identified for sure only at Ghana, but probably seen elsewhere

Wood Sandpiper *(T. glareola)*. First identified on marsh near Colombo, Feb. 14, but probably seen elsewhere also

Common Sandpiper *(T. hypoleucos)*. Apparently common everywhere from Agra to Ceylon

Common or Fantail Snipe *(Capella gallinago)*. Snipe seen frequently throughout trip; mainly, if not entirely, this American form

Little Stint *(Calidris minutus)*. Recorded only for Ghana, Jan. 26; and Kaziranga, Feb. 2 to 5

Recurvirostridae (Stilts)

Black-winged Stilt *(Himantopus himantopus)*. Agra, Jan. 25, several; also at Kaziranga, Madras (100's, and Ceylon

Burhinidae (Stone Plovers)

Great Stone Plover *(Esacus magnirostris)*. Wilpattu, Feb. 11; adults with young, at nests

Glareolidae (Coursers)

Indian Courser *(Cursorius coromandelicus)*. Wilpattu, Feb. 11; 1 or 2, identified by Badshah

Laridae (Gulls and Terns)

Brown-headed Gull *(Larus brunnicephalus)*. Madras, Feb. 6, scattered individuals along river; Colombo Harbor, Feb. 8 to 9

Black-headed Gull *(L. ridibundus)*. Thousands at Beirut and along Mediterranean Coast, Jan. 23; not sure of them in India

Whiskered Tern *(Chlidonias hybrida)*. Many in Ceylon, Feb. 8 to 15

Indian River Tern *(Sterna aurantia)*. Kaziranga, Feb. 2 to 5, common; Madras, Feb. 7, common

Black-bellied Tern *(S. acuticauda)*. Kaziranga, Feb. 2; a dozen or so with River Terns; not seen elsewhere

Columbidae (Pigeons, Doves)

Bengal Green Pigeon *(Treron phoenicoptera)*. Kaziranga, Feb. 3, a few; also on Ceylon (different race), Feb. 12

Common Pigeon or Rock Dove *(Columba livia)*. Widespread as in Europe and the Americas (would be "Indian" race here)

Rufous or Oriental Turtle Dove *(Streptopelia orientalis)*. Large groups en route from Agra to Ghana; not sure elsewhere

Collared Turtle or Indian Ring Dove *(S. decaocto)*. Abundant from Agra to Ghana; also at Delhi (?) and in Nepal (?)

Red Turtle Dove *(S. tranquebarica)*. A few with the above, en route to Ghana (quite distinctive)

Spotted Dove *(S. chinensis)*. Agra, Jan. 25, a few; Kaziranga, Feb. 2 to 5, abundant; Ceylon, Feb. 8 to 15

Little Brown Dove *(S. senegalensis)*. Delhi, Jan. 25, adult on and at nest at Craftsman Shop; not seen elsewhere

248

Emerald or Green-winged Dove *(Chalcophaps indica)*. Glimpse of one, brief but unmistakable, en route to Kaziranga, Feb. 1; many flushed along roadside in Ceylon, Feb. 12

Psittacidae (Parakeets)
Large or Alexandrine Parakeet *(Psittacula eupatria)*. Kaziranga, Feb. 3, 1
Rose-ringed Parakeet *(P. krameri)*. Abundant, nearly everywhere
Rose-breasted Parakeet *(P. alexandri)*. Kaziranga, Feb. 3 to 4, several
Slaty-headed Parakeet *(P. himalayana)*. Katana, Nepal, Jan. 28, several flocks (identified by Fleming)
Emerald-collared Parakeet *(P. calthorpae)*. Kandy, Ceylon, Feb. 9, half dozen or so in botanical gardens.

Cuculidae (Cuckoos)
Pied Crested Cuckoo *(Clamator jacobinus)*. Anuradhapura, Feb. 11, brief but definite glimpse of one (identified by Peters)
Indian Plaintive Cuckoo *(Cacomantis merulinus)*. Anuradhapura, Feb. 11 (1 female identified by Badshah)
Koel *(Eudynamys scolapacea)*. Kandy, Feb. 9. 1 male, 2 female in botanical gardens; daily thereafter in Ceylon
Crow Pheasant or Large Coucal *(Centropus sinensis)*. Fairly common and widespread, Agra, Ghana, Kaziranga, Ceylon

Strigidae (Owls)
Jungle Owlet *(Glaucidium radiatum)*. Kaziranga, Feb. 2 to 3, 2 seen closely, but could be *G. cuculoides*
Spotted Owlet *(Athene brama)*. Kathmandu, Nepal, Jan. 29, 3 young perched on Fleming's house

Caprimulgidae (Nightjar)
Indian Jungle Nightjar *(Caprimulgus indicus)*. Kaziranga, Feb. 2, 10 ± flushed from dirt road by car at night. (Could be any of several species; we decided on *indicus*.)

Apodidae (Swifts)
Alpine Swift *(Apus melba)*. Wilpattu, Feb. 1, 1 or more in flight
House Swift *(A. affinis)*. New Delhi, Jan. 25, many; Also common at Kaziranga and in Ceylon
Palm Swift *(Cypsiurus parvus)*. Kaziranga. Feb. 3 to 5, quite a few; Madras, Feb. 7

Hemiprocnidae (Crested Swifts)
Crested Tree Swift *(Hemiprocne longipennis)*. Anuradhapura, Feb. 11, several flying around rest house.

Alcedinidae (Kingfishers)
Small Pied Kingfisher *(Ceryle rudis)*. Keoladeo Ghana, Jan. 26, fairly common; Kaziranga, Feb. 2 to 4, a few; Ceylon, Feb. 12, 1 near Colombo
Common or Eurasian Kingfisher *(Alcedo atthis)*. Keoladeo Ghana, Jan. 26, 1 (or more); Ceylon, Feb. 11 to 12, 1 or more each day

Stork-billed Kingfisher *(Pelargopsis capensis)*. Ceylon, Feb. 12, 1 near Colombo.

White-breasted Kingfisher *(Halcyon smyrnensis)*. Common nearly everywhere, Jan. 26 to Feb. 14

Meropidae (Bee-eaters)

Blue-tailed Bee-eater *(Merops philippinus)*. Dambulla, Ceylon, Feb. 10, 1; seen almost daily thereafter in Ceylon

Green Bee-eater *(M. orientalis)*. Keolado Ghana, Jan. 26, several; Madras, Feb. 7 a few; Ceylon, Feb. 8 to 12, common

Coraciidae (Rollers)

Indian Roller *(Coracias benghalensis)*. Seen commonly at Ghana, Pokhara, Kaziranga, and in Ceylon

Upupidae (Hoopoe)

Hoopoe *(Upupa epops)*. New Delhi, Jan. 24, 1 in hotel gardens; Madras, Feb. 6, 1 in Theosophical Society gardens; Ceylon, Feb. 8 to 10, scattered individuals

Capitonidae (Barbets)

Great Himalayan Barbet *(Megalaima virens)*. Katana, Nepal, Jan. 28; beautiful specimen (identified by Fleming)

Green Barbet *(M. zeylanica)*, Ceylon, Feb. 8 to 14, seen almost daily throughout island

Lineated Barbet *(M. lineata)*. Kaziranga, Feb. 2 to 3, one each day; similar to and possibly conspecific with above

Yellow-fronted Barbet *(M. flavifrons)*. Kandy, Feb. 10, several along roadside

Blue-throated Barbet *(M. asiatica)*. Kaziranga, Feb. 2, one near rest house, the only one seen

Crimson-throated Barbet *(M. rubricapilla)*. Colombo, Ceylon, 1

Crimson-breasted Barbet or Coppersmith *(M. haemacephala)*. Pokhara, Nepal, Jan. 30, 1 at nest hole; Dambulla, Ceylon, Feb. 10, adults and immatures; also seen at Colombo, Kandy, and Anaradhapura

Jyngidae (Wryneck)

Wryneck *(Jynx torquilla)*. Keoladeo Ghana, Jan. 26; one netted, banded, photographed, and released

Picidae (Woodpeckers)

Small Scaly-bellied Woodpecker *(Picus xanthopygaeus)*. Kaziranga, Feb. 2, 1

Black-naped Woodpecker *(P. canus)*. Kaziranga, Feb. 3, 1

Lesser Golden-backed Woodpecker *(Dinopium benghalense)*. Keoladeo Ghana, Jan. 26, 1 netted, banded, and released; several others seen; Feb. 9, 2 in botanical gardens; Anuradhapura, Feb. 11, 1 at rest house

Brown-fronted Pied Woodpecker *(Dendrocopos auriceps)*. Godaveri, Nepal, 1 at boys' school

Fulvous-breasted Pied Woodpecker *(D. macei)*. Godaveri, Jan. 29, several in high forest

Alaudidae (larks)

Bengal or Rufous-winged Bush Lark *(Mirafra assamica)*. Dambulla, Ceylon, 1 or more. (We decided on this species rather than *M. javanica* or *M. erythroptera.)*

Crested Lark *(Galerida cristata)*. Agra to Ghana, Jan. 26, several in fields.

Eastern or Little Oriental Skylark *(Alauda gulgula)*. Probably widespread but positively identified only in Ceylon

Hirundinidae (Martins, Swallows)

Plain or Indian Sand Martin *(Riparia paludicola)*. Kathmandu, Jan. 27, colony in bank near airport; Kaziranga, Feb. 2 to 5, common

Dusky Crag Martin *(Hirundo concolor)*. New Delhi, Jan. 26, small colony nesting with House Sparrows

Barn Swallow *(H. rustica)*. Nearly everywhere, one of the world's most widely distributed birds

Wire-tailed Swallow *(H. smithii)*. Keoladeo Ghana, Jan. 26

Red-rumped or Striated Swallow *(H. daurica)*. Pokhara, Nepal, Jan. 30, several; Kaziranga, Feb. 2 to 5, many; Ceylon, Feb. 8 to 10, a few

Eurasian House Martin *(Delichon urbica)*. Ceylon, Feb. 12, one near Colombo

Laniidae (Shrikes)

Gray Shrike *(Lanius excubitor)*. Agra to Ghana, Jan. 26, several

Bay-backed Shrike *(L. vittatus)*. Keoladeo Ghana, Jan. 26, several

Rufous-backed or Black-headed Shrike *(L. schach)*. New Delhi, Jan. 24, 1; Kaziranga, Feb. 4, 1

Brown Shrike *(L. cristatus)*. Chapagaon, Nepal, Jan. 31, 1; Jorhat, Assam, Feb. 1, 2 or more at airport; Kaziranga, Feb. 2 to 5, many along road; Ceylon, Feb. 8 to 10, a few

Oriolidae (Old World Orioles)

Golden Oriole *(Oriolus oriolus)*. Madras, Feb. 15, female on campus.

Black-headed Oriole *(O. xanthornus)*, Kaziranga, Feb. 4 to 5, several each day; Ceylon, Feb. 8 to 10, quite common

Maroon Oriole *(O. traillii)*. Godaveri, Jan. 29, 1 female

Dicruridae (Drongos)

Black or Fork-tailed Drongo, King-Crow *(Dicrurus adsimilus)*. New Delhi, Jan. 24, 1; Agra to Ghana, Jan. 26, common; Pokhara, Jan. 30, common; Kaziranga, Feb. 2 to 5, common; Madras, Feb. 6

Gray or Ashy Drongo *(D. leucophaeus)*. Kaziranga, Feb. 3, 1

White-bellied Drongo *(D. coerulescens)*. Ceylon, Feb. 9 to 14, quite common

Hair-crested or Spangled Drongo *(D. hottentottus)*. Pokhara, Nepal, Jan. 30, 1

Artamidae (Wood Swallows or Swallow-Shrikes)

Ashy Swallow-Shrike *(Artamus fuscus)*. Ceylon, Feb. 12, several en route to Colombo

Sturnidae (Mynas)
  Gray-headed Myna *(Sturnus malabaricus)*. Pokhara, Jan. 30, 1—
    identified by Fleming; Kaziranga, Feb. 2, several
  Brahminy Myna *(S. pagodarum)*. Delhi, Jan. 25, 1
  Pied Myna *(S. contra)*. New Delhi, Jan. 24; Kaziranga, Feb. 2 to 5;
    several around rest house
  Common Myna *(Acridotheres tristis)*. Nearly everywhere, perhaps
    India's most abundant bird; widely transplanted into other countries
  Bank Myna *(A. ginginianus)*. Common, in association with *A. tristis* in
    northern India
  Jungle Myna *(A. fuscus)*. Nepal, Jan. 30, Kaziranga, Feb. 2 to 5; quite
    common
  Grackle or Hill Myna *(Gracula religiosa)*. Kandy, Feb. 9, 1 in botanical
    gardens; more at Anuradhapura, Feb. 10

Corvidae (Tree-Pies, Crows)
  Indian Tree-Pie *(Dendrocitta vagabunda)*. New Delhi, Jan. 24, 1;
    Kaziranga, Feb. 2 to 5, a few almost daily
  Himalayan Tree-Pie *(D. formosae)*. Godaveri, Jan. 28 to 29, several
  House Crow *(Corvus splendens)*. Abundant, especially in cities; all over
    India and Nepal
  Jungle Crow *(C. macrorhynchos)*. Widespread and abundant, more
    "rural" than House Crow; large roost (1,000's) in park in Kandy.

Campephagidae (Cuckoo-shrikes, Minivets)
  Pied Wood-shrike *(Hemipus picatus)*. Kandy, Feb. 8, pair seen
  Lesser or Indian Wood-Shrike *(Tephrodornis pondicerianus)*. Anurad-
    hapura, Feb. 10 to 11, several
  Scarlet Minivet *(Pericrocotus flammeus)*. Godaveri, Jan. 29, pair;
    Kaziranga, Feb. 4, pair seen at rest house; Kandy, Feb. 9
  Long-tailed Minivet *(P. ethologus)*. Katana, Nepal, Jan. 28, 1

Irenidae (Iora, Leaf Birds)
  Common Iora *(Aegithina tiphia)*. Kaziranga, Feb. 2, females; Feb. 4, 2
    females; Ceylon, Feb. 8 to 14, quite common, both male and female
  Golden-fronted Leaf Bird *(Chloropsis aurifrons)*. Ceylon, Feb. 8, 1
  Orange-bellied Leaf Bird *(C. hardwickii)*. Godaveri, Jan. 29, several

Timaliidae (Babblers, Laughing-Thrushes)
  Rufous-necked Scimitar Babbler *(Pomatorhinus ruficollis)*. Chapagaon,
    Nepal, Jan. 31, several
  Rusty-cheeked Scimitar Babbler *(P. erythrogenys)*. Katana Ridge, Jan.
    28, 1; more on Jan. 29 at Godaveri
  Red-billed Babbler *(Stachyris pyrrhops)*. Godaveri, Jan. 29, small group
  Red-capped Babbler *(Timalia pileata)*. Godaveri, Jan. 29, 1
  Common Babbler *(Turdoides caudatus)*. New Delhi, Jan. 24, 3 on hotel
    lawn, more in trees
  Jungle Babbler *(T. striatus)*. Common nearly everywhere, often in
    groups of 7 ("seven sisters")
  White-headed Babbler *(T. affinis)*. Madras, Feb. 15, several

White-throated Laughing-Thrush *(Garrulax albogularis)*. Godaveri, Jan. 29, groups passing rapidly through trees

Striated Laughing-Thrush *(G. striatus)*. Godaveri, Jan. 29, seen mostly in flight, but good views

White-crested Laughing-Thrush *(G. leucolophus)*. Godaveri, Jan. 29, Fleming saw many; I had a good view of white crest and head of one

Red-headed Laughing-Thrush *(G. eryrthrocephalus)*. Godaveri, Jan. 29, several in mountain forest

Hoary Barwing *(Actinodura nipalensis)*. Godaveri, Jan. 29, several in mountain forest

Rufous-vented Yuhina *(Yuhina occipitalis)*. Godaveri, Jan. 29, small flock in high forest

Chestnut-headed Tit-Babbler *(Alcippe castaneceps)*. Godaveri, Jan. 29, group of 10 ± feeding on sap of trees.

White-browed Tit-Babbler *(A. vinipectus)*. Godaveri, Jan. 29, 1 in high forest

Nepal Babbler *(A. nipalensis)*. Godaveri, Jan. 29, small flock moving fast in high forest

Black-capped Sibia *(Heterophasia capistrata)*. Godaveri, Jan. 29, abundant all through trees for a couple hours

Pycnonotidae (Bulbuls)

Black-headed Yellow Bulbul *(Pycnonotus melanicterus)*. Kaziranga, Feb. 3, 2 well camouflaged in tree

Red-whiskered Bulbul *(P. jocosus)*. New Delhi, Jan. 24, several; also at Agra, Keoladeo Ghana, and Kaziranga.

White-cheeked Bulbul *(P. leucogenys)*. New Delhi, Jan. 24, several; Godaveri, Jan. 29

Red-vented Bulbul *(P. cafer)*. Common nearly everywhere in India and Nepal

Striated Bulbul *(P. striatus)*. Godaveri, Jan. 29, 2 in high forest.

White-browed Bulbul *(P. luteolus)*. Colombo, Feb. 14, several

Rufous-bellied Bulbul *(Hypsipetes virescens)*. Pokhara, Nepal, Jan. 30 (identified by Fleming)

Gray or Black Bulbul *(H. madagascariensis)*. Godaveri, Jan. 29, large flock at boys' school

Muscicapidae (Old World Flycatchers)

Asian Brown Flycatcher *(Muscicapa latirostris)*. Wilpattu, Feb. 11, 1; Colombo, Feb. 13, 1 in city park

Red-breasted Flycatcher *(M. parva)*. Kaziranga, Feb. 2 to 3; 2 or more females or immature males each day

Orange-gorgetted Flycatcher *(M. strophiata)*. Godaveri, Jan. 29, several along fence row near boys' school

Verditer Flycatcher *(M. thalassina)*. Kaziranga, Feb. 2 to 3; male along brook both days

Gray-headed Flycatcher *(Culicicapa ceylonensis)*. Pokhara, Jan. 30, 1; Kaziranga, Feb. 2 to 5, pair at rest house, also along trail

253

Yellow-bellied Fantail Flycatcher *(Rhipidura hypoxantha)*. Pokhara, Jan. 30, 1

White-breasted Fantail Flycatcher *(R. aureola)*. Keoladeo Ghana, Jan. 26, 1 pointed out and identified by guide (Saxena)

Asian Paradise Flycatcher *(Tersiphone paradisi)*. Kandy, Feb. 9, 2 females in botanical gardens, another on the 12th

Black-naped Flycatcher*(Monarcha azurea)*. Kaziranga, Feb. 4, 1

Sylviidae (Old World Warblers)

Tawny-flanked or Plain Prinia *(Prinia subflava)*. Anuradhapura, Ceylon, Feb. 11, pair (?) "attacking" worms' nest

Ashy or Long-tailed Prinia *(P. socialis)*. New Delhi, Jan. 24, 1 at dump near hotel.

Tailor Bird *(Orthotomus sutorius)*. Common nearly everywhere

Orange-barred Leaf Warbler *(Phylloscopus pulcher)*. Godaveri, Jan. 29, apparently common but hard to identify

Yellow-browed or plain Leaf Warbler *(P. inornatus)*. New Delhi, Jan. 28, 1 on temple tour; Kaziranga, Feb. 2 to 5, a few identified

Yellow-rumped Leaf Warbler *(P. proregulus)*. Godaveri, Jan. 29, several (identified by Fleming)

Gray-faced Leaf Warbler *(P. maculipennis)*. Godaveri, Jan. 29, 1

Yellow-eyed Warbler *(Seicercus burkii)*. Godaveri, Jan. 29, 1

Gray-headed Warbler *(S. xanthoschistos)*. Katana, Jan. 28, 1; Chapagaon, Jan. 31, 1

Turdidae (Thrushes)

Eurasian Rubythroat *(Erithacus calliope)*. Chapagaon, Nepal, Jan. 31, 1 on ground in path; Bob says "rare"

Bluethroat *(E. svecicus)*. Keoladeo Ghana, Jan. 26, 1 captured, banded, and released.

Orange-flanked Bush Robin *(E. cyanurus)*. Godaveri, Jan. 29, male in road to iron mine, female seen earlier

Magpie Robin, Dayal *(Copsychus saularis)*. Common nearly everywhere, New Delhi to Ceylon

Black Redstart *(Phoenicurus ochruros)*. Common nearly everywhere, variable plumage (some might be *P. phoenicurus*?)

Hodgson's Redstart *(P. hodgsoni)*. Godaveri, Jan. 29, 1 at boys' school

Blue-fronted Redstart *(P. frontalis)*. Katana, Jan. 28, Chapagaon, Jan. 31

Plumbeous Redstart *(Rhyacornis fuliginosus)*. Godaveri, Jan. 29, male and female at fish hatchery

Spotted Forktail *(Enicurus maculatus)*. Godaveri, Jan. 29, wounded bird on ground, couldn't catch it

Stone Chat *(Saxicola torquata)*. Katana, Jan. 28, 1; Godaveri, Jan. 29, 1; Pokara, Jan. 30, 1; Kaziranga, Feb. 2 to 5, a few

Pied Bush Chat *(S. caprata)*. Katana, Jan. 28, male and female on hilltop; Godaveri, Jan. 29, more

Gray Bush Chat *(S. ferrea)*. Katana, Jan. 28, 1 (identified by Fleming)

White-capped River Chat *(Chaimarrornis leucocephalus)*. Godaveri, Jan. 29, male at fish hatchery

Indian Robin *(Saxicoloides fulicata)*. Very common, India and Ceylon

Chestnut-bellied Rock Thrush *(Monticola rufiventris)*. Godaveri, Jan. 29, 1 pointed out and identified by Fleming

Blue Rock Thrush *(M. solitarius)*. Kaziranga, Feb. 4, several

(Blue) Whistling Thrush *(Myiophoneus caeruleus)*. Kakana Ridge, Nepal, Jan. 28, 1 seen closely in path

White-collared Blackbird *(Turdus albocinctus)*. Godaveri, Jan. 29, 1 perched motionless for a long time

Paridae (Titmice)

Great Tit *(Parus major)*. Godaveri, Jan. 29, 1 at boys' school

Green-backed Tit *(P. monticolus)*. Godaveri, Jan. 29, 1

Yellow-cheeked Tit *(P. xanthogenys)*. Godaveri, Jan. 29, many

Yellow-browed Tit *(P. modestus)* Godaveri, Jan. 29, several

Red-headed Tit *(Aegithalos concinnus)*. Godaveri, Jan. 29, several

Sittidae (Nuthatches)

Chestnut-bellied Nuthatch *(Sitta castanea)*. Godaveri, Jan. 29, 1

White-tailed Nuthatch *(S. himalayensis)*. Godaveri, Jan. 29, 1 posed accommodatingly by iron mine

Certhiidae (Wall Creeper, Tree Creeper)

Wall Creeper *(Tichodroma muraria)*. Kakana Ridge, Nepal, Jan. 28, 2 flew across road. (Some classify this in Sittidae.)

Brown-throated Tree Creeper *(Certhia discolor)*. Godaveri, Jan. 29, 1

Motacillidae (Pipits, Wagtails)

Hodgson's Tree Pipit *(Anthus hodgsoni)*. Kakana Ridge, Nepal, Jan. 28, small group; Kaziranga, Feb. 2 to 5, common (?)

Eurasian Tree Pipit *(A. trivialis)*. Pokhara, Jan. 30, several (Bob called them *trivialis)*

Indian or Paddyfield Pipit *(A. novaeseelandiae)*. Pokara, Jan. 30, Ceylon, apparently the prevailing form in Ceylon (taxonomy confusing)

Yellow Wagtail *(Motacilla flava)*. Widespread—in dull winter plumage

Gray Wagtail *(M. caspica)*. Also widespread but easily confused with above in winter plumage

White or Pied Wagtail *(M. alba)*. Widespread and common in wet places

Hodgson's Pied Wagtail *(M. alboides)*. With conspicuous white forehead usually considered conspecific with *alba*

Large Pied Wagtail *(M. maderaspatensis)*. Madras, Feb. 15, 1 on campus, distinctive from *m. alba*

Dicaeidae (Flowerpeckers)

Thick-billed Flowerpecker *(Dicaeum agile)*, Kandy, Feb. 9, 1 in botanical gardens

Tickell's Flowerpecker *(D. erythrorhynchus)*. Kandy, Feb. 8, 1—thin-billed form

Fire-breasted Flowerpecker *(D. ignipectus)*. Godaveri, Jan. 29, male in forest

Nectariniidae (Sunbirds)

Purple-rumped Sunbird *(Nectarinia zeylonica)*. Common in Ceylon, Feb. 8 to 14

Loten's Sunbird *(N. lotenia)*. Dambulla, Ceylon, Feb. 10, 1; Colombo, Feb. 14, 1—amazingly long decurved bill

Purple Sunbird *(N. asiatica)*. Keoladeo Ghana, Jan. 26, pair at nest; also seen at Kaziranga; Madras; and in Ceylon, common

Nepal or Yellow-backed Sunbird *(Aethopyga nipalensis)*. Godaveri, Jan. 29, several in high forest

Fire-tailed Sunbird *(A. ignicauda)*. Godaveri, Jan. 29, 1

Little Spiderhunter *(Arachnothera longirostris)*. Kaziranga, Feb. 5, 1 at rest house (possibly *A. magna?*)

Zosteropidae (White-eye)

Oriental White-eye *(Zosterops palpebrosa)*. Godaveri, Jan. 29, 1; Kaziranga, Feb. 2 to 5, a few; Ceylon, Feb. 8 to 13, a few

Ploceidae (Weaverbirds, Munias)

House Sparrow *(Passer domesticus)*. Everywhere around human habitations

Eurasian Tree Sparrow *(P. montanus)*. Widespread but not as numerous as House Sparrows

Red Munia or Avadavat *(Estrilda amandava)*. Kaziranga, Feb. 2, flock in woodland road, only 1 bright male

White-rumped or Sharp-tailed Munia *(Lonchura striata)*. Kandy, Feb. 9, small group in gardens

Spotted Munia *(L. punctulata)*. Chapagaon, Jan. 31, 1; Anuradhapura, Ceylon, Feb. 11, small group

Chestnut Munia *(L. malacca)*. Wilpattu, Feb. 11, small group

Fringillidae (Finches)

Himalayan Green Finch *(Carduelis spinoides)*. Chapagaon, Jan. 31, several in tree by roadside

Common Rose Finch *(Carpodacus erythrinus)*. Godaveri, Jan. 29, small group at boys' school

Pink-browed Rose Finch *(C. rhodochrous)*. Godaveri, Jan. 29, single female on weed (identified by Fleming)

Total families: 59 (18 new)
Total species: 265 (222 new)

CHAPTER 12

Fabulous East Africa

AFRICA, THE "Dark Continent," has always been a major goal for explorers, naturalists, and—unfortunately—"developers." As a budding ornithologist I, too, had always dreamed of going to Africa sometime, but I never gave it serious consideration until my terminal year, 1971–1972, at MSU. At that time our department head, the late Dr. Charles Thornton, had a daughter in the Peace Corps in East Africa, which promoted a trip to Africa for him. Although by profession a morphologist (regeneration specialist), Dr. Thornton liked the out-of-doors, had spent several summers in the Tetons, and later had a cabin, accessible only by boat, on a remote lake in Ontario.

After his return from East Africa, Charles came into my office one morning bursting with enthusiasm. The animal life in the national parks was fantastic, he said. "You would go crazy seeing all the birds. You must go sometime." I thought it over—for a few seconds—and asked, "How soon can I get away?" Getting away was not difficult to arrange. In my final year I had no teaching responsibilities except continued guidance of my remaining graduate students. So in late January (how logical!), Martha and I joined an East Africa safari, sponsored by the American National Parks Association and organized and carried out by Club Tours, Inc., New York.

All of Africa seems inviting to the uninitiated, but many areas, even before the current political conflicts, have their drawbacks for visiting naturalists. Bird life in the inhospitable deserts is intriguing but limited. The steaming jungles are equally hazardous and the abundant animal life difficult to observe. And many other parts of Africa are overdeveloped and largely stripped of their native fauna and flora. In parts of Nigeria, for instance, there are almost no edible living animals surviving; even small

257

rodents have been trapped, snared, or captured by some other means by hungry natives.

But East Africa, particularly its national parks (there are thirteen of them) is an exception. Animal life abounds. Kenya alone has more than a thousand species of birds, almost double the number occurring regularly in North America north of Mexico. Roger Tory Peterson, who has been nearly everywhere, says that one can see more birds with less effort in East Africa than in any other place in the world. Some South American countries have more species, but many of them are rare or of limited distribution and observable only with great difficulty. East Africa's open savannas, by contrast, permit comparatively easy observation, even from cars.

Unlike our previous trans-Atlantic flights, this time we had no difficulties getting under way—no serious delays, no lost baggage, no unforeseen emergencies. A night flight from New York took us to Brussels, Belgium, where we visited a museum and brushed up on African wildlife in the museum's special exhibits of African animals. Then we were off on another night flight, to deplane in the early dawn at Entebbe, Uganda, on the shores of Lake Victoria. We were in Africa!

Uganda

As soon as I could slip through customs (which posed no real difficulties) I sneaked outside to look for birds. Even in the dim light the chattering Striped Swallows *(Hirundo abyssinica)* were readily identifiable as they flew to and from their mud nests under the eaves of the airport building. But specific identification of a colony of weaverbirds attending nests in a large tree was not so easy (there are more than 100 species of ploceids in East Africa). Peter Greaves, our British tour leader who met us at the airport, suggested that they might be Black-headed Weavers *(Ploceus cucullatus),* and he proved to be right. Next to appear—another easy one—was the Pied Crow *(Corvus albus),* much like our American Crow but with a broad white nuchal collar and white belly. Black Kites, which we had seen so often in India, were also much in evidence.

The fast thirty-mile drive from Entebbe to Hotel Apollo in Kampala afforded no opportunity for identifying birds—just tantalizing flashes of strange feathered forms along the way. But after getting settled at the hotel, several of us took the opportunity to wander around the hotel's gardens and lawn before our afternoon sightseeing tour of Kampala. As on our Indian tour, it is not practical to discuss in any detail all of the birds seen, which eventually totalled 292 species. They are given in an annotated list at the end of the chapter. But some of those of special interest are mentioned here.

A Woodland Kingfisher *(Halcyon senegalensis)* in the trees along the border of the lawn was the first of the five kingfisher species we were to see; and the Ruppell's Long-tailed Starling *(Lamprotornis purpuropterus)* and the Splendid Glossy Starling *(Lamprocolius splendidus)* were the first of the 10 starlings (Sturnidae). The Yellow-vented Bulbul *(Pycnonotus xan-thopygos),* which proved to be one of the commonest songbirds in East Africa, was the only pycnonotid we saw. Swallows (11 species seen) seemed to be everywhere in Africa; on the hotel grounds we observed the native Angola Swallows *(Hirundo angolensis)* with their short tails and ashy-gray belly mingling with our own similar Barn Swallows, which are nearly world-wide in distribution.

The afternoon was devoted largely to a tour of the better parts of Kampala, its fine parliament buildings, a historical and cultural museum, and the King's Tomb, a villa of neatly cane-thatched huts, which is one of the main tourist attractions in Kampala. The tomb itself, a newly remodeled hut that serves as a museum, is surrounded by a circle of smaller huts in which some of the descendents of the deceased king still live.

That evening we listened to a lecture by a Negro economist from the University of Uganda. It was a reasonably scholarly presentation that turned some of us off because, as might be expected from an economist, he deplored the amount of land devoted to national parks, land so badly needed for living space for people and for agricultural and other developments.

The next day we were up early with great expectations. The breakfast promised us in our room didn't arrive (we ate later downstairs), so we watched for birds from our balcony. One of my African *desiderata* ap-peared in the nearby trees—an Eastern Gray Plantain-eater *(Crinifer zonurus),* one of the 20 species of musophagids that occur only in Africa.

Our trip that day took us a hundred miles or more by car to Paraa Lodge on the Victoria Nile, which bisects the 1,557 square mile Murchison Falls National Park. En route, just outside Kampala, we stopped to view a colony of fruit bats clinging upside down in trees, some branches so heavily loaded that the bats looked like swarms of bees. Further on we stopped at a papyrus swamp but were warned not to leave the road because of poisonous snakes. The thick cane stands, still used for paper-making, we were told, didn't look very inviting anyway. A little later we paused at a waterhole teeming with birds. Two Hammerheads *(Scopus umbretta),* peculiar heronlike birds found only in Africa, were stalking prey in the puddle. With them were two Sacred Ibis *(Threskiornis aethiopicus),* a bird once so revered that specimens were often entombed with the pharaohs. Formerly (before they were displaced by pesticides) the ibis helped keep down the incidence of schistosomiasis (bilharzia) by feeding on the snails that carry the schistosome parasites. (The disease now has become a modern plague along parts of the Nile because dam building and irrigation create favorable conditions for the snails and their parasites.)

Near the waterhole was an active nesting colony of Maribou Storks *(Leptoptilus crumeniferus)* that Peter Greaves said was unusual at that time of year. And Martha spied, in the distance, our first two Crowned Cranes *(Balearica regulorum),* curiously, it seemed, perched high in a tall tree.

We stopped briefly at Masinda Hotel for a bounteous buffet luncheon with a good selection of fresh fruits, and for me an opportunity to find a Bronzy Sunbird *(Nectarinia kilimensis)* feeding at an enormous hibiscus blossom. Then we were off for Murchison Falls National Park, through barren-looking grass and scrub country via a narrow dirt road said to be impassable in the rainy season. Under a grove of trees we saw our first African elephants. They stood nearly motionless in the shade, as is their custom during the warmer parts of the day. A wart hog associated with the elephants, perhaps for easier scavenging, beat a hasty retreat, but the elephants remained unperturbed. We saw several herds of wild buffalo and several species of deer not readily identifiable at that time. Two large Ground Hornbills *(Bucorvus leadbeateri)* and a magnificent Kori Bustard *(Ardeotis kori)* were the only birds we identified from our car.

At the end of the long day's journey we crossed the Victoria Nile on a ferry, where I watched a Pied Kingfisher *(Ceryle rudis),* perhaps the most common of the African kingfishers, that seemed to be escorting us to the opposite shore. Then, before dark, we settled down at Paraa Lodge. After a welcome repast we watched a group of natives in picturesque costumes put on a perfectly respectable (it was rumored that it was not always respectable) performance of dancing, singing, and playing of native instruments.

During the night we heard a hippo splashing and bellowing in a ditch that drained from the lodge into the Nile. And at dawn we heard a chorus of avian voices, although January is not the optimum season for bird song. We tried to spot some of the singers from our balcony. One of them was a Black-headed Gonolek *(Lanarius erythrogaster),* a handsome red-breasted laniid that one would hardly take for a shrike. Then another prize: a Red-cheeked Cordon-bleu *(Uraeginthus bengalus)* hopped down onto the lawn below us. More grotesque, almost repulsive, were the Marabou Storks, seen in the distance at nests the day before, but here perched close by in trees or parading on the lawn. One group of trees was loaded with 30 or more Hooded Vultures *(Necrosyrtis monachus)* mingling with the storks.

Then we took the seven-mile launch cruise up the Victoria Nile, said to be (and I agree) one of the highlights of a trip to East Africa. Elephants (bulls, cows, and calves) lined the banks at close range; hippos sported in the water or wallowed in the mud along the banks; and huge crocodiles, said to be the largest specimens and the largest population in Africa, basked along the shores. Birds were numerous, of course, many of them close enough for identification. I listed about 20 new ones; probably a hundred species could be seen there with more time and effort. (The total park list runs close to 500 species.) Some of those of special interest to me were the Yellow-billed Storks *(Ibis ibis),* standing (often on one leg), or sitting on their tarsi, along the shore; the Goliath and Purple herons *(Ardea goliath* and *A. purpurea); *African Fish Eagles *(Cuncuma vocifer),* that resemble our Bald Eagles but with more white and with a chestnut belly; African Skimmers *(Rynchops flavirostris);* Green Wood Hoopoes *(Phoeniculus purpureus);* and a large colony of Red-throated Bee-eaters *(Melittophagus bullocki)* going in and out of their burrows in a steep bank.

Our launch took us to the foot of the falls that tumbled down through a deep cleft (20 feet wide) in the rocks, a more spectacular view I thought than that seen the previous day from the land. Then we returned to the lodge to catch our breath, to try to catch up on our notes, and to pick up a little nourishment before the afternoon excursion.

After lunch we went on a "game drive" in small observation cars whose tops open up for better views and for photography. Driving was a little dull at first, but out in the remoter ranges, especially on the plains bordering Lake Albert, animal life was abundant. In addition to the large mammals mentioned earlier, there were numerous lions, the females and their cubs so tame we could approach closely with cars without disturbing them. Here also was an excellent opportunity to study some of the less-known ungulates at close range—Jackson's hartebeest *(Alcelaphus buselaphus),* oribis *(Ouribia ouribi),* Uganda kobs *(Adenota kob),* and Defassa waterbucks *(Kobus defassa),* all beautiful animals that posed nicely for us. But a wary leopard did not pose for us; it slithered out of a tree and sneaked away before some of us had a chance to see it.

My bird list included 10 new species plus many repeats: three confusing harriers (see appended list), wintering wheatears from Europe, a Eurasian Kestrel, and—more exciting—a large flock of Tufted Guineafowl *(Numida meleagris),* two male Black-bellied Bustards *(Lissotis melanogaster),* and several Abyssinian Rollers *(Coracius abyssinica).* On the plains bordering

Lake Albert we also got closer views of large numbers of Sacred Ibis and Cattle Egrets that we had seen earlier, and a spectacular flock of Abdim's or White-bellied Storks *(Sphenorynchus abdimii)*.

Reluctantly, although anticipating more great adventures ahead, we left Paraa Lodge the next morning for the long drive back to Entebbe and the flight to Nairobi. But before leaving, I took a last look and saw a handsome Blue-spotted Wood Dove *(Turtur afer)* and a Scarlet-chested Sunbird *(Chalcomitra senegalensis)*. En route to Entebbe we paused at a waterhole long enough to watch a Saddle-billed Stork *(Ephippiorhynchus senegalensis),* one of the largest and handsomest of the storks. I had tantalizing glimpses of other birds as we sped along, but we couldn't stop to identify them.

Our flight from Entebbe to Nairobi was delayed, which afforded us some precious minutes in Entebbe Animal and Bird Sanctuary. The zoo with its caged animals was unimpressive, a little dismal, I thought, but many wild birds were present in the well-planted park. There were flocks of Golden-backed Weavers *(Ploceus jacksoni)*—males, females, nests, and young. Smaller numbers of Viellot's Black Weavers *(Melanopteryx nigerrimus)* were also attending nests. More exciting (a new order and a new family) were the Speckled Mousebirds *(Colius striatus),* those peculiar birds that sleep upside down in bunches and crawl around in trees like squirrels. After a welcome tea break on the lawn overlooking Lake Victoria, where I scanned the waters unsuccessfully for more birds, we were off for Nairobi. Then it was a long but interesting drive from the airport to the New Stanley Hotel where at about midnight we bedded down exhausted.

Nairobi and the National Parks of Kenya

After a morning of leisure (we needed it) we visited Nairobi National Park. For a park so close to a large and cosmopolitan city (all races and nationalities) like Nairobi, it has an amazing population of wild animals. On the outskirts of the park is an animal orphanage, where homeless, injured, or unwanted animals are cared for. It gave us an opportunity to see some unusual wildlife at close range. Then we went on a leisurely game-viewing drive through the park, stopping frequently to watch and photograph some of the larger animals—close-ups of giraffes browsing on sharp-spined acacia twigs, wart hogs grubbing in the dirt, and herds of zebras, wildebeests (gnus), hartebeests, and elands. And the highlight for me: my first Ostriches *(Struthio camelus),* the sole survivors of a once great order (Struthioniformes) of primitive birds. Red-billed Oxpeckers

(Buphagus erythrorhynchus) foraged on the backs of elands and on a giraffe, and several Spur-winged Geese *(Plectropterus gambensis)* grazed on the shores of a small pond in the park.

Back in Nairobi that evening we listened to a real down-to-earth lecture by a university faculty man. The three East African countries—Kenya, Uganda, and Tanzania—he said, were striving for economic and political unity but were having difficulties because of fears of losing tribal identities and sovereign powers. Dr. Safford, the physician in our party, asked about planned parenthood. We have it, the speaker told us, but it isn't working out well. The number of offspring a man has is considered a sign of virility, and people who need birth control the most often have the most children. And the decrease in infant mortality and increase in longevity are creating new population problems. Martha asked about the cost of education. We were told it is very high at primary and secondary levels and even higher, often prohibitive, at the college level. But one redeeming feature, in addition to increasing scholarships and other financial aids, is the obligation some feel toward helping their poorer relatives in school. He himself was helping out twenty-five relatives, some of whom he didn't even know. This proved to be true of one of our native drivers who, although he had children of his own, was helping some of his younger relatives finance their educations.

Next morning we visited the city's parliament buildings, the University of Nairobi campus, Snake Park, and the museum. The university grounds were surprisingly attractive with well-kept gardens and impressive buildings. Even with so brief a visit I found time to identify four new birds; the most interesting to me was a flock of Bronze Mannikins *(Spermestes cucullatus)* feeding on the heads of tall grasses. The Snake House had some truly intriguing specimens, and the avian exhibits in the museum were very good.

That afternoon we went back to the national park headquarters to hear another lecture, this time about the park and its problems: too many visitors, sometimes 10,000 children in a day; 100,000 cars a year, with parking and space problems; undue disturbance to animals—such as lions at their kill—which makes them too tame and facilitates poaching, a largely uncontrollable problem in Africa. The lecture was followed by an outstanding fifty-minute movie of underwater pictures—crocodiles feeding on their prey, otters catching fish and playing with a turtle, darters and cormorants pursuing fish, and rarely observed underwater activities of hippopotami.

That afternoon we visited Sidney (Ted) Downey's estate, a trip said to have been arranged especially for me. Mr. Downey, a former game hunter who had given up the gun for the camera, had a large aviary with a remarkable collection of living birds. More than 100 species—all but three of them (Ring-necked Pheasants, Harlequin Quail, and a Brazilian Cardinal) native species—were housed in a facility attempting to simulate natural habitats. Unfortunately it was a dark cloudy afternoon with thunder rumbling overhead, in spite of which I managed to secure a few passable pictures.

Not surprisingly, Martha and I (others in the party were "so-so" birders) joined the tea party at the house a little late. But that worked out well for us. Mrs. Leslie Brown (a neighbor of the Downeys), whose husband is a leading authority on African birds, was largely finished with her pouring duties and wanted to talk to us. The Browns, understandably, had entertained many American ornithologists, including Roger Tory Peterson; Dean Amadon, coauthor with Leslie Brown of the classic two-volume work *Eagles, Hawks, and Falcons of the World;* Walter Spofford (Syracuse), another authority on raptorial birds; and Tom Cade (Cornell), an authority on almost everything pertaining to birds. Leslie Brown was not home—he was camping in Ngorongoro Crater for his continuing study of flamingos.

En route to Nakuru National Park the following day, we stopped for a few hours at the Mayer ranch, a 6,000-acre estate with green lawns, flowering shrubs, and tall trees. The purpose of our visit was to see a Masai tribe whom the Mayers allow to camp on their premises and to put on demonstrations for tourists. A semicircle of low dung-plastered huts, surrounded by a thornbush barrier and "yellow fever," or acacia, trees, house junior warriors who put in a number of years (formerly twelve) of training at the *manyatta,* where they learn the art of primitive warfare and how to raise cattle, the main source of nourishment (milk and blood) for the youths. The young men, heavily painted, put on an amazing show for us, including dances and a sham battle in which they lined up and threw spears at the "enemy." Highly decorated skin shields warded off the spears. Another tribe, the Samburus, who do not live in the villa, came as invited guests and put on an equally remarkable performance of their own.

Women and children are not allowed to stay overnight in the encampment but come in during the day to sell beads and artwork. Unlike the warriors, who are fine physical specimens, the women and children are a sorry-looking lot, with shaven heads, facial sores, and flies crawling over their faces. The women did a good business that day—and so did Eastman Kodak!

But the day wasn't over. We were yet to see the flamingos at Nakuru

National Park, a sight that Sir Peter Scott, renowned British ornithologist, has called "the greatest ornithological spectacle in the world." After some delay at the park entrance, we proceeded directly to the lake, where we could see acres of flamingos. They looked like pink scum on the water as we approached, but resolved into individual birds on closer view. There were hundreds of thousands of them. In favorable years some of the larger concentrations are said to number one to three million birds. Most of them, perhaps 90 percent or more, were Lesser Flamingos *(Phoeniconaias minor),* the rest, Greater Flamingos *(Phoenicopterus ruber).* The adults were post-breeding birds that had nested elsewhere and then moved in to Lake Nakuru's alkaline rich waters to feed on the abundant algae, diatoms, and small invertebrates, which are scooped up as a rich muddy soup from which the edible portions are strained out by the sievelike lamellae in the peculiar bill. Associated with the flamingos were many Black-winged Stilts *(Himantopus himantopus)* standing in the shallow water on their ridiculously long legs, and scavenging Marabou Storks that had captured an injured flamingo and were rapidly disposing of it.

Birding was also good along the shores of the lakes as well as in a field en route to and from the park entrance. Wandering along the shore, Martha and I were able to identify some 13 species (mostly new for our African list) of gulls and terns, assorted shorebirds, and ducks. Three land birds were also of interest; a Drongo *(Dicrurus adsimilis),* the only Dicruridae we saw in Africa; a Yellow-throated Longclaw *(Macronyx croceus),* a motacillid reminding me of our meadowlarks; and an Anteater Chat *(Myrmecocichla aethiops),* a starlinglike thrush with white wing patches. Martha and I were late getting back to our car. But Andy, our driver, had waited for us; the others had gone on to Stag's Head Hotel in Nakuru for the night.

By this time Martha and I had been assigned more or less permanently to ride with Andy, the only one of the drivers who knew the native birds. Prior to that I had been largely on my own. I was the only fanatic bird watcher in the party; Peter Greaves, our British tour leader, was a good naturalist but was usually occupied with other matters, such as business arrangements and the collecting of butterflies for Williams' forthcoming book on the butterflies of East Africa. But Andy, who had been studying birds for three years, had remarkably sharp vision and could identify birds almost unerringly without binoculars. (He had had a pair but lost them in a car wreck—stolen while he was unconscious—so Martha gave him her binoculars when we left Africa.) Often, in hurrying from one place to another, we couldn't stop to identify roadside birds. But en route to Nakura that day, Andy had pointed out three species of hawks perched in trees or on wires along the way: a dozen or more Augur Buzzards *(Buteo rufofuscus)*, two Long-crested Hawk Eagles *(Lophoaetus occipitalis)*, and a Pygmy Falcon *(Poliohierax semitorquatus)*.

Mara Masai Game Reserve and the Serengeti

Our next station, and one of the best, was at Keekorok Lodge, 150 miles from Nakuru. We were off fairly early, but before departing I managed to sneak in a brief inspection of the almost birdless park near our hotel. Speckled Pigeons *(Columba guinea)* were the only birds of interest. It was a long ride to Keekorok Lodge in the Mara Masai Game Reserve in Kenya, which borders on Serengeti National Park in Tanzania. Our route took us through varied country and up over a high plateau where Andy made several stops for birds. At one place we found both Malachite and Golden-winged sunbirds *(Nectarinia famosa* and *N. reichenowi)*, which, like our hummingbirds, are among the jewels of the bird world. Here also we found several Streaky Seed-eaters *(Serinus striolatus)* and a flock of Yellow-rumped Seed-eaters *(S. atrogularis)*.

We stopped for lunch in an acacia grove, a sort of oasis surrounded by open plains. On the open plains I saw my first Secretary-birds *(Sagittarius serpentarius)*, long-legged, hawklike or cranelike birds roaming over the plains, and a White-bellied Bustard *(Lissotis melanogaster)*, perhaps the most attractively colored of the bustards. Both birds, especially the Secretary-bird, were high on my *desideratum* list. At the lunch stop our car had a flat tire; I offered to help but Andy suggested I look for birds. A Northern Brubru *(Nilaus afer)*, which is a striking black-and-white laniid; a D'arnaud's Barbet *(Trachyphonus darnaudii)*; and a Greater Honey-guide *(Indicator indicator)* were the best finds. The latter two are of special interest because of the parasitic relationship between them; female honey-guides enter the nesting cavities of barbets to lay their eggs. At hatching, the mandibles of the young honey-guides are equipped with sharp spines by means of which they "butcher" the young barbets as soon as the latter hatch. The spines are shed after they have accomplished their murderous mission.

Keekorok was a pleasant surprise—an outstanding setup of dormitories and a dining hall in a beautiful setting. We had a six-course dinner that evening while looking out over the spacious grounds where monkeys frolicked on the lawn. A sign post attractively set in a bed of flowers pointed the way to the numbered dormitories; a Pied Wheatear *(Oenanthe leucomela)*, obligingly, I thought, sat on the sign that pointed to our dormitory. We all loved Keekorok and wished that we could stay longer.

After a 6 A.M. tea the next morning, we were off for a three-hour game run in the Mara Masai Game Reserve, which Williams, in his *Field Guide to the National Parks of East Africa* has described in such glowing terms: "breath-taking vistas," "the largest population of lions—in Kenya," "vast assemblages of plains game—with associated predators," and a "profuse" birdlife (more than 400 species). Andy was in his element that morning. Although we saw some of the "vast assemblages" of game animals, we concentrated on birds. We got a dozen or so new species that morning, and I found many more around the lodge. Our car was late getting us back for breakfast, but we were fed royally nonetheless. We became known as the "birding car," and after each trip afield members of our party would ask how my bird list was coming.

Birds seen on the morning game run included Helmeted Guineafowl *(Numida mitrata),* Crested and Flappet larks *(Galerida cristata* and *Mirafra africana),* a White-browed Coucal *(Centropus superciliosus),* a flock of Gray-crested Helmet Shrikes *(Prionops cristata),* a Slate-colored Boubou *(Laniarius funebris),* and several Jackson's Widowbirds *(Drepanoplectes jacksoni).* Around the lodge, swallows were prominent, especially the Striped Swallows that nested on the buildings and competed with the White-rumped Swifts *(Apus caffer)* that often appropriated the swallow nests. But the beautiful Wire-tailed Swallows *(H. smithii)* and the large Mosque Swallows *(H. senegalensis)* were also prominent. Parrot species are scarce in Kenya, but we found a couple of Brown Parrots *(Poicephalus meyeri)* behind the lodge. Even more striking was a pair of White-crested Turacos *(Tauraco leucolophus)* attending a nest in a tree on the lawn, a flock of Red-necked Spurfowl *(Pternistis cranchii)* scuttling through the grass, and a pair of Verreaux's Eagle Owls *(Bubo lacteus)* well camouflaged as they perched motionless in a tree.

It was a short drive to Lobo Lodge, our next stop, so we had time for birding along the way. Again Andy was great. Often he would stop suddenly and say, "There's a bird over in that bush that would be new for your list." Usually he was right, but he was not infallible and didn't try to bluff us. He didn't profess to know many birds by song, and he hadn't worked out the obscure species of sylviids. We identified 14 new species of birds en route to Lobo and found two more in the evening at the lodge—a list of 75 species for the day. The en route birds were too numerous to describe here, but some of those that impressed me most were a Knob-billed Goose *(Sarkidiornis melanotus)* in a puddle beside the road, Pin-tailed Whydahs *(Vidua macroura)* being almost helplessly blown about by the wind because of their ridiculously long tails, several White-headed buffalo Weavers *(Dinemellia dinemelli),* a Bare-faced Go-away-bird *(Gymnoschizorhis personata),* and Cinnamon-breasted Buntings *(Fringillaria tahapisi).*

Lobo Lodge was another fabulous place—stone dormitories, a dining room, a lounge, and a swimming pool carved into gigantic rocks. A lookout on a high rock ledge afforded fine views of game animals on ranges below. Appropriately, a rock hyrax *(Heterohyrax brucei),* a rodentlike, woodchuck-sized mammal more closely related to elephants than to rodents, came out from his rocky den and whistled at us. African Rock Martins *(Ptyonoprogne fuligula)* also lived around the rocky ledges.

From Lobo we drove on to Fort Ikoma. Again we birded along the way and got 14 more new birds, including my first long-coveted sandgrouse (Pteroclidae), several raptors, rollers, shrikes, cuckoos, and more weaverbirds.

Fort Ikoma was another intriguing place, quite different from any of the other lodges. We were housed in small grass- and cane-thatched huts, usually one couple to a hut. Our abode had a stone floor with rugs, a bathroom with a sunken tub set in the stone floor and a picture window affording a spectacular view. Spacious gardens, vine-covered archways, and an open dining room where we were served several four-course dinners by waiters in costumes were other attractions.

Our various excursions afield from Lobo Lodge, Fort Ikoma, and Seronera (headquarters for the park) took us into various parts of Serengeti, the largest (over 5,600 square miles) and best known of Tanzania's five national parks. On these trips we concentrated on game animals, which Williams has called "the greatest and most spectacular concentration . . . found anywhere in the world." We witnessed some of the mass migrations, particularly of wildebeests and zebras, much as pictured in a recent *National Geographic* television show. Thousands of animals dashed across the road in front of and behind our moving cars; somehow—by some miracle, it seemed to me—the animals dextrously avoided colliding with our cars and went on their way at full speed. Giraffe also were plentiful in Serengeti, the most we saw anywhere. And there were gazelles (Grant's and Thompson's), impalas, topis, oribis, dik-diks, waterbucks, and elands, as well as hyaenas, mongooses, baboons, and many smaller mammals. I never did get them all properly classified. At the lodges we often dined on impala, topi, and zebra steaks; the former two were tender and tasty, the latter a little tough and not so well flavored. Surplus populations of grazing animals build up in the parks, we were told, and need to be culled.

268

Predators were quite plentiful in the park. I obtained close-up photos (from a car) of a pride of 25 sleeping lions stretched out on the grass, some lying on their backs with their feet up. Jackals (3 species) and cheetahs were also present and easily observed, but our drivers hunted long and diligently for our only leopard, a superb creature snoozing unperturbed by the cars that congregated under the tree for people to observe and photograph the magnificent beast.

Somewhat incidental to our big game observations, I continued to record birds, but I ended up a little confused as to what was seen where. I was intrigued by two tiny three- to four-inch tinkerbirds, the Golden-rumped and the Red-fronted *(Pogoniulus bilineatus* and *P. pusillus),* that were in sharp contrast to the huge Martial Eagle *(Polemaetus bellicosus)* we watched feeding on a carcass it had carried to a treetop. The black-and-white-patterned Blacksmith Plover *(Hoplopterus armatus)* was the most striking of the several plovers seen. We saw three species of sandgrouse, those strange birds that transport water in specially constructed, water-retaining breast feathers and carry it over miles of hot dry deserts for their thirsty young.

En route to Ngorongoro Crater from Fort Ikoma, we stopped at the Grzimek Research Institute, named in honor of the late Michael Grzimek who lost his life in a plane crash while studying the animal life of the Serengeti. Father and son (Bernard and Michael) had dedicated their lives to studying and preserving the Serengeti and its inhabitants. At the institute we visited the research lab and the well-stocked library and listened as employees explained the research projects being carried out in the Serengeti. Unfortunately, little or no money is available from the institute to finance such projects. Research workers have to find other means of support for the privilege of working in such a challenging setting.

We arrived at Olduvai Gorge, our next stop, in a deluge of rain. A small museum there depicts primitive man, his tools, and his way of life. All is carefully explained by an attendant on duty. From an observation hut we looked down into the gorge, where the Leakeys have made such remarkable discoveries of fossils of early man, particularly the two-million-year-old *Zinanthropus* remains, but the heavy rain prevented us from making closer inspections of the excavations.

We had to hurry on. Our drivers anticipated difficulties on the road ahead. How right they were! We soon came to a swollen stream, fed by a torrent of water from a cloudburst in the high surrounding hills. Peter and the drivers looked askance at the impassable river and suggested the gloomy prospect of having to wait, perhaps overnight, until the flood subsided. But

Male (black) and female (gray) Ostriches in Nairobi National Park.

Grazing animals, like these hartebeests and wildebeest (gnu) in Nairobi National Park, help flush insects for the Ostriches associated with them.

Giraffes, widespread in the savanna lands of East Africa, feed in part on thorny acacias.

Giraffes have thick-skinned lips and tough tongues that enable them to sort out succulent leaves from thorny acacia branches.

Yellow-billed Storks are common along the White Nile.

Pied Crows are common in cities like Kampala in Uganda.

Wild elephants, endangered in many parts of Africa, flourish under protection in some of the National parks.

Sleeping lionesses and cubs after a hearty meal. The male remained aloof from the pride at some distance.

A pair of Cape buffaloes, perhaps the most dangerous and most feared of the wild animals in Africa.

Dozing leopard, unperturbed by the tour vehicles and photographers gathered under the tree.

An eland in Ngorongora Crater. Large herds of grazing animals migrate into the crater when forage in the surrounding savannas becomes scarce.

then they went exploring upstream and thought they found a more shallow place that might possibly be forded. Andy was the first to try it. He shouted "Hang on!" We did hang on while he plunged his vehicle into the raging torrent and churned his way to the opposite bank. The car faltered, with spinning wheels, but finally climbed up the embankment. But the next car to cross got hopelessly mired. After breaking three tow ropes, the boys managed to extricate the car. Then, after a conference, the other three drivers decided to go back and try the original crossing, but that was no better. It seemed like hours before all five cars were safely across. The whole crew worked cooperatively at the task. They plunged into the water, removed stones from in front of and under the cars, and pushed and pulled. They accepted the challenge good-naturedly, talking loudly and shouting commands in Swahili. Perhaps they were swearing; if so, they nonetheless seemed to be enjoying themselves.

After the last car was free, we went on our way, but we soon faced another problem. A car with a flat tire was stuck in another stream. But our boys came to the rescue; they pushed the car out, fixed the tire, and we were on our way again. To revive our drooping spirits we sang hymns. Andy had an excellent voice and led the singing.

At Ngorongoro Crater Lodge we had other difficulties. The facilities were the poorest we encountered anywhere on our trip—someone in our party quipped that that was because it was run by Americans. But one obvious reason was crowded quarters. Because of the rain, a large number of visitors who were supposed to leave to make room for incoming guests didn't go. Martha and I were assigned to a "hole in the wall" with a narrow bed but no table or chairs. Wet and dirty, I looked forward to a hot shower, but the bathroom was down the hall and had no hot water.

During the night, however, the skies cleared some, affording us a breathtaking view down into the deep crater, a 102-square-mile expanse of luxuriant grass, marshes, and a brackish lake. Clouds and mist hung over the lake, partially obscuring it; only after we had descended into the 2,000 foot crater in jeeps with four-wheel drives did we get a clear view with the clouds above us.

The bottom of the crater was a fascinating place. Some herbivores, such as the rhinos and hippos, probably live there the year around, but many ungulates migrate into the crater when the grass on the outside ranges is depleted. We saw large herds of most of the grazing animals we had seen on the Serengeti plains, but the Black Rhino *(Diceros bicornis)* was new. One standing in a mud puddle faced us belligerently and started toward our jeep, but our driver shifted into reverse and backed away; the rhino didn't follow. Some say these rhinos are not really dangerous, that they have poor vision and charge in a straight line. All you need to do, it is claimed, is to step aside while the rhino continues to charge until it meets with some obstacle, like a tree, or forgets what it was mad about. We didn't try to test this theory.

Birds were also quite plentiful in the crater, but they were mostly birds seen earlier. It seemed strange to see a Northern Shoveler, our Michigan species, so far afield. A large assemblage of shorebirds, some of which went unidentified, included a flock of Ruffs *(Philomachus pugnax)* in winter plumage; we had not seen any in their striking breeding plumage in Europe. The crater also harbors a large population of flamingos. At our lunch stop in a grove of trees (rare in the crater) a flock of Speke's Weavers *(Ploceus spekei)* and several Superb Starlings *(Spreo superbus),* both species beauty-contest candidates in their respective families, came to lunch and reaped rich rewards.

Our stay in the crater was cut short. Rain was threatening again, and our drivers were concerned about climbing the 2,000-foot rise up out of the crater. So we returned to camp and spent a leisurely afternoon catching up on notes and visiting a Fig Tree House that served strong coffee and afforded a good view.

Next day we left the crater for Lake Manyara National Park. En route we passed through some pretty rugged country, over hills and through deep narrow canyons with dangerous curves, then out into more open country. Lake Manyara is noted for its wealth of bird life (more than 300 species) and for its tree-climbing lions, thought to climb into trees to escape annoying insects such as tsetse flies or, some say, to get a better lookout for prey. One of the unusual birds at Manyara is the Palm Nut Vulture *(Gypohierax angolensis),* which has largely forsaken the vulturine carrion-feeding habit to feast on the husks of oil palm nuts. We had a little time before and after a delicious buffet luncheon at the lodge, so Andy maneuvered around to find likely places for birds. We got a dozen or so new ones, including some Yellow-billed Oxpeckers *(Buphagus africanus)* feeding on the backs of buffaloes, some Kittlitz Sand Plovers *(Charadrius pecuarius)* that I tried to pass off as wheatears until Andy corrected me, a Blue-naped Mousebird *(Colius macrourus),* and a Wahlberg's Eagle *(Aquila wahlbergi)*—the latter perfectly silhouetted in a roadside tree. Lake Manyara was an inviting place—a beautiful lake, luxurious facilities on a ridge overlooking the lake, and an abundant bird life. We wished for more time there but had to stick to a schedule that called for an overnight in Arusha.

Arusha proved to be an attractive, prosperous-looking city. As we entered it, the market place was bustling with activity. Women in lavishly colored costumes were coming and going with baskets of produce on their heads. Pictures of the natives here are *verboten,* but I sneaked a few through the car window. One was of two gaily dressed children we passed at about 30 miles per hour; though it is somewhat blurred, I regard it as a choice picture. Our second-story hotel room window afforded a better view of street scenes below, including passing troops of school children in uniform. From our window we could see Mt. Meru, a rugged peak with streaks of snow in the gullies. The hotel grounds included spacious lawns and gardens that sloped down to a river, but a stroll in the morning produced wet feet and few birds.

We left Arusha in the morning, after casting a last lingering look at the busy crowds patronizing sidewalk sales. On the outskirts of the city we passed through pastoral country with many cattle and goats. We stopped briefly at an African Wildlife Management Office, where a staff man lectured on the functions of the institute. I skipped the lecture (at Peter's suggestion) and walked around the grounds to look for birds but found only two new ones—a Silvery-cheeked Hornbill *(Bycanistes brevis)* and several noisy White-necked Ravens *(Corvus albicollis)*. Suprisingly, the center had a good collection of birds in their museum.

We made a welcome stop at Marangu Hotel for lunch—a buffet luncheon that could be carried out into the rose gardens for consumption. Two Brown-headed Bush Shrikes *(Tchagra australis)* and a flock of a dozen or more Rufous-backed Mannikins *(Spermestes nigriceps)* afforded us good views as they foraged on the lawns.

Then we entered Tsavo National Park, Kenya's largest and perhaps most ecologically diversified park, one of the largest (8,034 square miles) in the world. Of course, we couldn't begin to cover the 500 miles of roads in the park, but our route to Kilaguni Lodge afforded a good representative sample. Beyond the park entrance the land was rather flat and barren and largely devoid of wildlife. Then we came into a hilly section with rounded peaks (The Five Sisters) and volcanic outcrops. Snowcapped Kilimanjaro, Africa's highest mountain, loomed up in the distance at times, but it was usually obscured by clouds. Andy identified some of the mammals for us, including gerunuks *(Litocranius walleri)* and oryx *(Oryx beisa),* which I had not noted previously. I got a dozen or so new birds along the way and a dozen more at Kilaguni Lodge, which proved to be an excellent place for birding. Special birds for me en route were the Yellow-necked Spurfowl *(Pternistis leucoscepus)* that walked or ran ahead of us in the road; Black-faced Sandgrouse *(Eremialector decoratus)*, also flushed from the road; and Namaqua Doves *(Oena capensis)*, the most attractive, I thought, of the nine species of columbids we saw in Africa. Best songbirds were the numerous Golden-breasted or Regal Starlings *(Cosmopsarus regius)*, and a choice Golden Pipit *(Tmetothylacus tenellus)*.

Kilaguni was quite different from the other lodges where we stayed. The buildings were constructed largely of stone; our dorm suggested a cold prison cell, but it was entirely adequate and had a porch with lounge chairs from which we could look out on a floodlighted waterhole where elephants and other animals came to drink and bathe at night. The dining room was open along one side. While we were eating, a huge bull elephant came in frighteningly close but didn't extend his trunk over the wall. Buffalo Weavers *(Bulbaornis albirostris)*, the largest of the weavers, and Layard's Black-headed Weavers *(Ploceus nigriceps)* did come in for handouts placed on the wall. Colonies of the latter, as well as Red-headed Weavers *(Anaplectes melanotis)*, had nests in the trees, but it was not their main breeding season and some of the nests were in a state of disrepair. Red-billed Hornbills *(Tockus erythrorhynchus)* wandered over the grounds like chickens. We saw several African Hoopoes *(Upupa africanus)*, thought by some taxonomists to be specifically distinct from the Eurasian form *(Upupa epops)*. Other special-interest birds included White-bellied Go-away-birds *(Corythaixoides leucogaster)*, Didric Cuckoos *(Chrysococcyx caprius)* that whistled a distinctive tune, an Orange-bellied Parrot *(Poicephalus rufiventris)*, and Paradise Wydahs *(Steganura paradisea)* being blown about by the wind.

On the afternoon of the second day in Tsavo we visited Mzima Springs, whose sparkling clear waters, frequented by hippos and crocodiles, gush out of the ground in sufficient quantities to supply the distant city of Mombasa with its water supply. We drank some of the cold water issuing from a pipe in the ground and then descended into an enclosure to view fish (barbels) through a glass window.

Next day (February 12) we were off for Mombasa on Kenya's Indian Ocean coast. Mombasa Beach Hotel, where we paused for lunch, is a millionaire's paradise with the traditional beach facilities—swimming pool, white sands, and outstandingly beautiful gardens. Here we encountered our first hot weather, and although the beach was reserved for hotel guests (we were hardly that) some of the girls couldn't resist plunging into the cool water with their clothes on. It was no problem to dry out quickly in the sun.

After an almost unbelievably sumptuous lunch, we left Mombasa for

Tilifi and the night's lodging at Mnarani Club. The facilities were in dismal surroundings but were among the best accommodations we had anywhere. Martha and I had an upstairs apartment with a fancy bathroom with wall mirrors and a spacious living room with sleeping cots entirely enclosed within a huge netting, presumably for protection from mosquitos. A balcony overlooked the bay, where fishing boats, gulls and terns, and people could be watched. We had a barbecue supper that night—roast pig and shish kebab.

The drive to Marine National Park at Watamu the following day took us along the famous migration route of the Carmine Bee-eaters *(Merops nubicus)*, said to be one of the most colorful ornithological spectacles in East Africa, but we saw only a few of the brilliantly colored birds. In fact, birds along the coast, where I had hoped to find many new species, were scarce. Apparently oblivious of the crowds beneath them, Golden Palm Weavers *(Ploceus bojeri)* attending nests in the park, were among the few seen.

At the marina we were taken in a glass-bottomed boat out over the blue waters of Turtle Bay to see the corals and bizzare fishes. A great variety of gaudy fishes came in close for bread crumbs tossed to them, but the corals were not as brilliant as those we had seen years earlier in the Bahamas. Some of the more adventurous members of our party went snorkeling.

En route to Mnarini Club for another night, we stopped at Gedi National Park to see the ruins of an ancient Arab city that had flouished from A.D. 802 to A.D. 1399. Portions of the Great Mosque and the crumbling walls of ancient buildings among the tall forest trees were truly impressive, awesome sights. Deep wells were the source of water for the city. At the time of our visit a local biologist was making a study of the strange animal life that still inhabits some of the wells.

For our last day on the coast we took a sightseeing and shopping tour of Mombasa and visited Fort Jesus, an ancient Portuguese fortification that is being restored. A historical museum featured pottery, implements of war, and various tools that depicted the way of life of the early coastal inhabitants. Introduced Indian House Crows *(Corvus splendens)* that live among the ruins came and scolded us, but the Bat Hawks *(Machaerhamphus alcinus)*, said to feed on bats there at night, did not put in an appearance.

Our return trip to Nairobi called for a flight from Mombasa, but serious doubts developed about the availability of a plane. After some discussion, our drivers agreed to take us on the long hard six-hour drive to Nairobi. En route I got my last bird—a Yellow-billed Hornbill *(Tockus flavirostris)* that flashed across the road in front of our speeding car.

In Nairobi we encountered more difficulties. We were scheduled for an early-morning flight from Nairobi to Rome, but it never materialized. In fact, we waited around the airport all day for a plane that didn't come in. We had a free (?) lunch, courtesy of the airlines, but to offset this we got charged $10 for excess baggage that we didn't have. We think that the luggage from another party got weighed in with ours and that we got charged for it. Eventually we were bused back to our hotel, presumably for another night, but then Lyman Perry, who had taken over supervision of affairs after Peter left us, arranged with Club Tours, Inc., to get us a midnight flight to Zurich and Brussels instead of going to Rome. Martha and I were disappointed with the change because we had never been in Italy; our schedule called for an overnight in Rome (paid for in advance) and a tour of the city's historical attractions the next day. But the flight to Zurich, Brussels, and New York came off without further delays. And after the usual confusion in New York, we caught a flight (not on our schedule) to Detroit and home.

Thus ended our fabulous tour of a small part of Africa, a rich experience with congenial companions, memorable trips through East Africa's parks, and 292 birds, 244 of which were new species for me.

References

Grzimek, B., and M. Grzimek. *Serengeti Shall Not Die.* New York: E.P. Dutton & Co., Inc. 1961.

Williams, J. G. *A Field Guide to the Birds of East and Central Africa.* (4th impression). London: Collins, 1969

_____. *A Field Guide to the National Parks of East Africa (3rd impression).* London: Collins, 1970.

An Annotated List of the Birds Seen in East Africa

(Except for minor updating, the names and sequence of families follows William's *A Field Guide to the Birds of East and Central Africa.*

Struthionidae (Ostrich)
   Ostrich *(Struthio camelus)*. Herd of nonbreeding males and females in

279

Nairobi National Park, Jan. 31; others in Serengeti, and Ngorongoro

Podicipedidae (Grebes)
Little Grebe *(Poliocephalus ruficollis)*. Nakuru, Feb. 3, 2 in a roadside puddle

Phalacrocoracidae (Cormorants)
Great or Common Cormorant *(Phalacrocorax carbo)*. Lake Nakuru, Feb. 2, several flying over flamingos (nearly world-wide species)

Pelecanidae (Pelicans)
(Eastern) White Pelican *(Pelecanus onocrotalus)*. Lake Nakuru, Feb. 2, several around flamingos; Lake Manyara, Feb. 9
Pink-backed Pelican *(P. rufescens)*. Lake Manyara, Feb. 9, 2 or more in group were *rufescens;* others *onocratalus?*

Ardeidae (Herons and Egrets)
Gray Heron *(Ardea cinerea)*. First on Victoria Nile, Uganda, Jan. 29; others occasionally throughout East Africa
Black-headed Heron *(A. melanocephala)*. First seen en route to Paraa Lodge, Jan. 28, along Victoria Nile, Jan. 29, frequent thereafter
Goliath Heron *(A. goliath)*. Victoria Nile, Jan. 29, two or more, hard to tell from following species without size comparison
Purple Heron *(A. purpurea)*. First along Nile, Jan. 29, frequent thereafter but some may have been *goliath*. Mzima Springs, Feb. 11
Great Egret *(Casmerodius albus)*. Common throughout East Africa (same species as our American form)
Little Egret *(Egretta garzetta)*. Common throughout East Africa
Cattle Egret *(Bubulcus ibis)*. Everywhere with grazing animals
Squacco Heron *(Ardeola ralloides)*. Victoria Nile, Jan. 29, several
Green-backed or Striated Heron *(Butorides striatus)*. Serengeti, Feb. 6, one on flooded bridge—the only one seen.
Black-crowned Night Heron *(Nycticorax nycticorax)*. Occasional throughout East Africa (world-wide species).

Scopidae (Hammerhead)
Hammerkop *(Scopus umbretta)*. Kampala, Jan. 28, 2 in roadside puddle; found only in Africa.

Ciconiidae (Storks)
White Stork *(Ciconia ciconia)*. Nakuru to Keekorok, Feb. 3, flock in field; Ngorongoro Crater, Feb. 8, many
Abdim's or White-bellied Stork *(Sphenorynchus abdimii)*. Common nearly everywhere—Murchison Falls, Serengeti, Ngorongoro, Tsavo
Open-billed Stork *(Anastomus lamelligerus)*. Kampala, Jan. 28, 2 in roadside puddle; Murchinson Falls, Jan. 29
Saddle-billed Stork *(Ephipporhynchus senegelensis)*. Murchison Falls, Jan. 30, 1 at roadside puddle
Marabou Stork *(Leptoptilus crumeniferus)*. Common nearly everywhere
Yellow-billed Stork *(Ibis ibis)*. Common in and around Murchison Falls,

Jan. 28 to 30; few seen elsewhere

Threskiornithidae (Ibises and Spoonbill)

Sacred Ibis *(Threskiornis aethiopicus).* Common to abundant throughout Murchison Falls and vicinity; few seen elsewhere

Hadada Ibis *(Hagadeshia hagedash).* Frequent in Murchison Falls, Jan. 29 to 30; not recorded again until Mzima Springs, Feb. 11

African Spoonbill *(Platalea alba).* Lake Nakuru, Feb. 2, brief view of 2 at flamingo colony

Phoenicopteridae (Flamingos)

Greater Flamingos *(Phoenicopterus ruber).* Lake Nakuru, Feb. 2, probably hundreds but greatly outnumbered by Lessers; Ngorongoro Crater, Feb. 8, many

Lesser Flamingo *(Phoeniconaias minor).* Lake Nakuru, Feb. 2, many thousands, possibly a million; also abundant in crater, Feb. 8

Anatidae (Ducks and Geese)

African Pochard *(Aythya erythrophthalma).* Lake Nakura, Feb. 2, 2 flocks flew over flamingo colony

Northern Shoveler *(Anas clypeata).* Ngorongoro Crater, Feb. 8, pair in puddle with shorebirds

African Black Duck *(A. sparsa).* Lake Nakuru, Feb. 3, in roadside puddle with Little Grebes—the only one seen

Cape Wigeon *(A. capensis).* Lake Nakuru, Feb. 2, small group, including 2 beautiful males, along lake shore; more in crater, Feb. 11

Hottentot Teal *(A. punctata).* Lake Nakuru, Feb. 2, small group with the wigeons along lake shore; more in crater, Feb. 11

Knob-billed Goose *(Sarkidiornis melanotos).* Serengeti, Feb. 4, female (no knob) in roadside puddle; small group, including males later in day

Egyptian Goose *(Alopochen aegyptiacus).* First at Victoria Nile, Jan. 29, common thereafter, in pairs, family groups, and flocks; many in crater, Feb. 11

Spur-winged Goose *(Plectropterus gambensis).* Nairobi, Jan, 31, 3 along shores of small pond

Sagittariidae (Secretary Bird)

Secretary Bird *(Sagittarius serpentarius).* Nakuru to Keekorok, Feb. 3, 2 on plains; Serengeti, Feb. 5, and later, several

Aegypiidae (Old World Vultures—included in Accipitridae in American classifications.)

African White-backed Vulture *(Pseudogyps africanus).* Widespread throughout East Africa; perhaps the most common of the vultures

Lappet-faced Vulture *(Torgos tracheliotus).* Ngorongoro Crater, Feb. 8, 1, not seen elsewhere; largest of the vultures seen

White-headed Vulture *(Trigonoceps occipitalis).* Quite common throughout East Africa, but sometimes hard to tell from *africanus;*

immatures confusing

Hooded Vulture *(Necrosyrtus monachus)*. Widespread and common throughout East Africa; one of the smallest vultures seen

Egyptian Vulture *(Neophron percnopterus)*. Murchison Falls, Jan. 29, 1; Ngorongoro Crater, Feb. 8, 1

Palm Nut Vulture *(Gypohierax angolensis)*. Lake Manyara, Feb. 9, 1 in palm nut tree, others in flight.

Falconidae (Falcons, Kites, Hawks, Eagles, Harriers—includes our Accipitridae)

Eurasian Kestrel *(Falco tinnunculus)*. First at Murchison Falls (Lake Albert), Jan. 29, frequent thereafter along roadsides

Lesser Kestrel *(F. naumanni)*. Fort Ikoma, Feb. 5, 1 en route

Pygmy Falcon *(Poliohierax semitorquatus)*. En route from Nairobi to Nakuru, Feb. 2, 1 on roadside wire; several others later

Black Kite *(Milvus migrans)*. First at Kampala, Jan. 29; common and widespread thereafter

Tawny Eagle *(Aquila rapax)*. Common and widespread in East Africa

Wahlberg's Eagle *(A. wahlbergi)*. En route to Arusha, Feb. 9, perfect silhouette in tree (exactly like picture in field guide)

Martial Eagle *(Polemaetus bellicosus)*. Lobo Lodge (vicinity), Feb. 5, immature feeding on carcass in treetop, crop bulging

Long-crested Hawk Eagle *(Lophaetus occipitalis)*. En route from Nairobi to Nakura, Feb. 2, two perched in trees; several at later dates

Lizard Buzzard *(Kaupifalco monogrammicus)*. Gedi National Forest, Feb. 14, 1

Bateleur *(Terathopius ecaudatus)*. En route to Kampala, Jan. 30, 2; another at Entebbe, Jan. 30; others later

African Fish Eagle *(Cuneuma vocifer)*. First along Victoria Nile, Jan. 29; frequent thereafter in other places

Augur Buzzard *(Buteo rufofuscus)*. En route from Nairobi to Nakuru, Feb. 2, a dozen or more; perhaps the most common of East African hawks; melanistic phase seen at Ngorongoro Lodge·

Gabar Goshawk *(Micronisus gabar)*. Fort Ikoma, Feb. 5, female with barred tail, quite tame

Pale Chanting Goshawk *(Melierax poliopterus)*. En route to Fort Ikoma, Feb. 5; several others later

Montagu's Harrier *(Circus pygargus)*. First at Lake Albert, Jan. 29, frequent thereafter in open savannas

Pallid Harrier *(C. macrourus)*. Lake Albert, Jan. 29, several; more later in other places

African Marsh Harrier *(C. ranivorus)*. Lake Albert, Jan. 29, several; a few others later in other places

Harrier Hawk *(Polyboroides typus)*. Murchison Falls, Jan. 30, 1

Phasianidae (Francolins, Spurfowl)

Crested Francolin *(Francolinus sephaena)*. Serengeti, Feb. 7, good view of one from car

Red-necked Spurfowl *(Pternistis cranchii)*. Keekorok Lodge, Feb. 3, small group flushed several times, fairly tame

Yellow-necked Spurfowl *(P. leucoscephus)*. En route to Kilaguni Lodge, Feb. 10, good views (and pictures) from car of birds in road; more in Tsavo, Feb. 10 to 11

Numididae (Guinea-fowl)

Helmeted Guinea-fowl *(Numida mitrata)*. Lobo Lodge, Feb. 4, small groups seen en route to and around lodge

Tufted Guinea-fowl *(N. meleagris)*. Lake Albert, Jan. 30, large flocks, then smaller groups (I missed the Vulturine Guinea-fowl that some others saw)

Rallidae (Crakes)

Black Crake *(Limnocorax flavirostra)*. Murchison Falls, Jan. 29, 2; Serengeti, Feb. 7, 2

Gruidae (Cranes)

Crowned Crane *(Balearica regulorum)*. Kampala, Jan. 28, 2; also in Nairobi, Serengeti, and Tsavo parks.

Otididae (Bustards)

Kori Bustard *(Ardeotis kori)*. Murchison Falls, Jan. 28, 1; Tsavo, Feb. 11, 1—displaying

White-bellied Bustard *(Eupodotis senegalensis)*. En route to Keekorok, Feb. 3, 1; several later in Serengeti

Black-bellied Bustard *(Lissotis melanogaster)*. Murchison Falls, Jan. 29, 2 males; Mara Masai, Feb. 3, 2

Burhinidae (Stone Plovers or Thickknees)

Stone Plover *(Burhinus sp.)*. Victoria Nile, Jan. 29, 1 along bank but I didn't check species carefully; probably *B. senegalensis*?

Jacanidae (Jacana)

African Jacana *(Actophilornis africanus)*. Murchison Falls, Jan. 28, 1 in puddle in park; seen frequently thereafter

Charadriidae (Plovers)

Ringed Plover *(Charadrius hiaticula)*. Lake Nakuru, Feb. 2, several

Kittlitz's Sand Plover *(C. pecuarius)*. Lake Manyara, Feb. 9, several on sandy ground, running around like larks

Caspian Plover *(C. asiaticus)*. Serengeti, Feb. 5, half dozen or more

Gray or Black-bellied Plover *(Pluvialis squatarola)*. Mombasa Feb. 14, 1 along beach, the only one seen

Crowned Plover *(Stephanibyx coronatus)*. Nairobi, Jan. 31, several among game animals; fairly common thereafter—Serengeti, Keekorok Lodge, Tsavo

Senegal Plover *(S. lugubris)*. Serengeti, Feb. 5

Spur-winged Plover *(Holopterus spinosus)*. Victoria Nile, Jan. 29, many

Blacksmith Plover *(H. armatus)*. Serengeti, Feb. 7, several; Ngorongoro, Feb. 8, good-sized flock in crater

Recurvirostridae (Avocets and Stilts)

Pied Avocet *(Recurvirostra avosetta)*. Lake Nakuru, Feb. 2, several along shore with flamingos

Black-winged Stilt *(Himantopus himantopus)*. Victoria Nile, Jan. 29, quite a few; Mara Masai, Feb. 3; associated with flamingos at Nakuru and Ngorongoro

Scolopacidae (Sandpipers)

Little Stint *(Calidris minuta)*. Nakuru, Feb. 2, several along beach; Ngorongoro, Feb. 8; apparently common in marshy habitats

Ruff *(Philomachus pugnax)*. Ngorongoro, Feb. 8; large flocks in crater, in winter plumage but a few showing white ruffs; also at Lake Nakuru, Feb. 2

Common Sandpiper *(Tringa hypoleucos)*. Apparently quite common throughout East Africa, but I didn't stop to check them very often

Green Sandpiper *(T. ochropus)*. Seronera Lodge (vicinity), Feb. 6, one on flooded bridge

Marsh Sandpiper *(T. stagnalis)*. Victoria Nile, Jan. 29 several; a few in other places

Greenshank *(T. nebularia)*. Victoria Nile, Jan. 29, a few; also at Lake Nakuru, Feb. 2

Common Redshank *(T. totanus)*. Lake Nakuru, Feb. 2, a few; not noted elsewhere

Whimbrel *(Numenius phaeopus)*. Mombasa, Feb. 14, lone "curlew" on shore believed to be this species

Glareolidae (Coursers)

Temminck's Courser *(Cursorius temminckii)*. En route to Fort Ikoma, Feb. 5, 4; Serengeti, Feb. 6; small flock

Laridae (Gulls and Terns)

Gray-headed Gull *(Larus cirrocephalus)*. Lake Nakuru, Feb. 2, dozen or so flying over flamingos; also at Lake Manyara and along Kenya coast

Lesser Black-backed Gull *(L. fuscus)*. Lake Manyara, Feb. 9, 2 or more

Sooty Gull *(L. hemprichii)*. Common along coast, noted especially from balcony at Mnarani Club

Gull-billed Tern *(Gelochelidon nilotica)*. Lake Nakuru, Feb. 2, several around flamingos

Lesser Crested Tern *(Sterna bengalensis)*. Apparently common along coast; in harbor at Mnarani Club

White-winged Black Tern *(Chlidonias leucoptera)*. Lake Manyara, Feb. 9, 1 adult and several immatures over lake

Rynchopidae (Skimmers)

African Skimmer *(Rynchops flavirostris)*. Victoria Nile, Jan. 29, large group (hundreds) resting on sand bar in river

Pteroclidae (Sandgrouse)

Chestnut-bellied Sandgrouse *(Pterocles exustus)*. Serengeti, Feb. 5, 3 or 4 flushed from road

Black-faced Sandgrouse *(Eremialector decoratus)*. Tsavo, Feb. 10, several flushed from road

Yellow-throated Sandgrouse *(E. gutturalis)*. Serengeti, Feb. 7, many flushed by car, some merely running ahead in road or stepping aside for car to pass

Columbidae (Pigeons and Doves)

Speckled Pigeon *(Columba guinea)*. Nakuru, Feb. 3, dozen or so in and around city park

Pink-breasted Dove *(Streptopelia lugens)*. Tsavo, Feb. 11, 2 females— the only ones seen

Red-eyed Dove *(S. semitorquata)*. Kampala, Jan. 27, first one in tree at Hotel Apollo; 2 more at Stag's Head Hotel in Nakuru, Feb. 2 to 3; several at Ngorongoro, Feb. 8

Ring-necked Dove *(S. capicola)*. Murchison Falls, Jan. 30, common in park; the most frequently seen dove in East Africa

Laughing Dove *(S. senegalensis)*. Nairobi, Feb. 1, 1 on university campus; also recorded at Serengeti and Tsavo

Namaqua Dove *(Oena capensis)*. Tsavo, Feb. 10 to 11, very common throughout park, flushed repeatedly, not seen elsewhere

Emerald-spotted Wood Dove *(Turtur chalcospilos)*. Serengeti, Feb. 4, 2 or more flushed (identified by Andy)

Blue-spotted Wood Dove *(T. afer)*. Paraa Lodge, Uganda, Jan. 31, 1 watched closely from balcony

Green Pigeon *(Treron australis)*. Kampala (en route to Masinda) Jan. 28, 1 flew past car—the only one seen in East Africa

Musophagidae (Turacos, Plantain-Eaters)

White-crested Turaco *(Tauraco leucocephalus)*. Keekorok Lodge, Feb. 3, pair at nest in tree on lawn

White-bellied Go-away Bird *(Corythaixoides leucogaster)*. Kilaguni Lodge, Feb. 11, 2 at lodge in morning, another in Tsavo in evening

Bare-faced Go-away Bird *(Gymnoschizorhis personata)*. Serengeti, Feb. 4, 1 (identified by Andy); more on Feb. 5 and 6 in park

Eastern Gray Plantain-Eater *(Crinifer zonurus)*. Kampala, Jan. 28, 1 in tree outside hotel window; more at Murchison Falls; not seen elsewhere

Cuculidae (Cuckoos and Coucals)

Black and White Cuckoo *(Clamator jacobinus)*. Serengeti, Feb. 5, 1; more the following day and in Tsavo, Feb. 10

Didric Cuckoo *(Chrysococcyx caprius)*. Kilaguni, Feb. 11, several chasing around and whistling at lodge

White-browed Coucal *(Centropus superciliosus)*. Serengeti, Feb. 4; in Tsavo, Feb. 10 to 11, quite a few

Psittacidae (Parrots)

Orange-bellied Parrot *(Poicephalus rufiventris)*. Tsavo, Feb. 11, 1

Brown Parrot *(P. meyeri)*. Keekorok Lodge, Feb. 4, 2 in back of lodge

Fischer's Lovebird *(Agapornis fischeri)*. Lobo Lodge, Feb. 5, 1; Ikoma Lodge, Feb. 6, sizable flocks

Coraciidae (Rollers)

European Roller *(Coracias garrulus)*. Serengeti, Feb. 5 to 6, and Tsavo, Feb. 10 to 11, common, also along coast

Abyssinian Roller *(C. abyssinica)*. Lake Albert, Jan. 29, 2

Lilac-breasted Roller *(C. caudata)*. Serengeti, Feb. 4, more later in Serengeti and Tsavo

Rufous-crowned Roller *(C. naevia)*. En route to Arusha, Feb. 10, 1

Broad-billed Roller *(Eurystomus glaucurus)*. Lake Manyara, Feb. 9, 2

Alcedinidae (Kingfishers)

Pied Kingfisher *(Ceryle rudis)*. Victoria Nile (Paraa Lodge), Jan. 28, 1 at ferry, more up the river on Jan. 29; Entebbe, Jan. 30, 10 at one place on wires; frequent thereafter in Kenya and Tanzania.

Pygmy Kingfisher *(Ispidina picta)*. Victoria Nile, Jan. 29, 2; may have been Malachite Kingfishers

Gray-headed Kingfisher *(Halcyon leucocephala)*. Victoria Nile, Jan. 29, common thereafter in most places

Striped Kingfisher *(H. chelicuti)*. Keekorok Lodge, Feb. 3, 1

Woodland Kingfisher *(H. senegalensis)*. Kampala, Jan. 27, 1 at hotel; Paraa Lodge, Jan. 28 to 29, several; Mara Masai, Feb. 4

Meropidae (Bee-eaters)

European Bee-eater *(Merops apiaster)*. Murchison Falls, Jan. 30, listed for park, not sure of my record

Carmine Bee-eater *(M. nubicus)*. Kenya Coast, Feb. 13 to 14, many seen, but not a mass migration as often occurs

White-throated Bee-eater *(Aerops albicollis)*. Murchison Falls, Jan. 30, 1 studied carefully at entrance to park

Little Bee-eater *(Melittophagus pusillus)*. En route to Fort Ikoma, Feb. 5, 1; more at Lake Manyara, Feb. 9

White-fronted Bee-eater *(M. bullockoides)*. Nairobi, Mayer's ranch; 2 pairs at ranch house

Red-throated Bee-eater *(M. bullocki)*. Victoria Nile, Jan. 29, large colony at nest sites in bank

Bucerotidae (Hornbills)

Trumpeter Hornbill *(Bycanistes bucinator)*. Gedi National Park, Feb. 13, 1 or 2 with flock of Silvery-cheeked at ruins

Black and White-casqued Hornbill *(B. subcylindricus)*. Ngorongoro, Feb. 9, 1 in tree tops in deep ravine

Silvery-cheeked Hornbill *(B. brevis)*. African Wildlife Management Office, Feb. 10, 1; Gedi National Park, Feb. 13, noisy flock

Gray Hornbill *(Tockus nasutus)*. Murchison Falls, Jan. 28, several, scattered; best view of one at falls.

Red-billed Hornbill *(T. erythrorhynchus)*. En route from Seronera to Fort Ikoma, Feb. 6, 1; common and quite tame at Kalaguni Lodge.

Yellow-billed Hornbill *(T. flavirostris)*. Mombasa to Nairobi, Feb. 14, unmistakable glimpse of one flying past car

Von der Decken's Hornbill *(T. deckeni)*. Fort Ikoma Lodge, Feb. 5 to 6; 1 or 2 each day; Tsavo, Feb. 16, 1 at nest hole

Ground Hornbill *(Bucorvus leadbeateri)*. Murchison Falls, Jan. 28, 2, several others later (some confusion between *B. leadbeateri* and *B. abyssinicus,* but we decided on *leadbeateri*)

Upupidae (Hoopoes)

African Hoopoe *(Upupa africana)*. Tsavo, Feb. 11, 4 seen. (Listed by Williams as specifically distinct from Eurasian form)

Phoeniculidae (Wood Hoopoes)

Green Wood Hoopoe *(Phoeniculus purpureus)*. Victoria Nile, Jan. 29, brief views of several from launch; others (dubious) later in parks.

Strigidae (Owls)

Verreaux's Eagle Owl *(Bubo lacteus)*. Keekorok Lodge, Feb. 4, 2, well camouflaged, in treetop back of lodge

Coliidae (Colies or Mousebirds)

Speckled Mousebird *(Colius striatus)*. Entebbe, Jan. 30, 6 or more climbing around in trees; quite common thereafter nearly everywhere

Blue-naped Mousebird *(C. macrourus)*. Lake Manyara, Feb. 9, 1; Tsavo, Feb. 11, several—better views

Capitonidae (Barbets)

White-headed Barbet *(Lybius leucocephalus)*. Lobo Lodge, Feb. 4, handsome bird in fig tree below lookout, more at Seronera Lodge on Feb. 6 and at Kilaguni Lodge on Feb. 11

Spotted-flanked Barbet *(Tricholaema lacrymosum)*. Keekorok Lodge, Feb. 3, 1

Red-fronted Tinker-bird *(Pogoniulus pusillus)*. Fort Ikoma, Feb. 6, 1 on lodge grounds, the only one seen for sure

Golden-rumped Tinker-bird *(P. bilineatus)*. Serengeti, Feb. 5; several seen—good views.

Red and Yellow Barbet *(Trachyphonus erythrocephalus)*. Tsavo, Feb. 10, 2

D'Arnaud's Barbet *(T. darnaudi)*. En route from Nakuru to Keekorok, Feb. 3, 1 at lunch stop; Seronera Lodge, Feb. 6, 2; Tsavo, Feb. 10

Indicatoridae (Honey-guides)

Greater Honey-guide *(Indicator indicator)*. En route from Nakuru to Keekorok, Feb. 3, 1 calling in treetop at lunch stop

Picidae (Woodpeckers)

Nubian Woodpecker *(Campethera nubica)*. Fort Ikoma, Feb. 7, 2 "courting" (I missed the Gray Woodpecker—*Mesopicos goertae*—that Martha saw.)

Apodidae (Swifts)

Nyzana Swift *(Apus niansae)*. En route from Nakuru to Keekorok,

Feb. 3, swifts flying over high plateau believed to be this species

House or Little Swift *(A. affinis)*. Nairobi, Feb. 1, many over city; apparently common in villages and around some lodges throughout East Africa

White-rumped Swift *(A. caffer)*. Keekorok Lodge, Feb. 4, colony usurping Striped Swallow nests; also at other lodges

Palm Swift *(Cypsiurus parvus)*. Entebbe and Kampala, Jan. 27, all over; common elsewhere around lodges and villages

Alaudidae (Larks)

Rufous-naped Lark *(Mirafra africana)*. Lake Nakuru, Feb. 2, 1; Mara Masai, Feb. 4, several on early morning game run

Flappet Lark *(M. rufocinnamomea)*. Mara Masai, Feb. 4, apparently common, with above.

Crested Lark *(Galerida cristata)*. Mara Masai, Feb. 4, apparently common (larks often heard and seen in flight, but not identified as to species)

Fischer's Sparrow Lark *(Eremopterix leucopareia)*. En route to Fort Ikoma, Feb. 5, saw both males and females

Motacillidae (Wagtails and Pipits)

African Pied Wagtail *(Motacilla aguimp)*. Common around all the lodges, coming in for handouts, some still in song

Eurasian Pied Wagtail *(M. alba)*. Less common than above (smaller species)

Gray Wagtail *(M. cinerea)*. A few throughout East Africa, mingling with the more abundant "blue-headed" form below and hard to distinguish from it in winter plumage

Yellow or Blue-headed Wagtail *(M. flava)*. Paraa Lodge, Jan. 29, 1; common nearly everywhere thereafter

Richard's Pipit *(Anthus richardi)*. Mara Masai, Feb. 4, 1 definite, others less certain

Golden Pipit *(Tmetothylacus tenellus)*. Tsavo, Feb. 10, Andy spotted one in flight ; better (superb) views later

Yellow-throated Longclaw *(Macronyx croceus)*. Nakuru, Feb. 2, perfect view of one in field by lake, a few others later

Pangani Longclaw *(M. aurantiigula)*. En route to Seronera, Feb. 6, 1

Rosy-breasted Longclaw *(M. ameliae)*. Serengeti, Feb. 7, 1

Pycnonotidae (Bulbuls)

Yellow-vented Bulbul *(Pycnonotus xanthopygos)*. First at Kampala, Jan. 27; common to abundant thereafter nearly everywhere

Muscicapidae (Old World Flycatchers)

Spotted Flycatcher *(Muscicapa striata)*. Fort Ikoma, Feb. 5, first definite one; hard to distinguish (Winter visitor from Europe)

White-eyed Slaty Flycatcher *(Dioptrornis fischeri)*. Mayer's ranch (Nairobi), Feb. 2, good view of one; another at Lake Manyara, Feb. 10

Paradise Flycatcher *(Tersiphone viridis)*. Mayer's ranch, Feb. 2, 1;

Seronera Lodge, Feb. 7, several; Tsavo, several

Gray Flycatcher *(Bradornis microrhynchus)*. Mombasa, Feb. 12, 1

Chin-spot Flycatcher *(Batis molitor)*. Fort Ikoma, Feb. 5, 1, identified from specimen in museum at Seronera.

South African Black Flycatcher *(Melaenornis pammelaina)*. Kilaguni Lodge, Feb. 11, 1 immature

Turdidae (Thrushes, Wheatears, Chats)

Olive Thrush *(Turdus olivaceus)*. Nairobi, Jan. 31, 2 in "orphanage"

Kurrichane Thrush *(T. libonyanus)*. Kampala, Jan. 27, 1 at hotel; Entebbe, Jan. 30, 2

European Rock Thrush *(Monticolor saxatilis)*. Mara Masai, Feb. 4, 1 on game run; others at Lobo Lodge, Feb. 5, and Kilaguni, Feb. 11

Little Rock Thrush *(M. rufocinerea)*. Mombasa, Feb. 12

Common Wheatear *(Oenanthe oenanthe)*. Murchison Falls, Jan. 29, dozen or so flushed; apparently common in open grassy areas

Isabelline Wheatear *(O. isabellina)*. Apparently common with above species, but hard to distinguish

Pied Wheatear *(O. leucomela)*. Keekorok Lodge, Feb. 4, 1 perched on sign post; others in Serengeti

Capped Wheatear *(O. pileata)*. Serengeti, Feb. 7, good view of one

Red-tailed Chat *(Cercomela familiaris)*. Paraa Lodge, Jan. 29, 1

Anteater Chat *(Myrmecocichla aethiops)*. Lake Nakuru, Feb. 2, several, perched and in flight; common in Ngorongoro Crater

Sooty Chat *(M. nigra)*. En route to Nakuru, Feb. 2, 1

Stone Chat *(Saxicola torquata)*. Ngorongoro Crater (Fig Tree House), Feb. 8, 1

White-browed Robin Chat *(Cossypha heuglini)*. Kampala, Jan. 27; Paraa Lodge, Jan. 28, 1 singing; Lobo Lodge, Feb. 5

Sylviidae (Old World Warblers)

Blackcap Warbler *(Sylvia atricapilla)*. Arusha, Feb. 9, male in tree outside hotel window (females overlooked earlier?)

Willow Warbler *(Phylloscopus trochilus)*. Fort Ikoma, Feb. 5, 2; 2 more next morning

Black-throated Apalis *(Apalis jacksoni)*. Keekorok Lodge, Feb. 4, 1

Rattling Cisticola *(Cisticola chiniana)*. Ngorongoro (Fig Tree house), Feb. 8, several "rattling," nesting(?)

Hirundinidae (Swallows and Martins)

Barn (European) Swallow *(Hirundo rustica)*. Kampala, June 27, abundant, almost daily thereafter, widespread and abundant

Angola or Uganda Swallow *(H. angolensis)*. Widespread and abundant, often with Barn Swallows

Ethiopian Swallow *(H. aethiopica)*. Victoria Nile, Jan. 29, many; noted frequently elsewhere

Wire-tailed Swallow *(H. smithii)*. Keekorok Lodge, Feb. 3 to 4, apparently nesting

Mosque Swallow *(H. senegalensis)*. Keekorok Lodge, Feb. 3 to 4, many.

(Seen on earlier and later dates, but I didn't record them)

Striped Swallow *(H. abyssinica)*. Entebbe airport, Jan. 27, many at nests; common thereafter at nearly all lodges

African Sand Martin *(Riparia paludicola)*. Murchison Falls, Jan. 28, common(?)

Bank Swallow or European Sand Martin *(R. riparia)*. Murchison Falls, Jan. 28, flying around with other martins

Banded Martin *(R. cincta)*. Murchison Falls, Jan. 28; Ngorongoro, Feb. 9

African Rock Martin *(Ptyonoprogne fuligula)*. Lobo Lodge, Feb. 4 to 5, some flying around rocky ledges

White-headed Roughwing Swallow *(Psalidoprocne albiceps)*. Murchison Falls, Feb. 28, 2 males flying around falls; Keekorok Lodge, Feb. 3 to 4; 2 females seen frequently

Campephagidae (Cuckoo Shrikes)

Black Cuckoo Shrike *(Campephaga sulphurata)*. Fort Ikoma, Feb. 6, 1

Dicruridae (Drongos)

Fork-tailed Drongo *(Dicrurus adsimilis)*. Lake Nakuru, Feb. 2; 1 at entrance (gateway) to park, seen frequently thereafter

Prionopidae (Helmet Shrikes)

Gray-crested Helmet Shrike *(Prionops poliolopha)*. Serengeti, Feb. 4, flock of 6

White-crowned Shrike *(Eurocephalus anguitimens)*. Serengeti, Feb. 5 to 6; several seen; more in Tsavo, Feb. 11

Laniidae (Shrikes)

Northern Brubru *(Nilaus afer)*. Mara Masai, Feb. 3, 1 at lunch stop

Fiscal Shrike *(Lanius collaris)*. Nairobi, Jan. 31, many on roadside wires; common thereafter

Long-tailed Fiscal *(L. cabanisi)*. Nairobi, Jan. 31, quite common here and throughout East Africa

Gray-backed Fiscal *(L. excubitorius)*. Kampala, Jan. 27, several on hill overlooking city; common thereafter

Lesser Gray Shrike *(L. minor)*. En route to Arusha, Feb. 9, 1

Red-backed Shrike *(L. collurio)*. En route to Seronera Lodge, Feb. 6, 1

Magpie Shrike *(Urolestes melanoleucus)*. En route to Fort Ikoma, Feb. 5, quite a few

Black-headed Gonolek *(Laniarius erythrogaster)*. Paraa Lodge, Jan. 29, 1

Slate-colored Boubou *(L. funebris)*. Lobo Lodge and vicinity, Feb. 4, quite a few

Brown-headed Bush Shrike *(Tchagra australis)*. Marangu Hotel, Feb. 10, 2 on lawn

Rosy-patched Shrike *(Rhodophoneus cruentus)*. Tsavo, Feb. 11, 1

Paridae (Tits)

Gray (Great) Tit *(Parus afer)*. Lobo Lodge, Feb. 4, 1

Oriolidae (Orioles)

African Golden Oriole *(Oriolus auratus)*. Serengeti, Feb. 7, glimpse of one in rain

Corvidae (Crows)

Pied Crow *(Corvus albus)*. Entebbe, Jan. 27, several around airport; common thereafter in Kampala and other cities

White-naped Raven *(C. albicollis)*. African Wildlife Management Center, Feb. 10, several in tall trees; Kilaguni Lodge, Feb. 11 to 12

Indian House Crow *(C. splendens)*. Mombasa, Feb. 12, common around city and at Fort Jesus Portuguese ruins

Cape Rook *(C. capensis)*. Ngorongoro Crater, Feb. 8, several

Piapiac *(Ptilostomus afer)*. En route to Entebbe, Jan. 30, several on backs of cattle.

Sturnidae (Starlings)

Wattled Starling *(Creatophora cinerea)*. Tsavo, Feb. 11, dozen or so in park (not very impressive compared to other starlings)

Blue-eared Glossy Starling *(Lamprocolius chalybaeus)*. En route from Kampala to Masinda, Jan. 28; apparently common in Uganda, less so in Kenya and Tanzania(?)

Splendid Glossy Starling *(L. splendidus)*. Kampala, Jan. 28, some at hotel; not noted (or not recorded) thereafter

Ruppell's Long-tailed Starling *(Lamprotornis purpuropterus)*. Kampala, Jan. 27, flock at hotel, then hundreds flew by; Victoria Nile, Jan. 29, several on backs of elephants

Golden-breasted or Regal Starling *(Cosmopsarus regius)*. Tsavo and Kilaguni Lodge, Feb. 10 to 11; quite common

Redwing Starling *(Onchognathus morio)*. Nakuru, Feb. 2, seen singing outside hotel; Lobo Lodge, Feb. 4 to 5

Superb Starling *(Spreo superbus)*. En route to Nakaru, Feb. 2; common thereafter at Ngorongoro, Kilaguni, Tsavo

Hildebrandt's Starling *(S. hildebrandti)*. Serengeti, Feb. 4, several; more on Feb. 6 at Fort Ikoma and Seronera, also at Tsavo

Red-billed Oxpecker *(Buphagus erythrohynchus)*. Nairobi National Park, Jan. 31, on backs of elands and giraffes

Yellow-billed Oxpecker *(B. africanus)*. Lake Manyara, Feb. 9, dozen or so on backs of buffaloes

Zosteropidae (White-eye)

Kikuyu White-eye *(Zosterops kikuyuensis)*. Ngorongoro Crater Lodge, Feb. 8, 3 in dripping moss in tree

Nectariniidae (Sunbirds)

Malachite Sunbird *(Nectarinia famosa)*. Mara Masai, Feb. 3, 1; Ngorongora, Feb. 8, 1

Bronzy Sunbird *(N. kilimensis)*. Masinda (Uganda), Jan. 28, 1 feeding on hibiscus blossom; also seen at Nairobi, Ngorongoro, etc.

Beautiful Sunbird *(N. pulchella)*. Entebbe, Jan. 30, male and female entering old car wreck repeatedly; also seen at Ngorongoro, Feb. 9

Golden-winged Sunbird *(N. reichenowi)*. Mara Masai, Feb. 3, 2 or more seen; also at Ngorongoro, Feb. 9

Variable Sunbird *(Cinnyris venustus)*. Nairobi (Downey's estate), Feb. 1, 1; also at Mayer's ranch (Nairobi), Feb. 2

Double-collared Sunbird *(Cinnyrus sp.)*. Ngorongoro, Feb. 9; 3 "double-collared" species (Eastern, Northern, and Southern) listed by Williams. Probably Eastern form *(C. mediocris)* in crater.

Amethyst Sunbird *(Chalcomitra amethystina)*. Downey's estate (Nairobi), Feb. 1, 1

Scarlet-chested Sunbird *(C. senegalensis)*. Paraa Lodge, Jan. 30, 1; had several later records but didn't record them

Ploceidae (Weavers, Waxbills and Allies)

Buffalo Weaver *(Bulbalornis albirostris)*. Tsavo and Kilaguni, Feb. 10 to 12; common

White-headed Buffalo Weaver *(Dinemellia dinemelli)*. Serengeti, Feb. 4 to 6; Kilaguni, Feb. 11 to 12, common, often in small groups

Rufous-tailed Weaver *(Histurgops ruficauda)*. Ngorongoro, Feb. 8, several, identified by a guide

White-browed Buffalo Weaver *(Plocepasser mahali)*. Tsavo and Kilaguni, Feb. 10 to 12, common, nesting at lodge

Black-capped Social Weaver *(Pseudonigrita cabanisi)*. Tsavo, Feb. 11, 1 (a rare bird?)

Gray-headed Social Weaver *(P. arnaudi)*. Serengeti, Feb. 5 to 6, common; also common at Seronera and Kilaguni

Speckled-fronted Weaver *(Sporopipes frontalis)*. Seronera, Feb. 6, apparently common but had hard time identifying them; Andy finally found specimen in museum at Seronera

Kenya Rufous Sparrow *(Passer rufocinctus)*. Common around lodges: Keekorok, Seronera, and Kilaguni.

Gray-headed Sparrow *(P. griseus)*. Murchison Falls, Jan. 30, quite common here and at other park headquarters

Black-headed Weaver *(Ploceus cucullatus)*. Entebbe, Jan. 27, colony at nests at airport, common elsewhere

Layard's Black-headed Weaver *(P. nigriceps)*. Kilaguni, Feb. 10 to 11, large colony at nests

Speke's Weaver *(P. spekei)*. Nairobi, Feb. 1, colony at nests on university campus; Ngorongoro, Feb. 8, many, tame, feeding from hand

Vitelline Masked Weaver *(P. vitellinus)*. Tsavo, Feb. 11, small colony in park

Golden-backed Weaver *(P. jacksoni)*. Entebbe, Jan. 30, many flocks in park (zoo), adult, young, and nests

Chestnut Weaver *(P. rubiginosus)*. Serengeti, Feb. 5, several identified among other weavers in park

Golden Palm Weaver *(P. bojeri)*. Common along Kenya Coast, Feb. 12 to 14

Holub's Golden Weaver *(Xanthophilus xanthops)*. Seronera Lodge (vicinity), Feb. 6, 1

Vieillot's Black Weaver *(Melanopteryx nigerrimus)*. Jan. 30, adults at nest tree in Entebbe city park

Reichenow's Weaver *(Othyphantes reichenowi)*. Nairobi, Feb. 1, 2 females on university campus; Ngorongoro, 2 males

Grosbeak Weaver *(Amblyospiza albifrons)*. Serengeti, Feb. 4, 1

Red-headed Weaver *(Anaplectes melanotis)*. Kilanguni, Feb. 11, male attending old or incomplete nests

Red-billed Quelea or Sudan Dioch *(Quelea quelea)*. Lake Manyara, Feb. 9, large flocks on the go

Red Bishop *(Euplectes orix)*. Serengeti, Feb. 6, 1

Yellow Bishop *(E. capensis)*. En route to Arusha, 1 flushed from roadside

Fan-tailed Widow-bird *(Coliuspasser axillaris)*. Ngorongoro, Feb. 8, many in crater, not seen elsewhere

Red-collared Widow-bird *(C. ardens)*. Ngorongoro, Feb. 8, 1 at lodge

Jackson's Widow-bird *(Drepanoplectes jacksoni)*. Serengeti, Feb. 4; several seen from car, others in crater

Bronze Mannikin *(Spermestes cucullatus)*. Nairobi, Feb. 1, group feeding on grass heads in Snake Park; male building nest under shingles on roof at Mnarani Club, Feb. 13 to 14

Rufous-backed Mannikin *(S. nigriceps)*. Seronera, Feb. 6, small flock; Hotel Manangu, Feb. 12, larger flock

Cut-throat *(Amadina fasciata)*. Tsavo, Feb. 11, 1

African Fire Finch *(Lagonosticta rubricata)*. En route to Arusha, Feb. 9, 1 perched (close) by roadside

Peter's Twin-spot *(Hypargos niveoguttatus)*. Keekorok Lodge, Feb. 4, 1; had difficulty with this one, but decided on this species

Red-cheeked Cordon-bleu *(Uraeginthus bengalus)*. Paraa Lodge, Jan. 29 to 30; both males and females on lawn; also at Keekorok and Mombasa

Angola Cordon-bleu *(U. angolensis)*. Seronera, Feb. 6, 1

Purple Grenadier *(Granatina ianthinogaster)*. Keekorok Lodge, Feb. 4 to 5, 1. (Checked with specimen in museum)

Pin-tailed Wydah *(Vidua macroura)*. Serengeti, Feb. 4, several, blown about by wind; also at Tsavo and other places

Paradise Wydah *(Steganura paradisea)*. Tsavo, Feb. 11, dozen or so being blown about by wind

Fringillidae (Finches)

Brimstone Canary *(Serinus sulphuratus)*. Serengeti, Feb. 4, small groups (look like Myrtle Warblers in flight)

Yellow-fronted Canary *(S. mozambicus)*. Tsavo, Feb. 10, 1

Yellow-rumped Seed Eater *(S. atrogularis)*. Nakuru, Feb. 3, flock in roadside tree

Streaky Seed Eater *(S. striolatus)*. Mara Masai, Feb. 3, several on high plateau; Ngorongoro (Fig Tree House), Feb. 8, several

Emberizidae (Buntings)

Golden-breasted Bunting *(Emberiza flaviventris)*. En route to Seronera, Feb. 6, 1

Cinnamon-breasted Bunting *(Fringillaria tahapisi)*. Serengeti, Feb. 4, a few along roadside

Total families: 62 (13 new)
Total species: 292 (244 new)

CHAPTER 13

Australia and New Zealand

AT THE MEETING of the International Ornithological Congress in Oxford, England, in 1966, we learned that the next congress, in 1970—or at least some future meeting—might be held in Australia. Then and there Martha and I resolved that, if possible, we would attend the Australian meetings to fulfill a long-cherished dream of visiting the continent "down under"—that intriguing land of primitive monotremes (egg-laying mammals), emus, kangaroos, koalas, and many other unique forms stranded on a continent long isolated from other land masses.

The date and place for the congress were finally announced for August 12 to August 17, 1974, in Canberra. Several birding tours were being organized in the United States, to include the congress and field trips to promising areas in that part of the world, but somehow a suitable tour for us never materialized. One that we had investigated never answered our inquiries as to dates, costs, and arrangements (as promised in the original announcement); I'm not sure if the tour ever got launched or not. Tours had also been organized in Australia for delegates to the congress—one of them an inviting extension to New Zealand—but the cost of all of these tours seemed prohibitive.

A colleague of mine, Dr. Lester Eyer of Alma College, and his wife, Alma, were also planning to attend the congress. So we got together and worked out an itinerary of our own. Les did nearly all of the spade work on arrangements. From the Central Travel Agency in Alma he obtained folders, brochures, and other information. Then he laid out a tentative day-by-day itinerary. Except for some unforeseen obstacles, such as the crippling transportation strikes then prevailing in Australia and the often uncooperative weather, our plans worked quite well.

After some juggling of travel plans, we decided on a "fly-drive" schedule, with car rentals (Avis and Hertz) to take us on the shorter trips. Our itinerary called for brief stops in Hawaii and Fiji and for nearly two weeks in New Zealand before attending the congress in Australia in August.

Unfortunately for my birding aspirations, August is winter in Australia (and even more so in New Zealand), so few birds were singing or engaged in courtship or nesting activities. And unlike East Africa, where excellent accommodations are available in the national parks, in Australia and New Zealand we usually had to stay in cities, then find our way out to good birding areas, a time-consuming operation. Nevertheless, we managed to work in many hours of birding, coupled with some sightseeing and some major tourist attractions, particularly in scenic New Zealand.

Hawaii

Except for a pleasant prelude in Chicago, when some Hawaiians in native costumes serenaded us with music before and after we boarded the plane, our flight to Hawaii was nonstop and uneventful. Soon the high bluffs framing the harbor at Honolulu loomed into view. We were in Hawaii—a new experience for all of us.

The transfer from the airport to our hotel by *wiki-wiki* (shuttle bus) and taxi, was too rapid to identify many birds. The most obvious ones, which proved to be abundant throughout the city, were the Barred or Peaceful Doves *(Geopelia striata)* and Spotted Doves *(Streptopelia chinensis),* both introduced species. Trying to identify birds in transit, however, was my undoing. When we reached our hotel, I discovered that my eyeglasses were missing. Presumably I had taken them off, as is my custom in looking through binoculars, and let them slip to the floor of the bus or taxi. In spite of persistent inquiries to the shuttle bus and taxi lines, I never recovered the glasses. But by rare good fortune, Les had an extra pair that I found usable. At least I could see to read with them and without them I would have been severely handicapped.

In the early morning Martha and I slipped out of our hotel and into the well-planted grounds of another hotel nearby to look for birds. We were rewarded by finding a group of Japanese White-eyes *(Zosterops japonica)* feeding among the blossoms of a flowering shrub, and a handsome male Red-crested or Brazilian Cardinal *(Paroaria cristata)* hopped over the lawn. After breakfast, Les and I took a longer jaunt to a small park bordering a canal, but we added only House Finches to my Hawaiian list. The male House Finches, unlike those in California, had yellowish or orange (rather than red) breasts. Of course we saw Starlings, House Sparrows, and

Common Mynas, but we had no opportunity to explore further for other birds.

Thus ended my efforts at birding in Hawaii—a total of eight species (all introduced), five of which were repeats of birds seen in other countries (United States and India). I still hope for a chance someday to visit some of the remoter islands to view Hawaii's really unique native bird life.

That afternoon, with some time on our hands before our evening departure for Fiji, we rented a car and drove to Pearl Harbor, took the launch ride across the bay, and viewed the awesome exhibits in the War Memorial Building. A particularly sobering sight was the long list of the 1100 officers and men who lost their lives in the Japanese surprise attack on Pearl Harbor. The rusting hull of the sunken battleship *U.S.S. Arizona,* left cluttering up the bay, was also a gruesome reminder of the Pearl Harbor tragedy. But en route back to our hotel we stopped at Fisherman's Wharf and fortified ourselves with a sumptuous seafood dinner, a cheering event.

The Fiji Islands

We had only a few hours to spend at Nadi (or Nandi), chief port on Vitilevu, one of the 200 or more islands that comprise the Fijian group. We held a brief council over a coffee table at the airport about what to do in our limited time. Then Les, ever the diplomat in dealing with people, engaged in conversation with a bystander who chanced to be a guide and taxi driver. He agreed to show us some of the island, including some of the local birds, for a reasonable price. His knowledge of birds turned out to be rather limited; although he spoke good English, he knew the birds only by their Fijian names, which was of little or no help to us. However, he did prove to be a congenial and jovial host who performed admirably in educating us about the islands. We saw much of the nearby country—high hills and farms, fields of sugarcane, and a long line of freight cars loaded with cane. One highlight was a visit to Viseisei Handicraft Center, an attractive native villa of thatch-roofed huts, a church, and the chief's house. A native girl guide, appropriately costumed, gave us an informative tour of the village and craft shops, where Martha bought a couple grass skirts for our grand-daughters.

In spite of obvious handicaps, I managed to work out seven new species of birds. The abundant Red-vented Bulbuls and the mynas (2 species) I had seen in 1969 in India. But during our stroll along a gravelly beach, a Reef Heron *(Demigretta sacra)* and a White-collared Kingfisher *(Halcyon chloris)* flew by. Small groups of swifts circling overhead had to be White-rumped Swiftlets *(Collocalia spodiopygia),* the only species listed in Mayr's *Birds of the Southwest Pacific* for the Fijian Islands. Pacific Swallows *(Hirundo tahitica),* considered by some authorities to be conspecific with *H. neoxena,* were numerous around the airport, where they nested on or in the buildings. A small thrushlike bird, dark blue above and rusty below, I decided (after much deliberation), must be a Vanikoro Broadbill *(Myiagra vanikorensis),* one of the muscicapid flycatchers. And the dark-backed, white-breasted, shrikelike birds perched on wires proved to be White-breasted Wood-swallows *(Artamus leucorhynchus).* But the most exciting find was a group of four green-backed, red-headed, red-rumped "finches" cavorting on the lawn at Viseisei village. I puzzled over their identity for days. Then, in a bookshop in New Zealand, Martha discovered Belcher's *Birds of Fiji in Colour.* In it was a full-page painting of our "finches"—the Red-headed Parrot Finch *(Erythrura cyanovirens).*

New Zealand

An uneventful flight from Nadi took us to Auckland (pronounced Oakland in New Zealand), where we had pleasant and comfortable overnight accommodations. Our stay here was too brief for birding, but a Song Thrush, introduced from England, was singing in a tree in front of the hotel. This set the pattern for passerine bird life on mainland New Zealand. Of the 15 species of songbirds we saw on the mainland, 12 were introduced from England—a bit of old England transplanted to a land where land birds are scarce. Another species, the White-backed Magpie *(Gymnorhina hypoleuca),* was introduced from Australia. And of the two "natives," one, the Silver-eye *(Zosterops lateralis),* probably reached New Zealand in several nineteenth-century invasions (the first in 1856) and subsequently spread over the islands. The New Zealand Pipit *(Anthus novaeseelandiae),* seen at the airport in Queenstown, was the only native passerine we saw on South Island.

To digress a bit from our travels: the paucity of native land birds in New Zealand does not mean a depauperate avifauna. Although many birds have been displaced or even eliminated by clearing of the land, the introduction of predators (cats, rats, oppossums), and perhaps introduced diseases, New Zealand's wealth of bird life lies in its coastal waters and off-shore islands where many water birds and displaced songbirds find sanctuary. And in the villages, in parks and gardens, and in outlying farmlands, the birds in-troduced from England are quite abundant. Probably they fill the void created by the scarcity of native songbirds that never reached New Zealand because of its geographic isolation.

After our brief sojourn in Auckland we took off by plane for Queenstown on South Island. The first stage of the flight took us to Christchurch and then to Timaru, over some breathtakingly spectacular terrain, with flocks of sheep and herds of cattle dotting the landscape below, and pristine lakes framed by towering snowcapped peaks. Then we were grounded by bad weather in Timaru and transferred to a bus that took us on the long journey to Queenstown.

Sometimes delays have their rewards. While grounded at Timaru, we saw our first South Island Pied Oystercatchers *(Haematopus finschi)*. A lady on the bus was so amused with the name that she said—jokingly—that she was going to report to her Audubon Society in Pennsylvania that she had seen a "South Island Pied Oystercatcher." White-backed Magpies *(Gymnorhina hypoleuca),* one of New Zealand's most conspicuous and strikingly marked birds, were quite common along the road to Queenstown. And our first New Zealand Harriers *(Circus approximans),* so much like our Marsh Hawks, were readily identified from the bus.

Eventually we reached Queenstown, one of the most delightful locales I have ever visited. The Frankton Motel, where we had reservations, is located on one arm of Lake Wakatipu, which, typically it seems for New Zealand, is beautifully framed by high snow-covered mountain ranges. Chaffinches inhabited the tall evergreens behind the motel, a Dunnock fed on the lawn outside our window, and Yellowhammers were flushed from a weedy field bordering the lake. On the lake we saw small rafts of New Zealand Scaup or Black Teal *(Aythya novaeseelandiae)* and Gray Ducks *(Anas superciliosa),* as well as the perhaps inevitable Mallards, Canada Geese, and Eurasian Coots. Later, on some pilings in the harbor, we spotted four Little Cormorants *(Phalacrocorax melanoleucus).* And in a park in town we found people feeding ducks and gulls that came in close, so that they afforded excellent opportunities for photographs. The Black-billed Gulls *(Larus bulleri)* were quite tame and very photogenic with their immaculate white mantles, but the Southern Black-backed or Kelp Gulls *(L. dominicanus)* were more wary and remained at a distance.

Next morning, after using hot water to melt the ice on the windshield of our car, we started off on a long day's trip to Manapouri and Te Anau, the launching place for our proposed flight to Milford Sound, one of the highly lauded scenic wonders in New Zealand. But several mishaps upset our plans. Not far out of Queenstown I lost a camera. My logical guess is that I set it on the hood of the car while looking at a bird and then forgot about it.

When we discovered it was missing, we backtracked many miles but didn't find it. I still had a camera with a telephoto lens but was severely handicapped thereafter without the camera with the regular lens. But the loss was not without some gain; Les and I exchanged slides for duplication and I got by far the best of the exchange deals.

The delay caused us to miss our planned launch ride over Lake Manapouri, another highly recommended tourist attraction in New Zealand. The only consolation, in addition to the spectacular scenery, was finding a handsome pair (the female more striking than the male) of Paradise Ducks *(Tadorna variegata)* feeding in a roadside field, and two White-faced Herons *(Ardea novaehollandiae)* in a roadside puddle.

At Te Anau the weather was miserable, so the morning flight for Milford Sound was canceled. In lieu of the trip we visited Fiordland National Park to look for birds, but all we found were more English imports—Greenfinches, European Goldfinches, and European Blackbirds. The park grounds, bathed in mists, were very attractive, but the cold wet weather drove us back indoors to view the exhibits in the museum.

Back in Queenstown we did more sightseeing. A major event was a cold but scenic launch trip across Lake Wakatipu to visit a sheep station. We were served tea and pastries (indoors in preference to the tables on the lawn), took a tour through the old homestead, then were given a demonstration of a sheep round-up with trained dogs. Mindful of the controversy about sheep-killing Keas *(Nestor notabilis),* which have been nearly exterminated by herdsmen because of the persistent belief that Keas kill sheep by pecking through the back to feed on kidney fat, I asked, as tactfully as I could, about the problem. Mr. Harrison, the shepherd, said he had never seen a Kea attack a sheep, but that the animals panicked whenever a Kea appeared. (Apparently, like our Golden Eagles, the Keas sometimes feed on dead or dying sheep but rarely attack healthy animals.) The sheep station had several Keas in a large outdoor cage, as an exhibit for visitors. Happily, the birds, like most other parrots, seemed well adjusted to captivity.

On the morrow we had to give up our planned trip to Mt. Cook, another of South Island's highly recommended scenic and recreational attractions. Accommodations at the resort were not available and because of bad weather planes were not landing. So we made another try for Milford Sound. It was a beautiful day (for a change), clear and crisp, so our prospects looked good. We boarded a small plane and flew over some incredibly beautiful country; then, to our surprise and chagrin, we landed back at the airport from which we had departed an hour or so earlier. The pilot explained that the landing field at Milford Sound was covered with ice and that planes could not land. We tried again for a possible afternoon flight, but that too was canceled. However, as a small consolation, our tickets were refunded, after we had had a free ride over part of the route!

Foiled in our efforts to get to Milford Sound, we substituted a trip by car to Arrowtown, a former gold-mining town reeking with history that we only partially absorbed. En route we passed Coronet Peak, one of New Zealand's most acclaimed ski resorts. We could see the headquarters far up on the mountainside but didn't attempt the steep climb.

From Queenstown we flew to Christchurch, the next lap on our journey. Along the Avon River that flowed past the motor lodge where we stayed were flocks of gulls, including some Red-billed Gulls *(Larus scopulinus)* that we had not seen previously; it is more of a coastal form than the Black-billed Gulls seen at Queenstown. In the morning, while Les and Alma attended services in Christchurch Cathedral, Martha and I took a long walk to the city's botanical gardens, a magnificent layout of flower-bordered paths and meticulously labelled plants. Birds were fairly active in the gardens and along the Avon River, but the only new one we saw was a pair of New Zealand Pigeons *(Hemiphaga novaeseelandiae),* the country's only native columbid.

In the afternoon we drove out to Birdling Flats and to Lake Ellesmere, reputed to be good places for waders and waterfowl. The flats looked promising, but we saw no waders there. Lake Ellesmere, however, had a good assortment of water birds. Mute Swans *(Cygnus olor)* and Black Swans *(C. atratus),* both introduced, were the most conspicuous, but on the far shore we could make out several Pied Stilts *(Himantopus leucocephalus)* and a group of mostly unidentifiable ducks. Among the latter, however, was one distinctive male New Zealand Shoveler *(Anas rhynchotus),* similar to but specifically distinct from our Michigan form. Presumably some of the unidentified ducks were female and immature shovelers. More interesting were the dozen or so Pukekos or gallinules *(Porphyrio melanotus),* feeding among cattle in nearby fields.

Our departure for Wellington the next morning got off to a bad start. We found our car keys locked in the car and had to call a Hertz man to the rescue. He came with a whole string of keys, but none of them fitted, so we took a taxi (for $2.95) to the airport and left the Hertz man trying to get into his company's car with a wire.

In Wellington, in another Hertz car, we made our way through the city's confusing traffic (Les doing the driving was in his element in such situations) to a government building to get a permit to visit Kapiti Island, a noted flora and fauna reserve, one of the last stands for some of New

301

Zealand's endemic species. Red tape at the government office seemed endless, but we finally got the required permit and were off early the next morning for Paraparauma, the port from which boats leave for Kapiti. We were taking our chances. In the winter, visitors are ferried to the island only by special arrangement—and then only if weather permits. By good fortune we found David Bennet, the boatman; he wasn't home but a man at a gas station had seen him earlier in the day and guessed where he might be—at the boathouse, lovingly inspecting his boat.

Down at the beach Bennet cast an appraising eye at the rough waters and said, "It's a bit choppy, but I think we can make it." We did, with only minor mishaps. We put our paraphernalia and the girls aboard, then pushed the boat out into deeper water by wading up to our knees. I scrambled aboard without a further dunking, but a big wave nearly engulfed Les before he climbed in.

Kapiti Island was a fantastic place. Approximately six miles long and one mile wide, it is comprised of nearly five thousand acres of grassland, swamps, shrubs, and kohekohe forest clothing slopes up to 1,709 feet. Once heavily farmed by a succession of Maori tribes, the island has suffered from overgrazing, devastating fires, and the introduction of mammalian pests. But now, largely abandoned and rapidly reverting to forest, it is a government reserve with a resident forest ranger.

The island afforded the best birding we found anywhere in New Zealand. In a short time we recorded 11 new species, including most of the island's specialties. Pied Shags *(Phalacrocorax varius),* Australian Gannets *(Sula serrator),* and White-fronted Terns *(Sterna striata)* cruised around the water. On shore we were greeted with the bell-like notes of the Tiu or Parson Bird *(Prosthemadera novaeseelandiae)* and the melodious songs of Bellbirds *(Anthornis melanura),* both species common on the island but scarce or local on the mainland. Kakas *(Nestor meridionalis),* an uncommon parrot nearly exterminated on parts of the mainland, were quite common and tame. During our picnic lunch a Weka *(Gallirallus—*a probable hybrid between *G. greyi* and *G. scotti)* peered out of the shrubbery, then came in close for a handout. Another Weka (rail) followed us along a trail like a puppy. New Zealand Pigeons, seen only once on the mainland where they were formerly heavily hunted, were quite common on the island.

After lunch we climbed a mountain trail through a dense jungle of trees and shrubs. Fantails *(Rhipidura fuliginosa)* put on spectacular aerial displays for us. Robins *(Petroica australis)* foraged in the underbrush along the side of the trail. And I caught a brief but near-perfect glimpse of a

Tomtit *(P. macrocephala)*. Whiteheads *(Mohoua albicilla)* darted in and out of the bushes along the beach but seldom sat still long enough for a good view.

Our next day's motor trip took us two hundred or more miles to Waitomo, through pastures dotted with sheep and cattle, wooded gullies with sharp, dangerous curves, and woodlands with tall pines and giant tree ferns. We made several stops en route. One was at Bushy Park Reserve, reached by ascending a steep, narrow, curving road nearly closed in by dense vegetation. It seemed odd to me, a dedicated lister, that the park, a bird sanctuary with a pretentious headquarters building and well-kept grounds, had no bird list, although we were told that botanists were working on a plant list for the reserve. We also took the time and effort to drive up Mt. Egmont, but heavy clouds, mist, and rain obscured the view from the lookout near the summit. The storekeeper at the rest house told us that it usually rained there quite steadily for three months of the year, making an annual rainfall of about 250 inches.

Our mission at Waitomo was to see the famous glowworm caves, underground passages with marvellous limestone formations of stalactites and stalagmites. Stairways (117 steps) and boardwalks make all parts of the cave accessible. The climax of the guided tour was a boat ride into Glowworm Grotto, where the roof overhead was lighted by millions of luminous glowworms *(Arachnocampa luminosa)* that shone like stars (at first I thought they were stars). The larvae of the glowworms live in mucous-coated hollow tubes suspended from the ceiling. The tubes are surrounded by sticky threads, or "fishing lines," that catch the numerous midges attracted to the light emitted by the glowworms. We were cautioned to remain silent, since any noise causes the glowworms to extinguish their lights. Eventually the larvae metamorphose into adult flies, which then start a new generation.

From Waitomo, we drove to Rotorua. Our accommodations at Travelodge, overlooking Lake Rotorua, were among the finest we found in New Zealand. The lake that evening, and in the morning, was a steaming, slightly smelly, sulphurous body of water teeming with gulls (3 species), Caspian Terns, a few ducks, and Pied Stilts.

At the lodge that evening, a Maori group of men and women put on a hilarious show for hotel guests—singing and lively dancing. The men demonstrated their method of greeting: rolling out their enormous tongues (supposedly a sign of affection) and rubbing noses. Near the end of their performance they mingled with the audience and picked out a guest to go onto the stage and dance with them. Les was selected and put on a very creditable performance. Alma got a flash picture of her husband rubbing noses with his female partner. (Next morning, for consolation or retaliation, Alma hugged one of the wooden male statues along the street.) I was a little disappointed, of course, that I didn't get chosen by one of the comely girls, but I have to admit that Les did a better job than I could have done.

The next day, outside Rotorua, we visited some of the thermal springs that abound in that part of the country. We missed the eruption of the main geyser (it spouted before we arrived), but we saw minor eruptions, bubbling pools, and the steaming mists that bathe the rocky ledges. A New Zealand Kingfisher *(Halcyon sancta vagans)*, a subspecies of the Sacred Kingfisher in Australia, seemed to be enjoying the mist. At the springs was a model Maori villa, with attractive, red-trimmed frame buildings, wood carvings of men with their tongues protruding, and decorative archways along the streets. Other stops en route to Auckland that day included Buried Village, an ancient Maori villa buried by an avalanche in the 1800's and now being restored, and Blue and Green Lakes, which were not blue and green at that time because of the cold cloudy weather. The swimming and picnicking beach at the park did not look inviting that chilly time.

En route to Auckland that day I got my last bird—a Wrybill Plover *(Anarhynchus frontalis)*, that unique form with a dextrally curved bill used to extract prey from under rocks, which the plover circles in a clockwise direction. I was disappointed not to see a wild kiwi *(Apteryx)*, New Zealand's famous national emblem. We had to settle for seeing them in a zoo in Auckland. Natives of whom we inquired knew about the bird; in some cases they specified where one might possibly be found, but no one we consulted had actually seen a kiwi in the wild. Kiwis are nocturnal, live in burrows, and are hard to find.

We spent a full day in Auckland. We went to the zoo, which was well stocked with native and exotic birds and other vertebrates, and then visited the war memorial museum, which had a good collection of New Zealand birds and a spacious hall with fine exhibits of Maori culture. Les and I made a final, futile attempt to find more birds; but the sewage disposal plant and its filtering beds, reputed to be good places for waders, were virtually birdless. And a nearby bird sanctuary was closed with a *Trespassing Strictly Forbidden* sign on the locked gate. So after another overnight in Auckland, we bade farewell to scenic New Zealand and flew to Australia for the congress meetings.

My final bird list for New Zealand totalled only 52 species, 32 of which were new for me—a low list, but it included many birds not found elsewhere in the world.

Canberra and the IOC

Our plane from Auckland to Sydney took us there expeditiously; but thereafter our troubles—not entirely unexpected—began. All National Airlines in Australia were on strike, and our flight to Canberra for the congress meetings had been canceled. Several representatives from the congress were at the airport to meet us and advise on procedures. They said they would wait for other incoming planes to bring in more congress members, then send all of us by bus to Canberra. The five-hour delay at the airport wasn't a complete loss; we met a few other stranded delegates from the United States and I snooped around the busy airport grounds to look for birds. Welcome Swallows *(Hirundo neoxema),* much like our Barn Swallows and the Pacific Swallows we had seen on Fiji (but usually considered specifically distinct) were flying around the airport; and a Nankeen Kestrel *(Falco cenchroides)* perched on high wires, apparently unmindful of the heavy traffic below.

It was a long hard ride to Canberra (nearly six hours), much of it after dark. Our driver needed an hour just to weave his way through Sydney's congested streets. Toward the outskirts of the city I began scanning lawns for birds. Among the few identifiable from the bus were Australian Ravens *(Corvus coronoides)* actually walking around on lawns, and Magpie-larks *(Grallina cyanoleuca),* the latter one of Australia's most abundant birds. Then it got too dark for bird watching.

In Canberra we were taken to the wrong motel, but our accommodating driver, after delivering other passengers, took us to our lodge—Forrest Motor Inn on the outskirts of town. In the morning I saw Sulphur-Crested Cockatoos *(Cacatua galerita)* flying around near the inn. An odd-looking bird outside our window I finally identified as a Red Wattle-bird *(Anthochaera carunculata),* one of Australia's 70 species of honeyeaters (Meliphagidae).

The Monday morning congress meetings were canceled; because of the air strikes many delegates, including some of the speakers, were stranded in far-off places. In lieu of the indoor sessions we were taken on local field trips. My group went to a gorge or ravine where a stream flowed over a rocky bed and where steep cliffs rose up on one side. A trail (pronounced "trial" in Australia) or "tramping track" through the woods made the steeper areas more accessible. Right away we were off to a good morning of birding. En route we saw a mother Australian Wood Duck *(Chenonetta jubata),* quite unlike our American species, escorting her family of young from a roadside field to the nearest water. A Black-shouldered Kite *(Elanus notatus)* was also readily identifiable from the bus. And then we got our

305

first view of Australia's notorious Kookaburra or Laughing Jackass *(Dacelo gigas)*. Later we heard its raucous laughter.

In the ravine I had my first real introduction to Australia's honeyeaters, a fantastic family of 160–170 nectar feeders, 54 of which are restricted to Australia; 16 others have spread out from Australia to other areas in the Pacific. Our guide pointed out and identified Yellow-faced, Yellow-tufted, and Eastern (Spinebill) honeyeaters. (See Chapter-end list for scientific names of these and the 18 other honeyeaters we saw later.) They darted in and out of foliage so rapidly that identification was difficult, even with the expert help of our guide.

Back in Canberra we found that the afternoon paper sessions also had been cancelled. As a replacement, several films were shown on birds. Then that evening the congress meetings got off to a belated start with explanations and good-natured apologies for the delays. The theme of the whole congress, the first ever held in the southern hemisphere, was "The Two Hemispheres," a program appropriately designed to illustrate the biological differences between the northern and southern continents.

In the morning, before a full day of somewhat rejuggled papers, early risers were taken on tours of the Canberra Botanic Gardens, 100 acres of plantings, many of which were especially attractive to birds. The Eyers and the Wallaces got lost trying to find the gardens and arrived just as the other parties were breaking up. However, all this worked out to our advantage. One of the guides took us on a personally conducted tour and helped us with our numerous identification problems. Some birds I especially remember—and cherish—were the Superb Blue Wrens *(Malurus cyaneus),* a truly superb Australian specialty featured on the cover of the brochure about the gardens; Scarlet Robins *(Petroica multicolor)* and Yellow Robins *(Eopsaltria australis)*; a Spotted Pardalope *(Pardalotus punctatus)*, one of those stubby-tailed, brilliantly marked flowerpeckers (Dicaeidae); numerous White-winged Choughs *(Corcorax melanorhamphus);* and a couple more hard-to-identify honeyeaters. Martha and I forfeited breakfast in order to spend a little more time with a knowledgeable guide who helped us identify the 17 species we saw that morning.

The rest of the day was spent at the formal congress meetings. In the forenoon there were five concurrent sessions going on simultaneously in different rooms, which made it impossible for a person to attend many of them. I did poorly running from room to room to try to hear a desired paper. In fact the whole congress was rather hopeless in this respect. There were 11 different symposia, consisting of 61 papers, and many concurrent general sessions comprised of 130 "selected" papers—all crowded into three days. That evening we had a choice of viewing more films or attending the symposium on "Origins of Australasian Avifauna." We chose the latter and found it well worthwhile. A panel of six authorities threshed out paleornithological problems; then Ernst Mayr and D. Schodde wound up the session with a discussion and summary.

Wednesday was reserved for an all-day excursion, a welcome break from the paper sessions. We were taken to Tidbinbilla Nature Reserve, some 40 kilometres from Canberra. In spite of miserable weather—intermittent rain and winds of near-gale proportions—it was a successful outing. Kangaroos and emus, once extirpated from the region, had been reintroduced when the area became a sanctuary. Two emus came to breakfast for handouts. After a hasty meal consumed while we huddled against the lee side of buses, we climbed a steep wooded trail to look for lyrebirds but saw only their mounds. We did find a sleepy koala, however, eyeing us warily from its home in a eucalyptus tree. In a sheltered cove we found a White-throated Tree Creeper *(Climacteris leucophaea)*, Brown Thornbills *(Acanthiza pusilla)*, a Gray Shrike-thrush *(Colluricincla harmonica)*, and both male and female Golden Whistlers *(Pachycephala pectoralis)*.

In another deluge of rain we stopped for lunch at the reserve's information center where we could look out on the lawn and watch Flame Robins *(Petroica phoenicea)*, both males and females, feeding in the rain. At this point part of our party (2 busloads) called it quits and returned to Canberra. The rest of us elected to stick it out. It was worth it. First we stopped at a feeding station in the reserve and were rewarded by close views of Eastern and Crimson rosellas *(Platycercus eximus* and *P. elegans)*, Pied Currawongs *(Strepera graculina)*, and a pair of Satin Bowerbirds *(Ptilorhynchus violaceus)*, all feeding on the abundant fruit in the feeders. (Martha lost her wristwatch here; she hopes a bowerbird found it to decorate his bower.) At a small pond near the feeders, we saw an Australian Little Grebe *(Podiceps novaehollandiae)* alternately diving and then eyeing us with its head and neck out of the water. Associated with the grebe were several Chestnut Teal *(Anas castanea)*, Gray Teal *(A. gibberifrons)*, and Australian Black Ducks *(A. superciliosa)*.

We made another try for birds in another area, saw more koalas and a few more birds—including a strikingly patterned (black, white, and yellow) Eastern Shrike-tit *(Falcunculus frontatus)*. By late afternoon we gave up, wet and tired but quite content.

The New Zealand Alps—rugged, fog-bound, beautiful—framed in the pristine waters of Lake Manapouri on South Island.

Kaka, a rare parrot once widespread on mainland New Zealand, now largely confined to coastal islands where they are protected.

Black-billed Gull at Queenstown on South Island.

Red-billed or Silver Gull, common in both New Zealand and Australia.

Australian Crane (Brolga) at Brisbane.

Magpie Goose, chosen as the avian symbol for the 16th International Ornithological Congress held in Canberra, Australia in 1974.

Melbourne, Hatta Lakes, and Alice Springs

With some reluctance, after discussing matters with the Eyers, we decided to forego the last part of the congress meetings in order to see more of Australia. In Melbourne, our next station, I wanted to visit Phillip Island to witness the parade of Little Penguins to and from their breeding grounds on the island, but it was the wrong season; the penguins were out at sea and probably would not return to land until spring. So we went to Healsville Bird Sanctuary instead—a long hard drive through congested city traffic. Then we found that the "sanctuary" was really a zoo with birds in cages, but they were well housed and it gave us an opportunity to study them at close range. Many birds, some perhaps escapees, were outside the pens. My standard of ethics may not be as high as it should be: I was able to convince myself that a flock of King Parrots *(Alisterus scapularis)* in a tree over one of the cages, Crested Pigeons *(Ocyphaps lophotes)* and Peaceful Doves *(Geopelia striata)* feeding around the stands, and Red-browed Finches *(Aegintha temporalis)* outside the "finch" house were really wild and unrestrained birds.

But our birding highlight in the Melbourne-Mildura area was at Hattah Lakes National Park, where, with the good help of the park ranger, we recorded more birds in a few hours than in any other place in Australia. The ranger pointed out and identified a half dozen or so new birds for us around park headquarters, then told us the best places to go for other birds. In the limited time available, I recorded some 40 birds, nearly half of them new to me. My list of 40 included 2 grebes (some of the many Great Crested in full display), 3 cormorants, 3 ardeids, 3 ducks, 2 raptors, 5 parrots, 5 honeyeaters, and a few miscellaneous species. The Black-backed Blue Wrens *(Malurus melanotus)* effectively supplemented the Superb Blue Wrens we had seen in the botanic gardens in Canberra. In the road in front of our car a Willie Wagtail *(Rhipidura leucophrys)* put on a hilarious show for us by swinging its tail and body vigorously from side to side. Along the lake shore we found five Black-fronted Dotterels *(Charadrius melanops)*. Noisy Miners *(Manorina melanocephala)* came to lunch with us, and a pair of Galahs *(Eolophus roseicapillus)* had a nest hole in a tree beside our picnic table. A Striped Honeyeater *(Plectorhyncha lanceolata),* the ranger said, was quite rare and the best find of the day.

Our next station—and our biggest adventure—was at Alice Springs in the interior desert (outback). In contrast to the humid east coast, Alice Springs was hot and dry. Too late we learned that it was a winter resort for Easterners and that we should have had reservations *twelve months* in advance. (Our travel instructions advised getting reservations *twenty-four hours* in advance.) A rodeo in full swing at the time didn't help matters. But fortune smiled upon us. After seemingly hopeless searching, we did find a hotel that had had a last-minute cancellation. The facilities weren't the best, but they were good enough for four weary travelers. Rather dismal-looking aborigines were nearly everywhere, dozing on doorsteps with hats over their faces and camping along a dry riverbed.

A major goal at Alice Springs was to see Standley's Chasm, said to be one of the most colorful spectacles in the outback. It was! At noon the sun shines down into the deep cleft in the rocks and illuminates the vertical walls with wonderfully soft shades of red. Some crevices in the rocks supported clumps of white flowers. It was a notable and inspiring sight—not as grand as the Grand Canyon—but still remarkable.

The long drive to and from the chasm was spectacular in a different way. Flat dry fields, sparsely clothed with yellow, blue, and purple flowers and a few gnarled trees, were bounded on one side by high bluffs of red and gray sandstone. Birding was not very rewarding at the springs (although fly catchers should have found good hunting among the flies that crawled all over our faces); perhaps the best was on our leisurely return trip from the chasm. Hawks hunting over the open fields were fairly numerous, but the only ones we positively identified were the Spotted Harriers *(Circus assimilis)* and a Gray Falcon *(Falco hypoleucus)* in pursuit of a larger unidentified hawk. The best find of the day was a Rainbow Bird *(Merops ornatus),* Australia's only bee-eater (Meropidae), a truly beautiful sight as it spread its long tail in flight and displayed its rainbow colors. Another interesting observation was a small flock of Crimson Chats *(Ephthianura tricolor)* feeding in weedy stubble and leapfrogging around for presumed insect prey.

On the morning of our departure from Alice Springs, I took a final check of the local park and the nearly dry stream bed that bordered the park. A Red-backed Kingfisher *(Halcyon pyrrhopygia)* posed nicely on a telephone pole by the creek, and I flushed a flock of Zebra Finches *(Taeniopygia guttata)* from a nearby field. At the airport, in addition to more Crimson Chats and Zebra Finches and the mud nests of Magpie-larks, I found some real wild Budgerigars *(Melopsittacus undulatus)* and decided that the miners there were the White-rumped species *(Manorina flavigula).*

Cairns and the East Coast

Our long flight to Cairns took us over a vast expanse of red and gray sands before the more heavily vegetated slopes of the eastern mountain ranges loomed ahead. Cairns was a welcome climatic change—Canberra

311

and Melbourne had been too cold and rainy, Alice Springs too hot and dry. But during our three days around Cairns we had mostly pleasant weather and fair birding. There were, to be sure, some frustrations. We had planned on a boat trip to Great Barrier Reef, but we found that here, also, reservations needed to be made far in advance. We hung around the boat dock for an hour or more that first morning in hope of a cancellation, but there was none.

However, our drive to Lake Barrine and Lake Eacham, high up in the hills west of Cairns, was a good substitute. At Lake Barrine we had three Brush Turkeys *(Alectura lathami)* come to lunch: a dominant male, an immature male, and a female. To see a megapode or moundbuilder, of which the Brush Turkey is an example, was high on my Australian priority list. Their nesting habits are unique. The male builds a huge mound of soil and decaying vegetation, three to four feet high and ten or more feet in diameter. In it one or more females deposit up to 30 eggs that are then covered over with decaying vegetation which, with some solar heat, provide the only means of incubation. The male tests the temperature in the mound by thrusting his naked head into it, then regulates the temperature (at about 92° F.) by covering or uncovering the eggs as needed. When the eggs hatch, the chicks, already in their juvenal plumage, dig their way out of the mound and *fly* away, without any further parental care.

Another prize at Lake Barrine was a Wompoo Pigeon *(Megaloprepia magnifica),* a green-backed, blue-headed, violet-breasted bird, one of the many gorgeously attired fruit pigeons that are restricted to the tropical and subtropical regions of the Old World.

Then we took a cruise over the lake in hope of seeing some water birds, but we found none of particular interest. However, we did see a Square-tailed Kite *(Lophoictinia isura),* pointed out and identified by our skipper. He also spotted a huge python basking on a log protruding out into the water. A nature trail led from the shore of the lake up into a dense rain forest, where the huge trees (Les and Alma, holding hands, couldn't reach halfway round the trunk of one of them) were festooned with lichens. We could hear birds twittering in the treetops but couldn't identify them. We puzzled for a long time over several small, dark-plumaged birds scuttling around in the underbrush. I finally decided—with tongue in cheek because the species isn't listed by either Slater or Macdonald for the region—that they must have been the dark phase of the Rufous Scrub-bird *(Atrichornis rufescens jacksoni),* one of the two endemic species in the primitive passerine family Atrichornithidae. Then later, on the road back to Cairns, we spotted a Banded Rail *(Rallus philippensis)* examining a dead rail, presumably its mate, crushed on the pavement.

The next day, with our hopes for a trip to Great Barrier Reef frustrated a second time, we went on a "wild cassowary" chase. We were told that cassowaries were frequently seen along the Palmerston highway to Palmerston National Park, one of the few places in Australia where those birds occur. We didn't find any; and we had to settle for seeing them in pens in Bird Park in Cairns. It was far from a lost day, however. At a gas station stop I found a Forest Kingfisher *(Halcyon macleayi)* perched on a roadside wire, and in and around Innisfail we saw both Spine-tailed and Fork-tailed swifts *(Hirundapus caudacutus* and *Apus pacificus)*. White-breasted Wood-swallows *(Artamus leucorhynchus)* were common in and en route to the park.

In the park we had lunch in an open area surrounded by dense woods that seemed alive with birds that we usually couldn't see well enough to identify. There and along the way, however, we did find two more honeyeaters, an Eastern Silver-eye *(Zosterops lateralis),* a little Grassbird *(Megalurus gramineus)* "beep-beeping" on a roadside wire, and, best of all, a gorgeous Green-winged Pigeon *(Chalcophaps indica).*

Next morning, before our departure for Brisbane, we explored the beach along Esplanade Avenue, where there was a good assortment of curlews, godwits, gulls, and herons. The curlews were the Eastern species *(Numenius madagascariensis),* a new bird for me, as were the Black-tailed Godwits *(Limosa limosa).* The more numerous Bar-tailed Godwits *(L. lapponica)* I had seen on the Farne Islands in England in 1964. Birds were also active in the trees along the avenue. We picked out a handsome male Yellow Figbird *(Sphecotheres flaviventris)* with two dull-colored females, and a grotesque Helmeted Friarbird *(Philemon novaeguineae).* Then we visited Bird Park, which has one of the most complete collections of living birds in Australia. The ferocious male cassowaries were penned in for the safety of visitors, but the young roamed freely, as did the Brolgas (cranes), Magpie Geese, and other semicaptive birds. Wild birds were also numerous in the park. New ones for me were the Black-faced Cuckoo-shrike *(Coracina novae-hollandiae)* going to a nest in a tree, a Rufous Whistler *(Pachycephala rufi-ventris),* and a flock of Chestnut-breasted Finches *(Lonchura castaneo-thorax)* along and outside the park fence.

Near Brisbane, our next major stop, we visited Surfer's Paradise at Southport, where there were numerous shorebirds and water birds, but the only new one for me was the Crested Tern *(Sterna bergii).* A launch trip (at $3 per person) around Brisbane's canals proved to be an appraisal of the real estate along the shore rather than the water-bird trip we had planned on; our skipper knew the owners and the cost of most of the houses. More interesting was our visit to the well-known (and well-patronized) Lorikeet Sanctuary in Brisbane, where hundreds if not thousands of Rainbow Lorikeets (and fewer Scaly-breasted Lorikeets) come in twice daily or oftener to be fed. It was a fantastic display of color watched by hundreds of visitors. Exotic peacocks in full display added to the spectacle.

In the late afternoon we went to another bird sanctuary that had a more varied assortment of birds, both wild and caged. Among the latter were lyrebirds, bowerbirds, pittas, hawks, owls, and frogmouths—mostly native birds that we did not see in the wild. One of the wild birds, a Whistling Kite *(Haliaster sphenurus),* had a huge nest in a large tree in the sanctuary; we were warned about passing under the tree because of fecal droppings, but the adults were not at the nest. Later we saw one in another part of the park.

Our last days in Australia, in Sydney, were marked by confusion, delays, and heavy rains. The airport was being remodeled and everything was disrupted. Somehow Les and Alma managed to get a bowl of soup at the crowded airport restaurant, but Martha and I couldn't get waited on. We tried to settle for a candy bar but found the candy counter blocked off. Part of Les' baggage was missing, but we had a long wait anyway and the missing baggage came in on a later plane. Our requested Avis car was not available, so we had to take a taxi to our motel in a far corner of the city. One advantage: the motel was located just across from the University of New South Wales. I looked for birds on the attractive campus both in the evening and the next morning and got a few pictures, but I found no new birds except the introduced Red-whiskered Bulbul, new for my Australian list.

That evening Les and Alma managed to get an Avis car rental and went to a concert in the multimillion dollar Sydney Opera House; Martha and I, less ambitious, elected not to go. Next day we all visited the opera house, viewed with awe its magnificent facilities, looked wistfully at the fancy seaside dining room, then dined on hamburgers in the less expensive grill, where fashionable ladies in furs mingled with teenagers in shoddy jeans. Nearly all our sightseeing had to be in sudden dashes between showers or views from the car.

One bright (but damp) spot at Sydney was a visit to Royal National Park, south of the city. The potential for birds seemed great, but rains drove us to shelter whenever we tried to look for birds. The ranger told us the best place was out on the Curra Moors. We tried it with some success; the rain slackened to intermittent drizzles, so we hiked along a densely wooded trail and out onto the moors, which were ablaze with flowers. Birds were fairly active; we saw more honeyeaters, a Fan-tailed Cuckoo *(Cacomantis pyrrhophanus),* Striated Thornbills *(Acanthiza lineata),* and, best of all, I got two glimpses of an elusive but very vocal Eastern Whipbird *(Psophodes olivaceus),* Australia's famous "whipcracking" babbler so often heard but so seldom seen.

Next day's visit to Ku-Ring-Gai Chase National Park north of the city was even less propitious. Rains had become a deluge by now, and some streets were under water. I'm still wondering what we might have seen on a better day. (The park had a checklist of 163 birds.)

Getting out of Sydney for our flight to the States also had its setbacks. On our arrival at the airport in the early evening we learned that our plane would be delayed four hours—to repair or replace a faulty engine. Then the next announcement was that our flight had been postponed until morning. We were bused back into the city and put up (courtesy of the airline) at a luxurious hotel and served dinner and breakfast. It was all attended by much confusion, and seemingly interminable delays. Martha and I, fagged out and ready for bed, decided to have our belated dinner in the grill (a quick ample meal for a paltry $17), but Les and Alma wanted to patronize the fifth floor garden restaurant. They waited more than two hours to get served and their bill (on the house) was $21.

There were more delays in the morning—and profuse apologies—but we finally took off and got home without further delays. We had a brief stop in Fiji but weren't supposed to leave the terminal; I tried but didn't get away with it. Our stop in Honolulu was during the night, with long lines and more confusion for customs and baggage inspection. We were shuttle-bused to another waiting station on a bus with standing room only; then Martha and I had to be brought back *alone* on a three-car train. Because of the delays, we had lost our reservations for the flight from San Francisco to Chicago. But we were lucky in catching a substitute flight and another substitute flight from Chicago to Lansing.

Thus ended our eventful sojourn and travels in New Zealand and Australia—sight-seeing, attending the congress meetings, and looking for birds. My total list for Australia was 139 species, of which 110 were new. My total for the trip was 184, of which 152 were new.

References

Belcher, W.J. *Birds of Fiji in Colour*. Auckland and London: Collins, 1972.

Falla, R.A.; R.B. Sibson; and E.G. Turbott. *A Field Guide to the Birds of New Zealand*. Boston: Houghton Mifflin, 1967.

Macdonald, J.D. *Birds of Australia*. Sydney, Wellington, and London: A. H. and A. W. Reed, 1973.

Mayr, E. *Birds of the Southwest Pacific*. New York: Macmillan, 1945.

Peterson, R.T. *A Field Guide to Western Birds*. Boston: Houghton Mifflin, 1961.

Slater, P. *A Field Guide to Australian Birds: Non-Passerines*. Wynnewood, Pennsylvania: Livingston, 1971.

_____. *A Field Guide to Australian Birds: Passerines,* Wynnewood, Pennsylvania: Livingston, 1975.

My Hawaii-Fiji-New Zealand-Australian Bird Lists
(July 26 to August 26, 1974. New species *)

Hawaii
(Nomenclature from Peterson)

Spotted Dove *(Streptopelia chinensis)*. Honolulu, July 26 to 27, all over city

*Barred Dove *(Geopelia striata)*. Honolulu, July 26 to 27, all over city

Indian Myna *(Acridotheres tristis)*. Honolulu, July 26 to 27, all over city

*Japanese White-eye *(Zosterops japonica)*. Honolulu, July 26 to 27, hotel grounds and city park

*Red-crested (Brazilian) Cardinal *(Paroaria cristata)*. July 26 to 27, hotel grounds and city park

(Also Starlings, House Sparrows, and House Finches)

Summary: 8 species (all introduced), 3 new

Fiji Islands
(Nomenclature from Belcher and Mayr)

*Reef Heron *(Demigretta sacra)*. Nadi, July 29, 1 (dark phase) flying along beach

*White-rumped Swiftlet *(Collocalia spodiopygia)*. Nadi, July 29, small groups flying over fields and road

*White-collared Kingfisher *(Halcyon chloris)*. Nadi, July 29, 1 flying along beach

*Pacific Swallow *(Hirundo tahitica)*. Nadi, July 29, many around airport, apparently nesting on buildings; possibly conspecific with *H. neoxema*

Red-vented Bulbul *(Pycnonotus cafer)*. Nadi, July 29, common, introduced from India

316

*Vanikoro Broadbill *(Myiagra vanikorensis)*. Nadi, July 29, 1 seen in Viseisei villa (a Muscicapidae)

*White-breasted Wood-swallow *(Artamus leucorhynchus)*. Several shrike-like birds perched on wires

Indian Myna *(Acridotheres tristis)*. Nadi, July 29, common

Jungle Myna *(A. fuscus)*. Nadi, July 29, several seen

*Red-headed Parrot-finch *(Erythrura cyanovirens)*. Nadi, July 29, group of 4 cavorting on lawn at Viseisei villa

Summary: 10 species (3 introduced), 7 new.

New Zealand
(Nomenclature and sequence of families from Falla *et al.*)

Sulidae (Gannet)
   *Australian Gannet *(Sula serrator)*. Kapiti Island, Aug. 6, 1 cruising along beach, made spectacular dive

Phalacrocoracidae (Shags and Cormorants)
   Black Shag *(Phalacrocorax carbo)*. Queenstown, Aug. 1, 1 flew over road (our "Common" or "Great" Cormorant)
   *Pied Shag *(P. varius)*. Kapiti Island, Aug. 6, several flying over
   *Little Shag *(P. melanoleucos)*. Queenstown, July 31, 4 or 5 perched on pier; Te Anau, Aug. 1, 1 light-phase bird on lake

Ardeidae (Herons)
   *White-faced Heron *(Ardea novaehollandiae)*. Auckland, July 30, 2 flew by motel; Manapouri, Aug. 1, 2; Auckland, Aug. 9, 1

Anatidae (Ducks, Geese, Swans)
   Mute Swan *(Cygnus olor)*. Lake Ellesmere, Aug. 4, many adults and immatures on shallow lake
   *Black Swan *(C. atratus)*. Lake Ellesmere, Aug. 4, many, originally introduced from Australia, now widespread in New Zealand
   Canada Goose *(Branta canadensis)*. Auckland, July 31, 2 on Lake Wakatipu; Lake Ellesmere, Aug. 4, many
   *Paradise Duck *(Tadorna variegata)*. Timaru, July 30, pair in field; Manapouri, Aug. 1, pair in field
   *Gray Duck *(Anas superciliosa)*. Queenstown, July 31 to Aug. 2, many, tame and hand-fed in park
   Mallard *(A. platyrhynchos)*. Queenstown, July 31, common; Lake Ellesmere, Aug. 4, common
   *New Zealand Shoveler *(A. rhynchotis)*. Lake Ellesmere, Aug. 4; 1 well-marked male, 2 females and 1 immature (?)
   *New Zealand Scaup *(Aythya novaeseelandiae)*. Queenstown, July 31, common on Lake Wakatipu; also at Te Anau and Lake Rotorua

Accipitridae (Hawks)
   *New Zealand Harrier *(Circus approximans)*. Timaru, July 30, 2 seen from bus; common thereafter

317

Phasianidae (Pheasants)
  Ring-necked Pheasant *(Phasianus colchicus)*. Auckland, July 30, 1 flew past motel
Rallidae (Rails, Coot, Gallinule)
  *Weka *(Gallirallus greyi scotti)*. Kapiti Island, Aug. 6, apparently common and quite tame, flightless
  Eurasian Coot *(Fulica atra)*. Queenstown, July 31, several on Lake Wakatipu
  *Pukeko *(Porphyrio melanotus)*. Birdling Flats, Aug. 4, a dozen or so, in field with cattle; Kapiti Island, Aug. 6, several
Haematopodidae (Oystercatchers)
  *South Island Pied Oystercatcher *(Haematopus finschi)*. Timaru, July 30, 2; Auckland, Aug. 10, 4; apparently widespread
Charadriidae (Plovers)
  *Spur-winged Plover *(Lobibyx novaehollandiae)*. Queenstown, Aug. 1, several
  *Wrybill *(Anarhynchus frontalis)*. Auckland, Aug. 9, several along roadside puddles
Recurvirostridae (Stilt)
  *Pied Stilt *(Himantopus leucocephalus)*. Lake Ellesmere, Aug. 4, 5 or more on far shore; Lake Rotorua, Aug. 8, several (conspecific with *H. himantopus?*)
Laridae (Gulls and Terns)
  *Southern Black-backed or Kelp Gull *(Larus dominicanus)*. Widespread in New Zealand—Auckland, Queenstown, Christchurch, Lake Rotorua
  *Red-billed Gull *(L. scopulinus)*. Christchurch, Aug. 6, many along Avon River; common in coastal areas
  *Black-billed Gull *(L. bulleri)*. Queenstown, July 31, abundant; widespread and common in New Zealand
  Caspian Tern *(Hydroprogne caspia)*. Lake Rotorua, Aug. 8, 4
  *White-fronted Tern *(Sterna striata)*. Kapiti Island, Aug. 6, several
Columbidae (Pigeons)
  *New Zealand Pigeon *(Hemiphaga novaeseelandiae)*. Christchurch, Aug. 4, 2 in botanical gardens; Kapiti Island, Aug. 6, common
  Rock Dove *(Columba livia)*. Well established in towns and cities, feral along some coastal cliffs
Psittacidae (Parrots)
  *Kaka *(Nestor meridionalis)*. Kapiti Island, Aug. 6, common. (Saw Keas—*N. notabilis*—only in captivity)
Alcedinidae (Kingfishers)
  *Sacred Kingfisher *(Halcyon sancta)*. Widespread: Te Kiuti, Rotorua, Blue Lake; bathing in mist at Thermal Springs *(H.s. vagans* is New Zealand race of Australian species)

318

Alaudidae (Larks)
  Skylark *(Alauda arvensis)*. Well established in rural areas; in nearly full song around Manapouri, Aug. 1

Muscicapidae (Old World Flycatchers)
  *Fantail *(Rhipidura fuliginosa)*. Kapiti Island, Aug. 6, many in full display
  *Tomtit *(Petroica macrocephala)*. Kapiti Island, Aug. 6, brief view of one along mountain trail
  *Robin *(P. australis)*. Kapiti Island, Aug. 6, several along woodland trail

Sylviidae (Whitehead)
  *Whitehead *(Mohoua albicilla)*. Kapiti Island, Aug. 6, many in coastal shrubbery

Turdidae (Thrushes)
  Song Thrush *(Turdus philomelos)*. Auckland, July 30, 1 singing at motel, also on Aug. 9 to 10; Christchurch, Aug. 4, several
  Blackbird *(T. merula)*. Apparently well established in New Zealand

Prunellidae (Accentors)
  Hedge Sparrow, dunnock *(Prunella modularis)*. Well established in New Zealand

Motacillidae (Pipit)
  *New Zealand Pipit *(Anthus novaeseelandiae)*. Queenstown, Aug. 3, several on airport field. (Conspecific with *A. richardii?*)

Meliphagidae (Honeyeaters)
  *Bellbird *(Anthornis melanura)*. Kapiti Island, Aug. 6; common, singing nicely.
  *Tiu or Parson Bird *(Prosthemadera novaeseelandiae)*. Kapiti Island, Aug. 6, common, singing; Bushy Gardens, Wanganu, Aug. 7, 1

Zosteropidae (White-eye)
  *Silver-eye *(Zosterops lateralis)*. Queenstown, July 31, small flocks in town; also at Te Anau, Christchurch, and Kapiti Island.

Fringillidae (Finches and Buntings)
  Greenfinch *(Chloris chloris)*. Te Anau, Aug. 1 to 2; singing at motel and in Fiordland National Park
  Goldfinch *(Carduelis carduelis)*. Te Anau, Aug. 1; a few seen.
  Common Redpoll *(Carduelis flammea)*. Queenstown, July 31; small flock on Bob's Peak
  Chaffinch *(Fringilla coelebs)*. Queenstown, July 30, pair at motel; seen commonly thereafter
  Yellowhammer *(Emberiza citrinella)*. Queenstown, July 31, 3 flushed in field by lake; seen commonly thereafter
  (All fringillids introduced from England. Not native to New Zealand)

Ploceidae (Weaverbird)
  House sparrow *(Passer domesticus)*. Well established in New Zealand

Sturnidae (Starlings, Mynas)
  Starling *(Sturnus vulgaris).* Abundant nearly everywhere
  Indian Myna *(Acridotheres tristis).* Well established on North Island
Cracticidae (Bell-Magpies)
  *White-backed Magpie *(Gymnorhina hypoleuca).* Widespread and
    common throughout New Zealand

Summary: 52 species (19 introduced), 32 new.

Australia
Nomenclature, family names, and sequence of families from
Slater and Macdonald)

Dromaiidae (Emus). (Dromiceidae in American classifications)
  *Emu *(Dromaius novaehollandiae).* Tidbinbilla Nature Reserve, Aug.
    14, reestablished in reserve after earlier extermination
Podicipedidae (Grebes)
  *Australian Little Grebe *(Podiceps novaehollandiae).* Tidbinbilla, Aug,
    14, 1 in puddle with ducks
  Great Crested Grebe *(Podiceps cristatus).* Hattah Lakes National Park,
    Aug. 16, large groups on lake, some in full display. (Widespread Old
    World bird)
Sulidae (Gannet)
  Australian Gannet *(Morus serrator).* Southport, Aug. 23, 1 flying over
    water along shore. (Same as New Zealand species)
Anhingidae (Darter)
  *Australian Darter *(Anhinga novaehollandiae).* Lake Barrine, Aug. 20, 1
    seen. (May be Australian race of *A. rufa*)
Phalacrocoracidae (Shags or Cormorants)
  Black or Common Cormorant *(Phalacrocorax carbo).* Hattah Lakes,
    Aug. 16, common on lake. (Nearly worldwide species)
  *Little Black Cormorant *(P. sulcirostris).* Hattah Lakes, Aug. 16,
    common on lake
  Little Pied Cormorant *(P. melanoleucos).* Hattah Lakes, Aug. 16,
    abundant; Lake Barrine, Aug. 20, 1. (Same as New Zealand's Little
    Shag
Ardeidae (Herons, Egrets)
  *White-necked Heron *(Ardea pacifica).* Hattah Lakes, Aug. 16, several
    flying around lake
  White-faced Heron *(A. novaehollandiae).* Hattah Lakes, Aug. 16, many;
    Alice Springs, Aug. 17, 1
  Cattle Egret *(Ardeola ibis).* Brisbane, Aug. 23, many in fields and
    pastures along highway
  Common or Great Egret *(Egretta alba).* Hattah Lakes, Aug. 16, com-
    mon (Nearly worldwide species)

320

Threskiornithidae (Ibis)
  *Australian White Ibis *(Threskiornis molucca).* Hattah Lakes, Aug. 16, 1 (or more?) flying over lake

Anatidae (Waterfowl)
  Black Duck *(Anas superciliosa).* Tidbinbilla, Aug. 14; Hattah Lakes, Aug. 16; Lake Eacham, Aug. 20; Royal National Park, Aug. 20. (Called Gray Duck in New Zealand)
  *Gray Teal *(A. gibberifrons).* Tidbinbilla, Aug. 14; Hattah Lakes, Aug. 16, many
  *Chestnut Teal *(A. castanea).* Tidbinbilla, Aug. 14, several in puddle
  *Australian Wood Duck *(Chenonetta jubata).* Canberra, Aug. 12, family group in roadside field; Tidbinbilla, Aug. 14; Hattah Lakes, Aug. 16

Accipitridae (Kites, Eagles, Harrier)
  *Black-shouldered Kite *(Elanus notatus).* Canberra, Aug. 12, 1 along roadside; Alice Springs, Aug. 17–18, several.
  Black Kite *(Milvus migrans).* Alice Springs, Aug. 17, several.
  *Square-tailed Kite *(Lophoictinia isura).* Lake Barrine, Aug. 20; 1 identified by skipper on boat.
  *Whistling Kite *(Haliastur sphenurus).* Brisbane, Aug. 23; large nest (inactive?) in sanctuary, kite in distance.
  *Little Eagle *(Hieraaetus morphnoides).* Hattah Lakes, Aug. 16, 2; Cairns, Aug. 22, 1
  *Wedge-tailed Eagle *(Aquila audax).* Tidbinbilla, Aug. 14, 1; Cairns, Aug. 20, 1
  *White-breasted Sea-eagle *(Haliaetus leucogaster).* Cairns, Aug. 22; adult over airport.
  *Spotted Harrier *(Circus assimilis).* Alice Springs, Aug. 18; several.

Falconidae (Falcons, Kestrels)
  Gray Falcon *(Falco hypoleucus).* Alice Springs, Aug. 17–18; 1 each day.
  *Nankeen Kestrel *(F. cenchroides).* Sydney, Aug. 11, female at airport; Alice Springs, Aug. 17, pair along river, others later

Megapodiidae (Mound Builders)
  *Brush Turkey *(Alectura lathami).* Lake Barrine, Aug. 20; 3 at picnic tables; others, including young, along road.

Rallidae (Rails, Moorhen, Coot)
  *Banded Rail *(Rallus philippensis).* Cairns, Aug. 20, crushed rail on road being inspected by live mate (?)
  *Dusky Moorhen *(Gallinula tenebrosa).* Brisbane, Aug. 23, large, dense flock on river in Lorikeet Sanctuary
  Eurasian Coot *(Fulica atra).* Tidbinbilla, Aug. 14; Hattah Lakes, Aug. 16

Haematopodidae (Oystercatcher)
  (European) Oystercatcher *(Haematopus ostralegus).* Southport, Aug. 23, 1 with gulls and terns

Charadriidae (Plovers)
*Masked Plover *(Vanellus miles)*. Cairns, Aug. 21, 6 in cemetery. (*V. miles* at Cairns and *V. novaehollandiae* at Hattah Lakes—may be same species but treated differently by different authors)
*Black-fronted Dotterel *(Charadrius melanops)*. Hattah Lakes, Aug. 16, 3 together, then 2 more; Alice Springs, Aug. 17 to 19, half dozen or more in nearly dry stream bed

Scolopacidae (Curlews, Godwits)
*Eastern curlew *(Numenius madagascariensis)*. Cairns, Aug. 23, several on mud flats.
*Black-tailed Godwit *(Limosa limosa)*. Cairns, Aug. 16, several on mud flats
Bar-tailed Godwit *(L. lapponica)*. Cairns, Aug. 16, many godwits, mostly Bar-tails, on mud flats

Recurvirostridae (Stilt)
Black-winged or Pied Stilt *(Himantopus himantopus)*. Alice Springs, Aug. 17, several on reservoirs. (White-headed or *leucocephalus* race; listed as separate species by some authors)

Laridae (Gulls and Terns)
*Silver Gull *(Larus novaehollandiae),* Cairns to Sydney, Aug. 20 to 26; abundant along coast (called Red-billed Gull in New Zealand)
Gull-billed Tern *(Geochelidon nilotica)*. Surfer's Paradise, Aug. 23; several seen on launch cruise of canals
*Crested Tern *(Sterna bergii)*. Southport, Aug. 23, several along beach

Columbidae (Pigeons and Doves)
*Wompoo Pigeon *(Megaloprepia magnifica)*. Lake Barrine, Aug. 20, beautiful specimen in treetop. Another on Aug. 21 in Palmerston National Park
Domestic Pigeon *(Columba livia)*. Common around cities, towns, farms
Spotted Turtle Dove *(Streptopelia chinensis)*. Cairns, Aug. 20, several in garden at motel, others en route
Peaceful Dove *(Geopelia striata)*. Apparently widespread and common (Same as Barred Dove in Hawaii)
*Green-winged Pigeon *(Chalcophaps indica)*. Cairns, Aug. 21, 1 along road in Palmerston National Park
*Crested Pigeon *(Ocyphaps lophotes)*. Melbourne, Aug. 15, several in Healsville Sanctuary; Hattah Lakes, Aug. 16, 3 perched in small tree, others in flight

Psittacidae (Lorikeets, Cockatoos, Parrots)
*Rainbow Lorikeet *(Trichoglossus haematodus)*. Southport, Aug. 23, small flock in roadside park; Brisbane, thousands at bird sanctuary.
*Scaly-breasted Lorikeet *(T. chlorolepidotus)*. Brisbane, Aug. 23, a few with Rainbows in sanctuary.
*Sulphur-crested Cockatoo *(Cacatua galerita)*. Canberra, Aug. 12, small flock at Forrest Lodge; Tidbinbilla, Aug. 14, "trees white with them"; common nearly everywhere

*Galah *(Eolophus roseicapillus).* Mildura, Aug. 16, small flock flying over; common nearly everywhere thereafter

*King Parrot *(Alisterus scapularis).* Melbourne, Aug. 15, small flock in Healsville Sanctuary; Aug. 26, a few in Royal National Park

*Crimson Rosella *(Platycercus elegans).* Canberra, Aug. 12, campus and botanical gardens; common thereafter

*Yellow Rosella *(P. flaveolus).* Hattah Lakes, Aug. 16, a few

*Eastern Rosella *(P. eximius).* Tidbinbilla, Aug. 14, many at feeding station; Royal National Park, Sydney, Aug. 26, a few

*Mallee Ringneck Parrot *(Barnardius barnardi).* Hattah Lakes, Aug. 16, common in park

*Red-rumped Parrot *(Psephotus haematonotus).* Hattah Lakes, Aug. 16, common in park

*Budgerigar *(Melopsittacus undulatus).* Alice Springs, Aug. 19, small group in "orchard" at airport

Cuculidae (Cuckoos)

*Fan-tailed Cuckoo *(Cacomantis pyrrhophanus).* Sydney, Aug. 25, quite a few at Curra Moors in Royal National Park

*Black-eared Cuckoo *(Chrysococcyx osculans).* Alice Springs, Aug. 17, 1 behind Piggly Wiggly store, others in town

Apodidae (Swifts)

*Spine-tailed Swift *(Hirundapus caudacutus).* Innisfail, Aug. 21, all over town and environs

*Fork-tailed Swift *(Apus pacificus).* Innisfail, Aug. 21, many all over, mingled with *H. caudacutus*

Alcedinidae (Kingfishers)

*Laughing Kookaburra *(Dacelo gigas).* Canberra, Aug. 12, along highway and in botanical gardens; common thereafter

*Forest Kingfisher *(Halcyon macleayi).* Innisfail, Aug. 21, 1 at gas station

*Red-backed Kingfisher *(H. pyrrhopygia).* Alice Springs, Aug. 19, 1 along nearly dry riverbed

Sacred Kingfisher *(H. sancta).* Cairns, Aug. 22, 2 at airport

Meropidae (Bee-eater)

*Rainbow Bird *(Merops ornatus).* Alice Springs, Aug. 18, 1; Lake Barrine, Aug. 20, 1; Australia's only bee-eater

Atrichornithidae (Scrub-bird)

*Rufous Scrub-bird *(Atrichornis rufescens).* Lake Barrine, Aug. 20, several dark-plumaged birds scuttling around and scratching in leaves on rainforest floor. Seems to fit only *A. r. jacksoni,* the dark race, but not listed by either Slater or Macdonald for the area

Hirundinidae (Swallows and Martins)

*Welcome Swallow *(Hirundo neoxema).* Sydney, Aug. 11, several around airport; common nearly everywhere thereafter

*Tree Martin *(Petrochelidon nigricans).* Hattah Lakes, Aug. 16, common; also at Alice Springs and Cairns

Motacillidae (Pipits)
Australian Pipit *(Anthus novaeseelandiae)*. Alice Springs, Aug. 18, several along dry weedy roadside. (Same as New Zealand form?)

Grallinidae (Magpie-lark)
*Magpie-lark *(Grallina cyanoleuca)*. One of Australia's most abundant birds; seen nearly everywhere; mud nests in tower at Alice Springs
*White-winged Chough *(Corcorax melanorhamphus)*. Canberra, Aug. 13, common in gardens (courting); Hattah Lakes, Aug. 16

Campephagidae (Cuckoo-shrikes)
*Black-faced cuckoo-shrike *(Coracina novaehollandiae)*. Cairns, Aug. 22, 1 at sanctuary entrance, flying to nest in tree

Pycnonotidae (Bulbul)
Red-whiskered Bulbul *(Pycnonotus jocosus)*. Sydney, Aug. 25, 1 singing on campus building; introduced

Turdidae (Thrushes)
Song Thrush *(Turdus philomelos)* Brisbane, Aug. 23, 1 singing in tree along city street
Blackbird *(T. merula)*. Canberra, Aug. 13; 1 in botanical gardens

Timaliidae (Babblers)
*Eastern Whipbird *(Psophodes olivaceus)*. Sydney, Aug. 25, heard repeatedly along trail on Curra Moors, seen twice

Maluridae (Australian Wrens—included in Sylviidae by some authors).
*Superb Blue Wren *(Malurus cyaneus)*. Canberra, Aug. 13, 1 in botanical gardens
*Black-backed Wren *(M. melanotus)*. Hattah Lakes, Aug. 16, 2 males and 2 females

Sylviidae (Grassbirds and Thornbills, the latter put in Acanthizidae by Slater.)
*Little Grassbird *(Megalurus gramineus)*. Cairns, Aug. 21, 1 "buzzing" on roadside wire
*Striated Thornbill *(Acanthiza lineata)*. Several indefinite records at Canberra, etc., then several groups seen closely along wooded trail in Royal National Park, Sydney, Aug. 25
*Brown Thornbill *(A. pusilla)*. Canberra, Aug. 13, 1 in botanical gardens, identified by guide; Tidbinbilla, Aug. 14, small group along trail; Cairns, Aug. 20, several along shore of Lake Eacham

Muscicapidae (Old World Flycatchers)
*Lemon-breasted Flycatcher *(Microeca flavigaster)*. Cairns, Aug. 22, 1 in Bird Park
*Scarlet Robin *(Petroica multicolor)*. Canberra, Aug. 13, pair in gardens
*Flame Robin *(P. phoenicea)*. Tidbinbilla, Aug. 14, males and females on lawn at lunch stop
*Hooded Robin *(P. cucullata)*. Lake Eacham, Aug. 20, good view of one
*Eastern Yellow Robin *(Eopsaltria australis)*. Tidbinbilla, Aug. 14, several along wooded trail

Gray Fantail *(Rhipidura fuliginosa)*. Canberra, Aug. 12, several in ravine; Sydney, Aug. 5, common in Royal National Park, displaying. (Same as New Zealand species)

*Willie Wagtail *(R. leucophrys)*. Mildura, Aug. 16, 1 singing in park; Hattah Lakes, Aug. 16, 1 displaying in road; common elsewhere

Pachycephalidae (Whistlers, Shrike-thrushes, and Shrike-tits—Muscicapidae of other authors).

*Rufous Whistler *(Pachycephala rufiventris)*. Cairns, Aug. 22, 1 in Bird Park

*Golden Whistler *(P. pectoralis)*. Canberra, Aug. 13, female in gardens; Tidbinbilla, Aug. 14, 2 males and female along trail

*Gray Shrike-thrush *(Collurcincla harmonica)*. Tidbinbilla, Aug. 14, 2 or more along trail

*Eastern Shrike-tit *(Falcunculus frontatus)*. Tidbinbilla, Aug. 14, 1 along forest edge in rain, identified by guide

Ephthianuridae (Australian Chats—Sylviidae of other authors)

*Crimson Chat *(Ephthianura tricolor)*. Alice Springs, Aug. 18, small group along road, more at airport on Aug. 19

Climacteridae (Australian Tree-creepers—Neosittidae of other authors)

*White-throated Tree-creeper *(Climacteris leucophaea)*. Tidbinbilla, Aug. 14, several along trail

Dicaeidae (Flower Peckers)

*Spotted Pardalote *(Pardalotus punctatus)*. Canberra, Aug. 13, 1 in gardens, pointed out by guide

Zosteropidae (Silver-eye)

Eastern Silver-eye *(Zosterops lateralis)*. Palmerston National Park, Aug. 21, 1 at lunch stop, another at bridge; Sydney, Aug. 25, group on campus of New South Wales

Meliphagidae (Honeyeaters)

*Scarlet Honeyeater *(Myzomela sanguinolenta)*. Cairns, Aug. 21, 1 male in Palmerston National Park

*Eastern Spinebill *(Acanthorhynchus tenuirostris)*. Canberra, Aug. 12, several in gorge, more on Aug. 13 in botanical gardens

*White-eared Honeyeater *(Meliphaga leucotis)*. Tidbinbilla, Aug. 16, common(?) along trail, also on Aug. 13 in botanical gardens

*Yellow-faced Honeyeater *(M. chrysops)*. Canberra, Aug. 12, several in gorge, also on Aug 13 in botanical gardens

*Fuscous Honeyeater *(M. fusca)*. Cairns, Aug. 21, 1; nest in Bird Park on Aug. 22

*White-plumed Honeyeater *(M. penicillata)*. Alice Springs, Aug. 18, seen earlier (and later) but first identified at Alice Springs; common

*Yellow-tufted Honeyeater *(M. melanops)*. Canberra, Aug. 12, 1 or more in gorge

*Bridled or Mountain Honeyeater *(M. frenata)*. Palmerston National Park, Aug. 21, several at bridge on mountain

*White-naped Honeyeater *(Melithreptus lunatus)*. Melbourne, Aug. 15, 1 in Healsville Sanctuary

*Blue-faced Honeyeater *(Entomyzon cyanotis)*. Hattah Lakes, Aug. 16, 1 flying from ranger's house to lake and back repeatedly

*Striped Honeyeater *(Plectorhyncha lanceolata)*. Hattah Lakes, Aug. 16, 1 at ranger's house

*Little Friar-bird *(Philemon citreogularis)*. Hattah Lakes, Aug. 16, several at ranger's house; Brisbane, Aug. 23, several in sanctuary

*Helmeted Friar-bird *(P. novaeguineae)*. Cairns, Aug. 22, 1 along beach

*Noisy Friar-bird *(P. corniculatus)*. Brisbane, Aug. 23, 1 at sanctuary

*New Holland (White-eyed) Honeyeater *(Philidonyris novaehollandiae)*. Sydney, Aug. 25, common on Curra Moors

*Crescent Honeyeater *(P. pyrrhoptera)*. Canberra, Aug. 13, 1 in botanical gardens

*Tawny-crowned Honeyeater *(P. melanops)*. Sydney, Aug. 25, perfect view of one on Curra Moors

*Bell Miner *(Manorina melanophrys)*. Melbourne, Aug. 15, several "stealing" feed around feeders

*Noisy Miner *(M. melanocephala)*. Hattah Lakes, Aug. 16, common, coming to lunch; also along coast

*Yellow-throated or White-rumped Miner *(M. flavigula)*. Alice Springs, Aug. 17 to 18; common

*Spring-cheeked Honeyeater *(Anthochaera rufogularis)*. Hattah Lakes, Aug. 16, several around ranger's house

*Little Wattle-bird *(A. chrysoptera)*. Sydney, Aug. 25, many on Curra Moors

*Red Wattle-bird *(A. carunculata)*. Canberra, Aug. 12, 1 at Forrest Lodge, also in gardens on Aug. 13, and at Mildura on Aug. 16

Spermestidae (Grass Finches—Ploceidae of other authors).

*Red-browed Finch *(Aegintha temporalis)*. Melbourne, Aug. 15, several feeding outside pens in Healsville Sanctuary

*Zebra Finch *(Taeniopygia guttata)*. Alice Springs, Aug. 19, small flocks (males and females) near hotel and at airport

*Chestnut-breasted Finch *(Lonchura castaneothorax)*. Cairns, Aug. 20, several along fence and in field at Bird Park

Ploceidae (Weavers)

House Sparrow *(Passer domesticus)*. Widespread in southeast: Sydney, Melbourne, Mildura, Brisbane, Cairns.

Sturnidae (Starlings, Mynas)

Common Starling *(Sturnus vulgaris)*. Widespread in southeast: Sydney, Melbourne, Mildura, Brisbane north to Cairns.

Indian Myna *(Acridotheres tristis)*. Abundant on a school playground in Sydney; also in Cairns: airport and city

Oriolidae (Old World Orioles)

*Yellow Oriole *(Oriolus flavocinctus)*. Lake Barrine, Aug. 20, brief but unmistakable view of one in rainforest

326

*Yellow Figbird *(Sphecotheres flaviventris).* Cairns, Aug. 23, a handsome male and brownish female in large tree on Esplanade Avenue

Artamidae (Wood-swallows)

White-breasted Wood-swallow *(Artamus leucorhynchus).* Quite common in the Cairns area, Aug. 21 to 23 (Same species as on Fiji)

*Black-faced Wood-swallow *(A. cinereus).* Alice Springs, Aug. 17, several flying around reservoirs

Cracticidae (Butcher-birds, Magpies and Currawongs)

*Pied or black-throated Butcher-bird *(Cracticus nigrogularis).* Alice Springs, Aug. 18, 1

*Gray Butcher-bird *(C. torquatus).* Hattah Lakes, Aug. 16, 1 in tree along lake shore; also at Alice Springs and Cairns

*Black-backed Magpie *(Gymnorhina tibicen).* Common nearly everywhere (except extreme southeast); may be conspecific with *G. hypoleuca* in New Zealand but listed separately by Slater and Macdonald

*Pied Currawong *(Strepera graculina).* Common throughout eastern Australia (not at Alice Springs)

Ptilonorhynchidae (Bower-birds)

*Satin Bower-bird *(Plilinorhynchus violaceus).* Tidbinbilla, Aug. 14, both males and females at feeders in reserve

Corvidae (Ravens and Crows)

*Australian Raven *(Corvus coronoides).* Sydney, Aug. 11, many on lawns; also around Canberra and Alice Springs (large flock at dump)

*Australian Crow *(Corvus orru).* Cairns, Aug. 22, not noted elsewhere. (Given as *C. cecilae* in Macdonald, but may be local race—*C. orru cecilae.)*

Summary for Australia: 139 species (8 introduced), 110 new.

Total for trip (Hawaii, Fiji, New Zealand, Australia): 184 species (11 introduced), 152 new.

CHAPTER 14

The Golden—and not so Golden—Years

Pending Retirement

IN THE LATE 1960's, when I began thinking seriously about retirement, Michigan State University had a commendably flexible retirement policy. A staff person could retire after 25 years of service, which in my case would have been at age 60, or wait until age 62, 65, or 68. If still in reasonably good health at 68, and wishing to remain longer with the university, one could make arrangements to continue in some nonteaching or nonadministrative capacity. Retirement at the earlier ages, of course, carried less compensation in pensions.

I chose to retire at 65, after 30 years at the university. Probably I would have remained for another three years, if conditions for ornithological work had been more favorable. But ornithology at MSU, as at many other institutions, was low on the totem pole compared to other disciplines. My hopes and plans for better facilities never seemed to materialize. For more than twenty years I tried to develop an ornithology laboratory in our natural science building. Actually, one lab was mainly for bird classes, but over the years, at different times, a dozen or more other classes, desperate for a place to meet, moved in on me. Laboratory space was always an acute problem at MSU. Hence, my birds invariably were getting mixed up with calculating machines, aquaria, fruit-fly bottles, test tubes, and other nonornithological materials. The opportunity never came to develop an exclusively ornithological laboratory.

Once we formed a research committee to seek grants for financing construction of an animal house to house living birds and other vertebrates for research, but the hoped-for grants were never forthcoming. An even more improbable ambition of mine was to set aside one of the campus woodlots with outdoor and indoor facilities for ornithology students, but the combined efforts of all the natural sciences—at least five different departments—were barely able to preserve any of the woodlots from encroachments by dormitories, other buildings, and access roads for the ever-increasing traffic.

I had additional difficulties trying to get grants for my graduate students. Some of my potential students defected to entomology, where grants for pest control were so readily available. Other students transferred to a new department of fisheries and wildlife, which split off from zoology in the early 1950's. During the DDT period we made a good start in assessing the effects of DDT on reproduction in birds, but my application to the National Institute of Health for a grant to continue such studies was turned down in no uncertain terms. Later, an official from NIH, who visited the campus to promote applications for grants from that agency, remarked wryly that I would stand a better chance if I were working with monkeys instead of birds.

Nonetheless, in spite of frequent setbacks and frustrations, I had 30 mostly rewarding years at MSU—challenging classes, many superior graduate students going into productive careers, and good opportunities for research—especially in the field. Unlike many staff people at MSU, I had a private office, much appreciated although it lacked a research annex, which most zoologists had. Our department had a reasonably good study collection of Michigan birds, which we were continually augmenting over the years. And the university museum, especially after Dr. Rollin Baker came as the director in 1955, had a nearly worldwide collection of specimens. In looking back, I wonder if I could have done any better elsewhere. Slow progress resulted in part from my own shortcomings, among them a lack of aggressiveness; yet it is well known that the overly aggressive often get into trouble with their colleagues or superiors, while the overly meek, rather than inheriting the earth, are seriously handicapped in competitive enterprises.

For my final academic year (1971–1972) I asked to be put on a consultantship basis, which meant a gradual phasing out of academic duties rather than a sudden termination of responsibilities. My chief obligations were to see my remaining graduate students over their last hurdles, to continue on certain (but fewer) committees, to carry on whatever research I cared to, and to get my office and ornithological materials in order for a successor. During the fall term I taught an adult education evening bird class by choice, took part of the winter term off for the trip to East Africa, and spent much of the spring term working at our retirement home in Northern Michigan.

Our Retirement Home

We decided not to remain in East Lansing after retirement. The relatively quiet residential area where we had lived for 30 years, so conveniently close to the campus, was rapidly deteriorating. Some of our longtime neighbors had died, others moved away, and the vacated houses were taken over by students—mostly needy, deserving students, but who soon became over-crowded in houses designed for single families; the three-bedroom house next to us (within a few feet) sometimes had ten or more students living in it. Increased traffic on the narrow streets, inadequate parking facilities, and sometimes riotous parties late into the night created problems for aging homeowners. Another distressing factor for us: after two defeats at the polls, liquor was finally legalized in previously "dry" East Lansing, pur-portedly to justify and help finance a seventeen-story hotel within a few blocks of our house. Actually, it never did get built, but apartment houses and a several-story parking ramp did get constructed in our area. However, we have few regrets; after so many years in a pleasant neighborhood, it was time to move.

Coincident with plans for retirement came the problem of finding a new home north, south, east, or west—and each direction had inviting features. In two trips to southeastern Arizona—a veritable paradise for wintering or permanently retired ornithologists—I was fascinated not only with the local bird life but also with the boulder-strewn canyons and the cactus plains. Yet somehow, the homes blasted into the scantily vegetated rock walls of canyons did not appeal to us for a permanent home; nor did the otherwise intriguing deserts, so barren and unproductive for homesites without borrowing water from the already depleted Colorado River.

In some respects Florida seemed more appealing. Martha's three sisters and a brother and their spouses had retired to Florida and were happy there. But the easy-going pleasant life in Florida's trailer courts, mobile homes, and condominiums was not what we were looking for. Texas, of course, has everything, but we didn't give it very serious consideration.

But both of us had a liking for northern Michigan. Martha, born and raised in Rockford (Kent County), was practically a northern native. And from my many trips north from Ann Arbor and East Lansing, I learned to appreciate the north country. Perhaps it was the nearest I could come, climatically and ecologically, to my native Vermont, where today's high land values and high taxes discouraged a return. We liked the Upper Peninsula: Whitefish Point with its unique bird life; Tahquamenon Falls for its sheer beauty; the Keweenaw Peninsula where we once spent a delightful

330

week on Gratiot Lake; the Porcupine Mountains for its woods and waterfalls; and other Upper Peninsula areas we had visited over the years. But it seemed remote from our continuing interests in southern Michigan, and the severity of the long winters would have been a drawback. Sites along the Lake Michigan and Lake Huron shorelines, perhaps the best migratory pathways for birds, were also appealing, but real estate values were prohibitively high and the best locations already overcrowded.

Eventually the Grayling area in Crawford County won out. On numerous occasions when our children were small we had camped in the then relatively undeveloped county park (now an overdeveloped state park) on Higgins Lake. During my years at MSU I had brought advanced students north almost annually to see Kirtland's Warblers (Crawford County has a disproportionate share of the world's supply), to watch the Sharp-tailed Grouse on their dancing grounds, to observe the Ospreys and herons at Michelson's, and to hike the trails through the Hartwick Pines.

Our quest for a home ended when a letter from a realtor in Grayling, with whom we had left our name and a brief statement of our needs, sent us a description of a house and added, "This may be just what you are looking for." It was a one-story, seven-room house located on a largely wooded ten-acre plot seven miles southwest of Grayling. The main structure was about eleven years old, but at later dates a new garage, a breezeway from the house to the garage, and some other remodeling had been done.

Two features in particular appealed to us immediately. A well-lighted, fairly spacious addition on the south side of the house seemed ideal for my office and library, where I could continue writing and study. And the open space north of the house looked ideal for one of Martha's essential requirements—a vegetable garden. The previous owners, the Skolaskys (who, incidentally, moved to Arizona but didn't like it and came back to Michigan) had had a garden there. In fact, since we bought the place in April 1970, but couldn't occupy it until June, the Skolaskys obligingly put in part of a garden for us before they left.

The garden was an important concern. In East Lansing during and following World War II we had had a series of Victory Gardens and even won a blue ribbon on one occasion. Thereafter Martha and her mother continued gardening on a rented plot an inconvenient mile and a half from our house; then the sale of the whole area for a housing development ended that project. Now to have a garden close to the house would fulfill a long-cherished dream. Another of Martha's ambitions was to raise chickens and so have a constant supply of meat and fresh eggs. After a crude makeshift arrangement in an old shed behind the house, we had a poultry house

331

constructed, adequate for housing several dozen hens. Both garden and chickens have served us well.

Another decided attraction for both of us was the approximately eight acres of woods behind the house. Although largely second-growth beech-maple in composition—hence, not harboring a great variety of birds—it included a fine stand of white birches and interspersed aspens, a few large, 50-to-100-year-old hemlocks and pines that had escaped the axe, several large red oaks, and about 20 other species of trees. Two old wood roads, largely grown over, crisscrossed the woodlot. I opened these up for foot trails to provide easier access to the otherwise dense woods. Sugar maples are scattered throughout the woods. True to my Vermont heritage, I tap a dozen or so of the maples each spring and boil down the sap in the old shed behind the house. Because of the need for some initial equipment, especially a wood-burning stove, I estimate that my first gallon of syrup cost about $60.00, but costs thereafter declined to practically nothing except hard work.

Our woodlot, like much of northern Michigan's second-growth hard-woods, is primarily a Red-eyed Vireo—Ovenbird—redstart—flycatcher (3 species) habitat and thus a little disappointing from the standpoint of avian variety. A better area for observing birds was along an old grass-grown lane that divided our property from our neighbors on the north. The lane had been used as a logging road in the late 1890's and early 1900's, when the whole area was largely cut over, then kept more or less open by hunters, berry pickers, and morel mushroom collectors. Until the trail and its borders were almost completely destroyed in 1975 by the Crawford County Road Commission for a road that no one really needed, this was my best area for studying birds. It was bordered on both sides by many fruit-bearing trees and shrubs attractive to birds—wild cherries (3 species), wild apple, hawthornes, shadbush, sumac, and blackberries. During the spring and fall migration periods I made almost daily (or oftener) observations along the lane. Between 1971, the first year of spring records, and 1976, when I discontinued observations because the lane had become (temporarily) a public highway, I recorded a little over a hundred species of land birds. About half of these were summer residents or summer visitors.

As soon as we got partially settled in our new abode, I began taking inventories of the flora and fauna on our property. I found 28 species of trees, all native to northern Michigan except the large weeping willow *(Salix babylonica)* in the front yard (a tree in which I have recorded some 58 species of birds). Additional shrubs (10 or more species), some natives, some introduced, complete the listing of woody plants. Other plant lists

332

are still incomplete. So far I have identified 121 species of wildflowers, but have not tackled the grasses and sedges nor worked out all of the goldenrods and asters. My list of 13 ferns and fern allies (Pteridophytes) is probably complete, but my list of mushrooms and fungi (about 30 species) is only a beginning.

I have attempted some fern and wildflower gardening in our heavily shaded backyard—reminiscent of my more extensive plantings at Pleasant Valley Sanctuary in Massachusetts. Many native species are lacking in our woods, so I am attempting to introduce some of them—trilliums (several species), hepaticas, may-apples, orchids, ferns, and other forms. A reminder of the old farm in Vermont is the patch of tansies *(Tanacetum huronense)* planted in my rock garden, and several clumps of maidenhair fern *(Adiantum pedatum)* brought in from Vermont.

Vertebrate Fauna

Vertebrates other than birds are scarce here: about 15 mammals, 4 snakes, a toad, a hyla, a salamander, and no turtles or fish. Most prominent among the mammals are the squirrels—blacks (the most common), grays, reds, fox, and (more rarely) flying squirrels. The black squirrels (presumably the black color phase of the gray squirrel) patronize and often dominate the bird feeders in the winter; I have counted eight or more around the feeders at one time, although in the severe winter of 1976–1977 all squirrels were largely lacking. In March the hibernating chipmunks emerge and take over, and still later the 13-striped ground squirrels *(Citellus tridecemlineatus)* become a nuisance in the garden. I have disposed of the latter periodically but have merely deported the excess chipmunks, which our grandchildren enjoy so much. On two occasions flying squirrels *(Glaucomys sabrinus)* have invaded our house; the first one was caught and fatally injured (we kept it alive for a few days) by our neighbor's cat. The other one we captured in the house, kept it alive for a few days, then released it. Flying squirrels in a house can be spooky. One morning in the dim early light I saw a picture on the wall tremoring as if in a passing earthquake. It was an eerie feeling and I wondered if I was really awake. Investigation disclosed a flying squirrel hiding behind the picture. In our earlier days in Lenox, Massachusetts, the attic of the old sanctuary house, built by a Revolutionary War officer, was sometimes haunted with flying squirrels. One evening when we pulled down the bed covers a flying squirrel "flew" out!

Another "friendly neighbor" was a skunk that insisted on taking up its abode under our chicken house. One winter the skunk shared its home—peacefully, as far as we could tell—with a raccoon. The skunks dig for grubs in our garden and so far have not molested the chickens or stolen any eggs. One summer our next-door neighbors had a woodchuck family in a burrow in their blackberry patch, but the animals did not invade our garden. The neighbors' dog, to its own detriment, "discovered" a porcupine in the woods next to ours.

Of course we have numerous smaller mammals. There are woodmice *(Peromyscus)* in the woods and sometimes in the basement and in the garage, meadow voles *(Microtus)* around the lawn and garden, and occasional shrews (only *Blarina* so far). We see deer tracks in the mud and snow along the old lane, and one summer deer raided our neighbors' gardens, but as yet they have not scaled our garden fence. A red fox, and tracks of its presumed prey, the snowshoe rabbit, are sometimes seen in and around our woods, and a few cottontails occur along the roadways.

Our four snakes are the common garter snake *(Thamnophis sirtalis),* green snakes *(Opheodrys vernalis),* a milk snake *(Lampropeltis triangulum)* (donated by a neighbor who feared it might be a rattlesnake), and two red-bellied snakes *(Storeria occipitomaculata),* one of them found crushed on the gravel road in front of our house. The other, I regret to say, was decapitated by my lawnmower.

We have noted only three amphibians—the American toads *(Bufo americana)* in and around our garden, the hylas *(Hyla crucifer)* in our woods, and numerous red-backed salamanders *(Plethodon cinereus)* in our basement and in any other damp and shady place they can find.

Our Birds

My annual bird lists from 1971 through 1975 ran from a low of 87 to a high of 97 with a total of 125 for the five-year period. But in 1976 and 1977, when I discontinued counts along the destroyed lane, my annual lists dropped to 73 and 75. With no lakes, ponds, streams, or marshes on or near our ten acres, we rarely see any water birds; the only exceptions so far have been Canada Geese sometimes seen or heard flying over in the spring or fall, and, on April 7, 1973, a flock of about 75 Whistling Swans in passage. Killdeer are local summer residents and sometimes visit our garden. Woodcock have dancing grounds nearby, and on July 6, 1970, I flushed an injury-feigning adult along our trail as it tried to hide its well-camouflaged young among the leaves.

Most of us have our favorite birds. Ours here are the Eastern Bluebirds, Whip-poor-wills, and Purple Finches in the spring and summer, and the

334

Black-capped Chickadees in winter. When we bought the property in April 1970, we were delighted to find that we were acquiring, without extra charge, a pair of bluebirds. Each year since then (until 1978) we have had one or two pairs nesting in our boxes; their soft mellow notes and flashing colors are a special treat for Martha when she is working in the garden in the early morning hours. We also cherished the Whip-poor-wills that used to serenade us in the evening, often (sometimes too often) coming to our bedroom windows and keeping us awake. (They didn't return in 1977 or 1978.) Then in early spring the Purple Finches make the air ring with their melodious songs.

The chickadees, always among my favorite birds, so retiring and unobtrusive in the woods in summer, come out in full force in late fall and winter. We favor them by putting out small tubes of sunflower seeds that the aggressive Blue Jays and Evening Grosbeaks are hesitant about patronizing. We call the tubes "Whiting feeders," because Bob Whiting does a landslide business selling them for the Michigan Audubon Society. Seed-filled, narrow-mouthed glass jars hung from a clothesline, and doughnuts suspended on strings or wires, are also especially for chickadees. Only they (and once a red squirrel) enter the jars; but squirrels, woodpeckers, and other birds demolish the doughnuts. I have only a rough estimate of how many chickadees we feed. In March 1975, I tried to get a banding trap count; I caught 43 different ones in three days and still had unbanded chickadees around.

Winter feeding of birds always gives us a great deal of pleasure; watching them often interferes with other pursuits. Winters in the northern snow belt are notably severe, so that few birds remain with us at that season. Only five species are regular patrons at our feeding stands. Bold, saucy Blue Jays, equalling or possibly outnumbering the chickadees in some winters, add a welcome touch of color to the snowy landscape. Two or more pairs each of Hairy Woodpeckers, Downy Woodpeckers, and White-breasted Nuthatches complete the five regulars. Sometimes we are swamped with ravenous Evening Grosbeaks, but they are irregular both in numbers and in frequency of appearance; often they show up in the morning, then disappear for the rest of the day. In the record-breaking cold winter of 1976–1977 they deserted us almost completely, and most of the rest of northern Michigan as well. Yet that same winter four Tree Sparrows came almost daily to our feeders; they had not remained over winter with us in milder years. In late winter of 1975 a Red-breasted Nuthatch stayed with us for the first time. It was so tame I could sometimes stroke it on the back while it was absorbed in eating suet.

Of course we have a few less regular winter visitors. Goldfinches often

Our retirement home in its winter setting near Grayling, Michigan.

Black-capped Chickadee, always one of my favorite birds. Chickadees are star-boarders with us from November to April, then disappear into the woods.

Beaver Lane in late March 1974 before bulldozing.

Beaver Lane in September 1975 during bulldozing and grading operations—all to provide an additional access to one house and a trailer.

appear for a brief spell, then disappear until spring; sometimes they are accompanied by a few Pine Siskins. Purple Finches, so prevalent in spring and summer, desert us in late fall, as do the crows, but reappear in late February or March. The cawing of crows during the first premature mild spell in late February is a welcome hint of coming spring. During four winters we have had invasions of Common Redpolls (a biennial invader) with counts up to 80 or more in and around the feeders. Pine Grosbeaks are more irregular—one to three in three different winters. And on November 24, 1975 we had a brief visitation (for only a few minutes) of five in our garden. I have no winter records of crossbills here, but on August 23, 1972, a flock of a dozen Red Crossbills appeared in our garden and remained off and on until the sunflowers were completely harvested in late October. Northern Shrikes have put in a brief appearance on three occasions; an adult and an immature (at different times) in 1972, and an adult in February 1977.

Occasionally, but quite rarely in winter, we catch a fleeting glimpse of a Cooper's Hawk dashing for cover or see a Redtail along the road. When chickadees and nuthatches "freeze," I look for a shrike or a hawk, but rarely find one that way. A Barred Owl often starts hooting in our woods in March, then lapses into silence for much of the year. A sharp-eyed neighbor, who often sees things that I don't, once reported seeing a "big white hawk" (presumably a Snowy Owl) perched in a tall tree in our yard, but I didn't see it. Twice I have seen large flocks of Snow Buntings in the open field across from our house, but our open space is too limited to attract them to our acres. Once two Ruffed Grouse roosted in the willow tree in our yard; sometimes I flush a covey or see their tracks in the back-woods, but I have not heard one drumming here in the spring. Hunters seem to be more successful at finding "pats" than I.

The scarcity of winter birds makes spring, when it finally comes, all the more welcome. On most days in late March and throughout April and most of May, I can look out our picture windows at the feeders, bird bath, lilac bush, or weeping willow and see one or more new arrivals. I have recorded 30 species (and once, at dawn, a doe deer) at the bird bath, 37 at the feeders, and 58 in the willow.

First to come are some of the birds that winter in southern Michigan but usually not here—Purple Finches, goldfinches, Tree Sparrows, and juncos. Then Redwings, grackles, and cowbirds arrive. Overlapping with the fringillids and icterids come the real harbingers of spring—robins, bluebirds, and Song Sparrows, all especially appreciated after the long winter. Then comes a flurry of April arrivals—more sparrows, Eastern

Phoebes, Tree Swallows, both kinglets, perhaps a Brown Creeper or two, Yellow-bellied Sapsuckers, sometimes a Hermit Thrush and Winter Wren (both local summer residents but not on our acreage), then the first warblers, led by the Myrtles or Yellow-rumped species. During May nearly a hundred species may appear sometime during the month—warblers, vireos, thrushes, more fringillids and icterids, then the belated cuckoos, hummingbirds, and late flycatchers. Spring waves of warblers have always been a challenge to me, but, unfortunately, we are not often blessed with heavy flights in this part of the state. Of the 23 species recorded on our property so far, only two—the Ovenbirds and American Redstarts—remain to nest in our woods.

About 30 of the birds are regular summer residents on our ten acres. Some others are irregular (not here every summer) or, like the Turkey Vulture and Chimney Swifts, are nonnesting summer visitors. Some of my favorites are the musical Veeries along our north boundary; a Wood Thrush that sometimes serenades us with its deep bell-like notes for a week or more in May, then seems to disappear; the Northern Orioles so conspicuous around the garden and yard; and the less-noticeable Scarlet Tanagers back in the woods. The numerous Rose-breasted Grosbeaks sometimes put in a premature appearance in early May, then are driven by adverse weather to patronize our feeders. In mid-May of both 1974 and 1975 cold weather caused flocking. On May 15 in 1974, Martha counted 13 males and 5 females outside the kitchen window; a row of 10 males lined up on the clothesline was a spectacular sight, much appreciated by a class of grade-school students who chanced to be here on a field trip that day.

We have tried in vain to entice our neighbors' phoebes to nest in the brackets placed on the garage, shed, and chicken house, but by leaving the sliding door of the shed ajar we finally persuaded the Barn Swallows to nest there. They raised five young in 1976 and, to our great amusement, lined them up on a wire outside our dining room window for post-nest feeding.

In 1973 and in 1974 a pair of Cooper's Hawks, one of Michigan's most endangered species, nested successfully in our woods. But in mid-April of 1975 the road crew came in with chainsaws and cut out more than 200 trees along the lane near the nest, and the hawks deserted. But in 1976, when the new road was largely abandoned, a pair of Red-shouldered Hawks, more tolerant of human disturbances than Cooper's Hawks, appropriated the nest and raised two young. Marsh Hawks, the male and female separately, are sometimes seen cruising over the field across the road and probably nest nearby, but a pair of American Kestrels at a horse farm a half mile south of us in the summers of 1972 and 1973 has not returned in subsequent years.

Other Activities

Bird watching, plant and animal surveys, trail maintenance, care of the grounds, cutting wood for the fireplace and sugarhouse, digging out in winter, gardening, and chicken farming do not take up all our time. MacArthur has said that "Old soldiers never die, they merely fade away." This applies equally well to retired professors. I have continued some teaching: substituting in the ornithology course at Central Michigan University one spring, conducting bird classes for senior citizens and for adult education courses, and trying (sometimes hopelessly, it seems) to help high school dropouts at a local boys' camp with their science lessons. Then there are bird talks for local clubs—Kiwanis, Rotary, Masons—and to Audubon Society chapters throughout the state. I have maintained memberships in about 20 ornithological, natural history, and environmental organizations, and try to keep up with their literature.

Writing is even more time-consuming: book reviews (more than a hundred since retirement) for two organizations, the third revision of my ornithology text (more work, it seemed, than the first two editions), a 100-page report for Argonne National Laboratory on *The Birds of the Lake Michigan Drainage Basin,* and, finally, trying to write this book from faded and often illegible notes. My addiction to scribbling means that Martha, in addition to household duties, outdoor chores, and trying to write a genealogy book, has had to keep her 45-year-old typewriter banging almost constantly (it finally gave up the ghost in 1977). We both wonder what it would be like to be retired!

The Not-so-Golden Years: The Problem

We had been reasonably happy with our new home, its surroundings, our neighbors, and the community. Then in the early spring of 1975, after nearly five years of relatively quiet living, a severe blow shattered our dreams. One morning, without any forewarning, a huge snowplow appeared and started plowing out our beloved lane. It gouged out massive hunks of sod, piled a high mound of snow against a medium-sized white pine along our fence row, and completely buried a group of red pines I had planted along the way. In response to our hurried inquiry, the operator of the snowplow merely informed us that they were "opening up the road."

Our concern about the new road was for the quarter mile along our north border, an acre of highly prized land. The part of the road leading in from the east was essential for access to the two 20-acre parcels of woods that were for sale; it provided access to and from Grayling (where the new owners lived) and to I-75 and all points north and south. The extension through our woods, where the greatest damage was done, was not really necessary; it was virtually a dead end leading by devious routes to almost nowhere.

The chainsaw crew soon followed the snowplow and cut a 30- to 40-foot swath along the lane, leaving stumps three feet high jutting out of the snow. After the cutting I counted 148 stumps of small and medium-sized trees along our quarter mile of the planned road. Our neighbors, who owned the other half of the lane bordering ours, lost fewer but larger and more valuable trees: a 12-inch red pine (stump diameter), a 10-inch white pine, several large black cherry trees, and several wild apple trees. Our losses included trees of 18 different species, among them our only balsam poplars *(Populus balsamifera),* several locally scarce scarlet oaks *(Quercus coccinea),* and a superb stand of 18 wild red cherries *(Prunus pennsylvanica).*

I regretted the loss of shrubs even more than the loss of trees. The shrubs included shadbush *(Amelanchier canadensis),* northern Michigan's most ornamental roadside shrub or tree; beaked hazelnut *(Corylus rostrata),* a food supply for the numerous squirrels and chipmunks; witch hazel *(Hamamelis virginiana),* so decorative in the fall with its yellow blossoms; maple-leaved viburnum *(Viburnum acerifolum)*; and a hundred or more staghorn sumacs *(Rhus typhina)* which were ablaze with color in the fall and furnished emergency rations for wildlife in winter.

Environmental Implications

Environmental damage was severe and much of it, I felt, unnecessary. Grading machines dug out a wide roadbed, leaving 2- to 3-foot banks in some places, with the roots of roadside trees exposed. Later some of the affected trees toppled over in the wind. A 40-year-old red pine had nearly half of its root system exposed. Deep ditches dug on either side of the road drain valuable water from the land, lower the water table in our woods and garden, increase soil erosion and pollution, and expose shade-loving ground flora on the banks to lethal rays of the sun.

Our tree losses included not only those cut down, but others off the road that were severely damaged. Careless bulldozing shoved a fallen birch log off the road onto a group of four 5- to 10-foot hemlocks and flattened them to the ground. Replacement costs with equivalent nursery stock would run to more than $72.00. Most of our white birches were spared temporarily; plans to put a power line through a superb grove of 56 birches were stalled, at least for a while. A severe loss was the fine stand of 18 fruiting pin cherry trees. Many choke cherries and several large black cherries, some of them outside the staked-off roadbed, were also cut down. Wild cherries are extremely valuable for birds over a long fruiting period. The pin cherries ripen in June, the choke cherries in July and August, and the black cherries in August and September.

Equally regrettable was the loss of the ornamental and fruit-bearing shrubs that formed a border between the taller trees and the grass-grown lane. One compact grove of 80 staghorn sumacs and many other scattered specimens were completely wiped out. Sumacs harbor an abundance of insects, useful at all seasons for insectivorous birds. Fruiting thornapples *(Crataegus* sp.) were scarce on our side of the lane but otherwise were well represented. Replacement costs of our ornamental shrubs would run to hundreds of dollars.

More than a hundred species of native herbaceous plants grew along the lane. Native wildflowers do not grow readily along graded or graveled roadways; they are replaced or crowded out by more hardy introduced weeds. Decimation of our plant life everywhere is appalling. An endangered plant gets little publicity, compared to eagles or Whooping Cranes, for instance; but all animal life is dependent, directly or indirectly, on plants for survival. The World Wildlife Fund reports that 20,000 species of plants throughout the world are "rare and endangered." The Smithsonian Institution gives the number in the United States as 3,000 "endangered, threatened and extinct." The Michigan Botanical Club has prepared a list of 324 rare, threatened, and endangered species in Michigan, including 24 that are already extinct here.

Six of the herbaceous species growing along the lane are on the botanical club's list of plants "protected by law"; six others are listed as "needing protection." Of special concern among these are the four species of club mosses or ground pines (*Lycopodium*), formerly so extensively exploited for Christmas decorations. *L. clavatum* was temporarily eradicated by the snowplow and bulldozers, but some specimens came up again the following year from underground roots. *L. complanatum* and *L. obscurum* were also well represented along the lane, *L. lucidulum* less so.

Among the wildflowers "protected" or "needing protection" were wild columbine (*Aquilegia canadensis*), many specimens of which were destroyed along the less shaded portions of the lane; fringed polygala (*Polygala paucifolia*), abundant along the wooded borders; pipsissewa *(Chimaphila umbellata),* a rare, infrequently flowering evergreen; shinleaf (*Pyrola* sp.); trailing arbutus (*Epigaea repens*), two splendid beds along our fence line—out of reach of the bulldozers but which may now die of dust and exposure; starflower (*Trientalis borealis*), fairly abundant; Indian pipe (*Monotropa uniflora*), a ghostly saprophytic plant that appears and disappears; and bluebells (*Campanula rotundiflora*), scarce along the lane but fairly common in nearby jack pines.

Other woodland plants growing along the more shaded portions of the lane were Canada mayflower *(Maianthemum canadense),* false Solomon seal (*Smilacina racemosa*), wintergreen (*Gaultheria procumbens*), and partridgeberry (*Mitchella repens*). At the open west entrance of the lane where the road builders constructed a 60-foot approach were fine stands of asters (chiefly *Aster laevis*) and goldenrods (*Solidago* sp.), both highly attractive to bees and butterflies. Also abundant along parts of the lane were spreading dogbane (*Apocynum androsaemifolium*) and common milkweed (*Asclepias syrica*). Many insects are partially or entirely dependent on milkweeds for completing their life cycles. The 1974 late brood of monarch butterflies (*Danaus archippus*), nurtured on milkweed, returned from their 2000-mile migration in 1975 only to find their life-support system destroyed. Beaver Lane indeed would have been eligible for dedication as a Natural Beauty Road had we known in time that it was slated for destruction.

Mammals were not conspicuous along the lane, but 13 or more species used it as an avenue of travel or for feeding grounds. None of them is in immediate danger of extinction, but all have lost living space or have been displaced. Many of their food plants, especially the wild apples and browse for deer and squirrels, have been lost. Dr. Lee Talbot, international authority on the status of endangered and declining species, has calculated that if the current rate of extinction of mammals continues to rise unabated, *all* the wild mammals on earth (more than 4000 species) will be extinct in about 30 years.

Over the years I have recorded a little over 100 species of birds along the lane; about 56 of these are, or were, summer residents or summer visitors. The most severe loss was our Cooper's Hawk, an endangered species that nested successfully in our woods in 1973 and 1974. In 1975, when the birds returned to the nest site, the road crew was already at work and the hawks deserted. Only one other Cooper's Hawk nest was reported that year in the whole state of Michigan, compared to 88 active eyries of the Bald Eagle and about 80 Osprey nests. Supposedly, killing, disturbing, or molesting an endangered species, or destruction or modification of its habitat, are prohibited by the Endangered Species Act.

Most other summer resident birds still persist in nearby habitats, but

343

Ruffed Grouse lost an important part of their food supply. Whip-poor-wills missed the rail fence that collapsed during bulldozing operations (they didn't return in 1977 or 1978). Indigo Buntings lost their blackberry patches. Trees in which American Robins, Rose-breasted Grosbeaks, Least Flycatchers, Red-eyed Vireos, and American Redstarts nested were cut down, and the homesites of several ground-nesting species were destroyed.

Many people also have been deprived of certain values. Over the years I have guided many visitors over the area, not only from Michigan but also from California, Texas, Georgia, South Carolina, Tennessee, Virginia, and several other Eastern states. Visitors have come from three foreign countries; Wayne Neily, a park naturalist from Yukon Territory; the Flemings (4 of them) from Nepal; and Dr. Rudolph Verheyen from Belgium. The latter, the director of the museum in Antwerp, was on a tour of the States and southern Canada to study our nature reserves as models for setting up similar projects in Belgium. I showed him our premises, the Hartwick Pines, a Kirtland's Warbler breeding site, and then took him to the University of Michigan's Biological Station at Douglas Lake. Such visitations are now largely a thing of the past.

Summary and Conclusions

Destruction or displacement of flora and fauna over so limited an area may seem a mere pittance with so much wild land still available in northern Michigan, but it is the pattern we see nearly everywhere now. And in this instance we deplore the unwarranted widening of Beaver Lane through our woods where an additional access route was not really necessary. We regard it as an unjustified invasion of private property, a callous disregard of landowners' rights, a lack of consideration for environmental laws, and a needless expenditure of public funds.

But we still trust that all is not lost. Chickadees and Evening Grosbeaks continue to accept our handouts in winter. Tree Swallows and (usually) bluebirds occupy their nest boxes, Purple Finches sing gloriously in the spring, squirrels and chipmunks frolic about the premises, and wildflowers bloom in what is left of our woods.

References

Federal Register, Part III, Vol. 39, Jan. 4, 1974, and Part IV, Feb. 22, 1977. U.S. Department of Interior, Fish and Wildlife Service. (Endangered Species)

Haak, Leo A. (ed.) *Alternatives after Retirement.* East Lansing: Michigan State University, 1971.

Michigan Department of Natural Resources, 1976. "Michigan's Endangered and Threatened Species Program." Lansing, Michigan, 1976.

Wagner, W.H.; E.G. Voss; J.H. Beaman; E.A. Bourdo; F.W. Case; J.A. Churchill; P.W. Thompson. "Endangered, Threatened, and Rare Vascular Plants in Michigan." *Michigan Botanist,* 16: (1977) pp. 99-122.

Wallace, G.J. "Birds of the Lake Michigan Drainage Basin." Vol. 14 in Environmental Status of the Lake Michigan Region. Argonne National Laboratory, Argonne, Illinois, 1977.